Numbers

Sign Markers

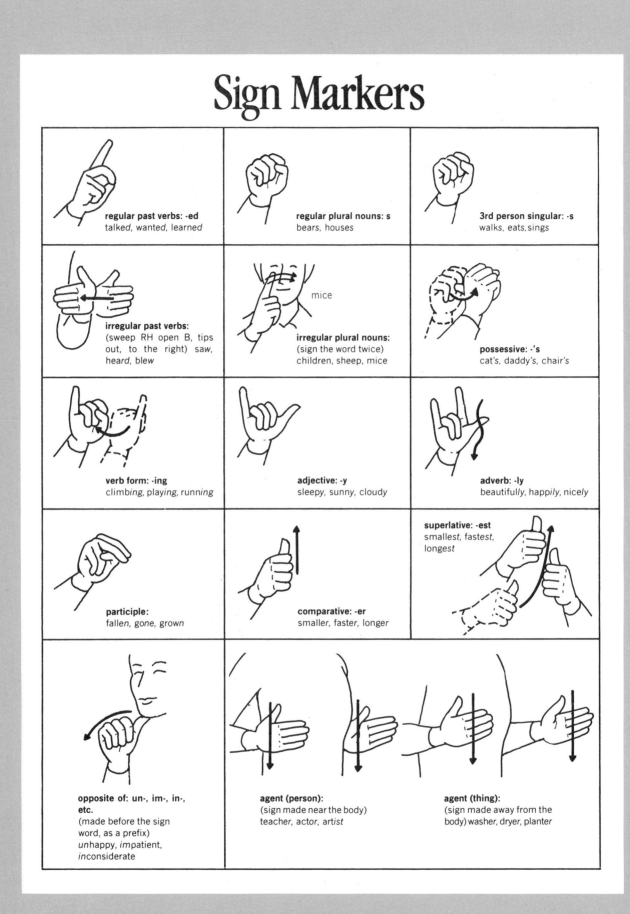

regular past verbs: -ed
talked, wanted, learned

regular plural nouns: s
bears, houses

3rd person singular: -s
walks, eats, sings

irregular past verbs:
(sweep RH open B, tips out, to the right) saw, heard, blew

mice

irregular plural nouns:
(sign the word twice)
children, sheep, mice

possessive: -'s
cat's, daddy's, chair's

verb form: -ing
climbing, playing, running

adjective: -y
sleepy, sunny, cloudy

adverb: -ly
beautifully, happily, nicely

participle:
fallen, gone, grown

comparative: -er
smaller, faster, longer

superlative: -est
smallest, fastest, longest

opposite of: un-, im-, in-, etc.
(made before the sign word, as a prefix)
unhappy, impatient, inconsiderate

agent (person):
(sign made near the body)
teacher, actor, artist

agent (thing):
(sign made away from the body) washer, dryer, planter

The Comprehensive Signed English Dictionary

Edited by   Harry Bornstein
Karen L. Saulnier
Lillian B. Hamilton

Illustrated by   Ralph R. Miller, Sr.

The Signed English Series
Clerc Books
Gallaudet University Press

Clerc Books
An imprint of Gallaudet University Press, Washington, DC 20002
© 1983 by Gallaudet University. All rights reserved

Published 1983. Eighth printing 1997
Printed in the United States of America

Library of Congress Catalog Number 82-82830
International Standard Book Number 0-913580-81-3

Contents

Titles in the Signed English Series

Level I. Beginning Books
Basic vocabulary, phrases, and simple sentences related to daily activities.

My Animal Book

A Book about Me

Circus Time

Count and Color

Fire Fighter Brown

My Toy Book

The Pet Shop

Police Officer Jones

With My Legs

Level II. Growing Up Books and Stories
High interest-level topics presented in simple, straightforward sentences.

The Clock Book

The Holiday Book

I Want to Be a Farmer

The Ugly Duckling

Level III. More Stories and Poems
Advanced language patterns. Classic fairy tales, some with complicated plots and more sophisticated vocabulary.

Be Careful

Jack and the Beanstalk

Little Poems for Little People

Oliver in the City

The Three Little Pigs

We're Going to the Doctor

Reference Books
Basic and specialized Signed English vocabulary, including illustrated signs and descriptions.

The Comprehensive Signed English
      Dictionary

The Signed English Starter

Signed English for the Classroom

Coloring Book
An all-time favorite with bold line drawings for hours of learning and fun.

Don't Be a Grumpy Bear

Flash Cards
Over 500 basic signs in an easy-to-learn flash card format.

Sign/Word Flash Cards

Preface

This dictionary is our attempt to provide a comprehensive volume for users of Signed English. It contains more than 3,100 sign words and 14 grammatical markers which, together with the manual alphabet, should meet most of the language needs of students from preschool through their adolescent years and beyond.

Two smaller and more specialized reference works, *The Signed English Starter* and *The Signed English Schoolbook,* provide additional vocabulary. These books are organized topically and focus on the vocabulary needs of teachers and parents.

Although the majority of the signs in this book are taken from American Sign Language, we have again included signs from a variety of sources, e.g., the Gallaudet community, the various SEE systems, the National Technical Institute for the Deaf, and other postsecondary programs. In our judgment, borrowing has become so commonplace that it no longer makes much sense to attempt to trace the true origin of a sign.

We have reviewed every sign in our previous works and improved either the drawing and/or the word description wherever it seemed useful. Of the added signs, three kinds are noteworthy: (1) We have added more lively, contemporary vocabulary such as *jog, mainstream, microwave, olympic, Disneyland;* (2) we present a number of single signs for some common double verbs and simple phrases such as *stick out, give up, get along, in charge of, line up;* and (3) we have provided some frequently found sign synonyms. These synonyms will be designated as "alternate" signs within the text. We have also dropped some signs that have been little used by teachers and deaf adults and some others which now seem awkward to us.

Other changes should be mentioned. There are suggestions on how to invent name signs. The section on numbers has been expanded. Our treatment of modals has been simplified somewhat. We offer some important new suggestions on how to use Signed English with older children and students. Finally, we make some observations on manual systems in Appendix A which we believe will be of value to parents and teachers.

This work, of course, builds upon the efforts of all those who contributed to the previous volume, *The Signed English Dictionary: For Preschool and Elementary Levels.* The most prominent of these early contributors include Howard L. Roy, Willard Madsen, and Gilbert Eastman. The work of the following artists is incorporated throughout this volume: Linda C. Tom, Nancy L. Lundborg, Ann Silver, and Jack Fennell.

While all the members of the Signed English Project contributed to every phase of the work, it is possible to describe the principal contributions of each to this volume:

Karen Luczak Saulnier compiled the English vocabulary and aided in the selection of the specific signs.

Lillian B. Hamilton wrote the description of the signs and organized the sign presentation and index.

Elizabeth Wheeler served as consultant on vocabulary and sign presentation and prepared the name sign section.

Harry Bornstein wrote the introduction and Appendix A and is the principal system designer.

Ralph R. Miller, Sr. designed pages 29–423 and redrew a large proportion of the signs. Lisa Ann Feldman designed the cover and the remaining pages.

Rosemary Weller, Shirley Stein, and James M. Pickett developed "A Model for the Visual Representation of Speech."

Harry Bornstein

The Elements of Signed English

Introduction:
About Signed English

This introduction focuses on the initial learning of Signed English, so it uses the young deaf child as its referent. However, the content is meant to apply to any person of any age level who might benefit from the Signed English materials.

Signed English is a reasonable manual parallel to English. It is an educational tool meant to be used while you speak and thereby help you communicate with deaf children and normal hearing individuals who, for a variety of reasons, are experiencing difficulty in development of spoken language.

Learn to use Signed English with your child *as early as possible in his or her life.* By doing so, you will help the child develop better English. Improved English will not in and of itself result in improved speech, but it should offer a better foundation for a speech training program and/or a reading program.

Here is the basic reason for developing a manual parallel to speech: Deaf children must depend on what they *see* to understand what others say to them. They must somehow get more information than do hearing children from what can be seen in other people's behavior. What does each of us see when we speak with one another? We see movement of lips, changes in facial expression and eye movement, different body postures, and natural gestures.

American Sign Language

Can most deaf children get enough information from these signals to learn English well? The answer to this question is a clear and very well documented no. Most deaf children do not learn English well. Recent surveys of the educational achievement of older deaf children indicate that, on the average, they equal the reading performance of hearing fourth or fifth graders. Not all deaf students do that well. This has caused some teachers and parents to consider using one or another manual system with very young children. One possibility is the American Sign Language (ASL). There are four major problems with this possibility.

- Only about 3 percent of the children in programs for the hearing impaired have two deaf parents, not all of whom use ASL. From 2 to 5 percent of the children have one hearing-impaired parent.* Research has shown that those homes with one hearing-impaired parent are least likely to use signs (Trybus and Jensema, 1978). Therefore, American Sign Language is *not* the language of the home nor of the neighborhood for 97 percent or more of deaf children in programs for the hearing impaired.

---

*The percentage of children in homes with one hearing-impaired parent varied from 2 to 5 percent depending upon the phraseology used in the question. When the word *deaf* was used, 2 percent responded yes; when *hearing impaired* was used, 5 percent responded yes. The latter figure probably includes hard-of-hearing as well as deaf individuals (Karchmer, M., personal communication, 1981).

2

- It is not possible to speak English and sign ASL simultaneously. Consequently, speech development and aided listening skills are necessarily limited when ASL is used.

- American Sign Language has no orthographic or print counterpart. Therefore, ASL is not encountered in a child's usual visual environment; for example, it is not found on display signs in stores, in advertising, on television, on road signs, or in books.

- For a variety of cultural reasons, North Americans do not readily take to the learning of second languages. Thus, it is unlikely that English-speaking parents would want their children, hearing-impaired or not, to learn a different language, especially when that learning might be dependent on the parents' own prior learning of ASL.

Because of these problems, some other people consider using a manual system parallel to speech. Signed English is by far the simplest of several manual systems in current use, and it is still far from simple to learn and to use. A brief discussion of various manual systems is given in Appendix A. More technical discussions can be found in journals which deal with sign language and the education of the deaf. As far as you are concerned, however, none of this other material is needed for you to use Signed English well. All you need is included in this section of the book.

Basic Vocabulary List

Signed English uses two kinds of gestures or signs: sign words and sign markers. Each sign word in this book stands for a separate entry in a standard English dictionary. The basic vocabulary list of more than 3,100 words was assembled from published lists of children's spoken language and from parent and teacher "language logs" of vocabulary used in the homes and classrooms of deaf children. Some of the vocabulary entries are specifically applicable to children, e.g., *fairy tale, Popeye, Walt Disney.* However, the majority of the sign words—e.g., *home, think, eat*—are considered basic to all communication situations.

The number and variety of signs in this book should meet a considerable portion of the linguistic needs of students and adults of diverse language abilities. We have also prepared a large number of teaching aids, some of which contain a few words not included in this dictionary. You do not need to worry about this because every teaching aid contains all the information you need to use it effectively.

The sign words are signed in the same order as words appear in an English sentence. Sign words are presented in this book in singular, nonpast form. Sign markers are added to these basic signs when you want to show, for example, that you are talking about more than one thing or that something has happened in the past. We recommend that you use 14 sign markers. All but one of these markers are signed after the sign word.

In Signed English you use either a sign word alone or a sign word and one sign marker to represent a given English word. When this does not represent the word you have in mind, use the manual alphabet and spell the word (see beginning of next section).

Please note that all drawings and descriptions in this book are for right-handed people. Left-handed people should simply reverse all references to right and left.

Although we have designed the *Signed English* series to be as simple as possible, we would like to note again that it is not easy to learn or to use. If you find there are parts of our system you are not able to use, then feel free to do without those parts or elements. Basically, we want Signed English to be a tool for your use. Some of you will learn to use it very well, some reasonably well, and some only in a very limited way. We think that your child can profit even from limited use. Of course, the more proficient you are, the more likely it is that your child will develop better language.

The Nature of Signed English

Before we describe Signed English in more detail let us introduce the manual alphabet which is shown on pages 14 and 15. As you can see, there is a manual representation of every letter in the English alphabet. There are two reasons why you should learn the alphabet. First, you can use the manual alphabet to spell any English word for which we do not have a sign; if you continue using Signed English with an older child, you will surely have a greater need to use the manual alphabet. Second, a great many sign words include a manual letter as a basic part of the sign. Many of the sign markers are simply manual letters. If you know the manual alphabet, it will be easier for you to form and to read the signs. Manual letters are also used in our word descriptions of the signs pictured in this book.

Because you can reproduce any English word by spelling it, you may wonder why signs are necessary. These are the reasons: Spelling is slow. For a very young child, it is relatively difficult to form and to read letters. It is a strain on both children and adults to attend to such fine signals for very long. Second, and perhaps most important, asking a child to read the manual alphabet is skipping a step in the usual order of things. Hearing children know English before they learn to read. If you fingerspell to an 18-month-old deaf child, you force that child to recognize letters and learn language at the same time. We do not know how many children can do this.

Most of the signs in Signed English are taken from American Sign Language. But these signs are now used in the same order as English words and with the same meaning. We use ASL signs where possible because it should make it somewhat easier for the child to communicate with people who use that language. American Sign Language is different from English, so do not be surprised if you have difficulty communicating with those deaf adults who depend exclusively on ASL.

Sign Markers

At this point we want to describe in more detail the second kind of sign used in Signed English, the sign marker. It is used to represent certain very basic and common English word form changes, usually inflections and endings, which change the meaning of the word.

When we say that you use a sign word and a sign marker to change a word such as *look* to *looked,* exactly what do we mean? First, of course, you must form the sign word for *look* as shown in the body of this text. Second, as

4

smoothly and as quickly as possible, you form the regular past sign marker described below and pictured on page 13. Additional time and effort are required to form this second gesture. How can you minimize the extra time and effort? Consider the diagram illustrated to the left. It shows the approximate position assumed by the hands when a signer pauses. It is reasonable to suppose, therefore, that the typical signer can execute his or her next sign with least effort from this position. Consequently, all of the frequently used sign markers are formed by the right hand in the area bounded by the rectangle. These sign markers are all newly developed. Those sign markers which are formed outside this area are used much less frequently in speech and, interestingly enough, are those which have been adopted from American Sign Language. These are the comparative, the superlative, the agent, and the opposite prefix. We will now discuss each of the 14 sign markers more specifically.

Nouns and Verbs

The most important words in an English sentence are usually the nouns and the verbs. A noun can stand for one (singular) or more (plural) things. Most often a noun is made plural by adding an s—*bear* becomes *bears, house* becomes *houses.* As can be seen in the sign marker chart on page 13, Signed English uses a manual alphabet S for this purpose. We call this the regular plural marker. When you want to show this kind of plural, you first form the sign word and then form the sign marker S. Now there are many other ways that nouns can be changed into plurals; for example, *child* becomes *children, foot* becomes *feet, mouse* becomes *mice,* etc. The sign marker for all of these ways of showing plural is simply repetition of the sign itself. We call this the irregular plural marker.

Verbs are words that express an action, the existence of something, or the occurrence of an event. We distinguish between things that happen in the past and those which do not happen in the past. The manual alphabet D stands for the most frequent past ending, *ed.* It is formed after the sign word. There are many other ways that a verb is changed into a past form; for example, *see* becomes *saw, hear* becomes *heard, blow* becomes *blew.* There is a special verb marker which represents all of these irregular past forms. It is an open B handshape, with palm left and tips out, swept from the center of the body to the right side.

There is a third class of actions which take place in the past, prior to some specified or implied time. In English, the past participle conveys this meaning. Examples include *gone, broken, eaten.* The participle sign marker is represented by the manual letter N.

Aside from the past and nonpast distinction, verbs have two other very common endings: *ing* and *s.* Thus *work* becomes *working* or *works, play* becomes *playing* or *plays.* A native speaker of English knows when these forms are used, without needing to think about it. When using Signed English, the signer adds a manual alphabet I, which he or she swings to the right for *ing,* and the manual alphabet S for *s.* All one need learn is to associate the hand signal with one's normal use of these endings.

There are three other important ways that English word changes are represented by sign markers. A noun has a possessive form *'s* which can be seen in *boy's house, girl's toy*, etc. This ending is represented by the possessive marker which is a manual alphabet S, twisted inward. Some nouns and verbs acquire a *y* ending when used as adjectives: *cloud* becomes *cloudy*, *sleep* becomes *sleepy*, etc. The manual alphabet Y is the sign marker for this ending. Finally, words can become adverbs by the addition of *ly* as in *quickly* and *happily*, etc. The sign marker for this ending is a simultaneous combination of the manual alphabet letters L and Y moving down.

So far we have described ten markers. They are the basic aspects of English structure which are represented in Signed English. If you are a hearing person, you already know this structure and use it without thinking about it.

Four Additional Markers

There are four other markers on the sign marker chart which parallel frequent word form changes in English. These are the comparative *er* and the superlative *est*, as in *taller* and *tallest*, and the agent (person or thing) as in *worker, sailor, librarian, mixer,* and *mower*. The fourth marker, the "opposite-of" marker, is a prefix and is the only marker formed before or ahead of the sign word. It represents the prefixes *in, un, im* as used in words such as *incapable, unhappy, impatient.* The opposite-of marker is formed by placing a right, A-shape hand, with palm left and thumb extended, under the chin and then moving it out. These last markers are taken directly from ASL and are commonly found in everyday language.

It should be obvious that these 14 sign markers will not permit you to parallel all of the changes in English word form. Why stop with so few markers? There are two important reasons: First, language used with and by small children often does not use most of the other changes in word form. Second, since each sign marker must be used in combination with a sign word, a large number of markers become a heavy learning burden and could make Signed English very cumbersome. To avoid this, users of Signed English are urged, with one exception, not to add more than one marker to a sign word at any one time.

There are a few more things to say about these markers which may make them easier for you to learn. It is usually easier to recognize something than it is to recall it from memory. So we will continue to show all 14 markers in our teaching aids. You may be able to recognize them even if you can't remember them when you try to communicate. For those who have difficulty learning to use all 14 markers, we suggest a reduced set of seven: the irregular past marker for *both* regular and irregular past tense verbs; the irregular plural for *both* regular and irregular plural nouns; the *-ing* verb form; the third person singular *s;* the adverbial *ly;* the adjectival *y;* and the possessive *'s.*

In those situations, where seven markers still appear to be too many, we would suggest that four markers be used: the possessive *'s,* the irregular past for both regular and irregular past tense verbs, the irregular plural for both regular and irregular plural nouns, and the *ing* verb form. We think that reduced systems are useful with adults who appear not likely to be facile with a gesture language. But the most important use for reduced systems is clearly with children who have profound language learning problems, such as the profoundly retarded, some autistic children, and some children with cerebral palsy. Most often, no markers are used with such children.

How to Use Signed English

As surprising as it may seem, we are still learning about how Signed English is best used with deaf students. Consequently, we have several suggestions to assist you in dealing with a child who should be fully capable of learning English. Signed English serves best as a model of the English language for young children. The sentence patterns you use with such children, while complete, are still relatively simple, and your speech rate is slower than you would use with adults. As the child gets into the upper elementary grades and beyond, you will use a larger vocabulary, somewhat more complex sentences, and may speak somewhat more rapidly.

Because signs take longer to form than words to speak, you may find it a burden to continue to use the full marker system under these circumstances. Fortunately, the meaning of some markers can be inferred from the rest of a sentence even when they are missing. We suggest that you consider deleting these sign markers *after* you have determined *without the slightest doubt* that the child knows them. A child can demonstrate this knowledge on the hands, on the lips, by speech, or in writing and reading. The markers that are the most likely candidates first to be deleted are the plurals and the third-person singular. The adjectival, the adverbial, and the participial are also readily inferred. You can also further simplify your signing burden somewhat by using some of the signs which represent common and useful double verbs. However, you must be careful to see to it that, at some early stage in the child's education, he or she is specifically taught that these signs represent two or more words rather than single words.

As the child grows older and displays a greater and surer command of English, you will become more concerned with simply communicating with him or her and less concerned with being a language model. Under these circumstances, you can delete some sign words as well as sign markers. The sign words that are usually deleted are articles and some of the prepositions, because they frequently do not convey important meaning. As noted earlier, we have also used single signs for some double verbs. When you delete words like these, you must make three judgments. First, the deleted word is not an important part of the message. Second, the redundancy inherent in English, which so often aids understanding, is firmly within the competence of the child so that he/she understands the message in spite of the deletion. And, third, the child no longer needs exposure to a complete manual mode.

Still another technique is available with adolescents. You can substitute ASL constructions rather than use a sign for each word in a phrase. Again, it is important that the child or adolescent know the meaning of the full phrase so that his or her speech, reading, and writing will not suffer.

These suggestions are easier to make than to implement. We urge you to be very careful in your judgments of competence, because, while comfort in signing is most desirable, it is not the basic reason for using a manual English system. Finally, please note that the reasons for deleting and substituting are quite different from that given earlier for using reduced marker systems. You delete and/or substitute *after* mastery for the sake of comfort. You use a reduced marker system, from seven to zero markers, when you have good reason to believe that (a) mastery is not likely to be achieved by the child, as is the case with some profoundly retarded and autistic children; and/or (b) the adult learner will not be facile with a complete set of markers, as is the case with some poorly educated parents.

7

Some Exceptions

While exceptions almost always complicate a system, there are a number of signs which are so well-established or so colorful that we thought it appropriate to make some exceptions to the following basic rules.

One sign for each English word: There are a number of phrases, proper nouns, and compounds, of two or more words, in this dictionary which are represented by a single sign word. These exceptions are, for the most part, idiographic, unambiguous ASL signs. Some examples are: *after a while, of course, Santa Claus, United States, Band-Aid, french fries, hot dog, ice cream, ice skate, jack-in-the-box, jack-o'-lantern, merry-go-round. Ping-Pong, rolling pin, tightrope walker, walkie-talkie,* and *yo-yo.*

One sign word for a separate English dictionary entry: There are two or more signs for a number of single English dictionary entries such as *back, blind, brush, fall, glass, right, watch.* The various signs represent different meanings of the same English word. For example, the noun *fall* and the verb *fall* are etymologically related; however, the common and well-established signs for these words are too ideographic to be used interchangeably. Thus the two words will be represented by two different sign entries.

Do not confuse the above exceptions to the "one sign for one English word" rule with the sign synonyms (alternates) also found in the Signed English dictionary. Sign synonyms or alternates are not locked into any specific meaning of a word. They simply offer the signer a choice of signs to use for an English word, regardless of the meaning that word imparts.

One sign word plus only one sign marker: Because use of the agent marker does not preclude a noun form further assuming a plural or possessive form, we permit the use of two sign markers in this one instance; for example, *work* + agent + plural, or *speak* + agent + possessive.

How to Learn Signed English

We recommend that you learn Signed English by using the teaching aids, especially the story books and posters that have been developed for the system. Each of these teaching aids is completely self-contained. Everything you need is in the teaching aid itself. The sign markers are used as they should be, without any reference to grammar or to the explanations given in this introduction. You do not need to learn grammar to use Signed English. With practice you will begin to use the markers in the right way without thinking about grammar. Also, you should use the teaching aids to learn the vocabulary of Signed English. Virtually all of the vocabulary in this book will be in those teaching aids. Learn by reading the stories to your child. This can be not only a delightful experience for both of you but also a more pleasant way to learn this artificial language than by trying to memorize lists of loosely connected words.

On page v you will find the titles of the teaching aids so far produced in the *Signed English* series. These have been organized into three different language levels. Level I material exposes the child to basic vocabulary, phrases, and simple sentences that relate to the child's daily experiences and activities. Level II material concentrates on the description of high interest-level topics and activities. Level III material covers those classic fairy tales which contain more complicated plots and more sophisticated vocabulary. It also deals with linguistic and conceptual material of a more advanced nature. In addition to varied language level, the subject matter of each of these aids has been developed to serve needs beyond those related to language development.

The stories in the *Signed English* series deal with some aspects of our heritage that should be familiar to all children. While these stories were designed to be read to children, they are also useful as scripts for skits and plays.

The poetry and song books in the series offer both parent and child an opportunity to practice signing parallel to spoken English rhythm. This language rhythm is important to English and often precedes specific vocabulary acquisition.

The *Signed English* beginning books are small and sturdy enough to be given to the smallest child. With beginning books, the child can look at, point to, and describe important parts of his or her environment. Other beginning books contain slightly more advanced language and describe behavior and things more important to toddlers.

The growing up books in the series are efficient tools for acquainting the child with the larger world. Apart from *Tommy's Day*—which should be the first book used by parents, because it provides the family with the language needed for a typical day—most of the growing up books depict experiences important to the child. It is usually helpful to the child if he or she can be exposed to these experiences through the medium of these books before the actual experiences take place. The child need not fully understand the contents of a book to profit from that exposure. A book such as *We're Going to the Doctor* not only describes the many things that happen during a check-up, but it also presents the vocabulary to talk about such a visit so that the child will have no fear of the instruments and procedures. This should make the child feel more comfortable and secure on a first visit to the doctor's office. In short, the carefully developed descriptions in the growing up books are designed to increase a child's understanding of and ability to cope with his or her environment. These, in turn, should aid personal adjustment and enhance language behavior.

The *Signed English* posters are designed to be used as decorations for home and classroom. The manual alphabet poster is particularly flexible in this regard. The letters are often cut out and rearranged in a variety of decorative patterns pleasing to the child and parent.

In addition to this dictionary, several references and companion volumes are available in the *Signed English* series.

The Sign Drawings

We would like to comment on the drawings of the sign words and markers in the dictionary and other teaching aids. There are two principal problems in drawing signs. First, there is the problem of sequence. We use arrows to show the movement of the hands and/or the fingers. When a sign requires two different hand positions, the starting position is shown by means of dashed lines. The final position is drawn with solid lines.

The second problem, showing movement through three dimensions, is difficult to solve by means of drawing alone. We have found that a verbal description is often helpful in the interpretation of some signs. This leads to what is perhaps the primary purpose of this book. It is a reference book. We suggest that you refer to the pictures and word descriptions in this book when the drawings in the teaching aids are not clear or if you just wish to browse while looking up a word. Otherwise depend on the teaching aids to learn the signs.

If you know the manual alphabet, it will help you to recognize and form the sign words. It will also help you to understand the word descriptions of a sign. In addition, the numbers one to ten and several other handshapes are also part of many signs. If you are familiar with all of these handshapes, it will help you to read the word descriptions. They are shown in the Key to Word Descriptions.

Unlike this dictionary, where signs are shown in isolation, the teaching aids depict the signs of English in complete English syntax. This means that both sign words and sign markers are presented together on the page. In these drawings, the marker is shown on the signer's right (your left) because that is where a right-handed signer would usually make it. It is drawn this way because the sign and the sign marker represent a single English word. English print, on the other hand, goes from left to right. This "mirror image" or reversal may confuse you at first, but with some practice it should cause little trouble. For some words, you may find it helpful to turn the book upside-down and align your hands with those of the singer. Those teaching aids which were prepared later in the program and all of those that have been reprinted include the numbers (1) and (2) to indicate the order in which the signs should be executed.

Sign and Rule Changes

During the last four years, we have felt obliged to change some signs and to make some exceptions to our rules. This section will detail the changes and the reasons for those changes.

There are about a dozen very important English words for which we were able to devise only rather clumsy signs in the past. They are *could, would, should,* their contractions, and the contraction forms of the verb *do.* After repeated efforts we have succeeded in developing what we believe are simple and easy-to-make signs for these words. For the above contractions, we simply add the appropriate markers to one or another contracted forms. The contraction subsystem is outlined and illustrated on pages 22–24. *Could, would,* and *should* are now shown in the text as repeated movements of *can, will,* and *must.*

Some sign words have been changed either because they are aesthetically objectionable to some deaf adults, were too easily confused with other existing signs, and/or were not as clear as alternative signs. These changes will be incorporated into the teaching aids as each is reprinted. We recognize that changing signs is a nuisance and an inconvenience, but we felt that continuing to use clumsy and unattractive signs would prove harmful in the long run. While we anticipate fewer changes in the future, we would like to note that a language-like tool such as Signed English will change through usage in ways that we cannot predict. It is both pointless and useless to resist such change.

Sign Variations

While on the topic of changing signs, there are certain other features of signing that are worth noting. Experienced signers do not always form a sign in the same way. For example, the first ten numbers and many of the signs for the days of the week are formed either with palm in or palm out. Often the movement is dependent upon the sign made just prior to that for the number or day. Normally, a signer will make the smallest possible number of wrist twists because this is easier and less awkward.

Direction of the movement of a sign varies in importance. For example, when you use the sign for *pull, turn,* or *push,* the direction in which you pull, turn, or push may or may not be important. As you become more adept in using Signed English, you will attend more and more to those features of a sign which add to meaning or to fluid movement. To simplify your task of learning these signs, however, we have tried to show each sign being formed in exactly the same way each time it appears in our teaching aids. Occasionally, our artists, all of whom are deaf, unconsciously draw a sign in a manner which reflects the aesthetics of the sign rather than our patterns. We sometimes fail to catch these deviations.

There is considerable age, regional, and socioeconomic variation in signs used throughout the United States. Consequently, you and your children will sometimes encounter different signs for some of the words in this dictionary. We suggest that you use them just as you might use two English words that have the same meaning, e.g. *small* and *little*. Debates about which sign is the "right" sign usually stem from differences in taste and past experience but, as in any language, correctness rests upon usage.

As for changes in sign markers, we began our work using 14 sign markers, reduced the number to 12, and returned to 14. Thirteen of the original 14 remain the same. The new 14th marker, the participle, is an important, although relatively infrequent, verb form change. The *ful* marker was dropped because of low frequency of use.

Final Words

We hope that we have given you enough information to learn and to use Signed English. It is not an easy way to communicate if you have used speech all your life. But we think it will be an effective way for your deaf child to develop English and progress into reading for further language growth and pleasure. We also think that a child's speech and speechreading ability will be enhanced by a better knowledge of the English language. If for any reason a manual signal system such as Signed English proves ineffective or irksome, you can always stop using it. But remember, the critical years of a child's life spent with little or no language can never be recovered.

Good Luck!

Sign Markers

Signed English uses two kinds of gestures or signs: sign words and sign markers. Each sign word stands for one English word from a basic vocabulary of more than 3,100 words used by and with children and adolescents. These are words such as *mother, balloon, tickle, pony,* etc. These sign words should be signed in the same order as words are used in an English sentence.

The sign markers should be used when you wish to change the meaning of some words in a sentence. This includes such things as changes in verb, number, possession, degree, etc. We recommend that you use the 14 sign markers pictured here.

All but one of these markers are signed after the sign word. The marker which stands for "opposite of" is the only marker that is signed before the sign word.

In Signed English you use either a sign word alone or a sign word and *one* sign marker to represent a given English word. When this does not adequately represent the word you have in mind, use the manual alphabet and spell the entire word.

If you use these markers properly, you will provide a better and more complete model of English.

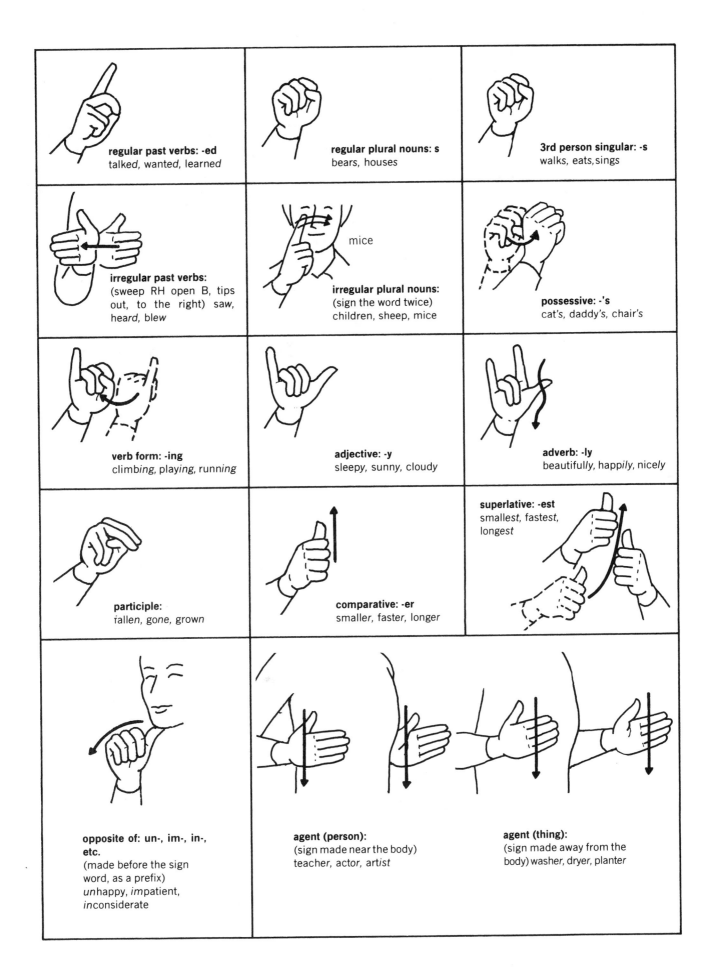

regular past verbs: -ed
talk*ed*, want*ed*, learn*ed*

regular plural nouns: s
bears, houses

3rd person singular: -s
walks, eats, sings

irregular past verbs:
(sweep RH open B, tips out, to the right) saw, hea*rd*, blew

irregular plural nouns:
(sign the word twice)
children, sheep, mice

mice

possessive: -'s
cat's, daddy's, chair's

verb form: -ing
climb*ing*, play*ing*, runn*ing*

adjective: -y
sleepy, sunny, cloudy

adverb: -ly
beautiful*ly*, happ*ily*, nice*ly*

participle:
fallen, gone, grown

comparative: -er
smaller, faster, longer

superlative: -est
small*est*, fast*est*, long*est*

opposite of: un-, im-, in-, etc.
(made before the sign word, as a prefix)
*un*happy, *im*patient, *in*considerate

agent (person):
(sign made near the body)
teacher, actor, art*ist*

agent (thing):
(sign made away from the body) washer, dryer, plant*er*

The American Manual Alphabet

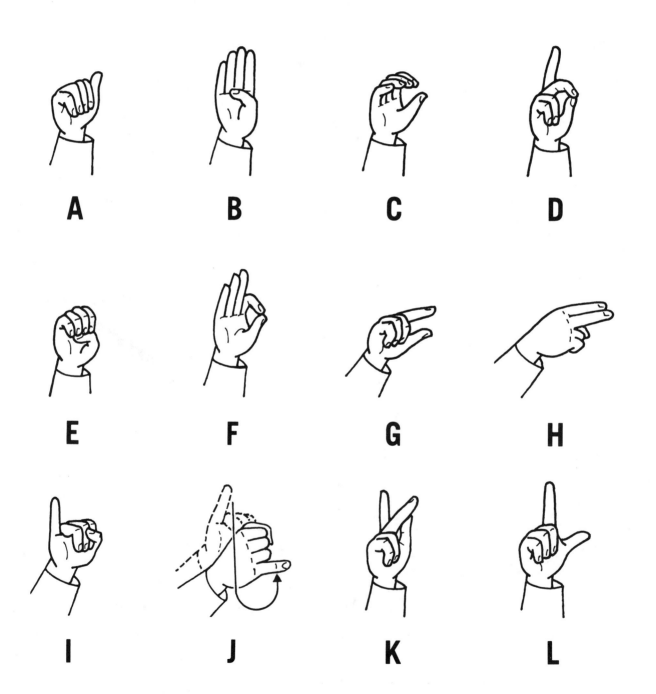

A   B   C   D

E   F   G   H

I   J   K   L

M

N

O

P

Q

R

S

T

U

V

W

X

Y

Z

Numbers

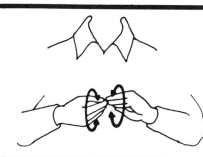

number
Flat O shape both hands, left palm in, right down, tips touching. Reverse positions.

0   1   2   3   4   5   6   7

8   9   10   11   12   13   14

15   16   17   18   19

20   21   22   23   24

25   26   27   28   29

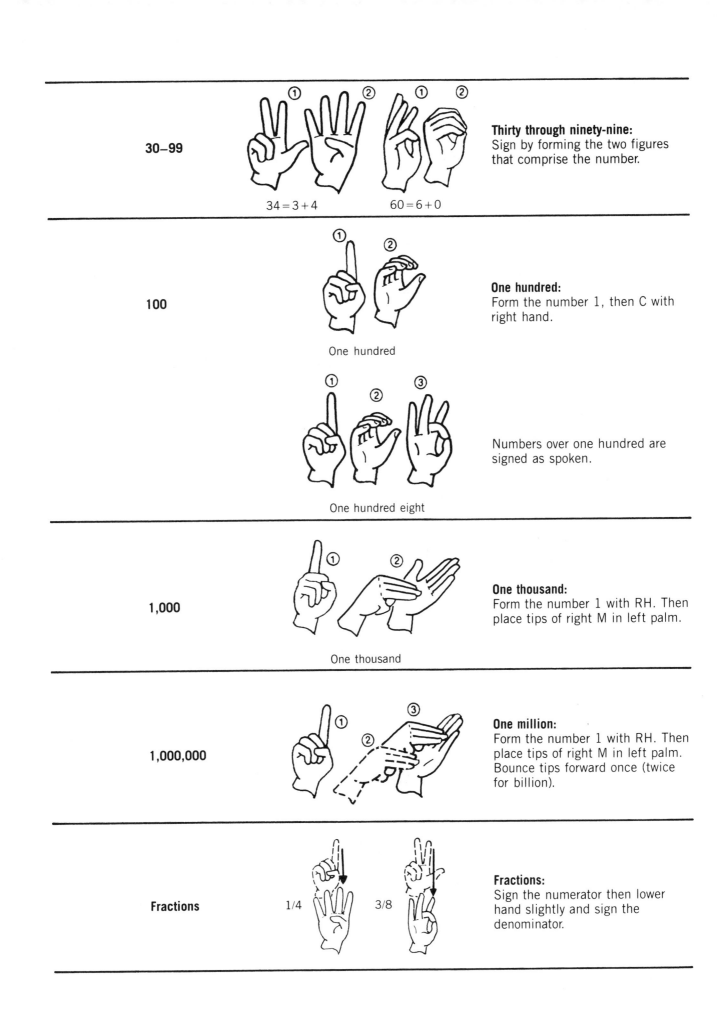

30–99

$34 = 3 + 4$ $60 = 6 + 0$

Thirty through ninety-nine:
Sign by forming the two figures that comprise the number.

100

One hundred

One hundred:
Form the number 1, then C with right hand.

One hundred eight

Numbers over one hundred are signed as spoken.

1,000

One thousand

One thousand:
Form the number 1 with RH. Then place tips of right M in left palm.

1,000,000

One million:
Form the number 1 with RH. Then place tips of right M in left palm. Bounce tips forward once (twice for billion).

Fractions

1/4   3/8

Fractions:
Sign the numerator then lower hand slightly and sign the denominator.

Numerical

Numerical:
Sign addresses, telephone numbers, and years as they are spoken.

Use abbreviated form when fingerspelling Street (St.), Road (Rd.), Avenue (Ave.), and Boulevard (Blvd.).

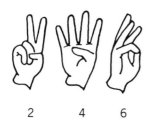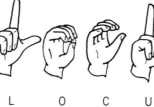

2   4   6   L   O   C   U   S   T   S   T

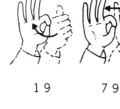

1 9   7 9   R D   A V E   B L V D

5-4-9-1-2-3-9

Money

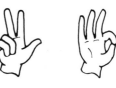

one-thirty-five

Money:
Sign money as it is spoken.

This approach to signing money is somewhat different from that used in ASL because Signed English parallels speech.

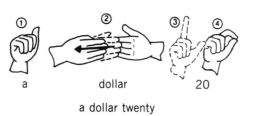

a   dollar   20

a dollar twenty

fifty cents

Percentages

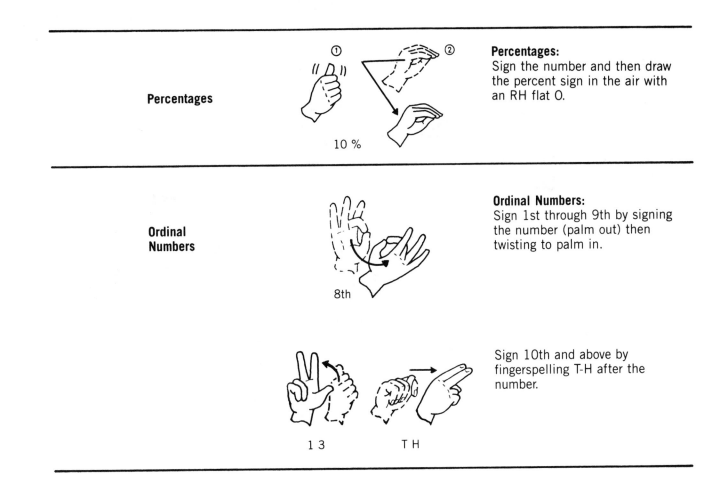

10 %

Percentages:
Sign the number and then draw the percent sign in the air with an RH flat O.

Ordinal Numbers

8th

Ordinal Numbers:
Sign 1st through 9th by signing the number (palm out) then twisting to palm in.

1 3   T H

Sign 10th and above by fingerspelling T-H after the number.

Contractions

The Basic Rule

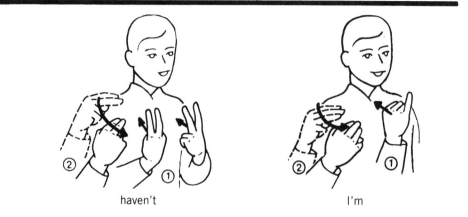

haven't   I'm

A simple and widely-used technique is followed in forming most contractions. As shown above, you first execute the sign word, then the right hand forms the appropriate manual letter and quickly twists it *inward*. The table below gives all the contraction parallels.

English Spelling:	'd	'll	'm	n't	're	've	's
Manual Letter:	D	L	M	N	R	V	S

The Modals
***Would*, *Could*, and**
Should

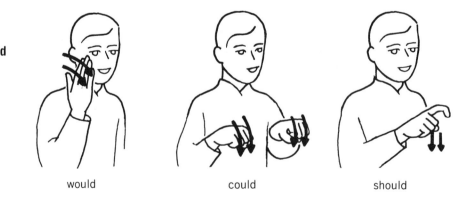

would   could   should

Signing the negative contractions of these words follows the basic rule. A right N is twisted inward after forming the base sign to produce *wouldn't*, *couldn't*, and *shouldn't*.

wouldn't   couldn't   shouldn't

Exceptions to the Rule

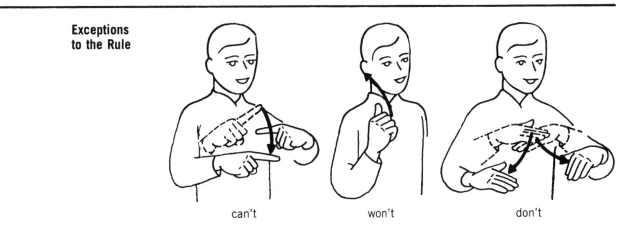

can't   won't   don't

There are three well-established exceptions to the rule for forming contractions: the words *can't, won't,* and *don't.* These are unique signs taken from the American Sign Language. They are *not* combinations of a base sign and marker.

The Verb *Do*

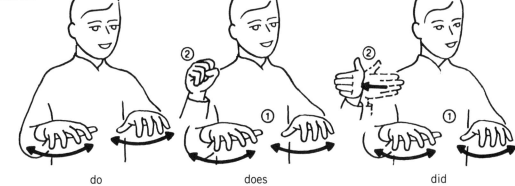

do   does   did

If the contraction rule were followed for these verbs, then *doesn't* would be represented by do + third person singular marker + n't. This violates the "one sign plus one marker" rule (and also demonstrates how clumsy unlimited combinations of sign markers can be).

Contractions (continued)

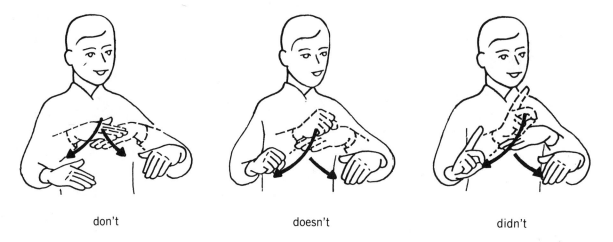

don't   doesn't   didn't

Initialize the ASL sign for *don't* to form the contractions *doesn't* and *didn't*.

Compounds

somewhere

everything

haystack

English contains a large number of compound words—words composed of two or more words—such as *somewhere, everything,* and *haystack.* About 150 compounds in this dictionary combine two sign words exactly like the combined English words. To save space, they are not shown as separate entries in the text but are listed in the index.

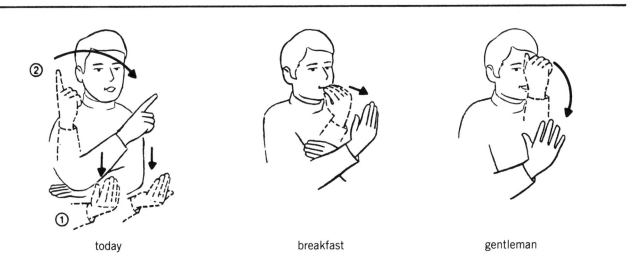

today

breakfast

gentleman

A number of English words, usually compounds, are represented by American Sign Language compounds that differ in order and kind from those found in the comparable English words. Three examples are given above: now + day represents *today;* eat + morning represents *breakfast;* man + fine represents *gentleman.* These signs and others of this group appear as separate entries in the text.

Compounds (continued)

sometimes

downstairs

toothbrush

Approximately 100 other English compounds in this dictionary are represented either by simple traditional or simple new signs, that is, signs which cannot be broken down into two other sign words. This type of sign usually suggests the meaning of the compound English word more directly, more graphically, and/or more traditionally than a combination of English sign words.

Key to Word Descriptions

In order to use this dictionary easily and effectively, you should be familiar with the names of your fingers, the manual alphabet, the signs for the numbers one through ten, and certain handshapes that are frequently used when making the sign words.

Positions of the handshapes are described by saying that the palms, (finger)tips, and/or knuckles, whichever the case may be, are facing in, out, up, down, right, or left. The dotted lines indicate the first position of a hand and the arrows show direction and/or repetition of movement.

Study the handshapes on this page and the arrows, letters, and numbers on the other pages. You should note that some letter shapes (A, B, F, S, V, Y) and number shapes (1, 3, 8, 9) are often used in making signs.

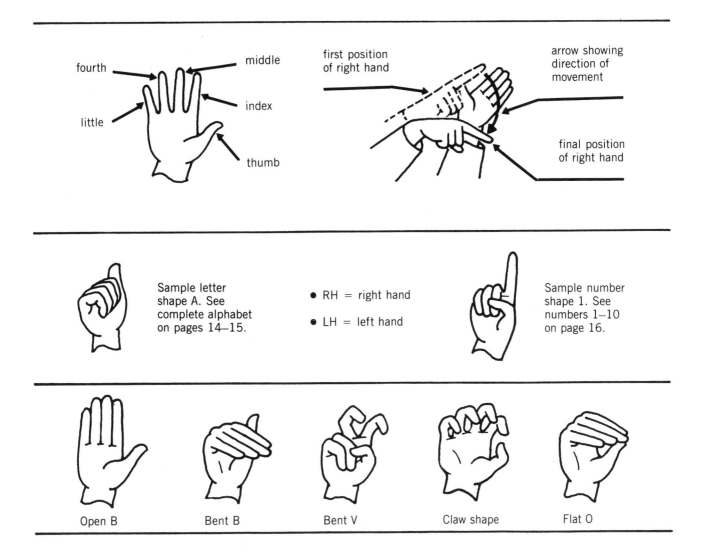

fourth   middle

little   index

thumb

first position of right hand

arrow showing direction of movement

final position of right hand

Sample letter shape A. See complete alphabet on pages 14–15.

• RH = right hand

• LH = left hand

Sample number shape 1. See numbers 1–10 on page 16.

Open B   Bent B   Bent V   Claw shape   Flat O

Key to Arrows

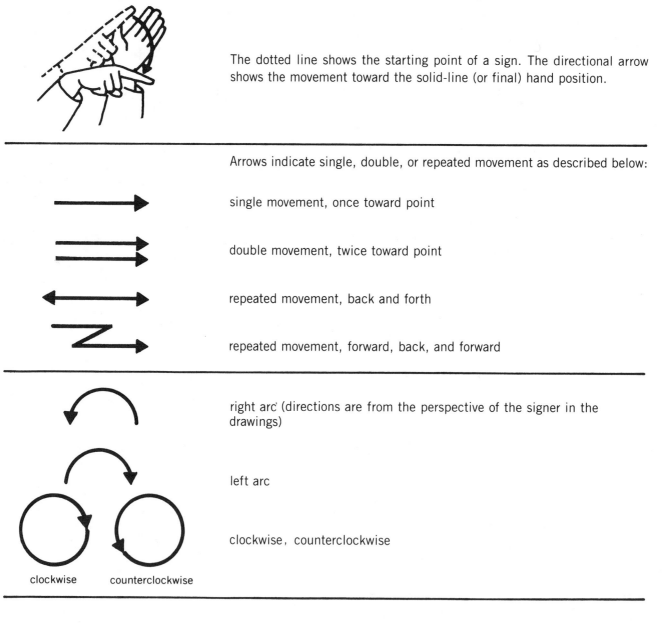

The dotted line shows the starting point of a sign. The directional arrow shows the movement toward the solid-line (or final) hand position.

Arrows indicate single, double, or repeated movement as described below:

single movement, once toward point

double movement, twice toward point

repeated movement, back and forth

repeated movement, forward, back, and forward

right arc (directions are from the perspective of the signer in the drawings)

left arc

clockwise, counterclockwise

clockwise   counterclockwise

motion markers indicate a slight wiggling movement

The Signs of
Signed English

A

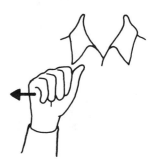

a
A shape RH. Move to right.

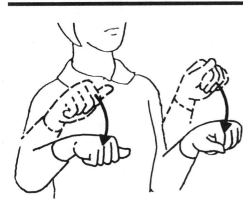

able
A shape both hands, knuckles down. Move down in forceful manner.

about
Point left index finger right, palm in. Circle with right index.

above
Open B both hands, palms down, left tips right, right tips slanted left. Place RH on back of LH, arc out and up.

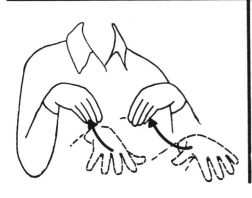

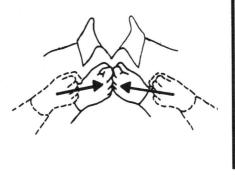

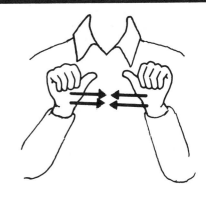

accept
Five shape both hands, palms down, tips out. Draw back toward chest into flat O shapes.

accident
S shape both hands, knuckles facing. Strike knuckles together.

ache
A shape both hands, thumbs extended, knuckles out. Move the thumbs back and forth toward one another.

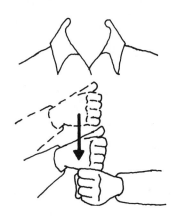

acorn

S shape LH knuckles right. A shape RH knuckles left. Tap left S with right A. Repeat.

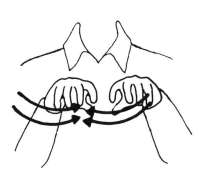

acrobat

A shape both hands, knuckles down. Move up and down alternately as if balancing. Follow with agent marker.

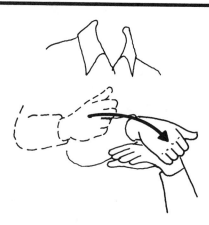

across

LH open B palm down, tips slanted right. Slide little finger edge of right A across back of LH.

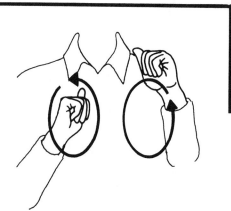

act

A shape both hands. Alternately move back in circles, brushing thumbs down chest.

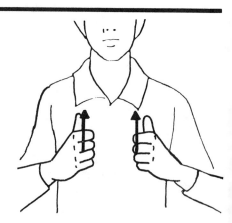

active

Claw shape both hands, palms down. Arc in toward each other several times.

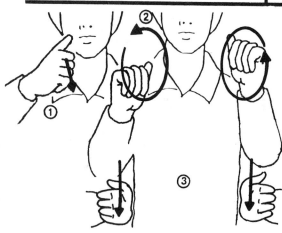

actress

Brush right thumb down right cheek, then form A shapes both hands. Move alternately in circles toward body. Follow with agent marker.

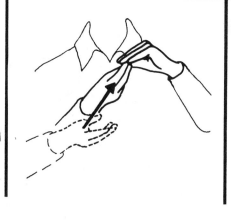

add

Hold left flat O, tips down, over right open palm. Close RH into flat O and bring up to left tips.

address

A shape both hands, palms in. Move up chest.

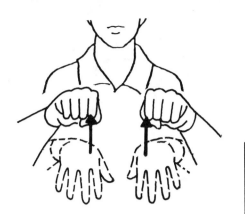

adopt
Five shape both hands, palms down. Move up, closing into S shapes.

adult
A shape RH. Place thumb at side of forehead then at side of chin.

advance
Bent B both hands, palms down, tips facing. Arc upward and forward several times.

adventure
Place right A against right side of head then arc down to the right.

advise
Place right A on back of LH then spread out into 5 shape.

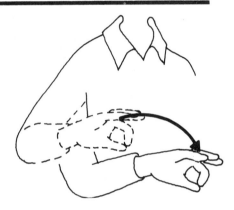

afford
F shape RH plam down. Mime placing in pocket and drawing out again.

afraid
Open 5 both hands, palms in, tips facing. Move back and forth several times, as if shaking in fright.

Africa
Hold right A at right side of face. Circle face to left, ending with thumb on mouth.

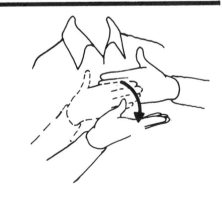

after
Open B both hands, palms in, left tips right, right tips left. Place right B on back of left. Turn out, ending with palm up.

after a while

LH open B palm right, tips up. Place thumb of right L in left palm and circle forward (about one-quarter turn).

afternoon

Hold left arm before you, palm down, tips right. Place elbow of right open B on back of LH and lower slightly.

again

LH open B palm up, tips out. RH bent B palm up. Arc RH left and place tips in left palm.

against

LH open B palm right, tips up. Strike palm with tips of right bent B palm down.

ago

Five shape RH palm left. Arc back over left shoulder.

agree

Place tip of right index finger on forehead. Bring down and place against left index which is held tip out, palm down.

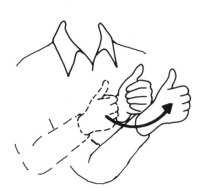

ahead

A shape both hands, thumbs up, knuckles facing. Place right knuckles on left wrist and move ahead of left A.

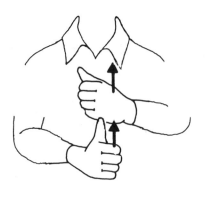

aid

A shape both hands, knuckles facing, right thumb extended. Place right A under left and push up.

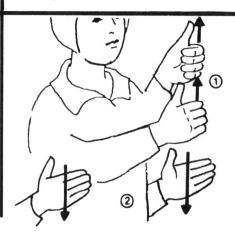

aide

A shape both hands, left knuckles right, right knuckles left. Place right A under left A and push up. Follow with agent marker.

aim
One shape both hands, right palm down. Place tip of right index on forehead then move directly to tip of left index.

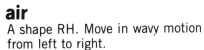

air
A shape RH. Move in wavy motion from left to right.

air force
Y shape RH, index finger extended. Move back and forth slightly.

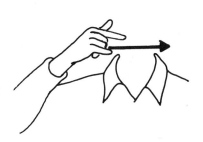

airplane
Y shape RH, index finger extended. Zoom to left.

airport
Cupped shape LH palm up. Y shape RH index finger extended. Hold at right shoulder and "zoom" down into left palm.

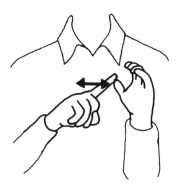

alarm
C shape LH palm right. Tap left thumb with right index several times.

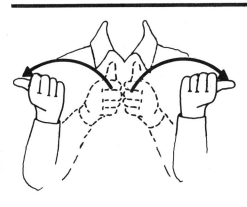

album
A shape both hands, thumbs extended, knuckles touching. Separate as if opening a book.

alike
Y shape both hands, thumbs almost touching. Move apart and back again.

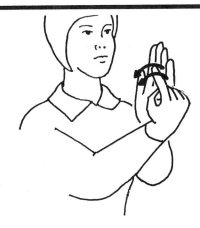

a little while ago
LH open B palm right, tips up. One shape RH palm in. Place RH against left palm and flick index finger toward body twice.

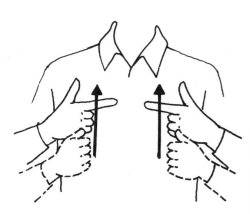

alive
A shape both hands, thumbs up. Place knuckles on chest and move up, changing to L shapes.

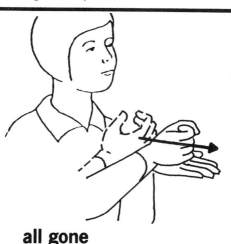

all
Open B both hands, left palm up, right palm down. Circle left with right, ending with back of RH resting in left palm.

allergic
A shape both hands, palms in. Place right A on forehead, left A on stomach.

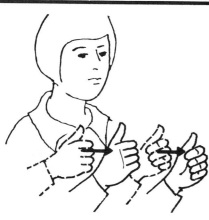

alley
A shape both hands, knuckles facing. Move forward in straight lines.

all gone
Place right C, palm in, on left palm then draw out, closing into S shape.

alligator
Five shape both hands, left palm up, right palm down, all tips out. Place right palm on left, interlocking fingers, then lift RH up (indicating huge jaws).

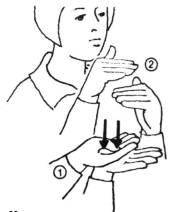

allowance
LH open B palm up, tips out. Tap palm of LH twice with back of right flat O. Change to bent B shapes, palms down, holding right B above left.

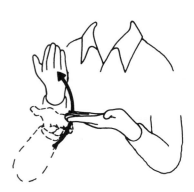

all right
Open B both hands, left palm up. Slide little finger side of RH across left palm and arc up.

almost
LH open B palm up, tips slightly right. Stroke back of left fingers with right fingers, bringing RH above LH.

34

alone

One shape RH palm in, tip up. Circle counterclockwise.

along

A shape RH knuckles down. Place on back of left wrist and slide up forearm.

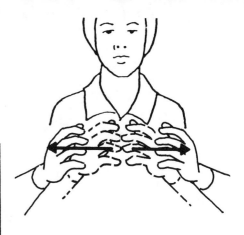

a lot (lots)

Claw shape both hands, palms facing, fingertips touching. Move hands apart quickly.

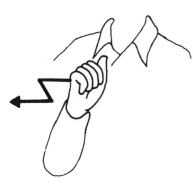

alphabet

A shape RH. Move down in Z motion.

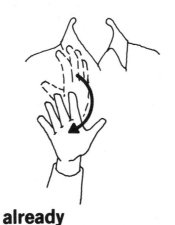

already

Five shape RH palm in and slightly to the right. Twist out so that palm faces out.

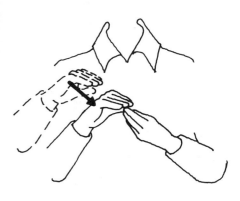

also

Flat O shape both hands, tips up, right O a little higher than left. Arc right tips over to left tips.

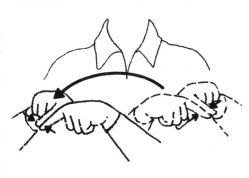

also (alt.)

One shape both hands, palms down, tips out. Tap index fingers together at left, then arc over to right and tap together again.

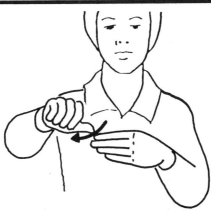

aluminum

B shape LH palm and tips slanted right. A shape RH with thumb extended. Scrape left tips with right thumb.

always

One shape RH palm left, tip out. Circle continuously.

am

Place right A on mouth and move out.

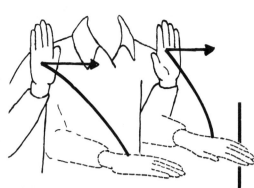

amaze

Open B both hands, palms down, tips out. Draw back to body, palms out and tips up, and push forward.

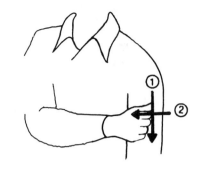

ambulance

Make cross on upper left arm with right A.

America

Interlock fingers, palms in, and circle from right to left.

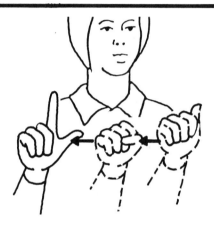

American Sign Language

Fingerspell A-S-L.

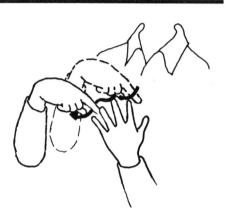

among

Five shape LH palm slightly right. Weave right index finger in and out of left fingers.

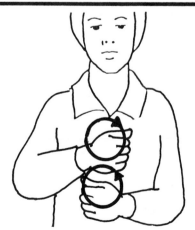

amusement

A shape both hands, palms in, right knuckles left, left knuckles right. Place on chest then circle RH clockwise and LH counter-clockwise.

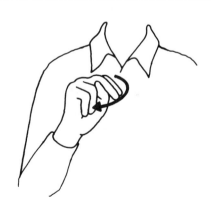

an

N shape RH palm in. Twist outward.

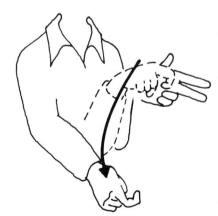

anchor

Three shape LH palm right, tips out. Place index finger of right X against left palm, swing down, then turn up, as if hooking anchor.

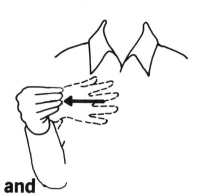

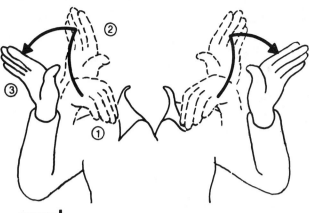

and

Five shape RH palm in, tips left. Move from left to right, closing into flat O.

angel

Place tips of curved open B shapes on shoulders. Swing palms out and flutter fingers slightly.

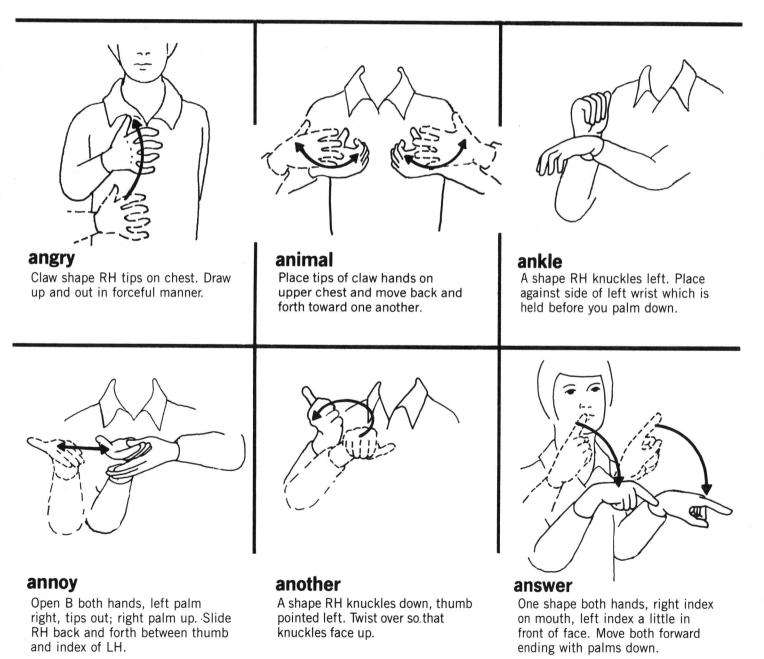

angry

Claw shape RH tips on chest. Draw up and out in forceful manner.

animal

Place tips of claw hands on upper chest and move back and forth toward one another.

ankle

A shape RH knuckles left. Place against side of left wrist which is held before you palm down.

annoy

Open B both hands, left palm right, tips out; right palm up. Slide RH back and forth between thumb and index of LH.

another

A shape RH knuckles down, thumb pointed left. Twist over so that knuckles face up.

answer

One shape both hands, right index on mouth, left index a little in front of face. Move both forward ending with palms down.

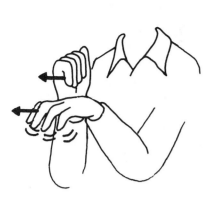

ant

Place base of right A on back of left claw hand which is held palm down. Move left claw forward in crawling motion.

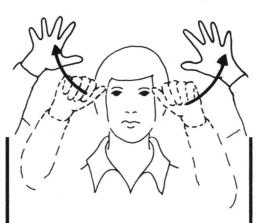

antler

A shape both hands. Place thumbs on temple and move up opening into 5 shapes.

any

A shape RH thumb up. Swing out to right.

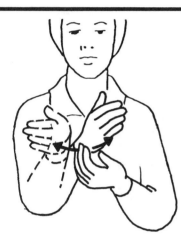

anyway

Curved LH open B palm up. Slap tips of fingers back and forth with little finger side of right open B.

apart

Bent B shape both hands, palms and tips in, backs of fingers touching. Draw apart.

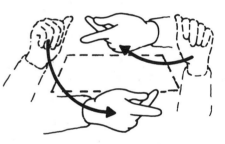

apartment

A shape both hands. Change into P shapes and bring left P behind right P, outlining shape of room.

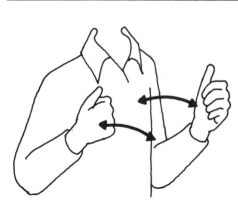

ape

A shape both hands, palms in. Beat alternately against chest.

apologize

Circle right A on chest.

appear (pop up)

LH open B palm down, tips out. Push right index up between left middle and index fingers.

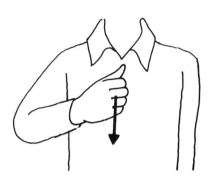

appetite
Place knuckles of right A on chest and move down.

apple
Press knuckle of right index finger into right cheek and twist forward.

appointment
Circle right A over left A, then drop on left wrist.

apricot
Place thumb of right A on right cheek. Twist forward and down into P shape.

April
LH open B palm in. Place knuckles of right A against left palm, slide over fingers and down back of hand.

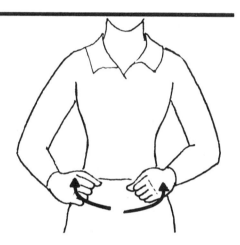

apron
A shape both hands, thumbs facing. Draw apart outlining small apron.

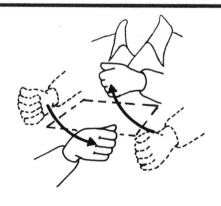

aquarium
A shape both hands, palms facing. Move right in front of left, palm in, and left behind right, palm in, forming box shape.

are
Place right R on lips, then move forward.

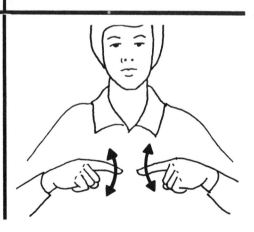

argue
One shape both hands, palms in, tips facing. Shake hands up and down simultaneously.

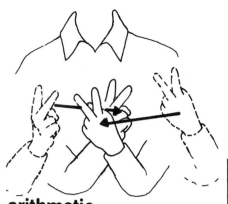

arithmetic
V shape both hands, palms in, tips up. Cross one another twice.

arm
Clasp left wrist with right C and run C up to left elbow.

army
A shape both hands, palms in. Place right A on left shoulder with left A just underneath, as if holding a rifle.

around
One shape LH palm in. Circle with right index which is held tip down.

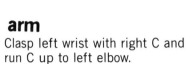

arrange
B shape both hands, palms facing, tips out. Move in short jumps to the left.

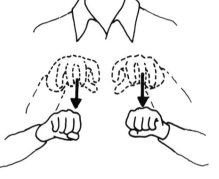

arrest
Claw shape both hands, palms down. Move quickly into S shapes, as if grabbing someone.

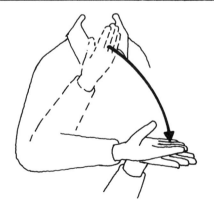

arrive
Open B both hands, palms up, tips out. Place back of right B in left palm.

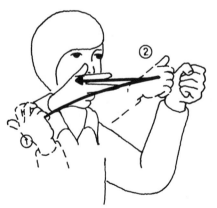

arrow
Mime pulling arrow from holder over shoulder, placing in bow string, and shooting.

art
LH open B palm right, tips up. Draw right little finger straight down left palm. Repeat.

artificial
A shape RH palm left. Brush across lips to the left.

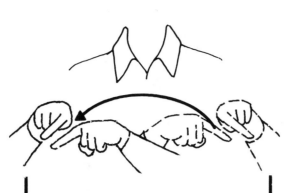

as
One shape both hands, palms down, tips out. Hold index fingers close together then arc from left to right.

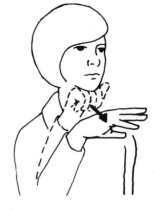

ash
Place back of right A under chin and open into 5 shape.

ashamed
Place back of RH on cheek, thumb up. Turn forward, opening fingers (to indicate blush spreading).

ashtray
Mime smoking cigar or cigarette then tapping ashes in cupped left hand.

ask
Palms together tip out. Arc back to body, ending with tips up.

asleep
Draw fingers of RH down over face, form A shape knuckles down, and place on upturned left A.

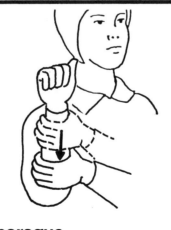

asparagus
A shape RH. Slide left C down right forearm.

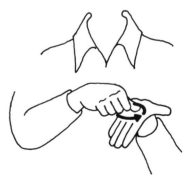

aspirin
A shape RH palm down, thumb extended. Place thumb in upturned left palm and circle.

assemble

Five shape both hands, palms and tips slanted out. Bring together in flat O shapes tips touching.

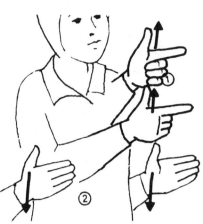

assistant

L shape both hands, index tips out, left palm right, right palm left. Place right L under left and push up. Follow with agent marker.

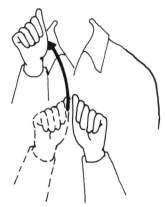

astronaut

A shape both hands, knuckles out, thumbs touching. Thrust right A forward and up forcefully.

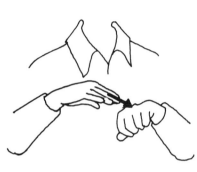

at

Touch back of left A with right fingertips.

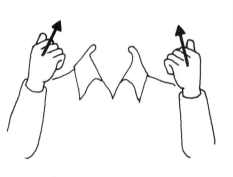

athlete

A shape both hands. Push up above shoulders, as if pushing up weights. (Make sign twice for athletic).

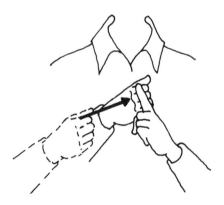

attack

Strike left index finger with right A from behind.

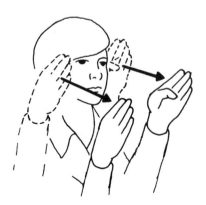

attention

B shape both hands, palms placed on temples. Move forward parallel to one another.

attitude

Circle heart with right A then touch chest.

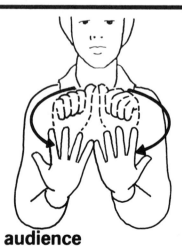

audience

A shape both hands, thumbs touching. Draw apart and around ending in 5 shapes palms in, little fingers touching.

audiogram

LH open B palm slanted right. Draw right A down left palm, change into G shape, then move forward on left palm.

audiology

Circle right A clockwise at right ear.

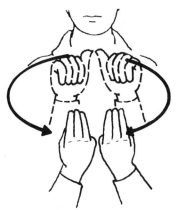

auditorium

A shape both hands, thumbs touching. Draw apart and around to front, ending in M shapes tips up. (Sometimes this word is fingerspelled A-U-D.)

August

LH open B palm in. Place knuckles of right A against left palm, slide over fingers and down back of hand, changing to G shape.

aunt

A shape RH. Wiggle at side of right cheek.

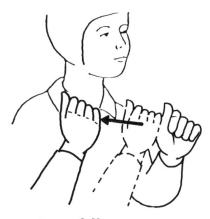

author

Mime writing across left upturned palm with right A. Follow with agent marker.

automobile

A shape both hands. Place little finger side of right A on left thumb, then draw back toward body.

avenue

A shape both hands, palms facing. Move forward as if following a path.

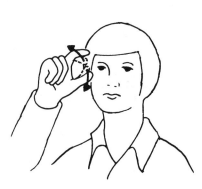

awake

Place right index finger and thumb over right eye, then snap open into L shape.

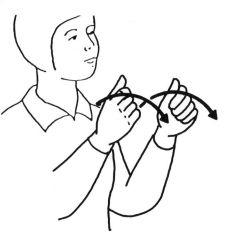

award

A shape both hands, knuckles facing. Arc both hands forward.

away

RH open B palm in, tips left. Flip away and out.

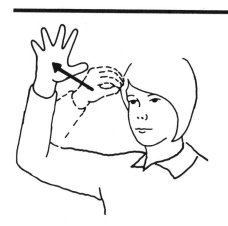

awful

Flat O shape RH. Place on temple and snap open into 5 shape palm out.

awhile

LH open B palm right, tips up. Place RH knuckles on left palm and shake index finger back and forth slightly.

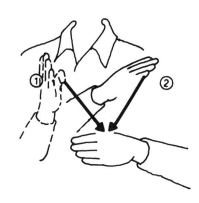

axe

Open B both hands, left palm right, tips out; right palm and tips slanted left. With little finger side of RH, chop left index finger backward then forward.

B

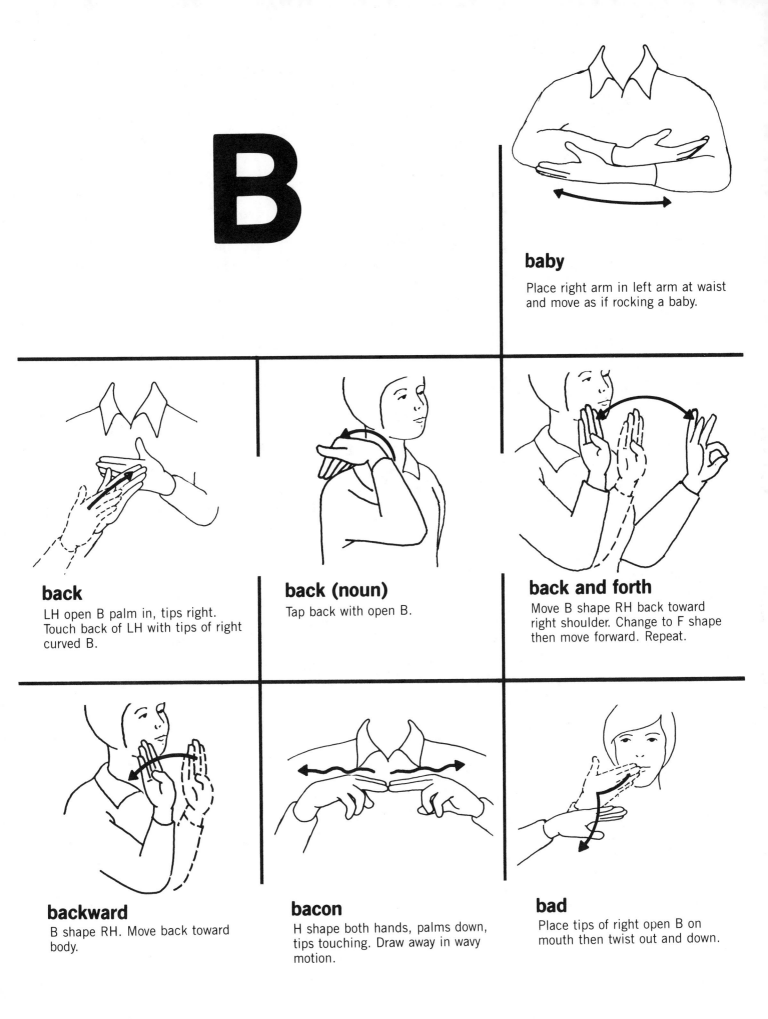

baby

Place right arm in left arm at waist and move as if rocking a baby.

back

LH open B palm in, tips right. Touch back of LH with tips of right curved B.

back (noun)

Tap back with open B.

back and forth

Move B shape RH back toward right shoulder. Change to F shape then move forward. Repeat.

backward

B shape RH. Move back toward body.

bacon

H shape both hands, palms down, tips touching. Draw away in wavy motion.

bad

Place tips of right open B on mouth then twist out and down.

badge

Place index and thumb side of right C on upper left chest (other fingers closed).

badminton

Hold right A above right shoulder then arc forward. Repeat motion.

bag

S shape LH knuckles down. Place index finger of right B on left S and circle under LH.

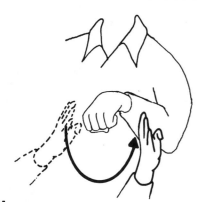

baggage

S shape LH knuckles down, arm extended. B shape RH palm left. Place index side of right B on left thumb then arc under to the left.

bake

Open B shapes both hands, left palm down, tips slanted right. Right palm up, tips slanted left. Slide RH under LH.

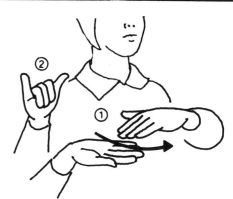

bakery

Slide right hand, palm up, under LH, then turn out into Y shape.

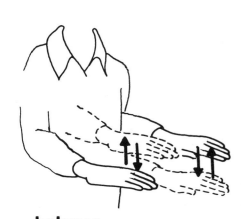

balance

B shape both hands, palms down, tips out. Move up and down alternately.

bald

Circle crown of head with right middle finger.

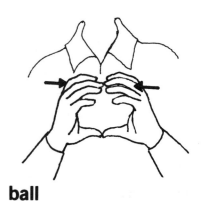

ball

Claw shape both hands, palms facing. Place tips together, outlining shape of ball.

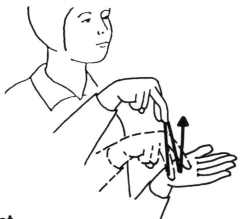

ballet

Place tips of right V in left palm. Lift up into right R then repeat.

balloon

S shape both hands at mouth, left in front of right. Move apart, opening into cupped shapes (as if blowing up and holding balloon).

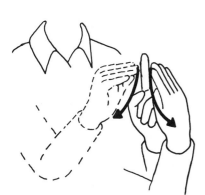

banana

Hold left index finger up. Go through motions of peeling a banana with tips of right flat O.

band

B shape both hands, index fingers touching. Move out in semicircle until little fingers touch.

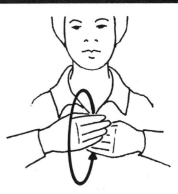

bandage

B shape both hands, palms in, left tips right, right tips left. Circle right B around left B.

Band-Aid

S shape LH knuckles down. Draw right H over back of left S.

bang (verb)

Open B shape LH palm right. Hit with right A.

bangs (noun)

Claw shape RH palm down. Place fingers on forehead imitating bangs.

banjo

B shape LH palm and tips slanted right. Mime strumming banjo strings with right fingers.

bank

C shape both hands, left palm out, right palm left. Place right C into left C.

bar

Slide base of right B forward on left index.

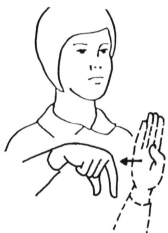

barbecue

Fingerspell B-Q.

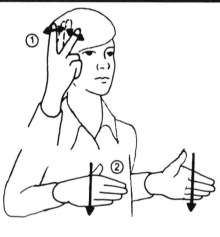

barber

Mime cutting hair with fingers of right V. Follow with agent marker.

bare

S shape LH palm down. Form circle on back of LH with tip of right middle finger.

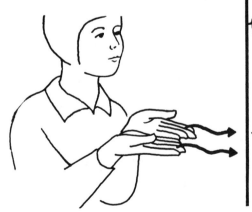

barge

Open B shape both hands, palms up, tips out, little fingers touching. Move forward.

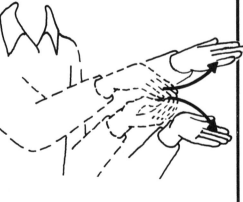

bark

Place right cupped hand on top of left cupped hand then open fingers quickly (indicating dog barking).

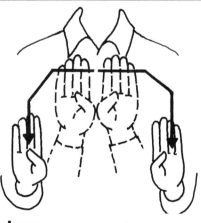

barn

B shape both hands, thumb knuckles touching. Draw apart and down outlining shape of barn.

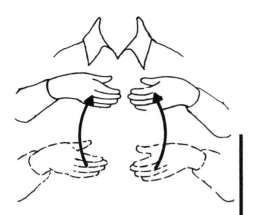

barrel
C shape both hands, palms and tips facing. Move up, indicating sides of barrel.

base
Open B both hands, palms down. Circle right B under left B counterclockwise.

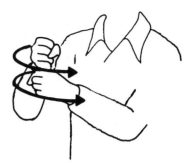

baseball
Mime grasping baseball bat with S shape hands and swinging at ball.

basement
LH open B palm down, tips right. Circle right A, thumb extended, under right B counterclockwise.

bashful
Place backs of A shapes on cheeks and twist forward.

basket
Place index finger of right B under left wrist and arc to elbow, ending with little finger side touching.

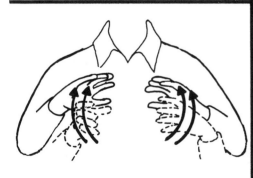

basketball
Mime holding ball then arc hands upward twice.

bat (animal)
Cross arms on chest holding hands with thumbs and index fingers touching. Flick index fingers up.

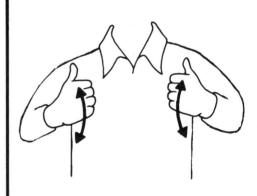

bath
A shape both hands, knuckles in, thumbs up. Make scrubbing motion on chest.

batter

C shape LH palm and tips right. Stir tips of right open B in left C clockwise.

battery

B shape LH. Strike left index finger with knuckle of right index finger twice.

battle

Four shape both hands, palms in, fingers facing and slightly bent. Simultaneously move hands to right, then to left.

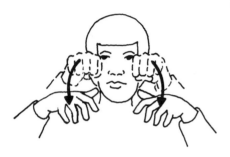

bawl

S shape both hands. Hold just under eyes and drop into 5 shapes palms down.

be

B shape RH palm left, tips up. Place index finger on mouth and move out.

beach

Open B both hands, palms down, left tips slanted right, right tips slanted left. Circle right B over left hand up to elbow and back.

bead

LH open B palm out. Make small O with right thumb and index tips, then bounce down left palm.

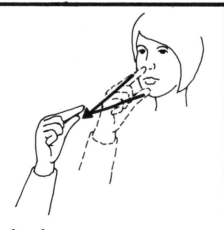

beak

Place tips of right G on nose and chin. Draw away, closing fingers.

bean

One shape LH palm right, tip out. Strike twice with tips of right G.

beanstalk

One shape LH palm right, tips out. Strike twice with tips of right G. Now slide right 1 up and through cupped LH in a wiggly motion.

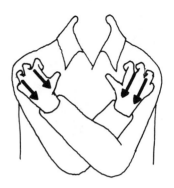

bear (noun)

Cross wrists of claw hands and scratch upper chest twice.

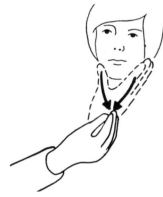

beard

Grasp chin with open B and draw down into flat O.

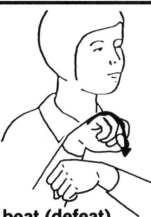

beat (defeat)

S shape LH palm down. Place base of right S on left wrist then arc RH down.

beautiful

Five shape RH palm in, tips up. Circle face from right to left ending in flat O. Then spread fingers, palm in, tips up.

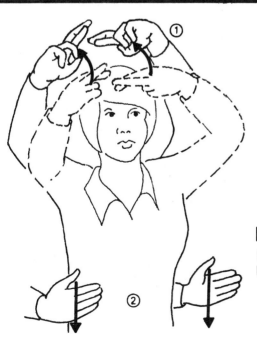

beautician

Mime rolling hair up with R shaped hands. Follow with agent marker.

beauty

Five shape RH palm in, tips up. Circle face from right to left, closing fingers into flat O shape. Follow with Y shape.

51

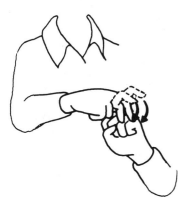

beaver
S shape LH palm down. Tap tips of right bent V on back of left S several times.

because
L shape RH palm in, index tip left. Place on forehead then draw back to right, ending in A shape thumb up.

become
Open B both hands, left palm in, right palm out. Place together and reverse positions.

bed
Place right palm on right cheek and tilt head slightly.

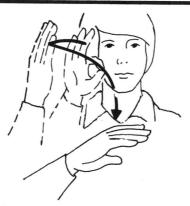

bee
Place thumb and index finger of right F on right cheek. Move away into open B shape, then brush down cheek with right fingertips.

beef
LH open B. Grasp LH between thumb and index with right thumb and index and shake.

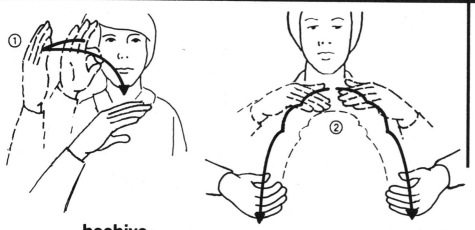

beehive
Place thumb and index finger of right F on right cheek. Move away into open B shape then brush right cheek lightly. Now outline shape of hive with open B shapes.

been
Place index finger of B shape RH on lips. Move out and form letter N.

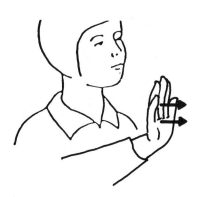

beep

Push right open B forward twice.

beer

Place right B against right cheek and circle forward.

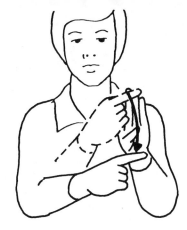

beet

B shape LH. Slice across left palm with right index.

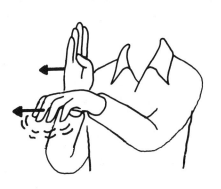

beetle

Rest base of right B on back of left claw hand which is held palm down. Move left claw forward in crawling motion.

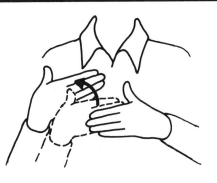

before

Open B both hands, palms in, thumbs up. Place RH against left palm then move RH back toward body.

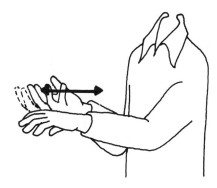

beg

Claw shape both hands, left palm down, right palm up. Place back of right claw on back of LH. Then move RH back and forth on LH.

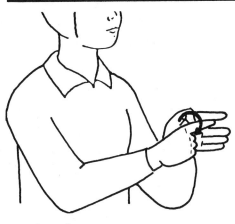

begin

B shape LH palm right, tips out. Place right index between left index and middle fingers and make a half-turn forward.

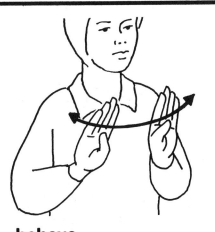

behave

B shape both hands. Swing back and forth from left to right.

behind

A shape both hands, knuckles facing, thumbs up. Place knuckles together and draw RH in back of LH.

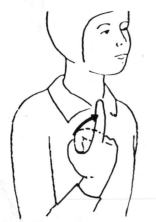

belch (burp)

Hold right S at base of throat and flick index finger up.

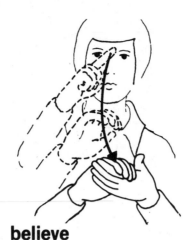

believe

Place right index on forehead then clasp both hands together.

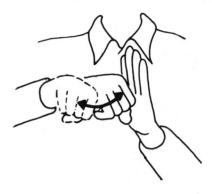

bell

LH open B palm right, tips up. Strike right S against left palm and pull away. Repeat motion.

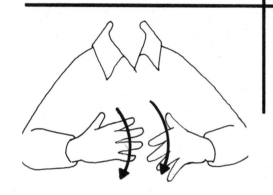

belly

Place hands on stomach then arc out and down outlining big stomach.

belong

F shape both hands, fingers spread, RH behind LH. Hook right index and thumb into left index and thumb.

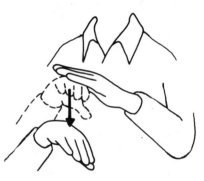

below

Open B both hands, palms down, left tips slanted right, right tips slanted left. Place RH under LH and move down.

belt

Run index fingers and thumbs from each side of waist to middle of stomach (as if fastening buckle).

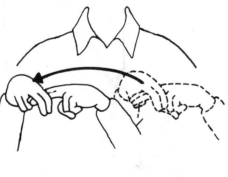

bench

H shape both hands, palms down, left tips out, right tips left. Hook right tips over left, lift up slightly, move both hands to right, and hook fingers again (indicating long chair).

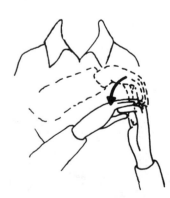

bend

LH open B palm right. Grasp tips with RH and bend down.

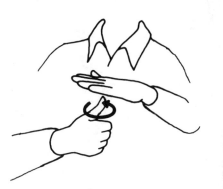

beneath

LH open B palm down, tips slightly right. Place right A, thumb extended, beneath left palm and circle counterclockwise.

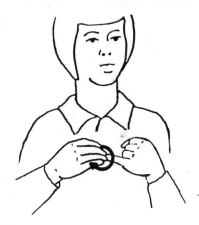

berry

Twist cupped RH around left little finger.

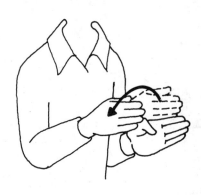

beside

B shape both hands, tips out, left palm right, right palm left. Place right B on left then move off to right, ending with palms opposite.

best

RH open B palm in. Place at mouth and move out. Then form A shapes, thumbs up. Brush right A up against left A.

bet

Open B both hands, palms up, tips out. Flip over toward one another ending with palms down. (Sometimes made with regular B shapes.)

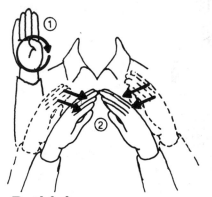

Bethlehem

Circle right B at shoulder. Then tap tips of both B shapes (palms facing) together.

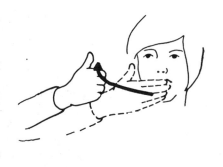

better

RH open B palm in, tips left. Place tips on chin then move upward into A shape with thumb extended.

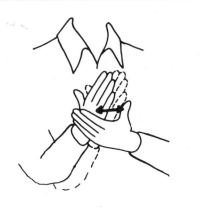

between

LH open B palm and tips slanted right. Place little finger edge of right open B between left thumb and index and move back and forth.

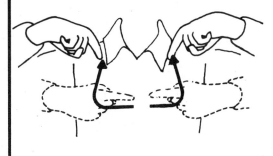

bib

One shape both hands, palms in, tips facing. Move up to collar, outlining bib.

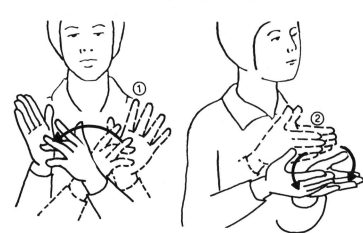

Bible

Open B both hands, palms facing. Place tip of right middle finger on left palm, then left middle tip on right palm. Now place palms together, thumbs up, and open as if opening book.

bicycle

S shape both hands, knuckles down, LH below RH. Circle up and down as if pedaling.

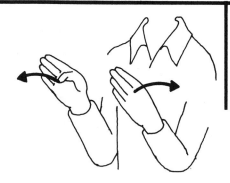

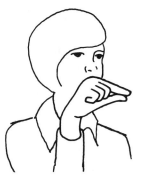

big

B shape both hands, palms facing, tips out. Move away from one another.

bill

B shape RH palm up, tips out. Move forward.

bill (bird)

Place back of right G (tips together) at mouth.

binoculars

C shape both hands, palms facing. Place on eyes and twist as if adjusting binoculars.

bird

G shape right hand, tips left. Place on chin and snap index and thumb together twice.

birthday

Open B both hands, left tips right, right tips left. Place right B on chest and flip over into left. Now place elbow of right D, palm left, on tips of left open B, palm down. Arc right D down to left elbow.

birthday (alt.)

Four shape RH palm in, tips left. Place on upper left arm then flip over onto left forearm.

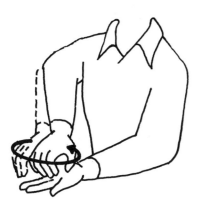

biscuit

LH open B palm up, tips slanted right. Twist cupped fingers of RH in left palm.

bit (small amount)

Hold RH palm up and flip thumb from under index finger several times.

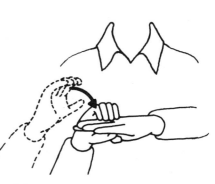

bite

B shape LH palm down, tips right. "Bite" LH with fingers of right C.

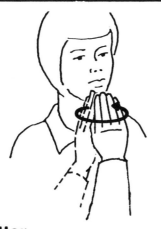

bitter

B shape RH palm left. Place index tip on chin and twist to the left.

black

Draw index finger across forehead from one brow to the other.

blade

B shape LH palm and tips slanted right. Slide right middle finger forward off left index.

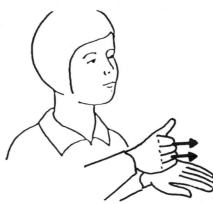

blame

B shape LH palm down, tips out. Slide right A, thumb extended, over back of LH twice.

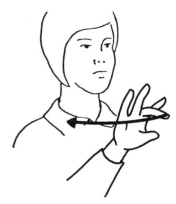

blank

Five shape RH middle finger bent. Draw a line in air from left to right.

blanket

B shape both hands, palms down, tips facing. Move toward chest, as if pulling blanket up to neck.

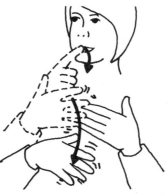

bleed

LH open B palm in, tips right. Place right index finger on lips then flutter right fingers across back of left fingers.

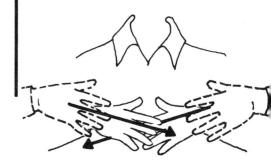

blend

Five shape both hands, palms in, tips facing. Place right fingers on back of left fingers.

bless

A shape both hands, knuckles facing, thumbs extended. Place on mouth then move out into 5 shapes palms down.

blind

Touch eyes with bent V.

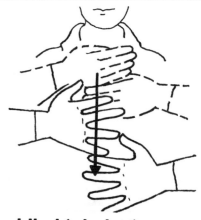

blind (window)

B shape both hands, palms in, left tips right, right tips left. Hold in front of face then drop and spread fingers.

58

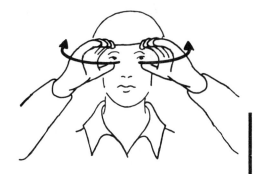

blindfold

C shape both hands, palms facing. Place on eyes and move back to temples, as if putting on blindfold.

blink

Snap right flat O in front of right eye.

blister

LH open B palm down, tips out. Place tips of right flat O on back of LH and spread slightly.

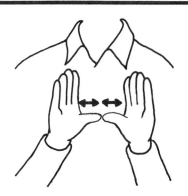

block

Open B both hands, palms out. Tap thumbs together twice.

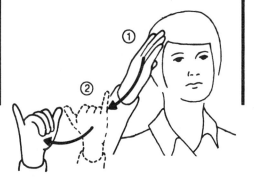

blonde

Touch hair with right open B. Then move down into Y shape and twist to palm out.

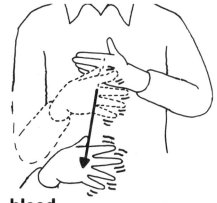

blood

LH open B palm in, tips right. Trickle right fingers down back of left (to indicate blood dripping).

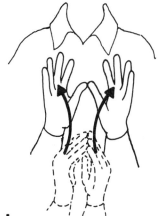

bloom

Place tips of flat O shapes together and open into 5 shapes thumbs touching.

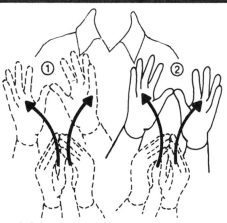

blossom

Place tips of flat O shapes together and open into 5 shapes thumbs touching. Repeat.

blouse

Bent B both hands, palms down, held at upper chest. Arc down, ending with palms up, little fingers against lower chest.

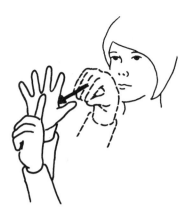

blow

Place right O on right edge of lips. Bring out into open 5 toward left index finger which is pointed up.

blower

Place left S at mouth, knuckles facing right. Loop right index out from left S and back again (indicating party horn).

blow up

S shape LH knuckles right. Place right hand on top of left S then raise up quickly.

blue

B shape RH palm left. Shake back and forth slightly.

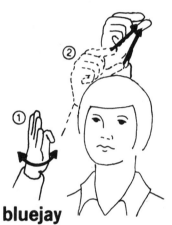

bluejay

B shape RH palm left. Shake slightly. Then place right G on head and move up closing index and thumb.

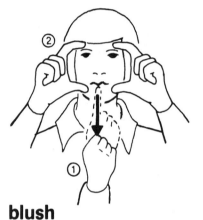

blush

Brush mouth with right index finger, then place index fingers and thumbs on cheeks.

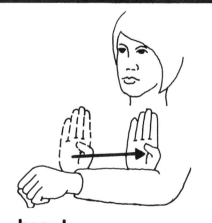

board

Run base of right B up left arm from wrist to elbow.

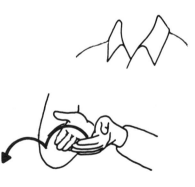

boat

Place little finger sides of open hands together, tips out, to form shape of boat. Move forward twice.

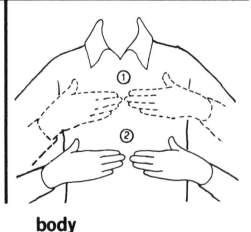

body

Open B shape both hands, palms in, tips facing. Pat chest, then stomach.

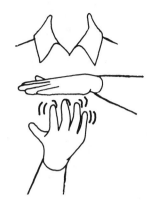

boil

LH open B palm down, tips right. Flutter fingers of RH beneath LH.

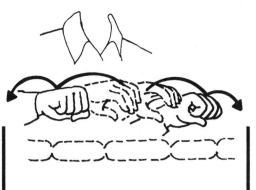

bologna

C shape both hands, palms down. Draw apart closing into S shapes. Repeat motion.

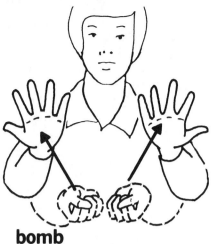

bomb

S shape both hands, palms up. Snap open and up into 5 shapes palms in.

bone

Three shape both hands, palms in. Cross wrists in front of chest.

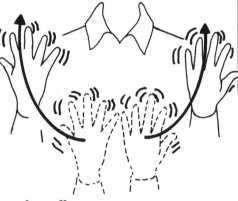

bonfire

Five shape both hands, palms in. Flutter fingers while moving up in semicircular motion.

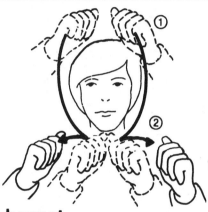

bonnet

A shape both hands. Mime putting on bonnet and tying strings under chin.

book

Palms together thumbs up. Open as if opening book.

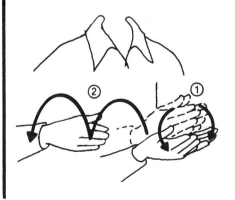

bookcase

Place palms together, thumbs up, and open as if opening book. Then form right open B, palm left, tips out, and move to right while dipping up and down.

boot

B shape LH palm down, tips out. Place in right C which is held palm up, then slide right C up to left elbow.

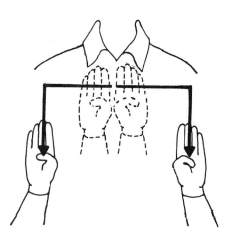

booth

B shape both hands held together. Move apart and down.

bore

Place right index on right side of nose and twist to left.

born

Open B both hands, palms in. Cross in front of chest and move away turning palms up.

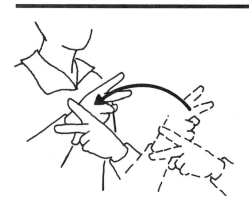

borrow

V shape both hands, left palm right, tips out; right palm in, tips left. Place right V on left and draw back to body.

boss

B shape RH, tips slanted left. Tap left upper chest twice.

both

V shape RH palm in. Place in left C which is held palm in, then draw down and out.

bother

LH open B palm right, tips out. Strike little finger side of right B several times between thumb and index finger of LH.

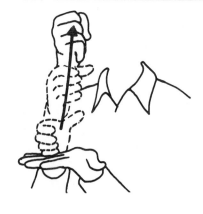

bottle

Place right C in left palm. Lift up closing into S shape.

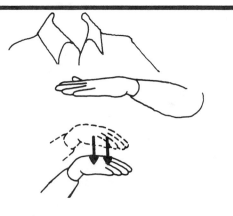

bottom

B shape both hands, palms down, left tips out, right tips left. Gently bounce right B under left B.

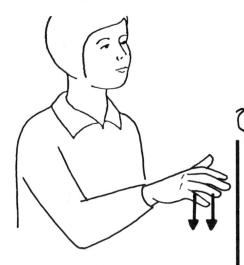

bounce

Five shape RH palm down, tips out. Bounce up and down as if bouncing a ball.

bow

Place knuckles of bent V shapes together, palms in. Draw apart into straight V shapes.

bowel movement

Fingerspell B-M.

bowel movement (alt.)

C shape LH palm right. Place right 5, palm in, in left C then draw into flat O shape.

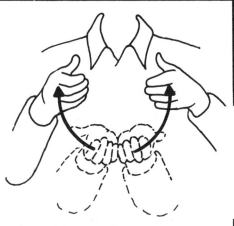

bowl (noun)

Hold cupped hands together palms up. Move apart and up, outlining shape of bowl.

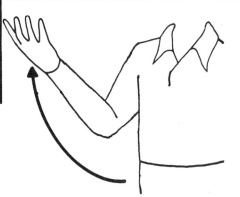

bowl (verb)

Mime throwing bowling ball.

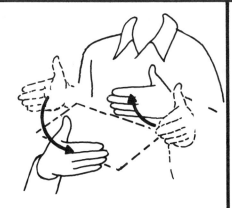

box

Open B both hands, palms facing, thumbs up. Turn LH right and RH left to form shape of box.

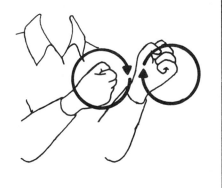

box (verb)

Move fists in circular motion as if getting ready to box.

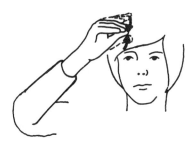

boy

Snap flat O at forehead twice, indicating brim of cap.

bra

L shape both hands, palms in, thumbs and index tips facing. Place on breast then draw apart, outlining bra.

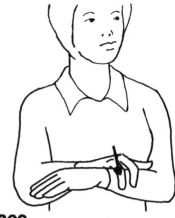

brace

Slap right 3 shape down on left forearm.

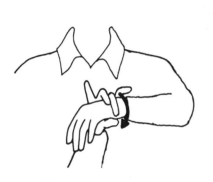

bracelet

Circle left wrist with right middle finger and thumb and twist slightly.

braces (teeth)

A shape both hands. Place thumbs on teeth.

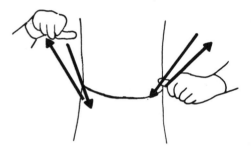

brag

A shape both hands, knuckles down, thumbs extended. Punch sides of body with thumbs alternately.

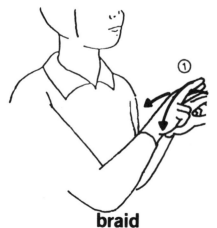
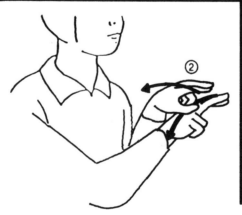

braid

R shape both hands. Place right R on top of left, draw back, and reverse motion (left on top of right).

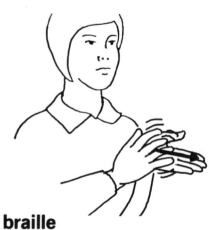

braille

Flutter right fingers slightly across left palm.

brain
Place thumb of right C on fore-head.

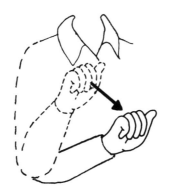

brake
A shape RH. Move forward quickly as if pushing brake.

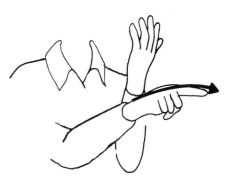

branch
Open B left hand palm in. Slide right index across back of left wrist.

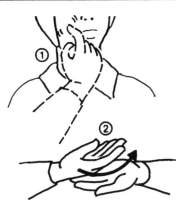

brand new
Rub index and thumb of RH, palm in, together at side of right cheek. Then brush back of right open B inward across left palm.

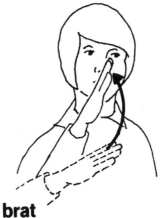

brat
B shape RH palm left. Arc up and hit tip of nose.

brave
Place claw hands on shoulders. Move out in strong movement, ending in fists.

bread
LH open B palm in, tips right. Draw little finger side of right hand down back of left fingers several times.

break
S shape both hands, knuckles down, thumbs and index fingers touching. Break apart.

breakfast
Place tips of right flat O on lips then move out into open B. Now place little finger side of left open B, palm in, tips right, in crook of right elbow and bring right arm up.

breakfast (alt.)

B shape RH palm in, tips left. Rotate tips at mouth.

breast

Bent RH open B palm in. Place tips on left breast then on right breast.

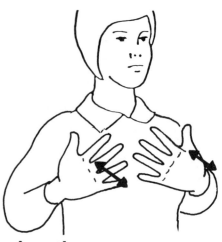

breath

Five shape both hands, palms in. Place on chest then move back and forth.

breathe

Place tips of claw hands on chest, left below right, then move in and out.

breeze

Open B both hands, palms in, tips up and slanted toward one another. Fan toward shoulders.

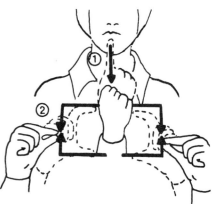

brick

Brush right index tip down lips, then outline shape of brick with index fingers and thumbs.

bride

Place index side of right B on right cheek then clasp hands together.

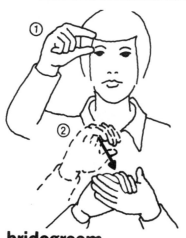

bridegroom

Place right G on forehead, tips left, then clasp hands together.

bridge

Hold left open B in front of body palm down, tips right. Place tips of right V under left wrist then arc to elbow.

66

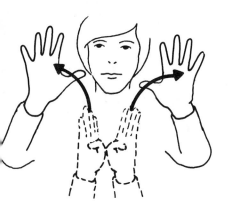

bright

B shape both hands, palms facing, tips up. Spread fingers and turn palms out.

brilliant

C shape RH palm left. Place thumb on forehead and move out.

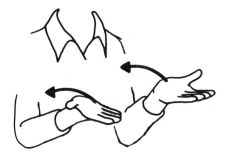

bring

Open B both hands, palms up, one slightly behind the other. Move toward body as if carrying something.

broccoli

B shape RH. Slide left C down right forearm.

broil

LH open B palm down, tips right. Flutter fingers of RH over back of LH.

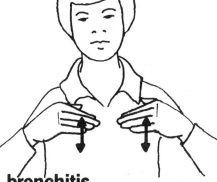

bronchitis

Bent B both hands, palms in. Place tips on chest and move up and down.

brontosaurus

Bent B shape RH. Move down from left to right in wavy motion (outlining back of dinosaur).

brook

Open B both hands, tips out, left palm up, right palm left. Slide little finger side of right B across left palm in wavy motion.

broom

S shape both hands. Mime holding broom and sweeping.

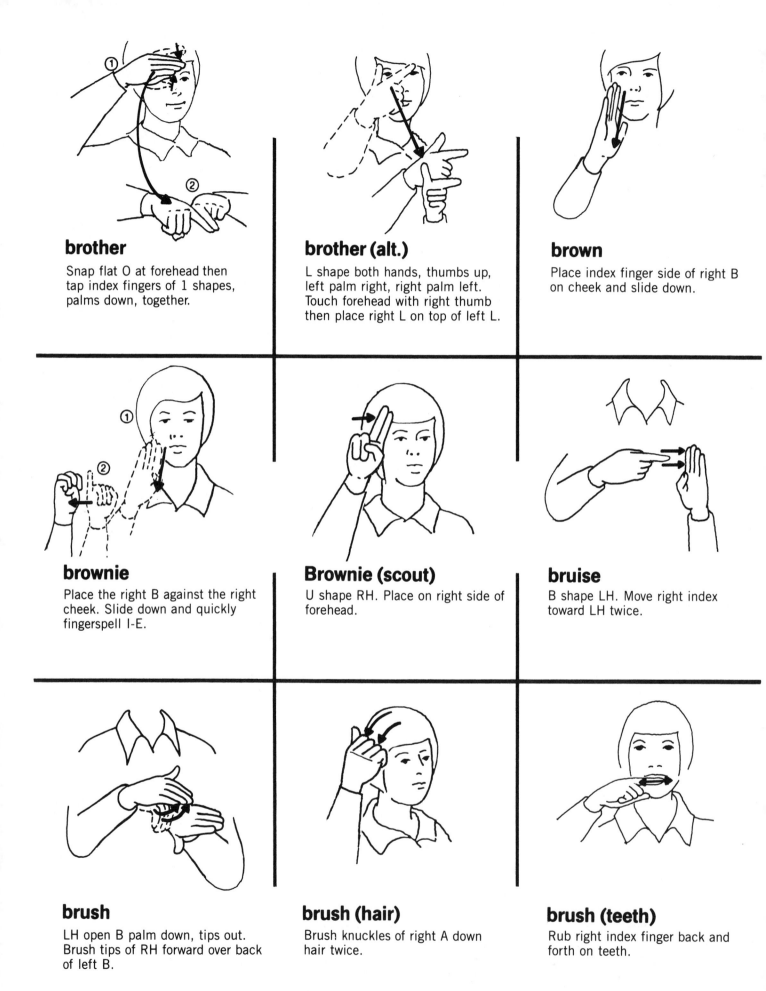

brother

Snap flat O at forehead then tap index fingers of 1 shapes, palms down, together.

brother (alt.)

L shape both hands, thumbs up, left palm right, right palm left. Touch forehead with right thumb then place right L on top of left L.

brown

Place index finger side of right B on cheek and slide down.

brownie

Place the right B against the right cheek. Slide down and quickly fingerspell I-E.

Brownie (scout)

U shape RH. Place on right side of forehead.

bruise

B shape LH. Move right index toward LH twice.

brush

LH open B palm down, tips out. Brush tips of RH forward over back of left B.

brush (hair)

Brush knuckles of right A down hair twice.

brush (teeth)

Rub right index finger back and forth on teeth.

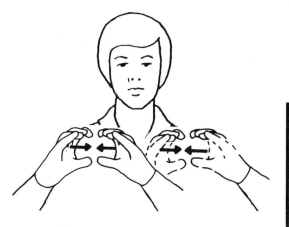

bubble
C shape both hands, palms and tips facing. Tap tips together at left, then at right.

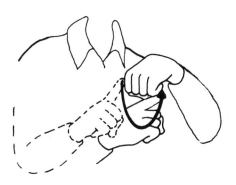

bucket
Hold left fist up as if holding handle of bucket. Place right index on thumb side then circle under to little finger side.

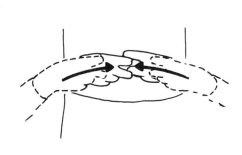

buckle
Bent V shape both hands, palms in, knuckles facing. Interlock at waist.

buffalo
I shape both hands. Place at side of head.

bug
Place thumb of right 3 on nose and crook index and middle fingers down.

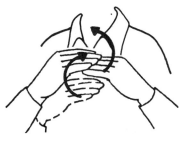

build
Open B both hands, palms down, tips facing. Alternately place one hand on top of other, moving upward.

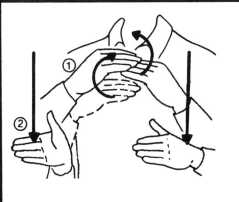

building
Open B both hands, palms down, tips facing. Alternately place one on top of other, moving upward. Then form sides of building, palms facing.

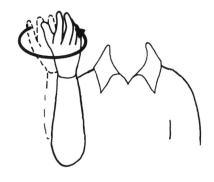

bulb
Mime screwing in light bulb.

bull

Place knuckles of right Y on forehead.

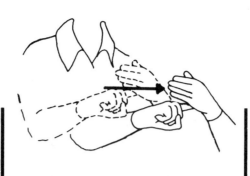

bulldozer

LH open B palm in, tips right. Place right index in left palm and push forward.

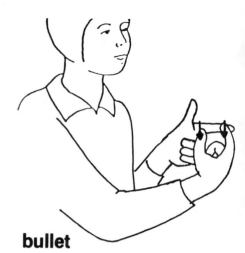

bullet

L shape LH palm right, index tip out. Draw tips of right G down tip of left index.

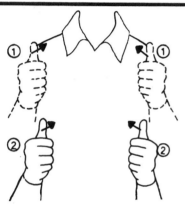

bulletin

A shape both hands, palms facing, thumbs extended. Hold before chest, punch forward, drop, and punch again.

bully

Curved L shape both hands, palms in, knuckles facing, index tips on eyebrows. Draw hands apart outlining eyebrows.

bump

Curved LH open B palm right, tips slanted out. Hit left palm with knuckles of right S.

bundle

Hold cupped hands in front of body. Circle up, right above left, closing into S shapes. Rest right S on left.

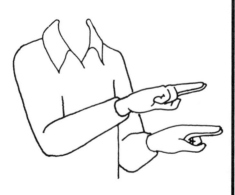

bunk

H shape both hands, palms down, tips out. Hold right above left.

bunny

B shape both hands, palms in, tips up. Cross wrists and flick fingers back toward body.

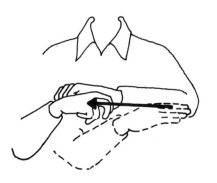

burglar

Place right B, palm down, tips left, against left elbow, then snatch back to wrist, ending in bent V.

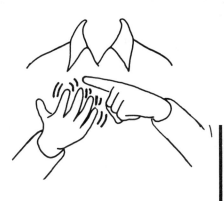

burn

One shape LH palm down, tip right. Flutter fingers of RH beneath left index.

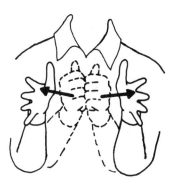

burst

A shape both hands, knuckles touching. Draw apart and push forward into 5 shapes.

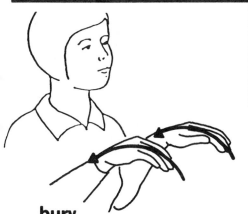

bury

Cupped hands, palms down, arc back toward body, outlining mound.

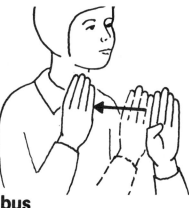

bus

B shape both hands, left palm right, right palm left. Place little finger side of right B against left index then draw RH back toward body.

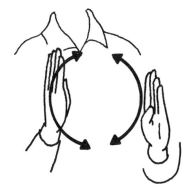

bus (alt.)

B shape both hands, palms facing. Mime holding steering wheel and turning.

bush

Five shape RH palm left, tips up. Place tips of left B on right wrist and wiggle right fingers.

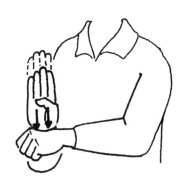

business

S shape LH palm down. B shape RH. Tap left wrist twice with base of right B.

busy

S shape LH knuckles down. Brush base of right B back and forth on inside of left wrist.

but
Cross index fingers and draw apart.

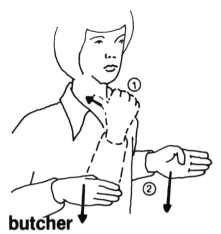

butcher
A shape RH knuckles down, thumb extended. Jab throat with thumb. Follow with agent marker.

butter
LH open B palm up, tips out. Brush twice with tips of right H.

buttercup
Place index side of right B on right cheek. Move over to left cheek, ending in C shape palm left.

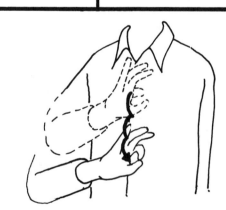

butterfly
Hook thumbs palms in and flap fingers.

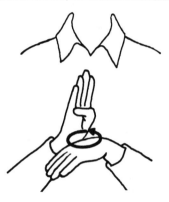

butterscotch
B shape LH palm down, tips slanted right. B shape RH palm left. Place base of right B on back of left B and make small circular motion.

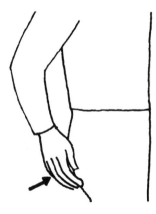

buttock
Place right hand on buttock.

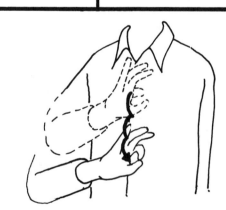

button
Curve index finger inside thumb. Tap three times on chest beginning at top.

button up
F shape both hands, palms facing. Place tips together on chest and alternately twist back and forth.

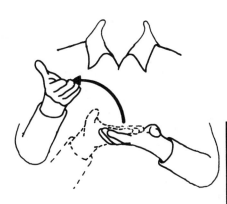

buy
Place back of right hand in left palm. Lift up and out.

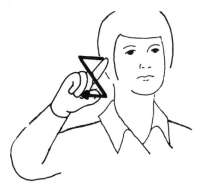

buzz
Place right index finger on ear then zigzag away to the right.

by
Fingerspell B-Y in quick succession as if one movement.

bye-bye
RH open B palm down, tips out. Wave up and down.

C

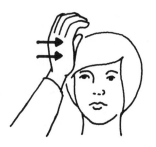

cabbage

Tap base of right C against right temple twice.

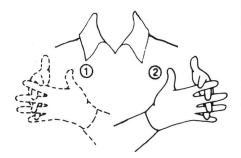

cabin

Interlock fingers and move from right to left.

cabinet

Place thumbs and index tips of both hands together. Mime opening up cabinet doors.

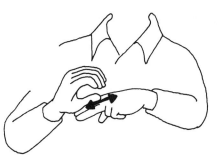

caboose

H shape LH palm down, tips out. C shape RH palm and tips left. Rub base of right C back and forth on left H.

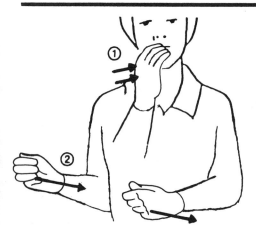

cafeteria

Place tips of flat O on mouth. Then form A shapes both hands, palms facing, and move from right to left.

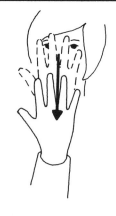

cage

Hold right 5 in front of forehead palm in. Drop to chin.

cake

LH open B palm up, tips out. Hold right claw, tips down, over left palm then lift up while spreading fingers.

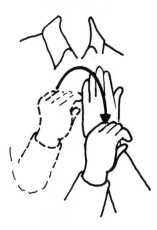

calendar

LH open B palm in. C shape RH palm and tips left. Place RH in left palm then slide over tips and down back of LH.

calf

Place thumb of right Y on right temple and twist forward. Then hold right bent hand over left bent hand and lower RH slightly.

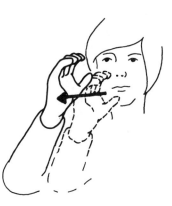

call

Place right C at right side of mouth and move out.

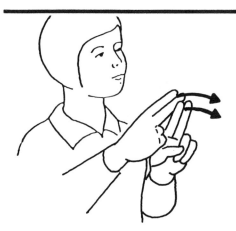

call (name)

H shape both hands, left palm right, right palm in. Place right H on left H then arc both hands forward.

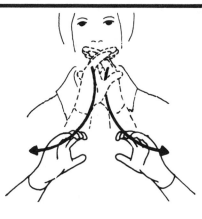

calm

C shape both hands, left palm right, right palm left. Cross at mouth then draw down and apart.

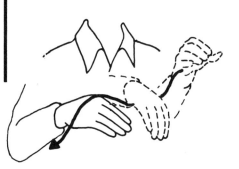

camel

C shape RH palm left. Beginning at left, slide down toward right then up and down again, outlining hump.

camera

Mime holding camera in front of face and clicking shutter.

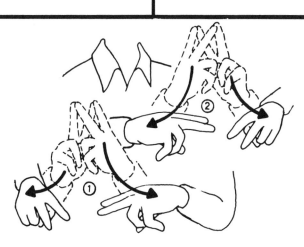

camp

V shape both hands, palms facing, tips touching. Draw apart ending with palms down. Repeat.

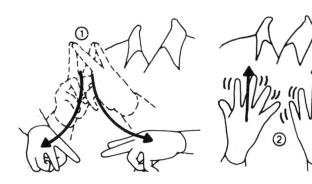

campfire

V shape both hands, palms facing, tips touching. Draw apart ending with palms down. Change into 5 shapes, palms up, and flutter fingers.

campus

Circle right C clockwise over back of LH which is held palm down, tips out.

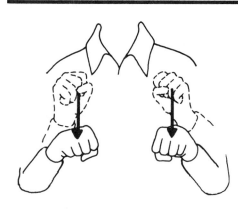

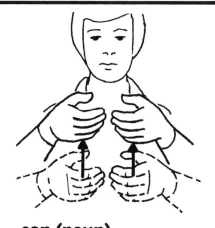

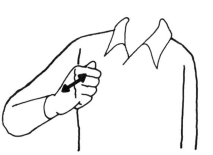

can (verb)

S shape both hands, knuckles down. Move down in forceful motion.

can (noun)

C shape both hands, palms facing. Move up, outlining shape of can.

Canada

Grab shirt with RH and tug back and forth slightly.

canary

LH open B palm up, tips out. C shape RH palm left. Place thumb of right C on chin then swing over left palm.

cancel

Make cross mark in palm of left open B with tip of right index finger.

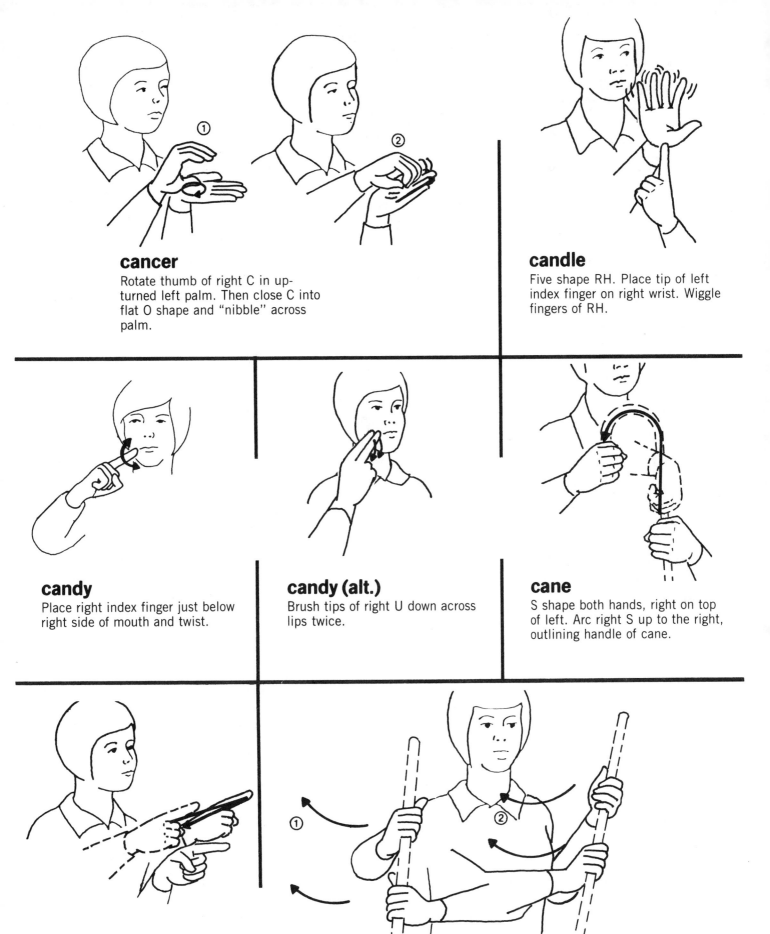

cancer
Rotate thumb of right C in up-turned left palm. Then close C into flat O shape and "nibble" across palm.

candle
Five shape RH. Place tip of left index finger on right wrist. Wiggle fingers of RH.

candy
Place right index finger just below right side of mouth and twist.

candy (alt.)
Brush tips of right U down across lips twice.

cane
S shape both hands, right on top of left. Arc right S up to the right, outlining handle of cane.

cannon
One shape both hands, left palm right, right palm left, tips out. Place right on top of left, shoot forward, then recoil.

canoe
Mime paddling a canoe.

can't

One shape both hands, palms down, tips slanted toward one another. Strike tip of left index with tip of right passing on down.

cantaloupe

C shape LH palm down. Thump back of left wrist with right middle finger.

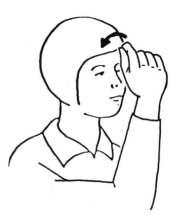

cap

Mime placing cap on head with thumb and index finger of RH holding brim.

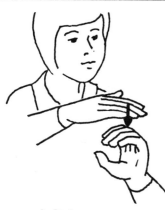

cap (alt.)

Tap top of left C with right palm.

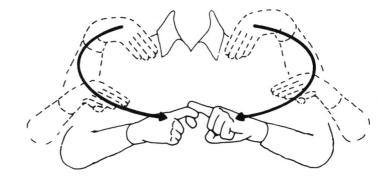

cape

Place curved hands on shoulders. Move forward in semicircles and hook index fingers.

capital

Rest thumb of right C on right shoulder.

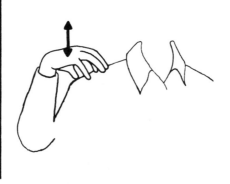

captain

Tap right shoulder with tips of right claw hand.

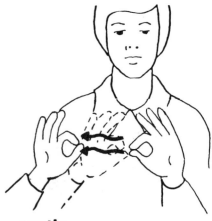

caption

F shape both hands, index fingers and thumbs touching. Wiggle right F to rignt (away from LH).

capture

Five shape both hands, left palm and tips slightly right; right palm down, tips out. Bring together quickly closing into S shapes, right on top of left.

car

C shape both hands. Place little finger side of right C on left index then draw back.

car (alt.)

C shape both hands. Mime holding and turning steering wheel.

caramel

Place thumb and index of right C against right side of mouth and brush down twice.

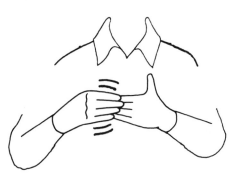

card

LH open B palm up, tips out. C shape RH palm down. Slide RH off left palm.

cardboard

LH open B palm in, tips right. Grasp left fingers with right fingers and wiggle back and forth.

care

V shape both hands, palms facing, tips out. Strike index side of left V with little finger side of right V. Repeat.

careful

V shape both hands, tips out. Place right V on left then circle both hands forward and back.

careless

V shape RH palm left. Pass across eyes, ending with palm down.

carnival

C shape RH palm left. Outline a "backward" S while changing to L shape.

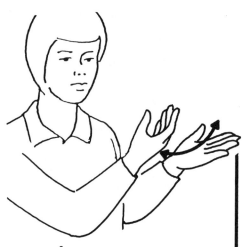

carol

LH open B palm up. Swing right C above left palm and forearm in rhythmic motion.

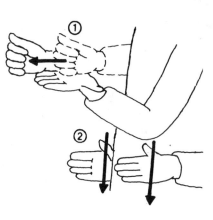

carpenter

LH open B palm up, tips out. A shape RH. Place A on base of left palm and push forward as if planing a piece of wood. Follow with agent marker.

carpet

LH open B palm down, tips out. Drag base of right C forward over back of LH.

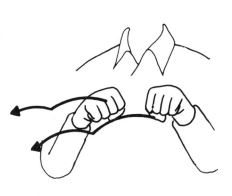

carriage

S shape both hands, knuckles down. Move forward as if pushing a carriage.

carrot

Hold right S up to mouth and twist slightly, as if eating carrot.

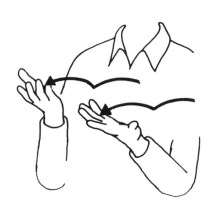

carry

Open 5 both hands, palms up, tips slanted left. Move from right to left or vice versa in front of body.

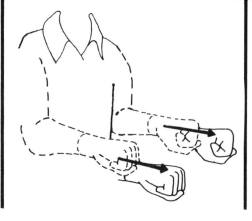

cart

S shape both hands, palms down. Push straight forward.

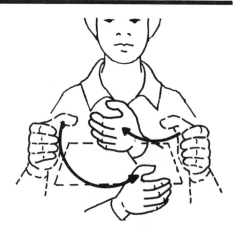

carton

C shape both hands, palms and tips facing. Turn LH right and RH left to form shape of box.

cartoon

Brush index finger of right C down nose twice.

carve

C shape LH palm and tips down. B shape RH palm left. Make carving motions across the left index and thumb with palm of right B.

case

C shape both hands, palms and tips facing. Change to S shapes then turn LH right and RH left, outlining box shape.

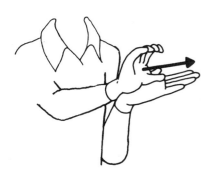

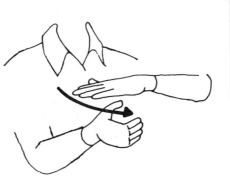

cash

LH open B palm up, tips out. Place base of right C on base of left palm and move forward.

casserole

LH open B palm down, tips right. C shape RH palm and tips left. Slide RH under left hand.

cast

LH open B palm down. Slide right C up left forearm.

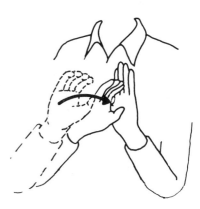

castle

Bent V shape both hands, palms facing. Move upward outlining shape of castle tower.

cat

Place thumb and forefinger of right 9 at side of mouth and pull away twice (indicating whiskers).

catch

LH open B palm right, tips up. Hit middle of left palm with index and thumb of right C.

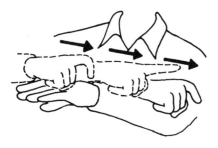

caterpillar

LH open B palm down, tips right. Rest knuckles of right X on back of LH. Crook and uncrook right index while moving hand up left arm.

Catholic

Describe a cross in front of face with right U shape.

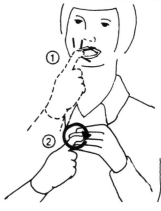

catsup (ketchup)

K shape RH palm out. Shake to left side.

cauliflower

Tap right side of head twice with heal of right F.

cave

C shape LH palm right. "Walk" right bent V into left C.

cavity

Tap teeth with right index. Then make circular movement on back of left bent B held palm in.

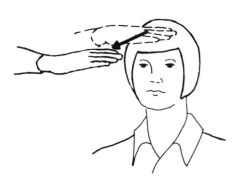

ceiling

B shape RH palm down, tips left. Place over head and move out.

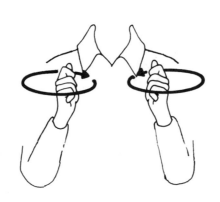

celebrate

X shape both hands, knuckles facing. Circle toward one another in exuberant manner.

celery

Bring right G up to mouth as if eating a piece of celery.

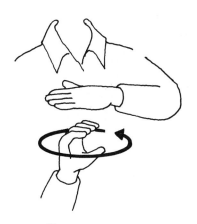

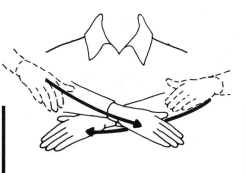

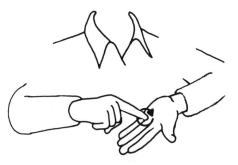

cellar

LH open B palm down, tips right. C shape RH palm and tips left. Circle RH under LH counterclockwise.

cemetery

Open B both hands, palms down, left tips slanted right, right tips slanted left. Cross hands, right over left.

cent

Circle right index finger in left palm.

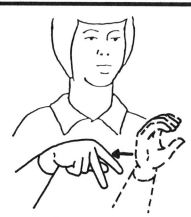

center

Circle tips of right open B over left palm, then drop tips in center of palm.

cereal

LH open B palm up, tips right. Place back of right C in left palm then lift to mouth.

cerebral palsy

Fingerspell C-P.

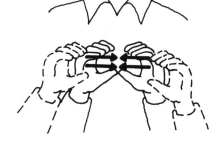

certain

C shape RH palm and tips left. Place at mouth then move out forcefully.

certificate

C shape both hands, palms facing. Tap thumbs together.

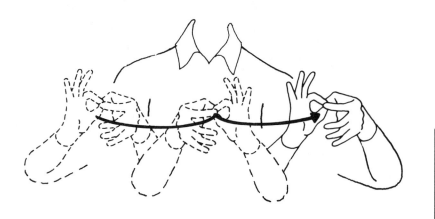

chain
Interlock index fingers and thumbs then reverse several times while moving to left.

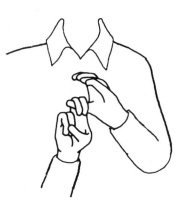

chair
C shape LH palm right. Hang right N over left thumb.

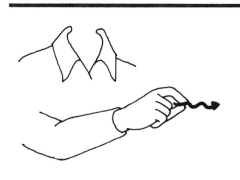

chalk
Mime writing on blackboard with chalk.

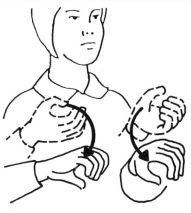

chance
C shape both hands, palms up. Flip over toward one another, ending with palms down.

change
A shape both hands, left knuckles up, right knuckles down. Place right wrist on left wrist, then reverse positions.

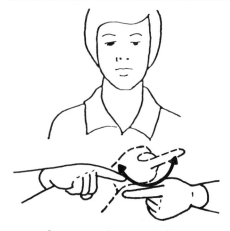

change (money)
Arc right index back and forth on left index.

channel
Fingerspell C-H.

chapel
S shape LH knuckles down. Form C shape with index and thumb of RH and tap back of left S twice.

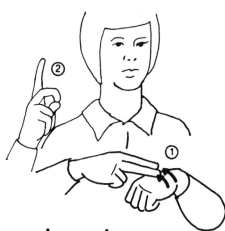

chapped

Rub tips of right H across back of left fist twice. Follow with regular past-tense marker.

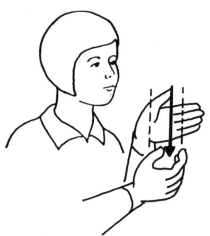

chapter

LH open B tips out. Draw tips of right C down left palm.

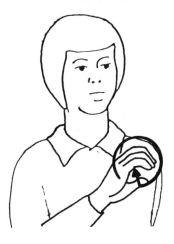

character

Circle right C, palm left, in front of left upper chest, then place on chest.

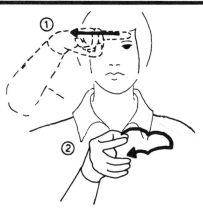

charcoal

Draw right index finger across brow from left to right and form the letter F. Move to left in short jumps and back to right as if placing coals on grill.

charge (pay later)

LH open B palm right. Brush knuckles of right C down left palm.

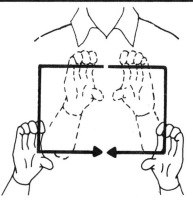

chart

C shape both hands held close together. Move apart, down, then back together.

chase

A shape both hands, thumbs up, right A behind left. Move right A toward left in circular motion.

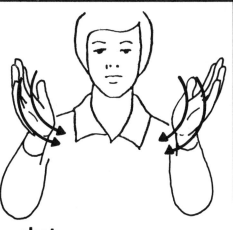

chat

Open B both hands, palms facing, tips out. Move up and down simultaneously.

cheap

LH open B palm right, tips out. Slap index finger side of right B down against left palm.

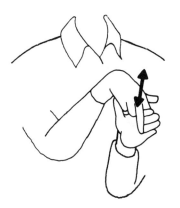

cheat

LH open B palm right, tips out. Straddle with index and middle finger of RH then move RH up and down.

check

LH open B palm up, tips out. Outline check mark in left palm with right index.

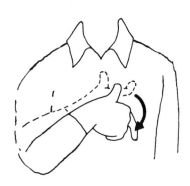

checkered

G shape RH palm in. Place tips on left upper chest. Then turn upside down so that index finger is on bottom.

checkers

Place tips of right 3 shape in left palm, then move in various directions, as if moving checker on board.

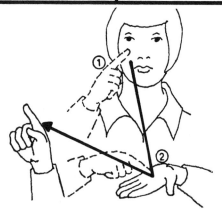

checkup

Place tip of right index under right eye. Move to center of left palm then up and out to the right.

cheek

Make circle on right cheek with right index tip.

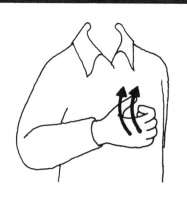

cheer

Place thumb of right C on chest and brush up twice.

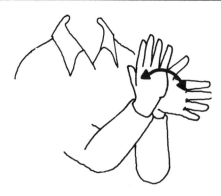

cheese

Twist heel of right palm on heel of left palm.

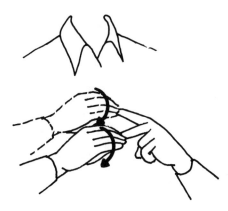

cherry

V shape LH palm down, tips right. Twist left index then middle finger with tips of right flat O.

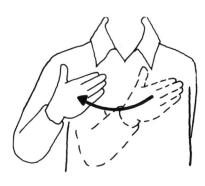

chest

Place tips of right open B on upper left side of chest then move over to right side.

chew

Bent V both hands, left tips up, right tips down. Circle right tips over left tips clockwise.

chick

LH open B palm up, tips slanted right. Place knuckles of right G in left palm and tap index and thumb together twice.

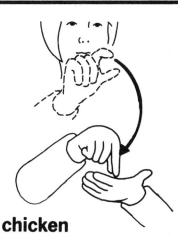

chicken

Place side of right G on mouth then place tips in left palm.

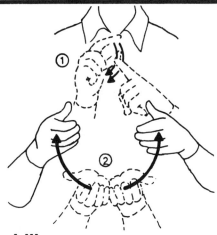

chief

A shape RH knuckles left, thumb extended. Raise up above shoulder level.

child

Lower RH, palm down, indicating height of child.

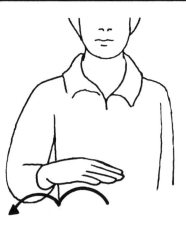

children

RH open B palm down. Bounce down two or three times to the right.

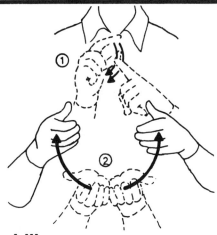

chili

One shape LH palm right, tips out. Strike twice with tips of right G. Now place cupped hands together, palms up, then move apart and up, outlining shape of bowl.

chill

Place right bent V on top of left bent V with thumbs touching. Rub back and forth (as if teeth chattering).

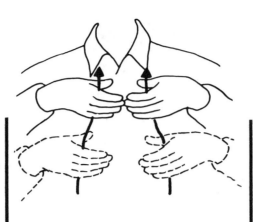

chimney

C shape both hands, tips almost touching. Draw up in shape of chimney.

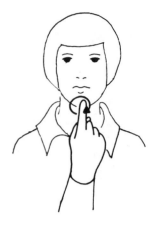

chin

Make circle on chin with index finger.

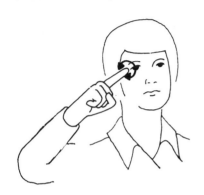

China

Place tip of right index on edge of right eye and twist forward.

chip

Strike tip of left index finger with thumb of right C.

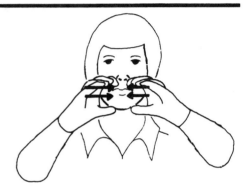

chipmunk

C shape both hands, palms facing. Tap tips together at mouth.

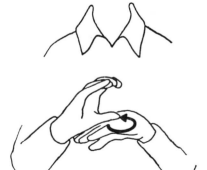

chocolate

Place thumb of right C on back of left hand and circle counterclockwise.

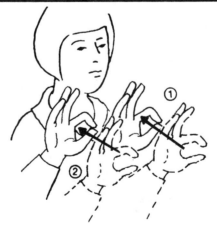

choice

Open F shape RH fingers spread. Move back, closing thumb and index. Repeat motion a little to the right.

choke

Grasp throat tightly with RH.

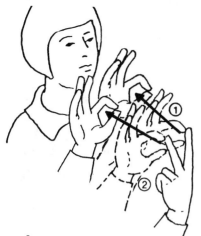

choose

V shape LH palm in. With right thumb and index, pick at left index and middle fingers, as if choosing something.

chop

Open B both hands, left palm up, tips slanted right; right palm and tips slanted left. Chop left palm with little finger of right open B.

chop (tree)

LH open B palm in. Chop back of left wrist with little finger side of right open B.

chore

S shape LH palm down. Brush base of right C back and forth across top of left S.

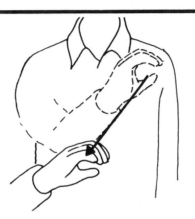

Christ

Place right C against left shoulder and move to right side of waist.

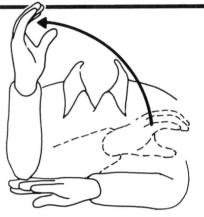

Christmas

Place elbow of right C on back of LH which is held before you tips right. Arc right C from left to right.

chubby

Place claw hands on cheeks.

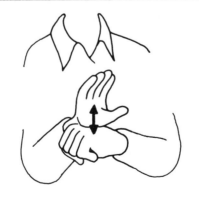

church

Tap right C on back of left S twice.

cider

Place thumb of right C on right cheek and twist forward.

cigar

Hold right R at right side of mouth tips out, palm down.

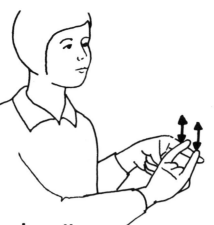

cigarette

Tap left index with right index and little finger several times.

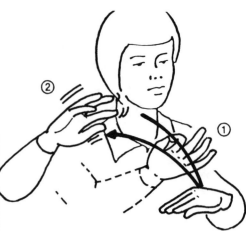

Cinderella

Strike little finger side of right F against back of LH. Change to 5 shape RH and move slowly up from LH while wiggling fingers (as if tapping Cinderella with wand and transforming her).

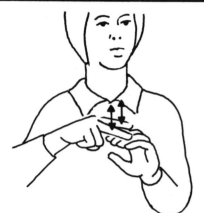

cinnamon

Tap right V on back of left C several times. (Sometimes the fingers of the right V alternate in motion.)

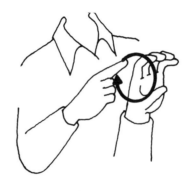

circle

C shape LH. Circle thumb side with right index finger clockwise. (Sometimes made without left C.)

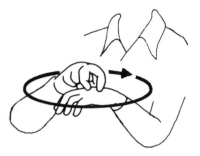

circus

Bent LH open B palm down. Place tips of right bent V on back of LH and circle both hands clockwise.

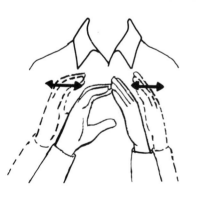

city

LH open B palm right, tips up. C shape RH palm left. Tap hands together twice.

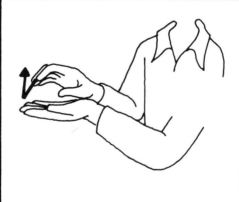

clam

LH open B palm up, tips out. Curved RH open B palm down. Place base of right B on base of left. Lower fingers then raise. Repeat.

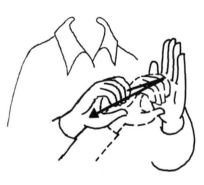

clang

LH open B palm right. Strike index and thumb of right C against left palm and swing back to the right.

clap

Open B both hands, palms facing. Clap together several times.

class

C shape both hands held close together. Draw apart and around to front ending in 5 shapes, little fingers touching.

claw

Claw shape RH palm out. Turn so that palm faces body.

clay

Put hands together and move slightly as if molding clay.

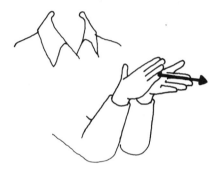

clean

Open B both hands, left palm up, tips out; right palm down, tips left. Brush right palm across left as if wiping clean.

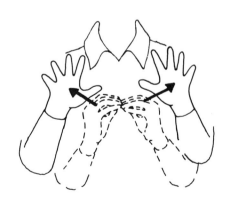

clear

Place tips of flat O shapes together, open into 5 shapes, and turn out.

clever

Place tip of right middle finger on forehead then flick out.

climb

RH bent V palm out. Move up in short circular movements.

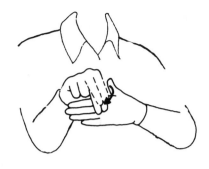

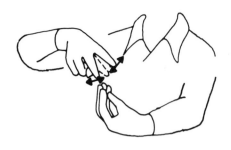

clip (noun)

LH open B palm in, tips right. Snap right index, middle finger, and thumb over left index.

clip (verb)

LH flat O tips up. V shape RH palm down, tips left. Snip right V over left tips.

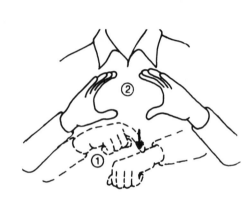

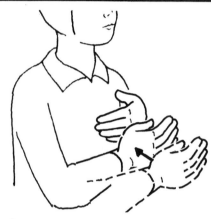

clock

Touch back of left wrist with right index finger. Then outline clock with double C shapes facing each other.

close (verb)

B shape both hands, palms facing, tips out. Turn toward each other so that index fingers touch.

close

Open B both hands, palms in, thumbs up, right B in front of left. Move RH close to LH without touching.

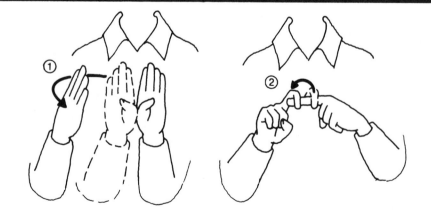

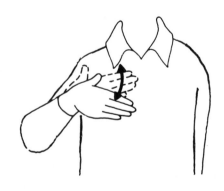

closet

B shape both hands, index fingers touching. Turn RH to right, then hook right index over base of left and move forward.

cloth

RH open B palm in, tips left. Rub up and down on upper right side of chest.

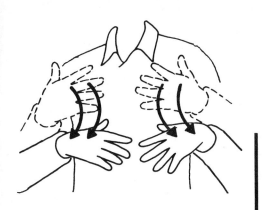

clothes

Brush open palms down chest twice.

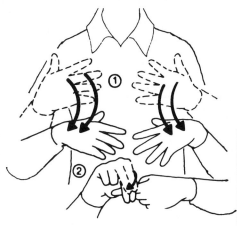

clothespin

Brush open palms down chest twice then snap right index, middle finger, and thumb over left index.

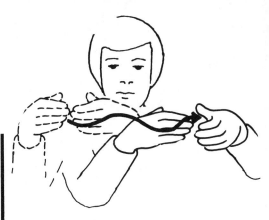

cloud

Cupped shape both hands, palms facing. Move from right to left with undulating motion. (Can also be made moving from left to right.)

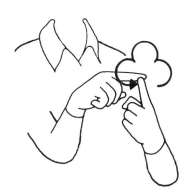

clover

One shape LH. Touch with right index and outline clover leaf.

clown

Place tips of right claw hand on nose and move back and forth several times. (Sometimes made with twisting motion.)

club

C shape both hands, thumbs touching. Draw apart and around, changing to B shapes palms in.

clumsy

Three shape both hands, palms down. Move up and down alternately once or twice.

coach

One shape LH knuckles down, tips slanted right. Rub right C back and forth on left index.

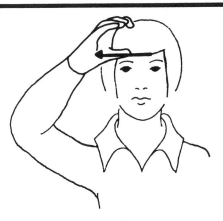

coal

Draw thumb of right C across eyebrows from left to right.

coat

A shape both hands. Trace shape of lapels with thumbs.

cocoa

Place thumb of right C (middle, fourth, and little fingers closed) on back of left hand and circle counterclockwise.

coconut

Mime holding coconut at right side of head and shaking.

cocoon

Interlock thumbs, palms in, and close fingers.

coffee

Place right S on left S and make a grinding motion counterclockwise.

coffin

LH open B palm right, tips out. Form lid with right open B, ending with thumbs touching.

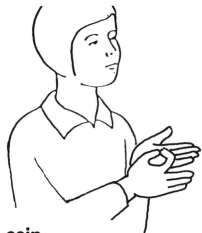

coin

Place thumb and index finger of right F in left palm, describing shape of coin.

Coke (Coca-Cola)

Hold left arm out. Stick upper arm with index finger of right L and wiggle thumb.

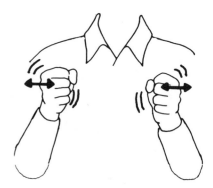

cold (adj.)

S shape both hands. Draw hands close to body and "shiver."

cold (noun)
Place right thumb and index on nose, then draw away as if using handkerchief.

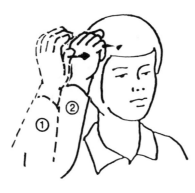

coleslaw
Tap right side of head with base of C shape RH. Change to S shape RH and tap head once more.

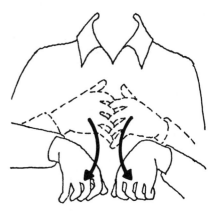

collapse
Claw shape both hands, fingers entwined, palms in. Drop apart suddenly, ending with palms down.

collar
G shape both hands, tips facing. Place at neck and outline collar.

collect
LH open B palm up. Scrape little finger side of right C across left palm twice.

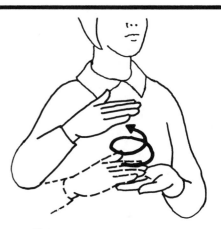

college
Clap hands together once then circle RH upward over left palm.

color
Five shape RH palm in. Flutter fingers at chin level.

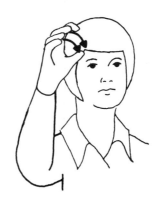

colt
Place thumb of right C against right temple and bend fingers forward twice.

comb

Brush open fingers through hair twice.

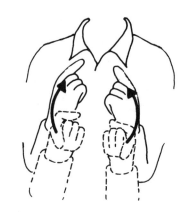

come

One shape both hands, knuckles up, tips out. Bring tips up and back toward chest.

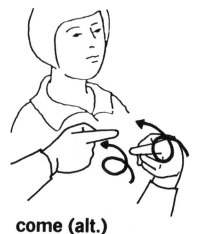

come (alt.)

One shape both hands, palms in, fingers facing. Roll in alternately toward body.

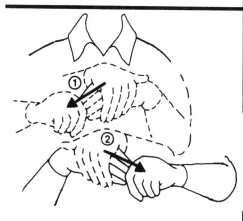

comfortable

Curved open B shape both hands, palms down. Place right palm on back of LH, slide off, then reverse motion.

comic

Place index tips of C shapes at side of mouth then move away from face. Repeat motion.

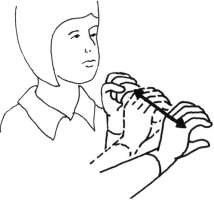

commercial

S shape LH palm right. C shape RH palm left. Place right C against left little finger, then move right C out and back several times.

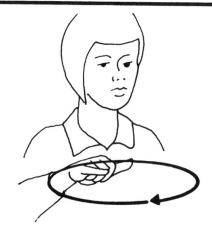

common

Y shape RH palm down. Move out in large clockwise circle.

common sense

C shape RH palm left. Place on right side of forehead then move out into S shape.

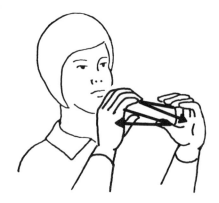

communicate

C shape both hands, palms facing. Move back and forth alternately at sides of mouth.

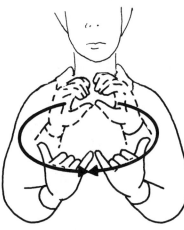

community

C shape both hands, thumbs touching. Draw apart and around to front, changing into Y shapes palms in, little fingers touching.

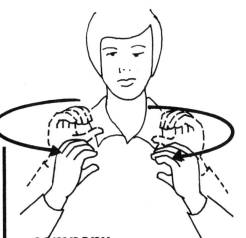

company

C shape both hands. Move apart in large semicircles, ending with palms in.

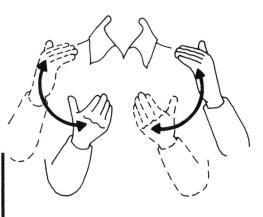

compare

Curved open B both hands, tips out, left palm up, right palm down. Turn each over, reversing positions. Repeat motion.

compass

Place knuckles of right 1 in left palm and wave index finger back and forth.

complain

Claw shape both hands, palms in, RH above LH. Strike chest twice with tips.

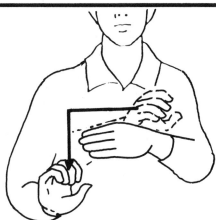

complete

B shape LH palm right, tips out. Slide right C off left index finger and drop down.

complicate

Claw shape both hands, palms down, tips facing, RH slightly above LH. Move in toward one another while wiggling fingers.

computer

LH open B palm down, tips out. Place base of right C on left wrist and move up arm in short bouncing motions.

concentrate

C shape both hands, palms facing, held at temples. Move forward parallel to one another.

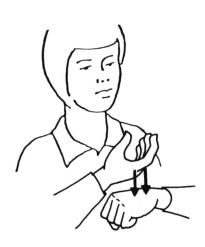

concrete

Strike back of left S with back of right C twice.

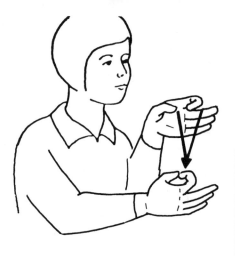

cone

F shape both hands, palms and tips facing. Place left F on top of right, then drop right F down indicating cone shape.

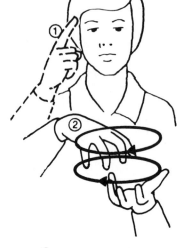

confuse

Place right index on temple. Alternately circle claw shape hands, right over left, in a clockwise motion.

congratulations

Place tips of right open B on mouth then move forward. Clap hands together twice.

connect

Lock right index and thumb into left index and thumb and wiggle slightly.

conscience

One shape RH palm down, tip left. Tap upper left side of chest twice.

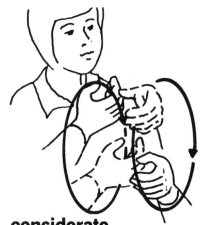

considerate

C shape both hands, left tips right, right tips left. Circle around one another.

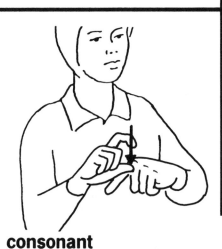

consonant

Place base of right C, fingers closed except for index, on top of left index.

constipate

A shape both hands, left palm right, right palm left, thumbs extended. Place right thumb in left A and shake slightly.

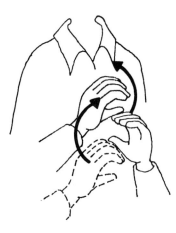

construction

C shape both hands, palms facing. Place one on top of the other alternately.

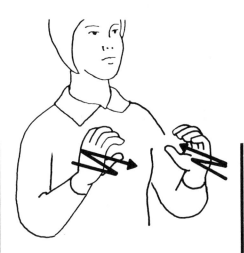

contest

C shape both hands, palms facing. Move back and forth alternately.

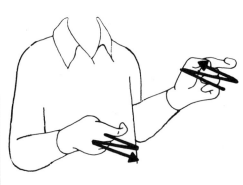

control

X shape both hands, palms facing. Move back and forth alternately as if holding reins.

convenient

Curved LH open B palm up. Brush little finger side of right C up back of left fingers twice.

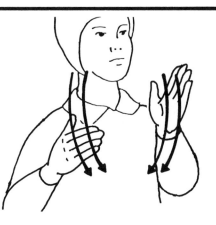

conversation

Open B both hands, palms facing. Swing down simultaneously. Repeat motion.

cook

Open B both hands, left palm up, right palm down. Place right palm on left and flip over, as if flipping pancakes.

cookie

LH open B palm up, tips out. Place tips of RH in left palm and twist as if cutting out cookies.

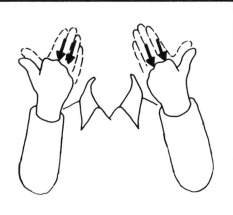

cool

Open B both hands, palms in, tips up and slanted toward one another. Hold above shoulders and wave fingers backward.

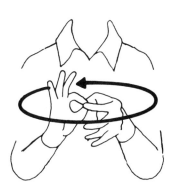

cooperate

Hook right index and thumb into left index and thumb then circle counterclockwise.

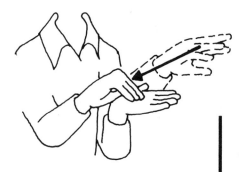

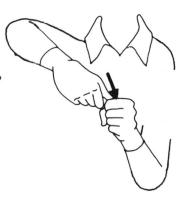

copy

LH open B palm up, tips out. Hold right hand palm down, fingers spread, above and slightly ahead of LH. Draw RH back into flat O shape and place in left palm.

cord

C shape LH palm out. Place tip of right little finger on side of right C and draw away to right in wiggly motion.

cork

S shape LH knuckles right. Press right thumb down on top of left S.

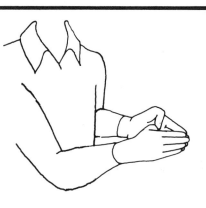

corn

Hands face each other in front of mouth as if holding an ear of corn. Rotate slightly.

corner

B shape both hands, left palm right, tips out; right palm in, tips left. Place tips together, forming corner.

correct (adj.)

One shape both hands, tips out, left palm right, right palm left. Place right 1 on top of left. Repeat.

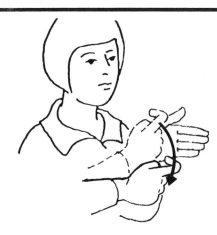

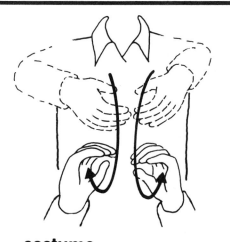

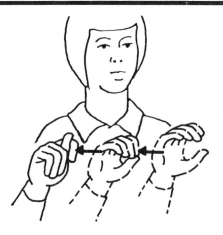

cost

LH open B palm right. Brush knuckle of right X down left palm.

costume

C shape both hands, palms facing. Brush down chest.

cot

Fingerspell C-O-T.

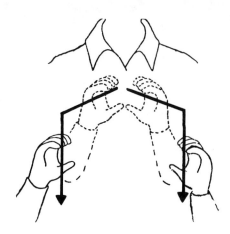

cottage

C shape both hands, palms out. Outline roof and sides of cottage.

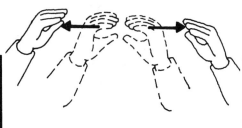

cotton

C shape both hands, palms facing. Draw apart into flat O shapes.

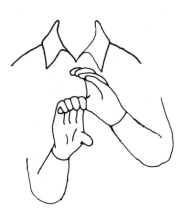

couch

C shape both hands, left palm out, right palm left. Hook right C over thumb of left C.

cough

C shape RH palm in. Place under throat with index and thumb touching chest. Rock up and down.

could

S shape both hands, knuckles down. Move down in forceful motion. Repeat.

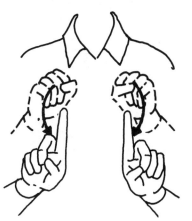

could (alt.)

S shape both hands, palms down. Move down, changing into D shapes.

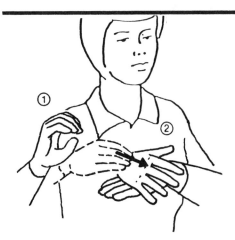

counsel

B shape LH palm down, tips slanted right. Place right C on back of LH then open into 5 shape.

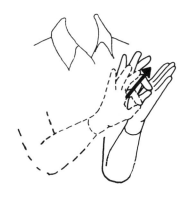

count

LH open B palm right, tips up. Run thumb and index finger of right 9 shape up left palm.

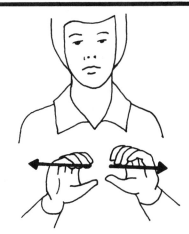

counter

C shape both hands held at waist level. Move apart.

country

Rub left elbow clockwise with palm of right open B.

county

Rub side of left elbow clockwise with index finger side of right C.

couple

V shape LH palm in. C shape RH. Tap index, then middle finger, of left V with thumb of right C.

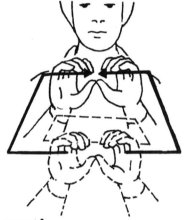

court

C shape both hands, thumbs touching. Draw apart, back, and then together, outlining a court.

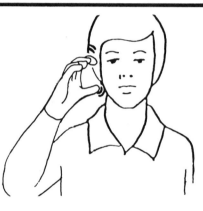

cousin

Shake right C at right side of head.

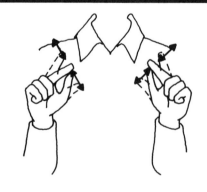

cover

Open B shape both hands, palms down, tips slanted toward one another. Slide right palm over back of left hand then lift up.

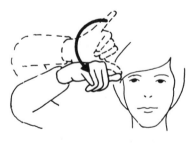

cow

Place thumb of right Y on right temple and twist forward.

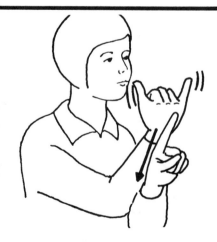

coward

One shape LH, Y shape RH. Place back of right Y on back of left index and shake while moving down.

crab

Modified L shape both hands, palms facing. Snap index fingers and thumbs together twice.

crack

LH open B. Outline crack on left palm with right index finger.

cracker

Tap left elbow several times with right A.

cradle

Place back of right index and middle fingers in left upturned palm. Rock both hands back and forth.

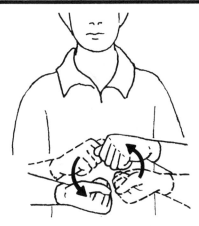

cramp

A shape both hands, right knuckles down, left knuckles up. Hold at stomach level and twist.

cranberry

Form C with RH. Then close fingertips of RH around left little finger and twist.

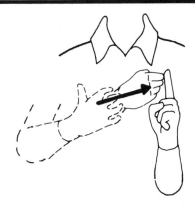

crash

One shape LH. Claw shape RH palm in. While closing fingers, strike RH against left index.

crawl

LH open B palm up. Place back of right V on left forearm. Move down arm slowly while crooking and un-crooking fingers.

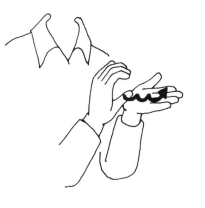

crayon

LH open B palm up, tips out. C shape RH. Move right thumb forward on left palm with small wave-like motion.

crazy

Circle right index around right temple several times.

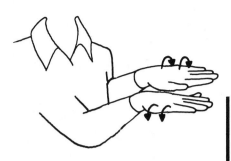

creak
Open B both hands, palms down, tips out, thumbs touching. Twist hands away from each other.

cream
LH open B palm up, tips out. Pass right C over left palm, closing into S shape (as if skimming cream).

creature
Place right C, palm and tips left, against chest and move upward.

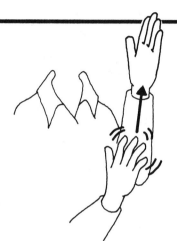

creep
Hold left arm in front of body palm in. Then right fingers creep up left arm from elbow to wrist.

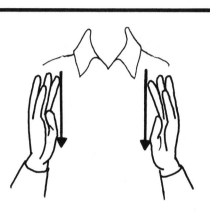

crib
Four shape both hands, palms facing. Lower hands slightly.

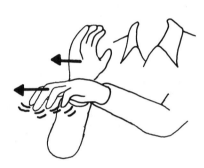

cricket
Place base of right C on back of left claw hand which is held palm down. Move left claw forward in crawling motion.

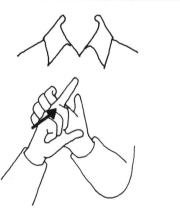

crime
C shape LH palm and tips in. Place right L against back of left C.

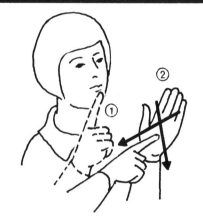

criticize
Touch lips with right index finger, then make a cross mark in left palm which faces right, tips up.

crocodile
Place right palm on left palm, tips out. Raise right hand up then drop back to original position.

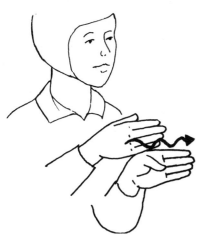

crooked
B shape LH palm right, tips out. Place little finger side of right open B on left index and wiggle forward.

croquet
Mime holding a croquet mallet and hitting ball through wicket.

cross (adj.)
Wiggle fingers of right claw hand in front of face.

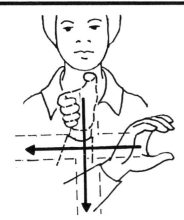

cross (noun)
Form cross with C shape RH.

cross (verb)
LH open B palm down, tips out. Slide little finger edge of right open B across back of LH.

crow
Place wrist of right G, tips out, on right side of chin and jerk up and down.

crowd
S shape both hands held tight against body. Push out in semicircles as if pushing through crowd.

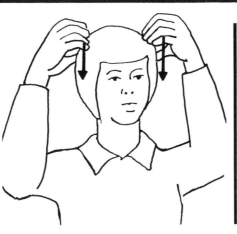

crown
C shape both hands, tips on either side of head. Move down as if slipping on crown.

cruel
A shape LH knuckles right. Hold tips of right claw shape at mouth, then brush down past left A rapidly, changing into A shape.

crumb

Strike tips of left index with thumb of right little C.

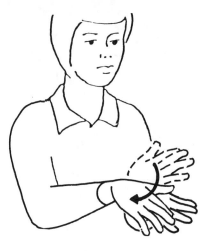

crush

Five shape both hands. Press base of right palm on base of left palm. Then slowly circle RH forward in crushing motion.

crust

LH open B palm down, tips out. Place base of right G, tips left, on left wrist and slide forward over back of hand.

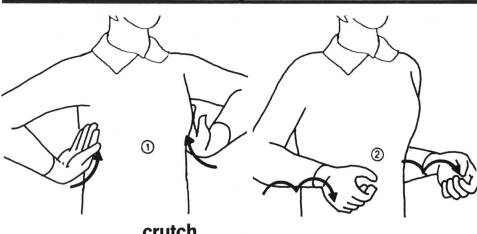

crutch

Mime placing crutches under arms, grasping the handles, and moving forward.

cry

Place index tips under eyes and draw down as if tracing tears.

cry (out)

C shape both hands, palms facing. Place at sides of mouth then move forward and out.

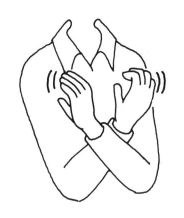

cub

Cross C hands, palms in, and tap upper chest lightly.

cube

G shape RH palm out. Turn over until palm faces up.

Cub Scout
Hold up U shape RH near right shoulder.

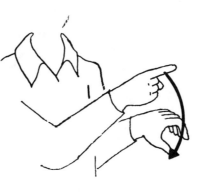

cucumber
C shape LH palm down. Slice side of left C with right index.

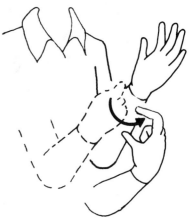

cuff
Hold LH up and outline wrist with right thumb and index (other fingers closed).

cup
LH open B palm up. Place little finger side of right X in left palm.

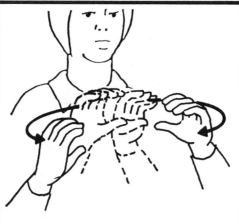

cupboard
C shape both hands, palms out. Place close together then swing apart, as if opening cupboard doors.

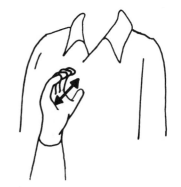

Cupid
Tap center of chest with C shape RH.

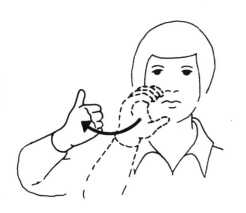

cure
Place right C on right cheek. Move upward into A shape with thumb extended.

curious
F shape RH palm in. Place thumb and forefinger on the throat and wiggle.

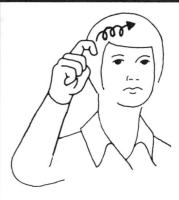

curl
With index finger of right X, outline ringlets and/or curls in hair.

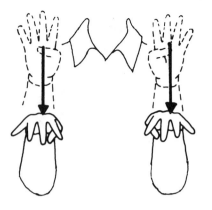

curtain

Four shape both hands. Drop forward and down, ending with palms down.

curve

Curve right C downward.

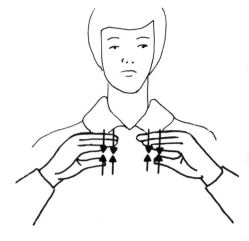

cushion

Flat O shape both hands, tips facing. Press fingers and thumbs together as if feeling soft cushion.

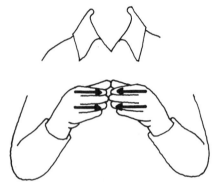

custard

C shape both hands, palms facing. Place tips together. Repeat.

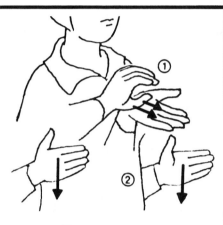

custodian

Hold LH palm up, tips out. Slide right C across left palm twice. Follow with agent marker.

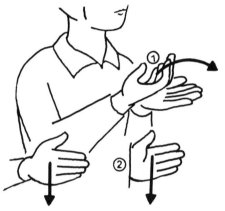

customer

Place back of right C in left palm then lift up and out. Follow with agent marker.

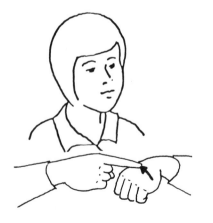

cut (noun)

S shape LH palm down. Draw right index to the right across back of left S.

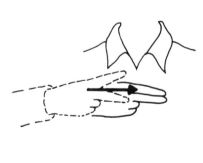

cut (verb)

V shape RH palm in, tips left. Move fingers as if snipping with scissors.

cute

Place index and middle fingers on chin. Move down, closing over thumb.

cymbal

A shape both hands, knuckles facing, thumbs extended. Hit together as if banging cymbals.

D

daddy

Five shape RH palm left, tips up. Tap forehead with thumb twice.

daffodil

Place right D on right side of nose than arc over to left side.

daily

A shape RH thumb extended. Brush forward on right cheek twice.

dairy

LH open B palm up, tips out. D shape RH. Twist heel of right D on heel of left palm.

daisy

Hold left index up and mime plucking petals with right G.

damage

A shape both hands, left knuckles up, right knuckles down. Brush right knuckles over left and back once.

damp

Form flat O shapes both hands, palms up. Tap thumb and fingertips together several times while moving hands to the right.

110

dance

LH open B palm up, tips out.
Sweep right V over left palm
several times.

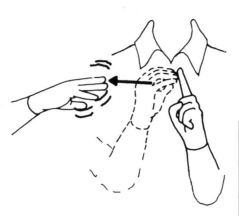

dandelion

Place tips of right flat O on left
index and flutter away to right.

dangerous

A shape both hands, thumbs up.
Bring right A up and place wrist on
back of left wrist.

dare

D shape RH palm left. Place on
chest then move out in short and
sharp motion.

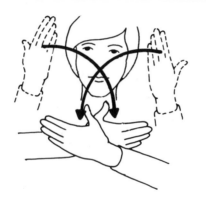

dark

Open B both hands, palms in, tips
up. Cross in front of eyes.

darling

Open B both hands, palms in. Fold
over heart.

date

LH open B palm right, tips up. Tap
middle of left palm with tips of
right D.

daughter

Place thumb of right A on right
cheek. Change into open B palm
up, tips left, and place in crook of
left elbow.

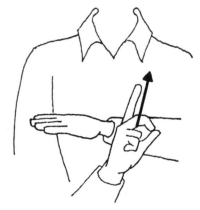

dawn

Hold left arm before you palm
down, tips right. Place right D,
knuckles left, against outer side
of left wrist and move up slowly.

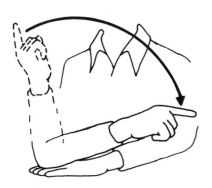

day

Hold left arm before you palm down, tips right. Point right index finger up. Then rest right elbow on back of left hand and arc down to elbow.

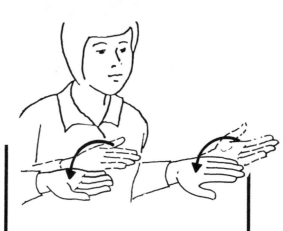

dead

Open B both hands, right palm down, left palm up. Simultaneously turn hands over to the right, reversing palm positions.

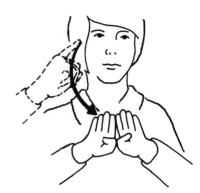

deaf

Point index finger to ear, then place index fingers of double B shapes together, palms down.

deaf (alt.)

Place right index at right ear, then at mouth.

deal (noun)

S shape LH palm down. Brush base of right D back and forth on left wrist.

dear

D shape both hands. Cross on chest over heart.

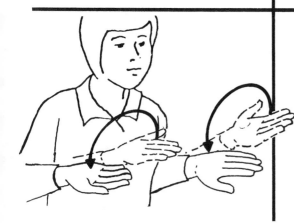

death

Open B both hands, left palm up, right palm down. Arc over to the right in exaggerated motion, ending with palms in reverse positions.

December

LH open B palm in. Place right D against left palm, slide over fingers and down back of hand.

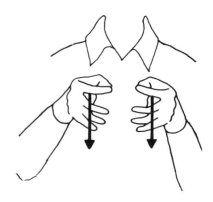

decide

F shape both hands, palms facing, tips out. Lower in decisive manner.

decorate

Flat O both hands, left palm up, right palm down. Touch tips and reverse positions several times.

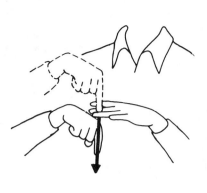

deep

LH open B palm down. Push right index down between left middle and fourth fingers.

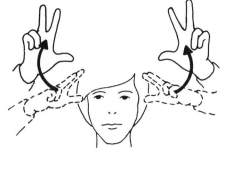

deer

Three shape both hands, palms out. Place thumbs on temples and move out and up.

defeat

S shape LH palm down. Drop right D over left wrist.

degree

Rub tips of right D up and down on left index.

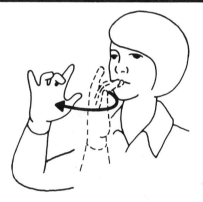

delicious

Place tip of right middle finger on lips and twist out.

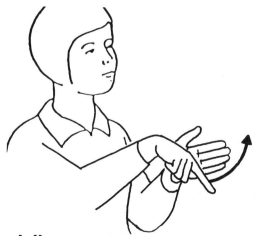

deliver

LH open B palm right, tips out. Place right index (tip down) against left palm then flip forward and up.

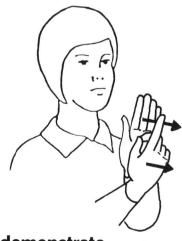

demonstrate

LH open B palm out. Place tips of right D in left palm and move both hands forward.

113

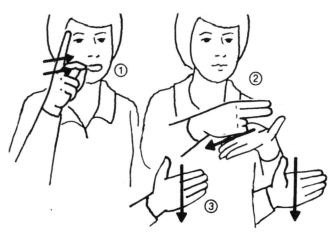

den

D shape both hands, palms facing. Turn LH to the right and RH to the left, indicating shape of room.

dental hygienist

Tap tips of right D twice at mouth. Now place base of right H on left palm and slide forward. Follow with agent marker.

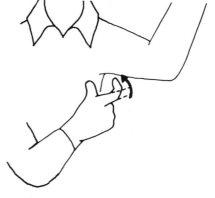

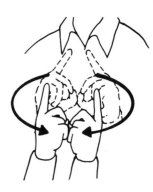

dentist

Tap right side of mouth with middle finger and thumb of right D.

deodorant

Mime spraying deodorant under arm.

department

D shape both hands, palms facing. Touch tips, move out in semicircles, and come together with little fingers touching.

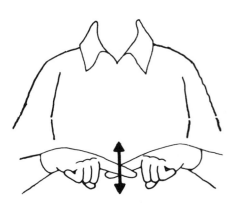

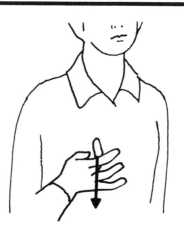

depend

Cross index fingers, right on top of left. Move down then up again.

depress

Draw middle finger of RH down chest.

describe

D shape both hands, palms facing. Move back and forth alternately.

desert
D shape both hands, palms facing. Arc in toward one another and out again.

design
LH open B palm right. Scribble down left palm with tips of right D.

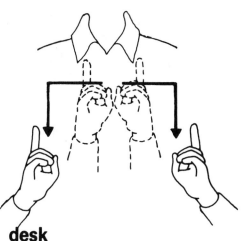

desk
D shape both hands, palms facing, thumbs almost touching. Draw apart and down.

desk (alt.)
Extend left forearm before body, palm down, tips right. Tap inside of left elbow with fingertips of right D.

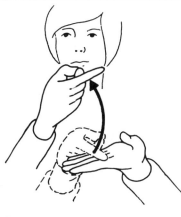

dessert
Place little finger side of right D on left palm, then raise to lips.

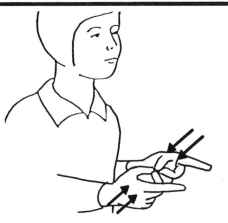

dessert (alt.)
D shape both hands, palms facing, tips out. Tap together twice.

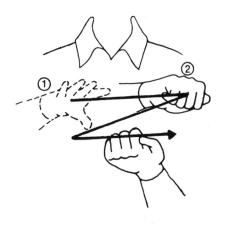

destroy
Five shape both hands, tips out, left palm up, right palm down. Close into A shapes, pass right over left and back again.

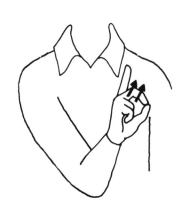

detective
Tap upper left side of chest with right D twice.

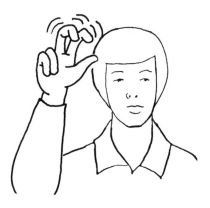

devil

Place tip of right thumb against right side of head then wiggle middle and index fingers.

diamond

Tap left fourth finger with right D.

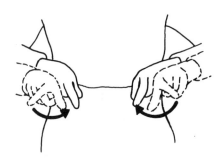

diaper

L shape both hands, palms down, held at waist. Close forefingers and thumbs.

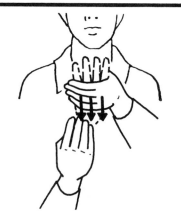

diarrhea

C shape LH palm right. Place 5 shape RH, palm in, in left C then draw down quickly into flat O shape. Repeat several times.

dice

D shape RH. Throw to the left opening into 5 shape.

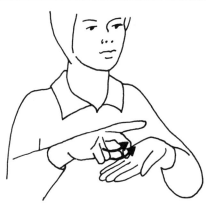

dictionary

LH open B palm up, tips out. Brush thumb and index tips of right D inward on left palm (as if turning pages).

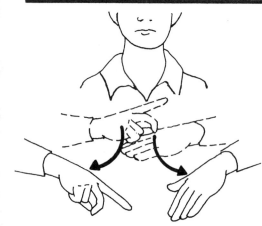

didn't

LH open B palm down. Place right D over LH then draw hands apart forcefully.

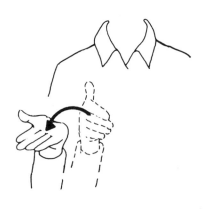

die

RH open B palm left, tips out. Turn so that palm faces up.

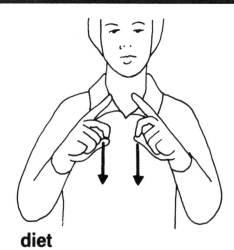

diet

Place tips of D shape close together on chest and slide down.

116

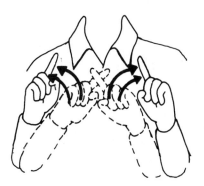

different
Cross index fingers and pull apart so that fingers point outward. Repeat.

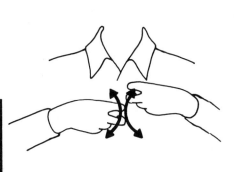

difficult
Bent V shape both hands, palms in, knuckles facing. Strike the knuckles together in up and down movements.

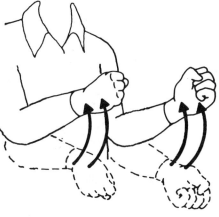

dig
S shape both hands, right behind left. Push down and up as if digging with a shovel.

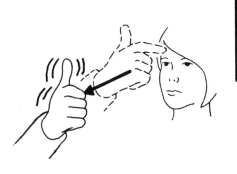

dime
Place right index finger on right temple. Bring out into 10 shape and shake.

dimple
Press tip of right index finger into right cheek.

dine
D shape RH knuckles left. Bring up to mouth as if eating.

dinner
Place tips of right flat O on lips. Hold left arm in front of body palm down, tips right. Turn right flat O over into open B palm down, and droop over left wrist.

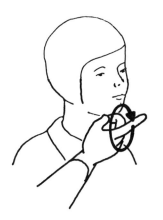

dinner (alt.)
D shape RH palm in. Rotate at mouth.

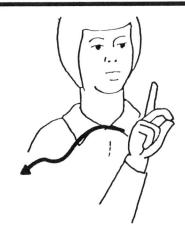

dinosaur
D shape RH. Move from upper left corner down to right in wavy motion.

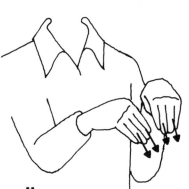

dip

Flat O both hands, tips down. Dip down twice.

diplodocus

D shape both hands, index fingers and thumbs touching. Move right D down to right in wavy motion.

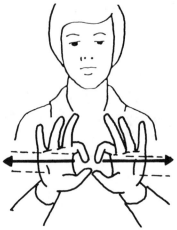

diploma

Small C shapes both hands, fingers extended, thumbs touching. Draw apart, outlining scroll.

direct

D shape both hands, palms facing, index tips out. Move back and forth alternately as if handling reins.

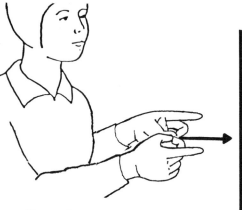

direction

D shape both hands, palms facing, index tips out, thumbs and middle fingers touching. Move right D forward.

dirt

Place back of RH, tips left, under chin. Wiggle fingers.

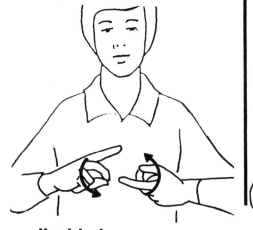

disabled

D shape both hands, left palm up, right palm down. Twist in opposite directions, reversing positions of palms.

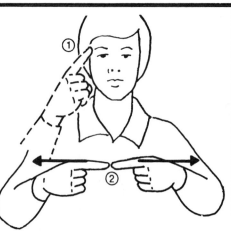

disagree

Touch forehead with right index, then point to left index finger and pull hands apart.

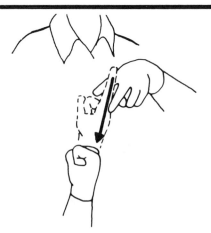

disappear

V shape LH palm down, tips slanted right. Place right index between V shape fingers and draw down into S shape.

118

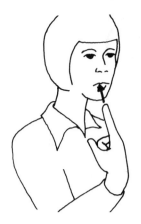

disappoint

Place tip of right index on chin.

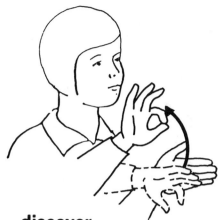

discover

Five shape RH palm down. Close thumb and index (as if picking up something) while brushing up past left open B which is held palm right.

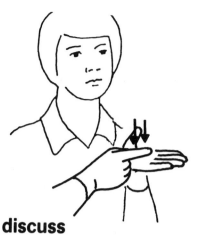

discuss

Tap right index finger several times on upturned palm of LH.

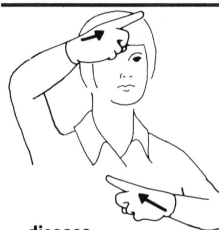

disease

D shape both hands, palms in. Place right D on forehead and left D on chest.

disguise

D shape RH palm left. Hold above shoulder level then pass down in front of face, ending with index tip pointing left.

disgust

Claw shape RH palm in. Circle clockwise on chest.

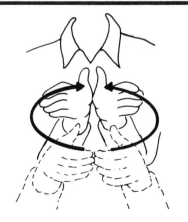

dish

Place tips of curved open B shapes together. Arc back so that wrists touch, outlining dish.

Disney

D shape RH. Place tips of thumb and middle finger on right temple then circle forward and out.

disobey

S shape RH palm in, knuckles up. Twist out forcefully.

disposal

LH open B palm up, tips out. Scrape little finger side of right B outward across left palm.

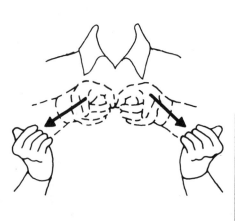

dissolve

D shape both hands, palms facing, tips touching. Draw down and apart ending in A shapes, knuckles out.

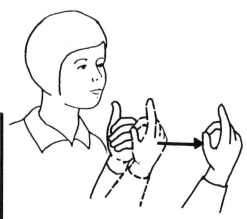

distance

A shape LH palm right. Place thumb and index tip of right D on fingers of left A, then move RH forward.

disturb

LH open B palm and tips slanted right. Tap thumb side of right D several times between left thumb and index.

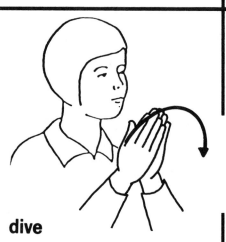

dive

Place palms together then make diving motion forward.

divide

Open B both hands, palms and tips slanted toward one another. Place little finger side of RH on left index. Swing hands apart, ending with palms down.

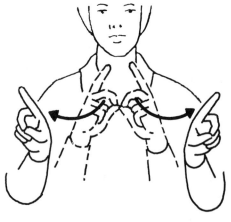

divorce

D shape both hands, thumbs and index tips touching. Break away ending with palms out.

dizzy

Circle right claw hand, palm in, clockwise in front of forehead.

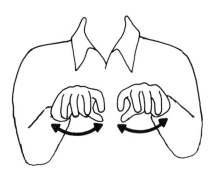

do
Claw shape both hands, palms down. Swing back and forth.

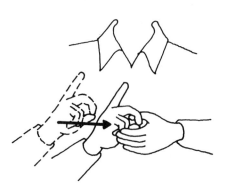

dock
C shape LH palm and tips right, little finger side down. D shape RH palm left. Slide right D into left C.

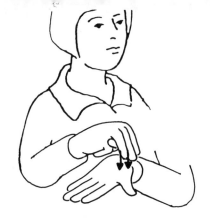

doctor
LH open B palm up, tips out. Tap left wrist with tips of right M.

doctor (alt.)
LH open B palm up, tips out. Tap left wrist with thumb and middle finger of right D.

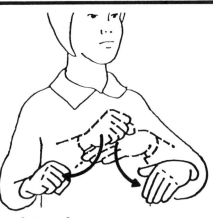

doesn't
LH open B palm down. Place right S over LH then draw hands apart forcefully.

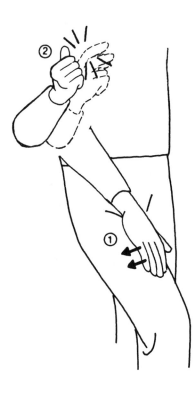

dog
Pat right thigh with RH twice then snap thumb and middle finger twice. (Can also be signed using either ① or ② alone.)

doll
Brush down tip of nose twice with right X.

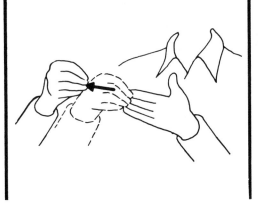

dollar
LH open B palm in, tips right. Grasp left fingers with right fingers and thumb. Draw RH back to right, ending in flat O shape.

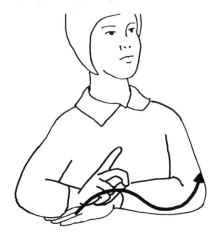

dolphin

Hold left arm before body, palm down, tips right. Move right D up outside of left arm to elbow in wavy motion.

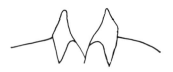

donkey

Place tips of right D on right temple. Move forward twice.

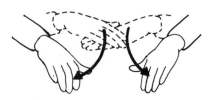

don't

Open B both hands, palms down, tips slanted toward one another. Place RH over LH and draw apart forcefully.

door

B shape both hands, palms out slightly, tips a little up. Place index fingers together then turn RH to the right, ending with palm up. Return to starting position.

doorbell

LH open B palm right. A shape RH thumb extended. Punch left palm with right thumb.

dope

Strike forehead with thumb and middle finger of right D.

dormitory

Place middle finger and thumb of right D on right edge of mouth then move to upper cheek.

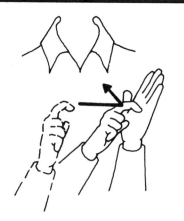

dot

LH open B palm right. Strike left palm with tip of slightly bent right index.

double

LH open B palm up, tips out. Place middle finger of right V in left palm then brush inward and up twice.

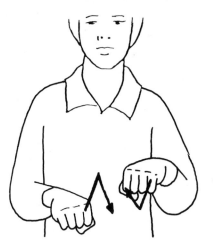

doubt

S shape both hands, palms down. Move up and down alternately.

doubt (alt.)

Hold right bent V in front of nose and crook and uncrook fingers several times.

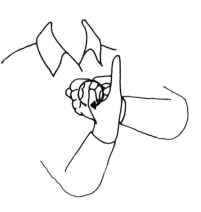

dough

S shape LH palm in, knuckles right. D shape RH palm in. Circle RH clockwise on back of left S.

doughnut

R shape both hands, palms out, fingers touching. Turn over, ending with R shapes touching, palms up.

dove

Place right D on chest then arc out and back against chest.

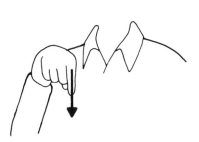

down

Point index finger down.

downstairs

Point index finger down and move up and down twice.

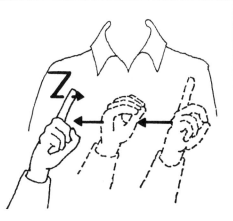

dozen

Fingerspell D-O-Z.

Dracula

Crook index fingers at sides of mouth and make an ugly face.

123

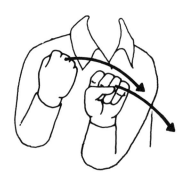

drag

S shape both hands, right held about shoulder level with knuckles in; left in front of chest. Move forward simultaneously.

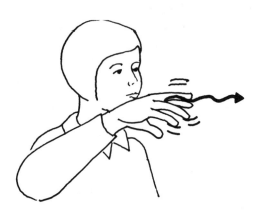

dragon

Five shape RH palm down, tips out. Place thumb near mouth then move hand forward while wiggling fingers.

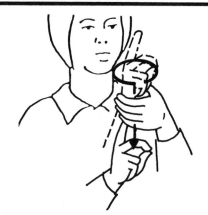

drain

Cupped LH palm right. D shape RH palm left. Circle RH slightly above LH then drop down below.

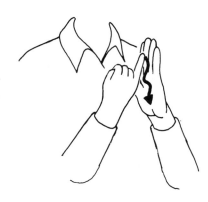

drapes

D shape both hands. Change to 4 shapes while dropping down.

draw

LH open B palm right, tips up. Draw right little finger down left palm in wavy motion.

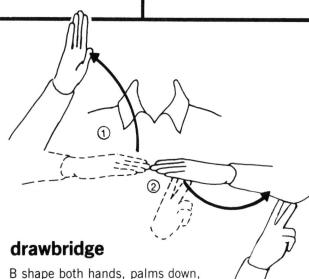

drawbridge

B shape both hands, palms down, tips touching. Raise RH up. Now hold left arm in front, palm down, tips right. Place tips of right V under wrist and arc to elbow.

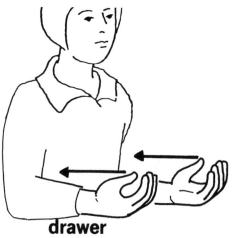

drawer

Hold cupped hands in front of body palms up, then draw back as if pulling drawer open.

dream

Place right index finger on fore-head. Move up and out crooking finger several times.

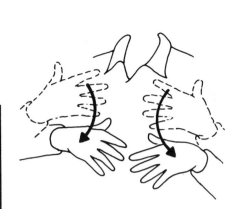

dress

Five shape both hands, palms in. Brush tips down chest while spreading hands apart slightly.

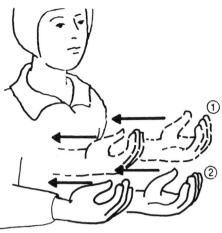

dresser

Hold cupped hands in front of body, palms up. Draw back as if pulling drawer open; lower hands and repeat motion.

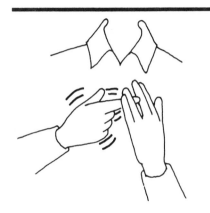

drill

LH open B palm right. Push index finger of right L between left middle and fourth fingers in jerky motion.

drink

Mime holding and drinking glass of water with C shape RH.

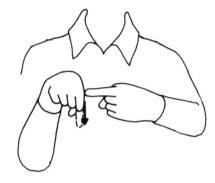

drip

One shape LH palm in, tip right. S shape RH palm down. Place left index tip on base of right index then flick right index down.

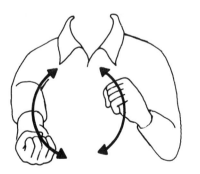

drive

A shape both hands. Move as if turning steering wheel of car. (Sometimes made with two D shapes.)

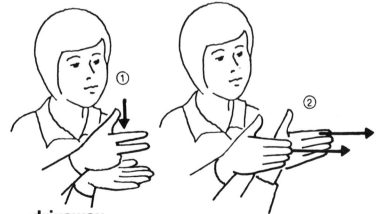

driveway

Place right 3 shape in left palm then change both hands to open B shapes, palms facing, tips out. Move out in straight line. (A compound of *drive* and *way* may also be used.)

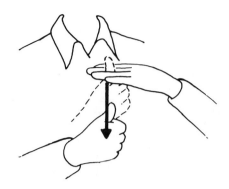

drop

Hold right S at shoulder level. Drop into 5 shape, fingers and palm down.

drown

LH open B palm down, tips right. Place extended thumb of right A between left middle and fourth fingers and pull down.

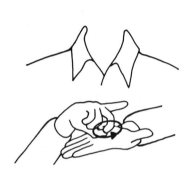

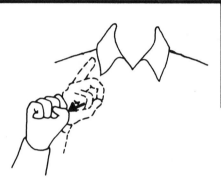

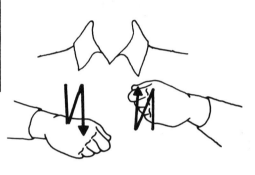

drug

Circle tips of right D on left palm.

drugstore

Fingerspell D-S in quick succession. (A compound of *drug* and *store* may also be used.)

drum

Mime holding drumsticks and beating drum.

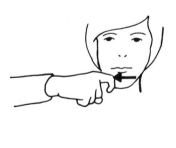

drunk

A shape RH thumb extended. Arc down in front of mouth, ending with thumb tip down.

dry

Draw bent index finger from left to right across chin.

duck

Snap thumb and index and middle fingers together at mouth (to indicate duck quacking).

duckling
Snap thumb and index and middle fingers of RH in palm of LH.

dull
D shape RH palm in. Place on left side of chin then slide over to the right side.

dumb
Hit forehead with knuckles of right fist.

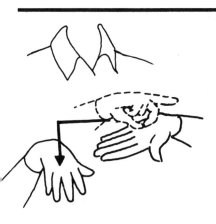

dump
LH open B palm up. Slide right D off left palm and drop down, opening into 5 shape.

during
D shape both hands, palms facing, held at right shoulder. Twist down and out.

dust
Circle back of right D on back of left S counterclockwise.

dustpan
LH open B palm up, tips slanted down. Mime sweeping dust into pan with right A shape.

127

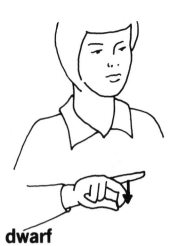

dwarf

D shape RH palm down, held at waist level. Lower slightly.

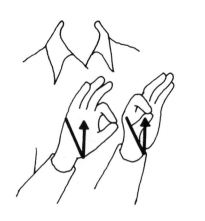

dye

F shape both hands, palms down, tips out. Dip up and down.

E

each
One shape LH. Slide knuckles of right A, thumb extended, down back of left index finger.

eagle
Crook right X around nose and turn slightly.

ear
Pinch lobe of right ear with right index and thumb (other fingers closed).

earache
Hold index tips at ear, then move tips back and forth toward one another several times.

early
S shape LH palm down, knuckles out. Place tip of right middle finger on back of left S, bend down and over.

ear mold
Place right index finger and thumb in right ear (other fingers spread).

earn
LH open B palm up. Pass right C over left palm and close into S shape.

129

earring
Grasp tip of right ear with RH thumb and index finger and wiggle.

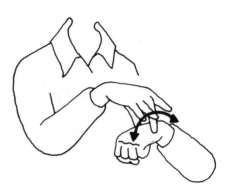

earth
S shape LH palm down. Place right thumb and middle finger on back of left hand near wrist and rock back and forth.

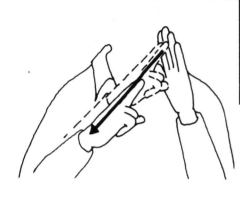

easel
LH open B palm right. Place tips of right H on left fingertips then draw away and down at angle.

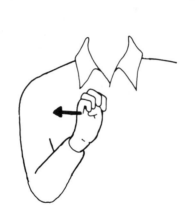

east
Hold right E a little to the left and move over to right.

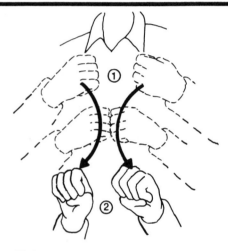

Easter
E shape both hands, knuckles facing. Bring together then draw apart, ending with knuckles out.

Easter (alt.)
E shape both hands. Circle away from each other.

easy
Cupped LH open B palm up. Brush up back of left fingers twice with tips of right open B.

eat

Place tips of right flat O on lips. Repeat several times.

eat (alt.)

Circle right A at mouth as if spooning in food.

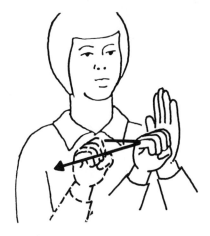

echo

LH open B palm slightly right. Strike thumb side of right E against left palm then pull away to right.

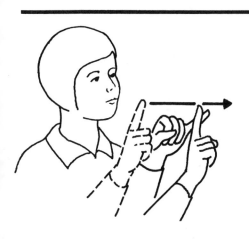

edge

I shape LH palm slanted right. Brush right index against left little finger and continue forward.

educate

E shape both hands, palms facing, held at temples. Move forward twice.

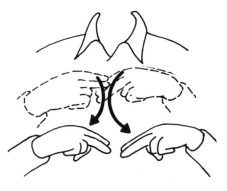

egg

H shape both hands, palms in. Hit left H with right H then draw hands apart.

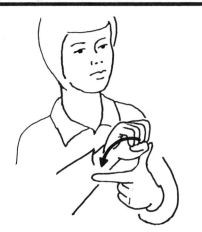

either

L shape LH index tip out. Place base of right E on left thumb and arc to tip of index.

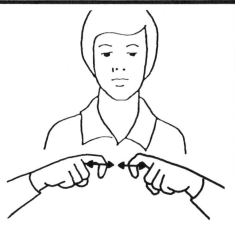

elastic

X shape both hands, palms down, knuckles facing. Move back and forth slightly as if stretching a rubber band.

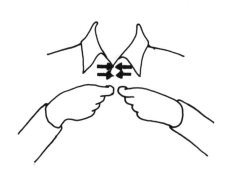

electric

X shape both hands, palms in. Tap together twice.

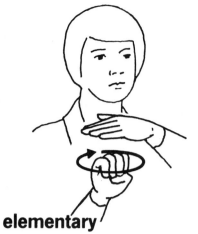

elementary

Circle right E clockwise under left palm.

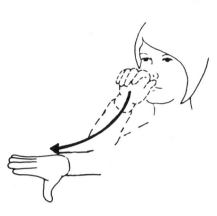

elephant

Place back of right curved open B on nose and trace trunk of elephant downward.

elevator

Slide knuckles of right E up and down left index finger.

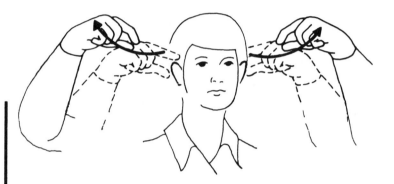

elf

G shape both hands. Place tips just in front of ears, then arc up and out, closing thumbs and index fingers.

else

E shape RH knuckles left. Twist wrist so that knuckles face up.

embarrass

Five shape both hands, palms facing. Move in circles alternately at sides of face.

emergency

Shake right E back and forth from left to right.

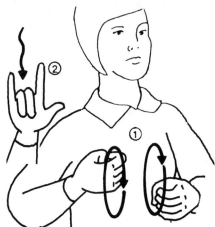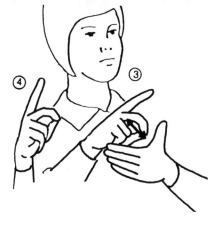

emotionally disturbed

E shape both hands, knuckles facing. Circle alternately on chest and follow with adverb marker. Now strike base of right D several times between thumb and index of LH. Follow with regular past marker.

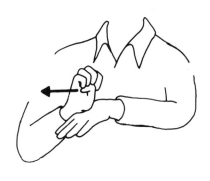

empty

LH open B palm down, tips out. Move base of right E out across back of LH.

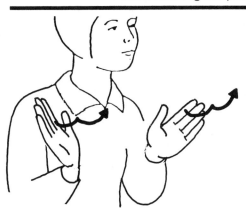

encourage

Open B both hands. Arc forward in stages as if pushing.

encyclopedia

LH open B palm up, tips out. Brush base of right E inward on left palm twice.

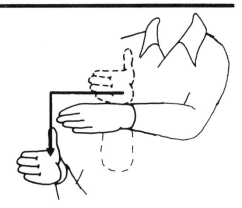

end

B shape LH palm right, tips out. Slide little finger side of right open B (palm in, tips left) forward on left index and drop down.

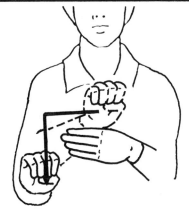

ending

B shape LH palm right, tips out. Slide base of right E forward on left index and drop down.

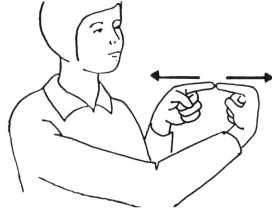

enemy

Place index tips together, right in front of left. Pull apart sharply.

133

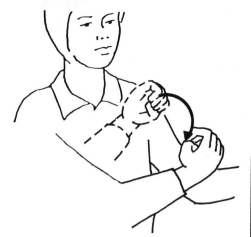

energy
Outline muscle of left arm with right E.

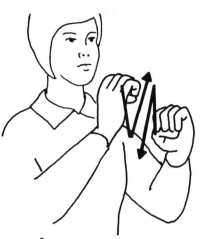

engine
E shape both hands, right palm left, left palm right. Place right E behind left E then move both hands up and down alternately.

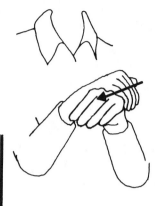

England
LH open B palm down, tips slanted right. Clasp with RH and draw back toward body.

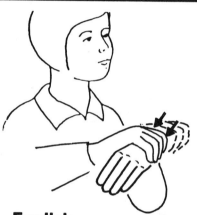

English
LH open B palm down, tips slanted right. Pat back of LH with palm of cupped RH.

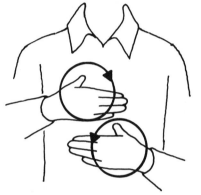

enjoy
Open B both hands, palms in, left tips right, right tips left. Place on chest. Circle RH clockwise and LH counterclockwise.

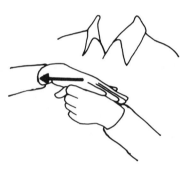

enough
S shape LH knuckles right. Brush right palm over left S away from body.

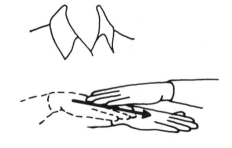

enter
Open B shape both hands, palms down, left tips slanted right, right tips slanted left. Slide RH under left palm.

envelope
C shape LH palm and tips right. Pass right open B across mouth then stuff tips into left C.

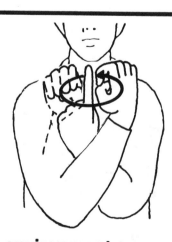

environment
Circle right E counterclockwise around left index, tip up.

134

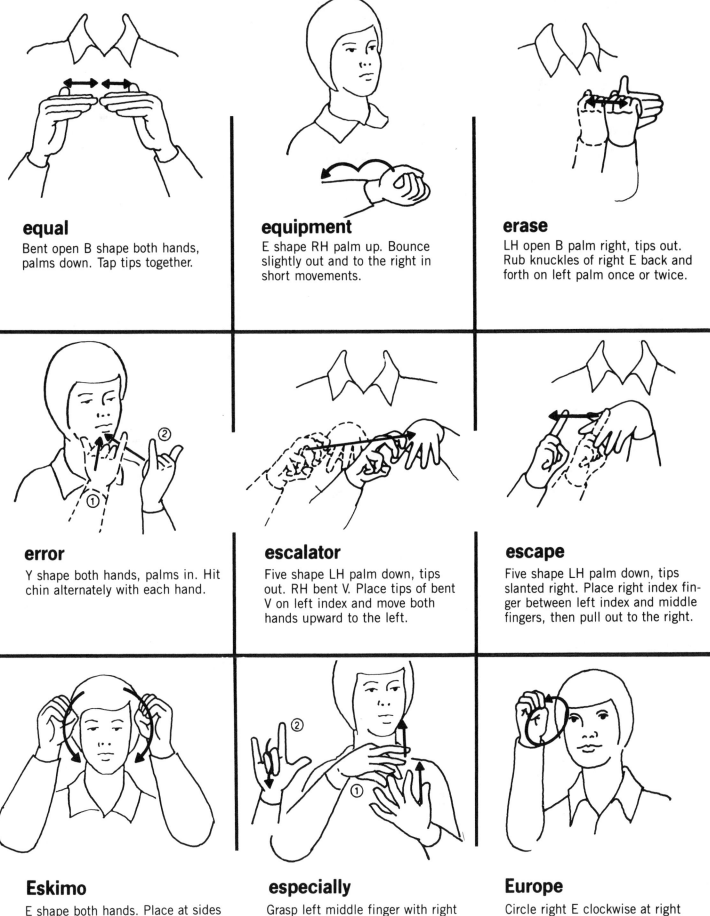

equal
Bent open B shape both hands, palms down. Tap tips together.

equipment
E shape RH palm up. Bounce slightly out and to the right in short movements.

erase
LH open B palm right, tips out. Rub knuckles of right E back and forth on left palm once or twice.

error
Y shape both hands, palms in. Hit chin alternately with each hand.

escalator
Five shape LH palm down, tips out. RH bent V. Place tips of bent V on left index and move both hands upward to the left.

escape
Five shape LH palm down, tips slanted right. Place right index finger between left index and middle fingers, then pull out to the right.

Eskimo
E shape both hands. Place at sides of head then move down, outlining shape of hood.

especially
Grasp left middle finger with right thumb and index. Pull both hands upward then follow with adverbial marker.

Europe
Circle right E clockwise at right temple.

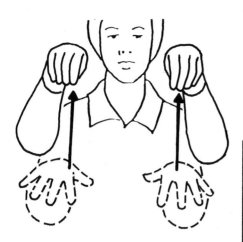

evaporate

Five shape both hands, palms down. Draw up into flat O shapes.

eve

LH open B palm down, tips right. Slide right E down inside left wrist.

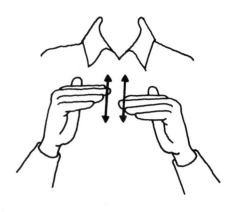

even

Bent open B shape both hands, palms down, tips almost touching. Alternately move up and down slightly.

evening

LH open B palm down, tips right. Tap back of left wrist twice with base of right cupped hand.

even though

Open B both hands, palms in, tips facing. Brush tips back and forth.

ever

E shape RH. Circle clockwise.

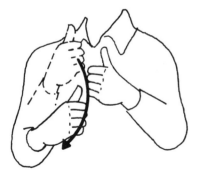

every

A shape both hands, thumbs up. Brush knuckles of right A down knuckles of left A.

evil

E shape RH knuckles in. Hold in front of mouth then twist out and down, ending with knuckles down.

exact

Closed X shape both hands, right hand held behind left. Tap thumbs and index tips together once.

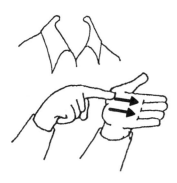

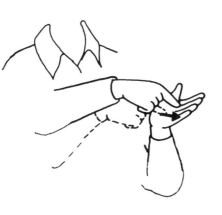

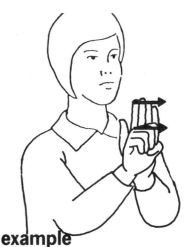

examination
LH open B palm up, tips out. Slide right index forward on left palm. Repeat motion.

examine
LH open B palm up, tips out. One shape RH palm down. Slide right index forward on left palm.

example
LH open B palm slanted out. Place thumb side of right E against left palm and push both hands out.

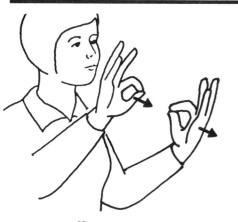

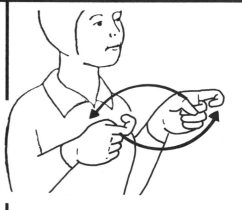

excellent
F shape both hands, left palm in, right palm out. Jerk both hands forward slightly.

except
Grasp left index finger with right thumb and index finger and pull up.

exchange
X shape both hands. Circle right X under left X and left over right, reversing positions.

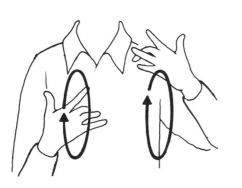

excite
Five shape both hands, palms in. Alternately brush tips of middle fingers upward on chest.

excuse
LH open B palm up, tips out. Brush edge of left palm twice with tips of RH.

exercise

S shape both hands, arms held above shoulders. Push up and out.

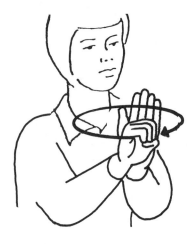

exhibit

LH open B palm out. Place thumb side of right E on left palm and move both hands out in a large circle.

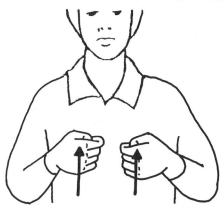

exist

E shape both hands, palms in, knuckles facing. Place on chest then draw up.

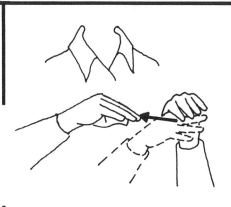

exit

Claw shape LH palm and tips down. Five shape RH palm down, tips left. Place in left claw then draw back to right, ending in flat O.

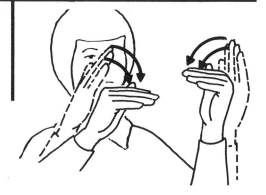

expect

Open B both hands, palms facing, RH near right side of forehead, LH held out at left side. Bend finger-tips of both hands to right angle and then unbend simultaneously. Repeat motion.

expensive

LH open B palm up. Place back of right flat O in left palm, lift up and out, then drop down, spreading fingers.

experiment

E shape both hands. Circle toward one another alternately, as if pouring from vials.

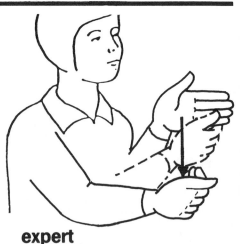

expert

Grab little finger side of left open B with RH. Pull RH down sharply ending in A shape.

explain

F shape both hands, palms facing, tips out. Move back and forth alternately.

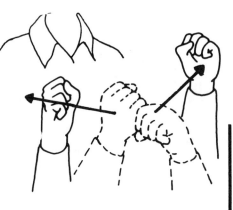

explode

S shape both hands, palms in. Place right S on left. Draw apart quickly, moving upward.

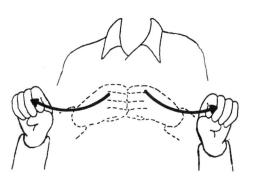

extension

E shape both hands, knuckles touching. Separate and turn out into correct E positions.

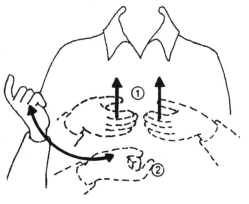

extinguisher

C shape both hands, palms and tips facing. Move upward. Form right X, palm up, and swing back and forth.

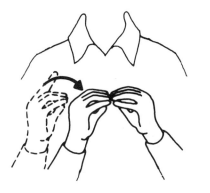

extra

Flat O shape LH palm down, tips right. One shape RH palm left. Change into RH flat O and touch tips of left flat O.

eye

Place tip of index finger on eye.

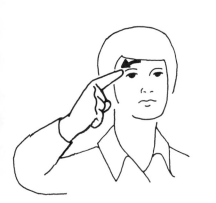

eyebrow

Outline eyebrow with tip of index finger.

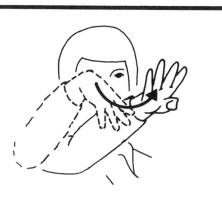

eyelash

Four shape RH tips out, palm down and slanted in. Place thumb side against right eye then flip hand up and out.

139

F

face
Circle face with index finger.

factory
S shape LH knuckles down. F shape RH palm left. Place right wrist on side of left S. Slide back into Y shape, then forward.

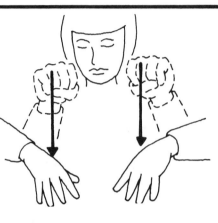

faint
S shape both hands, palms down. Drop into 5 shapes and bow head.

fair (adj.)
F shape RH palm left. Tap chin with middle finger of right F.

fairy
F shape RH. Dip forward as if touching something with a wand.

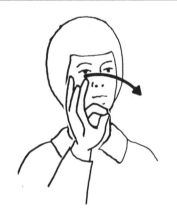

fake
F shape RH palm left. Brush across nose and lips from right to left.

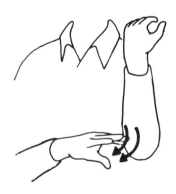

fall (season)
Hold left arm upright, palm in. Brush index finger of right open B (palm down, tips left) against left elbow.

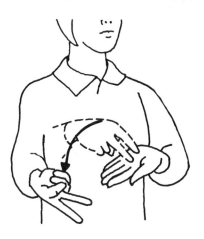

fall (verb)

LH open B palm up, tips out. Place tips of right V in left palm then flip forward and out, ending with palm up. (Sometimes made without LH as base.)

false

One shape RH palm left. Brush across lips, ending with index tip pointing left.

family

F shape both hands, palms out, thumbs and index fingers touching. Draw apart and around until little fingers touch.

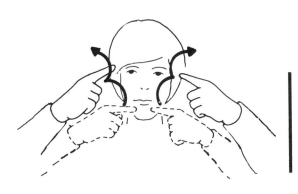

famous

One shape both hands, palms in. Place tips at sides of mouth then move up and out in semicircles.

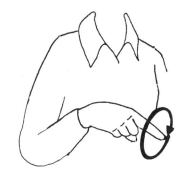

fan

One shape RH palm in, tip left. Circle rapidly.

fancy

Claw shape both hands, palms and tips out. Simultaneously circle in opposite directions, RH moving counterclockwise, LH moving clockwise.

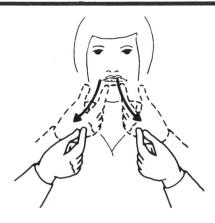

fang

G shape both hands, palms in, tips up. Place index fingers on sides of mouth. Bring down and apart, closing forefingers and thumbs.

fantastic

F shape both hands, fingers spread. Arc forward and out.

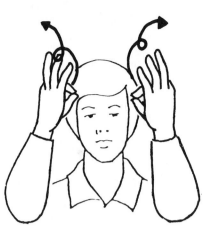

fantasy

F shape both hands held at temples. Circle forward alternately two or three times.

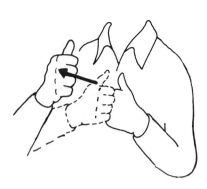

far

A shape both hands, thumbs up. Place right on back of left then move right A forward and out.

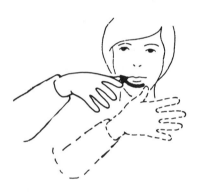

farm

Five shape RH palm in, tips left. Place thumb on left side of chin and draw across to right side.

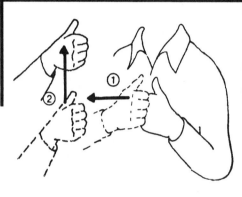

farther/further

A shape both hands, thumbs up. Place right on back of left then move right A forward. Follow with comparative marker.

fast

L shape both hands, palms facing, index tips out. Draw back quickly into S shapes.

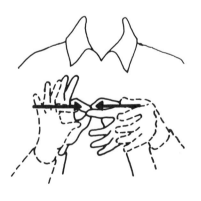

fasten

F shape both hands slightly open. Bring together, hooking thumbs and forefingers.

fat

Hold claw hands on cheeks, then move away (indicating puffy, fat face).

father
Five shape RH palm left. Place thumb on forehead and wiggle fingers.

faucet
Mime turning faucet with thumb, index, and middle finger of RH.

fault
LH open B palm down. Place little finger side of right A on back of LH.

favor
Place right open B on upper chest then swing out to the right.

favorite
Five shape RH palm in. Tap middle finger on chin twice.

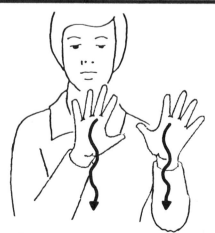

fear
Five shape both hands held to left of body. Shake hands while moving downward.

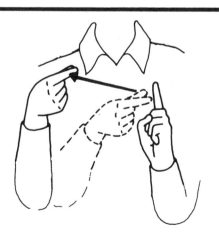

feather
Pluck at left index finger with right G as if plucking feathers from a fowl.

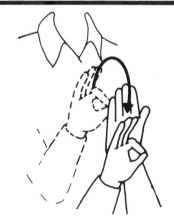

February
LH open B palm in. Place right F on left palm, slide over fingers and down.

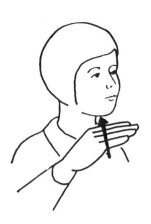

fed up
RH open B palm down, tips left. Raise up sharply, hitting underside of chin.

feed (verb)
O shape both hands, left in front of body, right on lips. Move right O down toward left O and shake both hands slightly.

feel
Strike right middle finger upward on chest.

feeling (noun)
Place tip of right middle finger on left side of chest then stroke upward twice.

female
Place thumb and index finger of right F on right cheek and slide down.

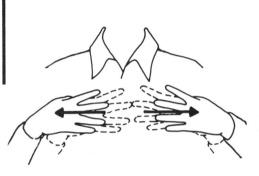

fence
Four shape both hands, palms in, tips facing. Place tips of middle fingers together then draw apart.

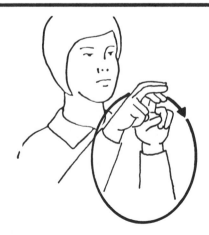

ferris wheel
Place right middle and index fingers on back of left middle and index fingers. Circle forward.

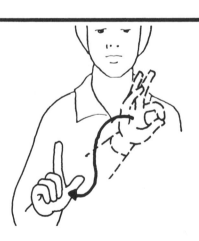

festival
Describe backward S shape in air with RH moving from F to L shape.

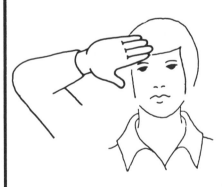

fever
RH open B palm out, tips left. Place back of hand on forehead.

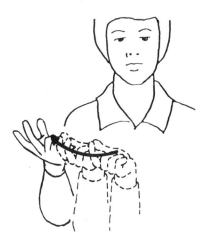

few

Loose A shape RH palm up. Pass thumb along first two fingers while opening them up.

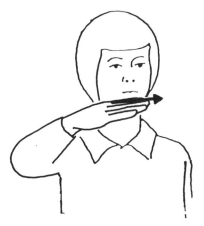

fib

RH bent B palm down, tips left. Brush across chin from right to left.

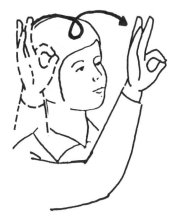

fiction

Place side of right F on right temple then circle up and forward.

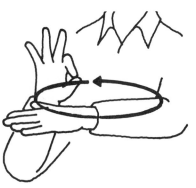

field

LH open B palm down, tips slightly right. Place right F on left wrist, circle counterclockwise over elbow, and return to original position.

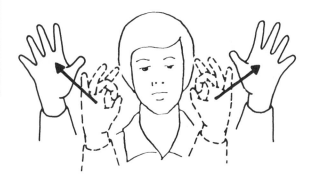

fierce

Eight shape both hands. Open quickly into 5 shapes while moving apart.

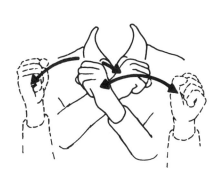

fight

S shape both hands, knuckles facing. Cross hands in front of body once or twice.

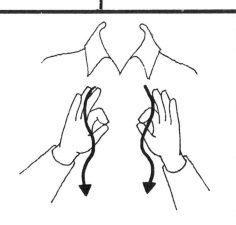

figure (noun)

F shape both hands. Move downward, outlining female shape.

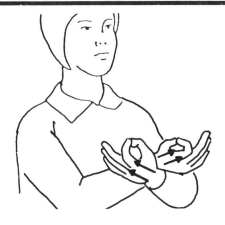

figure out

F shape both hands, palms up, left tips right, right tips left. Pass back of right F across left wrist. Repeat motion.

145

fill

C shape LH palm right, little finger side down. B shape RH palm down. Starting at bottom of left C move right B up to top.

film

LH open B palm and tips slanted right. Place base of right F in left palm and move back and forth.

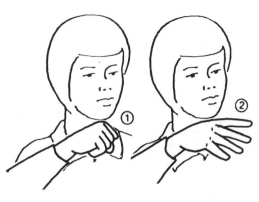

filth

S shape RH palm down. Place under chin then open sharply into 5 shape.

final

I shape both hands, left palm in, tip right; right palm left, tip out. Bring right I up in semicircle then down, striking the tip of left little finger.

find

Five shape RH palm down, tips out. Close thumb and index finger and raise hand as if picking up something.

find out

C shape LH palm right. Place tips of right F in left C then pull out.

fine

Five shape RH palm left. Place thumb on chest and move slightly up and out.

finger

Touch left index with right index.

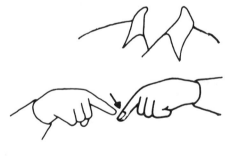

fingernail

Tap nail of left index with tip of right index.

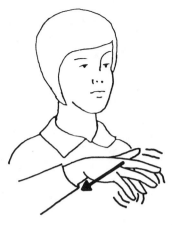

fingerspell

Five shape RH palm down. Wiggle fingers while moving from left to right.

finish

Five shape both hands, palms in. Turn suddenly so that palms and tips face out.

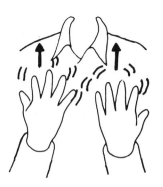

fire

Curved 5 shape both hands, palms in. Move up, fluttering fingers.

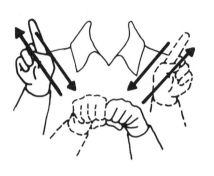

fireworks

S shape both hands, knuckles down, index fingers touching. Pop index fingers out and to the sides alternately.

first

A shape LH knuckles right, thumb up. Strike left thumb with tip of right index.

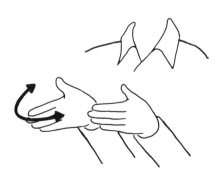

fish

Open B both hands, left palm in, tips right; right palm left, tips out. Place left tips on right wrist. Flutter right hand while moving forward.

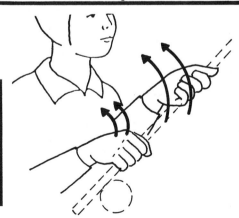

fishing or fish (verb)

Mime holding fishing pole and jerk up twice as if hooking fish.

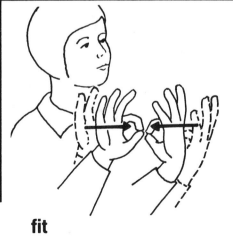

fit

F shape both hands, left palm slanted in. Touch tips of left index and thumb with tips of right index and thumb.

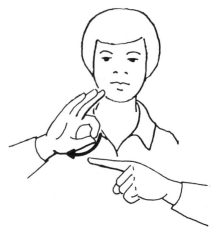

fix

F shape both hands. Place little finger side of right F on thumb side of left F. Twist hands in toward body.

flag

Place right elbow on back of left hand which is held before you. Wave right hand back and forth.

flake

Brush tip of left index with thumb of right F.

flame

Hold cupped hands in front of body, palms up, little fingers touching. Flutter fingers.

flannel

Brush thumb and index tips of right F on upper right chest.

flash

RH flat O tips out. Move quickly into 5 shape. Repeat several times.

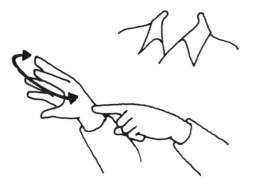
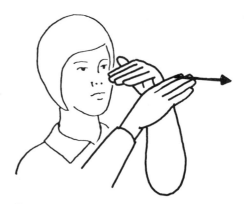

flashlight

Five shape RH palm down, fingers slightly bent. Place tips of left index on right wrist and move hands around, as if searching with a flashlight.

flat

Open B both hands, palms down, left tips right, right tips left. Place right index against left little finger then move RH forward.

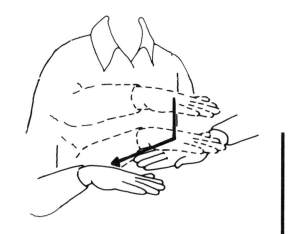

flatten

Open B both hands. Slap RH on left palm then slide forward.

flavor

F shape RH palm in. Tap chin twice with right thumb and index.

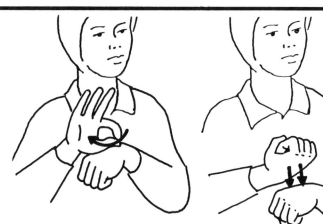

Flintstones (The)

S shape LH palm down. Brush left wrist with thumb and index of right F. Change right F to S shape and strike back on left S twice.

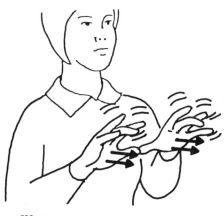

flirt

Five shape both hands, palms down, thumbs touching. Flutter fingers while moving forward (to indicate "batting" eyelashes).

float

Place little finger side of right A on back of left hand. Move both hands in floating motion.

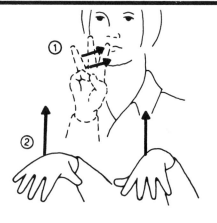

flood

Tap lips twice with index finger of right W. Then hold hands in front of body, palms down, and raise up.

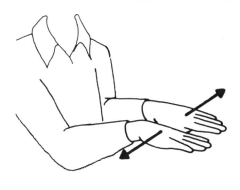

floor

B shape both hands, palms down, tips out, index fingers touching. Move apart.

flour

S shape LH palm in, knuckles right. Place index and thumb of right F on back of left S and circle clockwise.

flower

RH flat O. Place tips on right side of nose then arc to left side.

flu

Place back of right F on forehead.

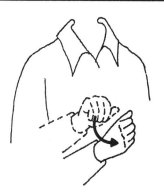

flush

Mime turning handle to flush toilet.

flute

Mime holding flute to mouth and playing.

fly (noun)

S shape LH palm down. Curved RH open B palm left. Brush RH across back of LH, ending in S shape (as if catching a fly).

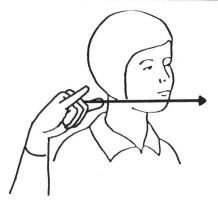

fly (verb)

Y shape RH palm left. Move in straight line from right to left.

fly (verb alt.)

Open B both hands held at shoulders. Flap from wrists two or three times.

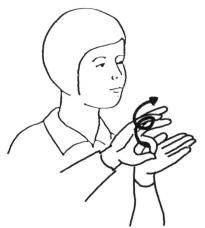

foam

F shape RH. Touch left palm with right thumb and index then spiral upward.

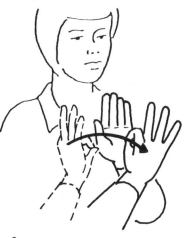

fog

LH open B. F shape RH palm in. Pass right F across front of LH.

foil (noun)

B shape LH palm in, tips right. "Wrap" right F around LH.

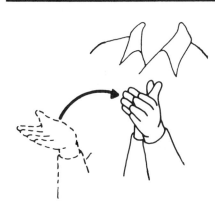

fold

Open B both hands, left palm right, tips out; right palm up, tips out. Bring right hand up and place against left.

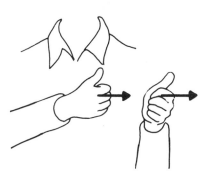

follow

A shape both hands, thumbs up, right behind left. Move both forward simultaneously.

food

Place tips of flat O on mouth.

fool

Y shape RH palm left. Shake at right temple.

fool (verb)

Grasp end of nose with right thumb and index and pull down slightly.

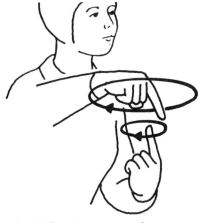

fool(ing) around

One shape both hands, right pointed down above left. Twirl both index fingers outward alternately.

foolish

Y shape RH palm left. Place at nose then arc down to the left.

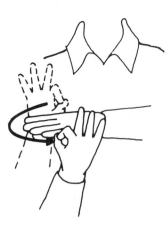

foot

LH open B palm down. Place thumb and index tips of right F on left thumb then circle around to left little finger.

foot (alt.)

LH open B palm down, tips slanted right. Brush thumb and index tips of right F down inside of left wrist.

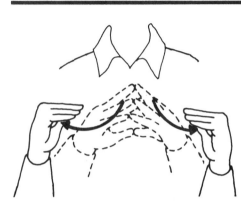

football

Five shape both hands, palms facing, tips touching. Draw apart into flat O shapes.

football (game)

Five shape both hands, palms in, tips facing. Mesh fingers together two or three times.

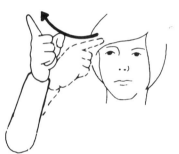

for

One shape RH palm in. Place tip on forehead, twist wrist, and point tip forward.

force

Hold right C just above right shoulder then push forward forcefully.

forest

F shape RH palm left. Place right elbow on back of LH and twist back and forth.

152

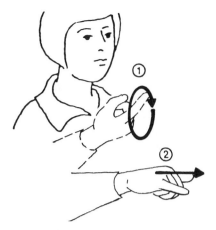

forever

Describe circle in air with right index, palm up. Change to Y shape palm down and move forward.

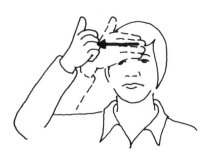

forget

RH open B palm in. Draw tips across forehead from left to right, ending in A shape.

forgive

LH open B palm up, tips out. Brush with right tips in strong sweeping movement. Repeat.

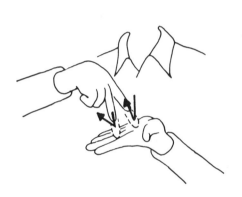

fork

LH open B palm up, tips right. Tap left palm with tips of right V.

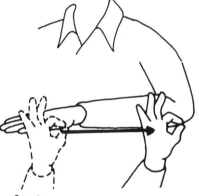

formula

LH open B. Tap fingers, then base, of left palm with thumb and index of right F.

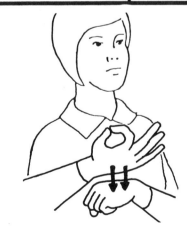

fort

Extend left arm before you palm down. Place index side of right F on left little finger and slide up to elbow.

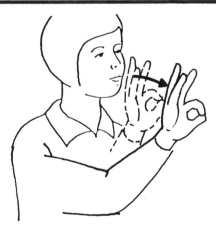

forward

Hold right F at right side of face then arc forward.

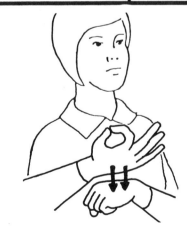

fossil

S shape LH palm down. Tap back of left S with back of right F.

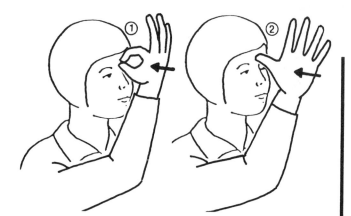

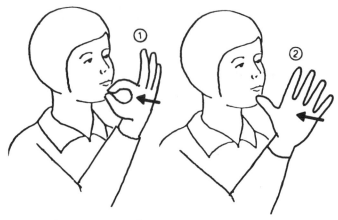

foster father
Tap forehead with thumb and index of right F. Open to 5 shape and tap forehead again with tip of thumb.

foster mother
Tap chin with thumb and index of right F. Open to 5 shape and tap chin again with tip of thumb.

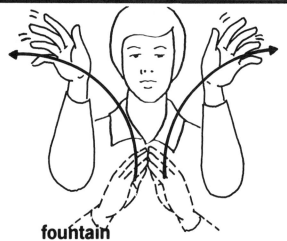

fountain
Flat O shape both hands, palms facing, tips touching. Move out and apart while wiggling fingertips.

fox
Enclose tip of nose with index and thumb of right F. Twist right wrist down and up.

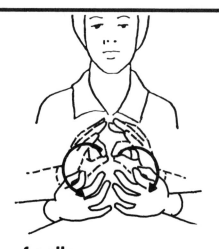

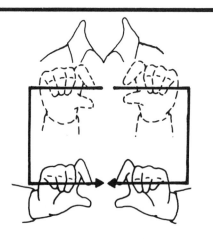

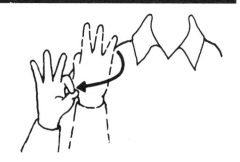

fragile
F shape both hands, palms down, thumbs and index fingers touching. Break apart.

frame
G shape both hands, palms out, hands held close together. Draw apart, down, and together again.

France
F shape RH palm in. Twist outward.

Frankenstein
F shape both hands. Touch sides of neck with tips.

frankfurter
F shape both hands almost touching. Draw apart in S shapes.

freckle
Bounce tips of right F from left cheek to the nose then to right cheek.

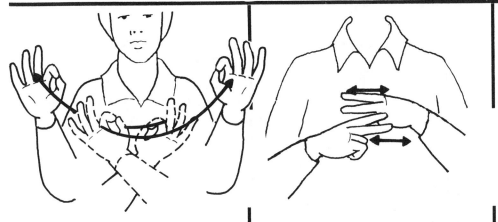

free
F shape both hands, palms in, wrists crossed. Break apart, turning palms out.

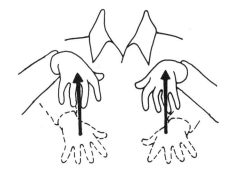

freeway
V shape both hands, palms down, tips facing. Brush back and forth, RH in front of left.

freeze
Five shape both hands, palms down, tips out. Bring up into claw shapes.

french fries
F shape RH palm down. Bounce to right.

frequent
LH open B palm up, tips out. Bounce tips of right F forward on left palm.

fresh
LH open B palm up, tips out. Brush back of right F across left palm from right to left.

155

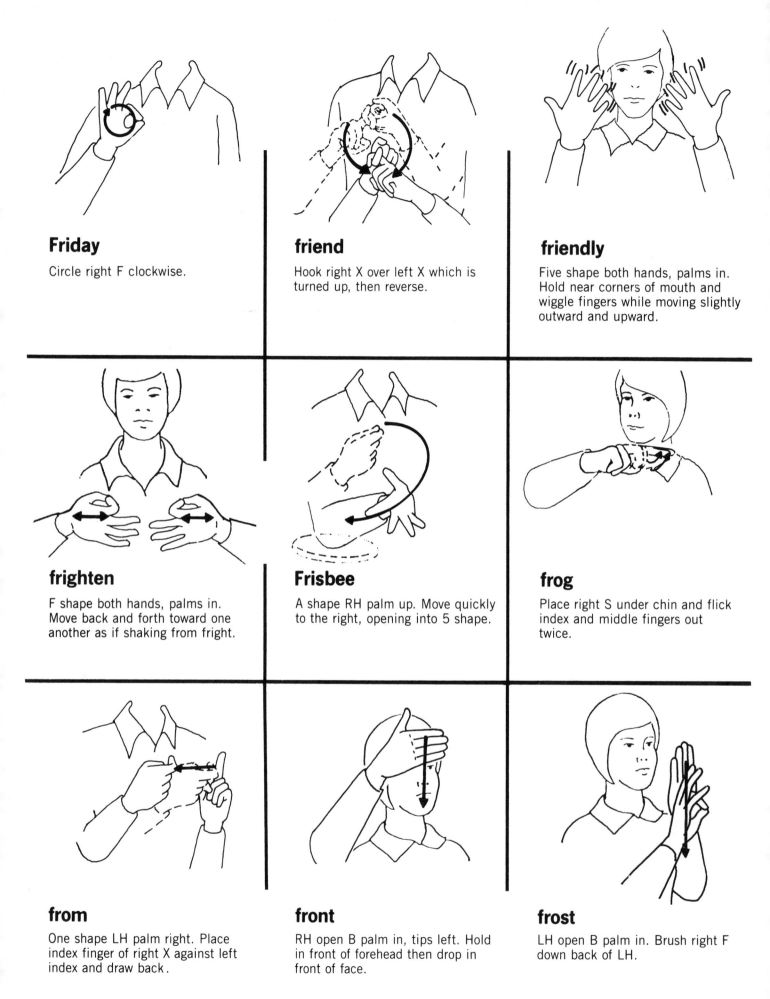

Friday

Circle right F clockwise.

friend

Hook right X over left X which is turned up, then reverse.

friendly

Five shape both hands, palms in. Hold near corners of mouth and wiggle fingers while moving slightly outward and upward.

frighten

F shape both hands, palms in. Move back and forth toward one another as if shaking from fright.

Frisbee

A shape RH palm up. Move quickly to the right, opening into 5 shape.

frog

Place right S under chin and flick index and middle fingers out twice.

from

One shape LH palm right. Place index finger of right X against left index and draw back.

front

RH open B palm in, tips left. Hold in front of forehead then drop in front of face.

frost

LH open B palm in. Brush right F down back of LH.

156

frosting
LH open B palm down. F shape RH tips left. Move RH in waves over LH from wrist to fingertips.

frown
Draw index fingers down sides of mouth, outlining frown lines.

fruit
Place the thumb and index of right F on right cheek. Twist, ending with palm in.

frustrate
Five shape RH. Flip up into face.

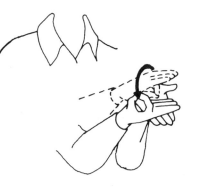

fry
LH open B palm up, tips out. Place thumb and index of right F in left palm and flip over.

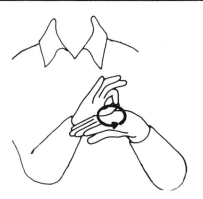

fudge
LH open B palm down. Describe circle on back of LH with base of right F.

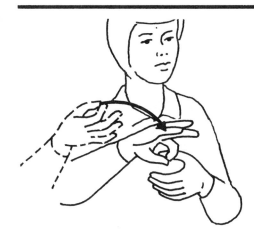

fuel
C shape LH palm and tips right, little finger side down. "Pour" tips of right F into left C.

full
S shape LH knuckles right. Brush right palm across left S toward body.

fun
H shape both hands, left palm down. Place right H on nose then on back of left H.

157

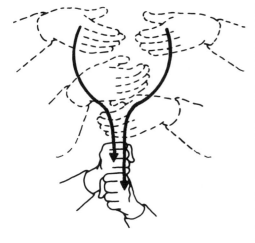

funny

Brush tip of nose twice with tips of right N.

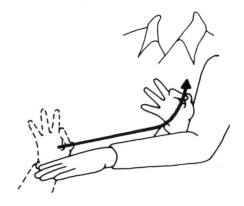

fur

Extend left arm before you, palm down. Run right F up left arm to shoulder.

funnel

Curved open B both hands, tips facing. Outline funnel shape while moving down, ending in S shapes, right on top of left.

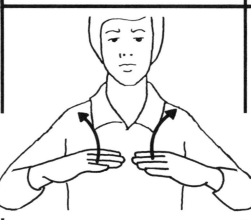

furious

Open B both hands, palms down, tips facing. Place against chest then flip hands up forcefully.

furnace

C shape LH palm and tips right. Flutter fingers of right 5 while moving up through left C.

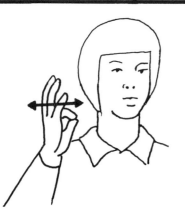

furniture

F shape RH. Move briskly back and forth sideways.

fuss

L shape RH palm left, little finger extended. Place index on lip and move back and forth quickly.

future

F shape RH palm left. Place at right temple then arc forward.

fuzz

Open B both hands, palms down, left tips slanted right, right tips slanted left. Rub back of left hand with right tips.

G

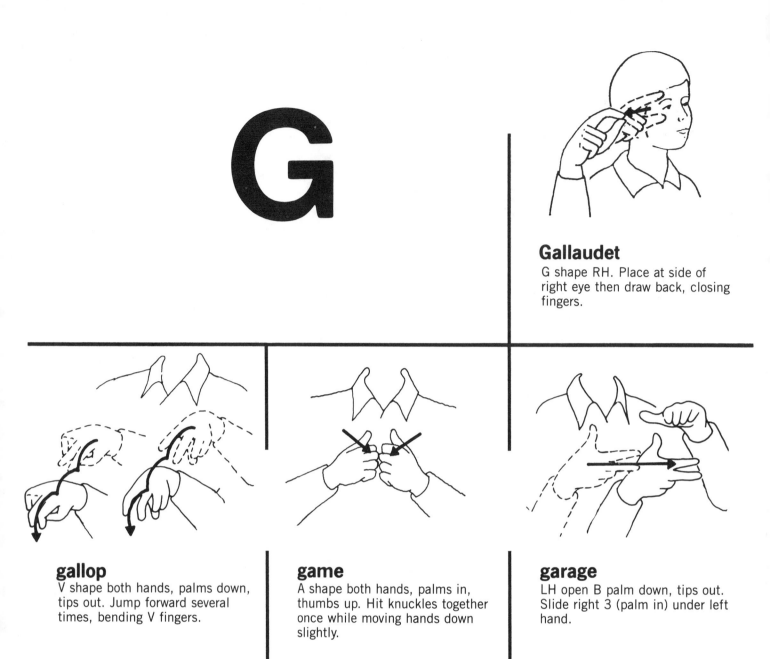

Gallaudet
G shape RH. Place at side of right eye then draw back, closing fingers.

gallop
V shape both hands, palms down, tips out. Jump forward several times, bending V fingers.

game
A shape both hands, palms in, thumbs up. Hit knuckles together once while moving hands down slightly.

garage
LH open B palm down, tips out. Slide right 3 (palm in) under left hand.

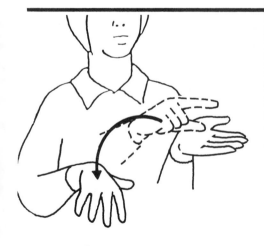

garbage
LH open B palm up, tips out. Place base of right G in left palm, lift up, then drop down, ending in 5 shape.

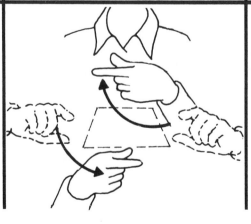

garden
G shape both hands, tips out. Move right G in front of left G, turning right tips left and left tips right (indicating square shape).

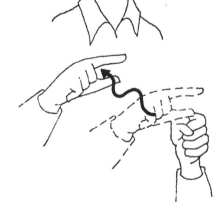

gas
S shape LH palm right. Place thumb of right G on top of left S, then move up in wavy motion.

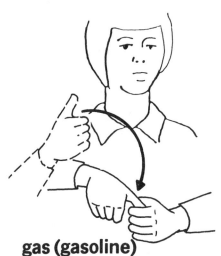

gas (gasoline)

S shape LH palm right, little finger side down. A shape RH thumb extended. Arc thumb of right A down into left S, as if pouring gasoline into tank.

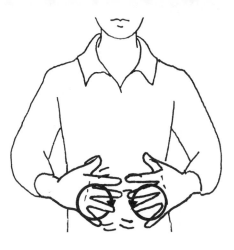

gas/flatulence (gas pains)

Five shape both hands, palms in, tips facing. Rotate hands in front of stomach in small circles while fluttering fingers.

gas/flatulence (passing gas)

Place back of flat O on buttocks then rapidly open into 5 shape.

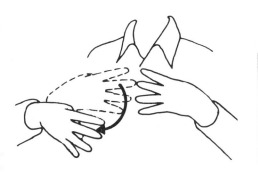

gate

Four shape both hands, palms in, fingers almost touching. Swing RH out from wrist, indicating gate opening.

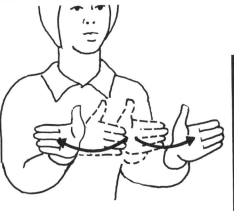

general

Open B both hands held parallel to one another. Move forward and spread apart.

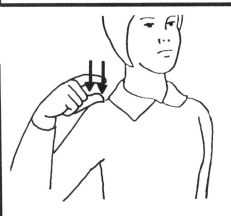

general (person)

Tap right shoulder with thumb of right G.

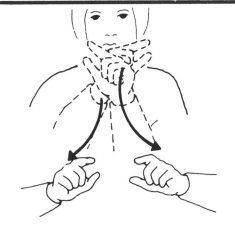

gentle

G shape both hands crossed in front of body. Separate and move down, ending with G shapes facing each other.

gentleman

Place thumb of right A on forehead. Bring down to chest, changing to open 5 palm left.

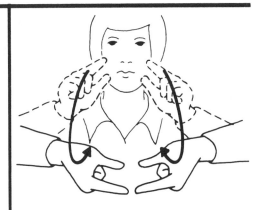

gerbil

G shape both hands, palms facing. Place tips on cheeks, arc down, and twist up slightly.

 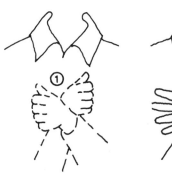 

germ

C shape LH palm and tips right, little finger side down. Form right G, change into flat O, and pass up through left C while spreading fingers.

Germany

A shape both hands, palms in. Cross at wrists and snap sharply into 5 shapes.

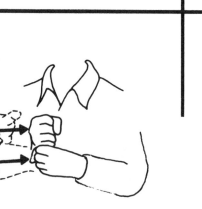 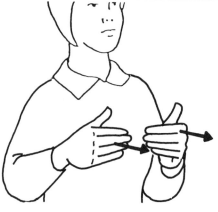 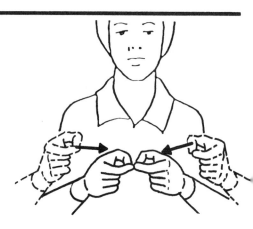

get

C shape both hands, right slightly above left. Move in toward body, closing into S shapes, right on top of left.

get along

Open B both hands, palms in, tips facing, held in front of chest. Move forward simultaneously.

get even

Closed X shape both hands, palms facing. Strike thumbs and index tips together.

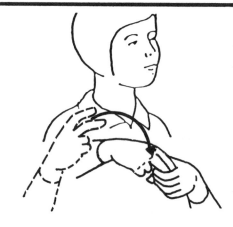 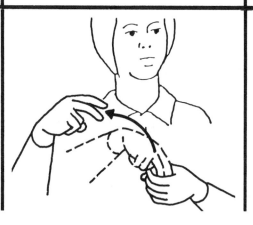 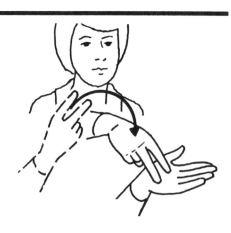

get in

O shape LH palm right. Place tips of right bent V in left O.

get out

O shape LH palm right. Place tips of right bent V in left O then pull out.

get up

Arc tips of right V over into up-turned palm of LH.

ghost

Open 8 shape both hands, left palm up, right palm down. Close right thumb and middle finger around left thumb and middle finger. Then slip RH up in wavy motion and close both hands into 8 shapes.

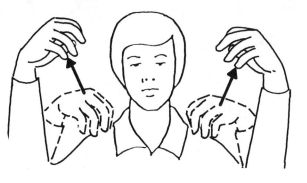

giant

Place tips of claw hands on shoulders then move up forcefully.

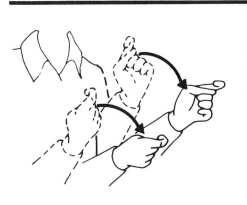

gift

X shape both hands, palms facing. Arc both hands forward.

giggle

L shape both hands, palms in, thumbs up. Wiggle index fingers at corners of mouth.

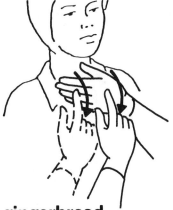

gingerbread

LH open B palm in, tips right. Draw thumb and index finger of right G down back of LH several times.

giraffe

Place right C on side of neck. Raise up, indicating long neck.

girl

A shape RH. Place thumb on right cheek and move down jaw line.

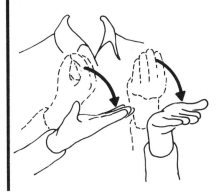

give

O shape both hands, palms up, left a little ahead of right. Move out, opening fingers.

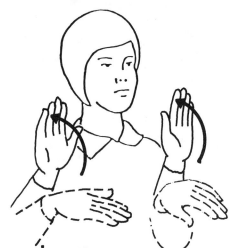

give up
Open B both hands, palms down. Move up and back sharply.

glad
Place thumb of right G on chest and brush upward twice.

glass (drinking)
LH open B palm up. Place little finger side of right C on left palm, then raise up, indicating shape of tall glass.

glass (material)
Tap upper right teeth with tip of right X.

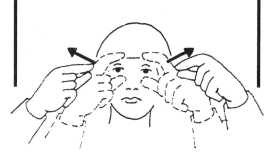

glasses
Place thumbs and index fingers at sides of eyes then draw back, closing fingers (as if outlining frame of glasses).

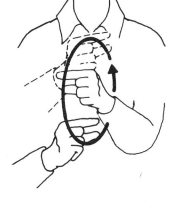

globe
G shape both hands, left tips right, right tips left. Place right G on left, circle foward and under, returning to original position.

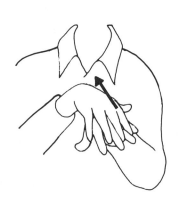

glove
Five shape both hands, palms down, tips out. Draw right fingers back over left fingers.

glow
Rest back of RH on back of LH then move RH up while wiggling fingers.

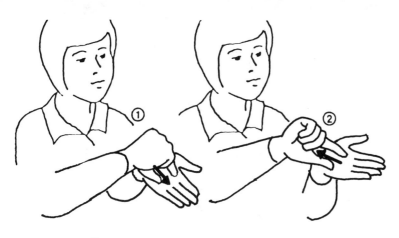

glue

LH open B palm up, tips out.
Place right G on left palm, slide
forward, flip over, and slide back.

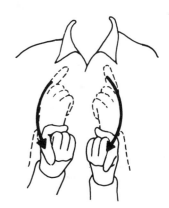

go

One shape both hands, palms and
index tips in. Flip index tips out,
ending with palms up.

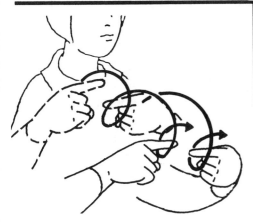

go (alt.)

One shape both hands, palms in,
tips facing. Rotate around one another while moving forward.

goal

One shape both hands. Place tip of
right index on forehead then point
toward left index.

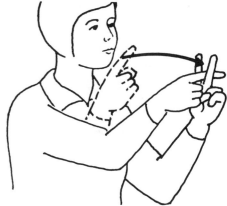

goal (game)

V shape LH palm in. Arc right
index finger forward, ending
between fingers of left V.

goat

Flick tips of right bent V on chin
then on forehead.

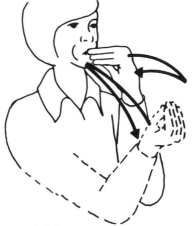

gobble

Flat O shape both hands, tips up.
Place tips on mouth alternately, as
if eating very fast.

God

B shape RH palm left, tips slanted
out. Arc up, back, and down, ending with tips up.

goggles
Place curved thumbs and index fingers at eyes.

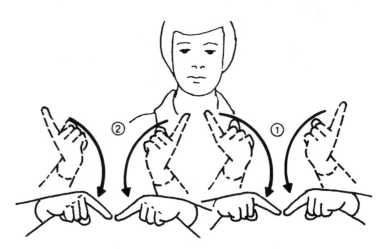

going on (happening)
One shape both hands, palms up. Twist downward, move hands to the right, and repeat motion.

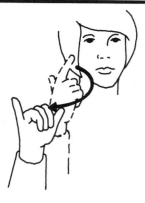

gold
Point right index finger to right ear then twist out, ending in Y shape.

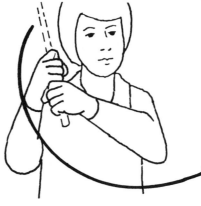

golf
Mime swinging golf club at ball.

good
Open B both hands, palms in, tips slanted up. Place right tips on mouth then move out and down, placing back of hand in left palm.

good-bye
Place right fingertips on mouth then move forward. Turn hand over and wave good-bye.

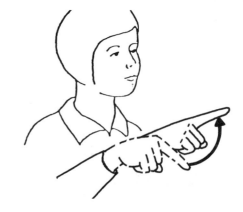

go on (continue)
One shape RH palm in, tip down. Flip index up.

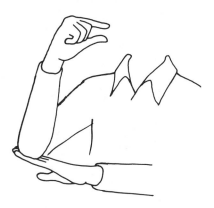

goose

LH open B palm down, tips right. G shape RH. Rest right elbow on back of left hand.

gopher

G shape both hands, palms facing. Tap tips in front of face.

gorilla

G shape both hands, tips facing. Beat alternately against chest.

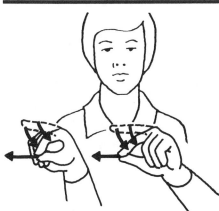

gossip

G shape both hands, palms out. Move from left to right while rapidly opening and closing thumbs and index fingers.

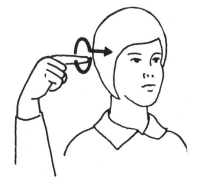

government

Circle and touch right temple with right index.

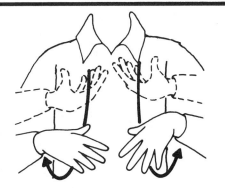

gown

Bent open B shape both hands, tips touching upper chest. Brush down and out, ending with palms down.

grab

C shape RH palm down, fingers slightly spread. Bring hand down and close into S shape.

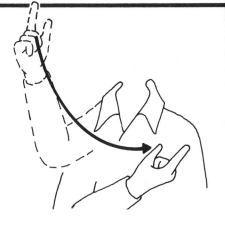

grace

Hold right G up then arc down to left shoulder.

grade (noun)

LH open B palm up, tips out. Circle right G clockwise over LH then drop into palm.

graduate

LH open B palm up, tips out. Place base of right G in left palm then spiral upward.

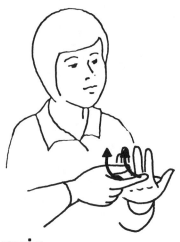

grain

Five shape LH palm up, fingers cupped. Brush thumb of right G up against back of left fingers several times.

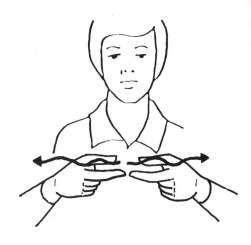

grammar

G shape both hands, tips facing. Wiggle while moving apart.

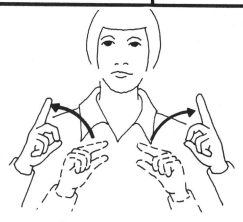

grand

G shape both hands, tips facing. Arc apart, changing into D shapes.

grandchild

G shape RH palm down, tips left. Place on forehead then move to chin. Then place right open B palm down at waist level, indicating size of child.

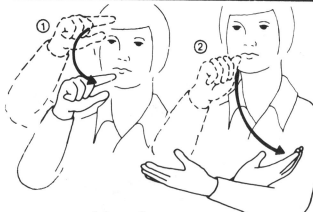

granddaughter

G shape RH palm down, tips left. Place on forehead then move to chin. Form right A, place thumb on right cheek, change into open B (palm up, tips left) and place in crook of left elbow.

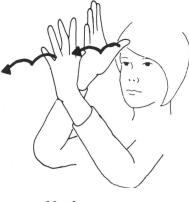

grandfather

Five shape both hands, left palm right, right palm left. Place right thumb on forehead and left thumb on edge of RH. Move out in two short jumps. (Sometimes made with RH only.)

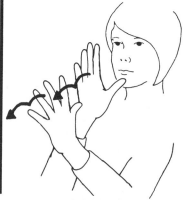

grandmother

Five shape both hands, left palm right, right palm left. Place right thumb on chin and left thumb on edge of RH. Move out in two short jumps. (Sometimes made with RH only.)

grandparent

G shape RH palm down, tips left. Place on forehead then chin. Change to P shape, placing middle fingertip on side of forehead then moving to chin.

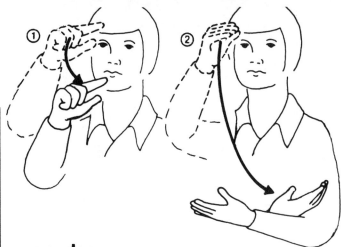

grandson

G shape RH. Place tips on forehead then move to chin. Place thumb side of right flat O on forehead. Arc down into crook of left elbow, opening into open B shape.

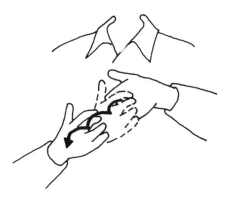

grape

LH open B palm in, tips down. Hop curved right fingers down back of LH, indicating a bunch of grapes.

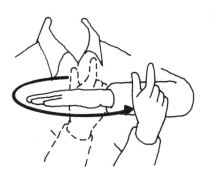

grass

B shape LH palm down, tips right. G shape RH. Outline left hand with right G.

grass (alt.)

Five shape both hands, palms up, fingers cupped. Brush back of right fingers up against back of left fingers.

grasshopper

Place right G on back of left bent V, palm down. Hop forward twice.

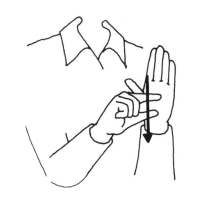

grave

LH open B palm right. Place right G against left fingers and lower to base of palm.

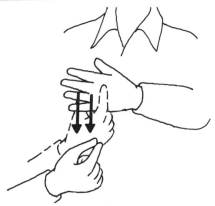

gravy

LH open B palm in, tips right. G shape RH. Grasp bottom of left palm with right index and thumb then slip fingers off into closed G. Repeat.

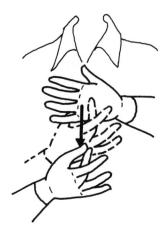

gray

Five shape both hands, palms in, tips facing. Move right fingers back and forth between left fingers. (Sometimes made like sign for *black,* using right G shape instead of index finger.)

grease

LH open B palm in, tips right. Grasp bottom of palm with right middle finger and thumb, then slip right fingers off into 8 shape.

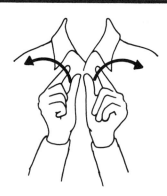

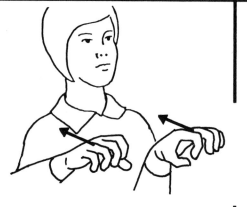

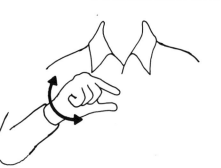

great

G shape both hands, palms and tips out. Arc hands apart.

greed

Claw shape both hands, palms down. Draw back toward body in forceful manner.

green

G shape RH. Shake back and forth.

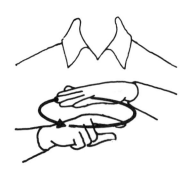

grill

LH open B palm down, tips slanted right. Circle right G counterclockwise beneath left palm.

grin

G shape both hands. Place tips on sides of mouth and arc up slightly.

grocery

Circle right G and up and out from mouth.

170

grouch

Place right G on right side of mouth then draw down right side of chin.

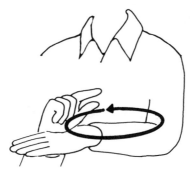

ground

LH open B palm down, tips right. Place base of right G on back of left wrist, then circle counterclockwise over elbow and return to original position.

grumpy

Hold right claw shape in front of face and crook fingers several times.

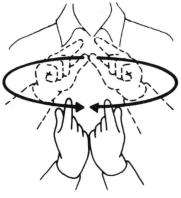

group

G shape both hands, thumb tips touching. Draw apart and around to front, ending with little fingers touching.

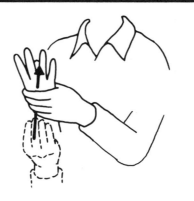

grow

Hold left C before body. Pass right flat O up through left C, spreading fingers as hand emerges.

growl

Grab throat with cupped hand.

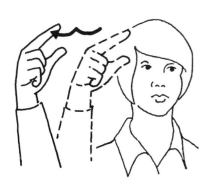

grown-up

Place thumb of right G on right temple then arc up to the right twice.

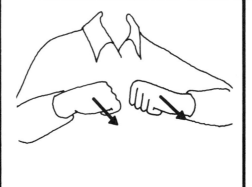

guard

S shape both hands, palms down, knuckles facing. Push forward forcefully.

guess

Cupped RH palm left. Move in quick grasping motion across face, closing into S shape.

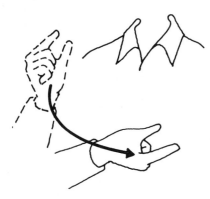

guest

G shape RH palm up. Make sweeping motion to the left.

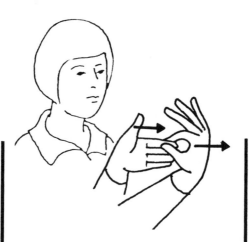

guide

LH open B tips out, palm right. Grasp tips with right thumb and index and pull forward.

guilt

Strike thumb side of right G against upper chest two or three times.

guinea pig

G shape RH tips left. Brush nose twice. Then place back of right open B under chin and flap fingers downward.

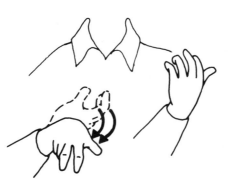

guitar

Mime holding, fingering, and strumming a guitar.

gull

LH open B palm down, tips right. G shape RH palm and tips out. Place right forearm against LH and dip G fingers down twice.

gulp

L shape RH palm left, tips slanted out. Draw back toward throat and down quickly.

gum

G shape RH knuckles and tips left. Place on left side of cheek and slide to right side, outlining gums.

gum (chewing)

Place tips of right V on right cheek and bend up and down rapidly.

gun

L shape RH palm left, index finger out. Crook thumb down.

guy

Place thumb of right G on right temple then move out slightly.

gym (class)

A shape both hands, knuckles facing. Hold above shoulders and move forward in circular movements. (Sometimes made with G shapes.)

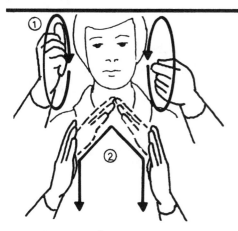

gymnasium

Hold A shapes above shoulder and circle forward alternately. Change to B shapes palms facing, tips touching; draw apart and down, outlining building.

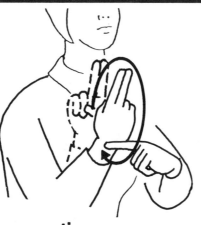

gymnastics

One shape LH palm in, tip right. Place base of right U on left index then circle forward and under, ending with palm in.

H

habit

S shape both hands, palms down. Place right S on left wrist and push both hands down.

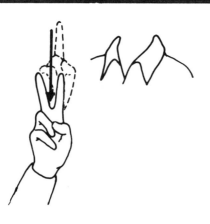

had

Place thumb and index tips of D shape hands on chest.

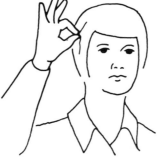

hair

Grab hair with right thumb and index finger.

hair dryer

L shape RH palm in, knuckles left. Circle clockwise at right side of forehead.

half

Form the number 1 and drop down into the number 2.

hall

H shape both hands, tips up. Move forward and out from sides of face.

174

hallelujah

Clap hands together once or twice. Then change to A shapes, thumbs up, and circle at both sides of head.

Halloween

H shape both hands, palms in, tips up. Place tips under eyes and circle around to ears.

ham

H shape LH palm and tips slanted right. Grasp left hand between thumb and index finger with right thumb and index and shake.

hamburger

Clasp hands together, reverse position, and clasp together again, as if forming patty.

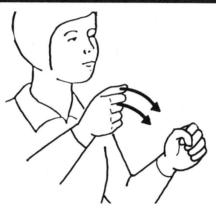

hammer

S shape LH knuckles right. A shape RH. Move right A toward left S as if hitting nail.

hamper (basket)

S shape LH palm down, arm extended. Place tips of right H against left wrist and arc down and up to elbow.

hamster

H shape both hands. Place tips on cheeks. Move down and turn palms up.

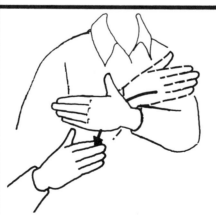

hand

Open B both hands, left palm slanted right, tips out. Draw little finger side of RH across left wrist in slicing motion.

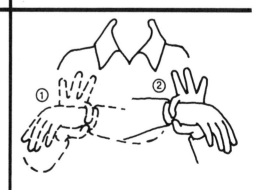

handcuff

Circle left wrist with right thumb and index finger, then circle right wrist with left thumb and index finger.

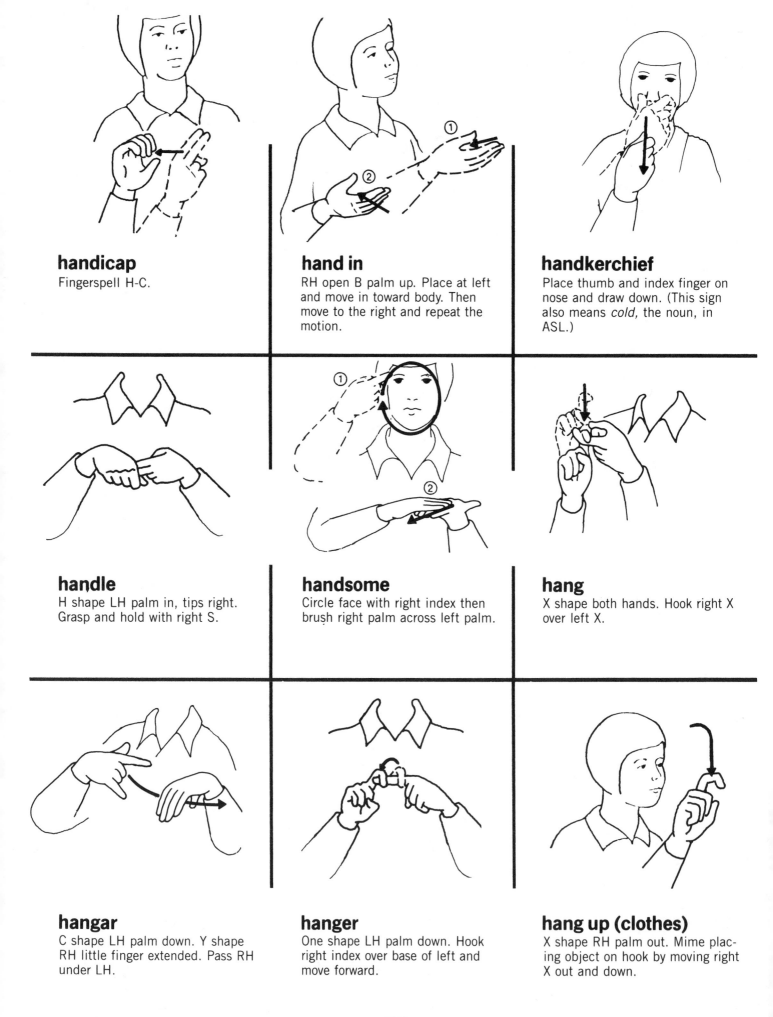

handicap
Fingerspell H-C.

hand in
RH open B palm up. Place at left and move in toward body. Then move to the right and repeat the motion.

handkerchief
Place thumb and index finger on nose and draw down. (This sign also means *cold*, the noun, in ASL.)

handle
H shape LH palm in, tips right. Grasp and hold with right S.

handsome
Circle face with right index then brush right palm across left palm.

hang
X shape both hands. Hook right X over left X.

hangar
C shape LH palm down. Y shape RH little finger extended. Pass RH under LH.

hanger
One shape LH palm down. Hook right index over base of left and move forward.

hang up (clothes)
X shape RH palm out. Mime placing object on hook by moving right X out and down.

hang up (telephone)
Y shape RH palm down. Mime placing receiver on base of telephone.

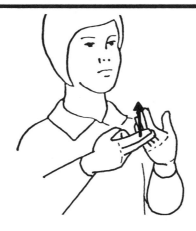

Hanukkah
H shape both hands, palms out, tips up. Place index fingers together and move away and up, outlining menorah.

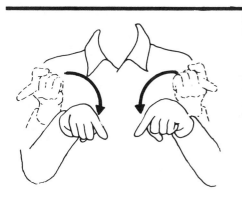

happen
One shape both hands, palms up, tips out. Twist toward each other, ending with palms down.

happy
RH open B palm in, tips left. Brush up chest twice with quick, short motion.

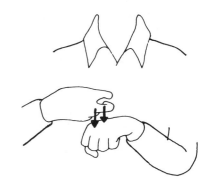

hard
S shape LH palm down. Hit back of left S with middle finger of right bent V. Repeat motion.

hard of hearing
Point to ear with right index finger. Change to H shape RH and bounce once to the right.

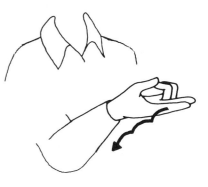

hardly
Cupped LH open B palm up. Slowly move middle finger of right H up back of left fingers.

hardware
H shape RH palm up, tips out. Move toward right in short jumps.

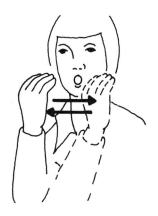

harmonica

Mime holding and playing a harmonica

harp

Mime plucking and strumming a harp with both hands.

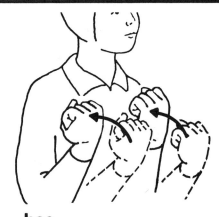

has

S shape both hands, palms in. Draw toward and touch chest.

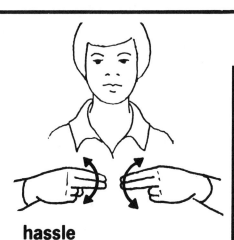

hassle

H shape both hands, palms in, tips facing. Simultaneously shake hands up and down.

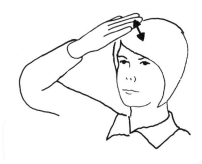

hat

Pat top of head with palm of RH.

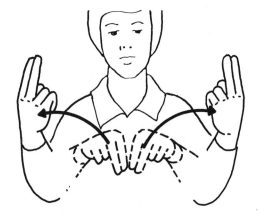

hatch

H shape both hands, palms down, index fingers touching. Draw apart, ending with palms up.

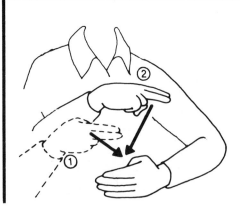

hatchet

B shape LH palm and tips slanted right. H shape RH palm and tips slanted left. Chop left index backward then forward with right H.

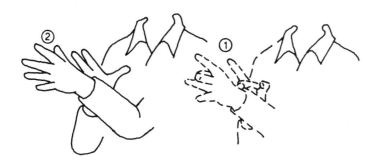

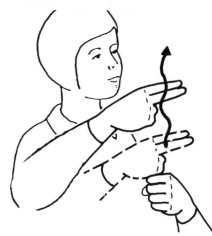

hate

Eight shape both hands, palms facing, tips out, left slightly in front of right. Flick middle fingers from thumbs.

haunt

S shape LH knuckles right. H shape RH palm in, tips left. Place RH on left S then wave upward.

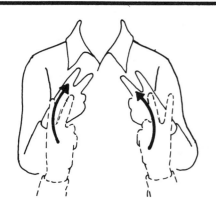

have

V shape both hands, palms in, tips up. Draw toward and touch chest.

have to

X shape RH palm out. Move down forcefully, ending with palm down.

hay

Cupped 5 shape LH palm up. Brush middle finger of right H up back of left fingers. Repeat motion.

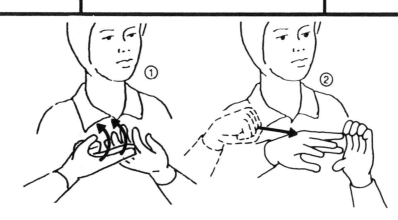

hayloft

Brush H shape RH up back of left cupped fingers twice. Then move right S into left C, ending with a 5 shape RH.

he

E shape RH palm left. Place on right temple, then move out slightly toward right.

head

RH bent B palm down, tips left. Place tips on right temple then on chin.

headache

One shape both hands, tips facing. Move back and forth in front of forehead.

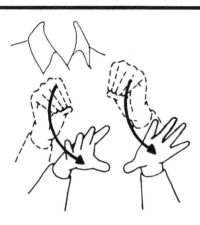

headlight

Flat O shape both hands, palms and tips out. Swing forward, opening into 5 shapes.

headphone

Claw shape both hands, palms facing. Place tips on sides of head, covering ears.

health

H shape both hands, palms in, tips facing. Place tips on upper chest then move down to stomach.

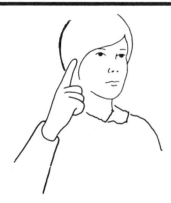

hear

Point index finger to ear.

hearing aid

Place right thumb, index, and middle finger on right ear (as if inserting aid).

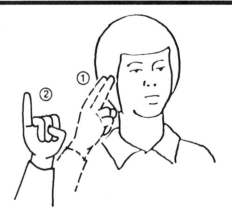

hearing impaired

Place right H, palm in, at ear. Move out, changing to I shape.

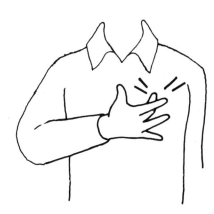

heart

Tap heart with right middle finger.

heart (alt.)

Trace a "heart" on left upper chest with middle fingers.

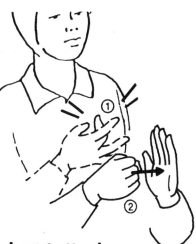

heart attack

Tap heart with right middle finger. Then hit palm of left open B with right fist.

heartbeat

LH open B palm in. A shape RH palm in. Strike left palm with knuckles of right A several times.

heat

Cupped shape LH palm up. Place RH under LH and wiggle fingers, indicating action of flames.

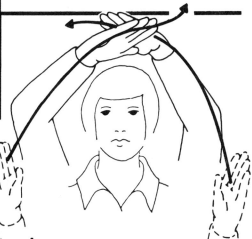

heaven

Open B shape both hands, palms facing. Circle up and toward one another, passing RH under LH.

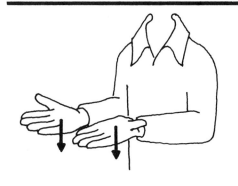

heavy

Open B both hands, palms up, tips out. Lower slowly.

heel

LH open B palm down, tips out. G shape RH palm up, tips out. Place RH under base of left palm.

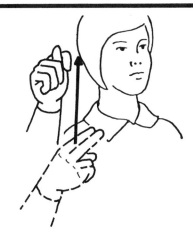

height

Right H changes to T shape while moving up.

181

helicopter

Support open right palm with left index finger and shake right fingers.

hell

H shape RH, palm left, tips out, slashes to the right, ending with palm out.

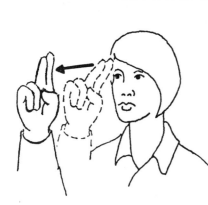

hello

Place index tip of H shape RH at side of forehead then move out.

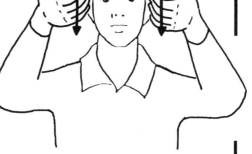

helmet

Mime pulling helmet down over ears using cupped hands.

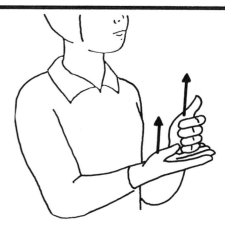

help

Place little finger side of left A, thumb up, in right palm. Raise right palm up.

hen

Three shape RH palm left, tips out. Tap thumb on chin.

her

R shape RH. Place on right cheek then move out slightly to the right.

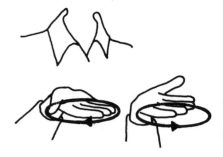

here

Open B both hands, palms up, tips out. Circle horizontally in opposite directions.

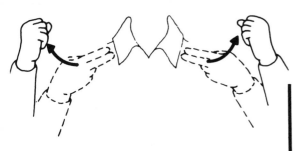

hero
H shape both hands, palms in, tips facing. Place on upper chest then move apart and up, ending in S shapes.

hers
Place tips of right R on right cheek then move forward. Form right S and move out slightly.

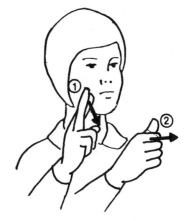

herself
Place tips of right R on right cheek then move out. Form A shape RH, thumb extended and push forward.

hey!
Place cupped hands around mouth.

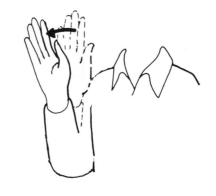

hi
Wave open palm from left to right. (This word is often fingerspelled.)

hiccup
One shape RH palm left. Place against chest and jerk up and down.

hide
LH bent open B palm down. Place thumb of right A on lips then move down and under LH.

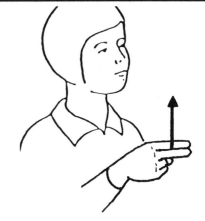

high
H shape RH tips out. Move up several inches.

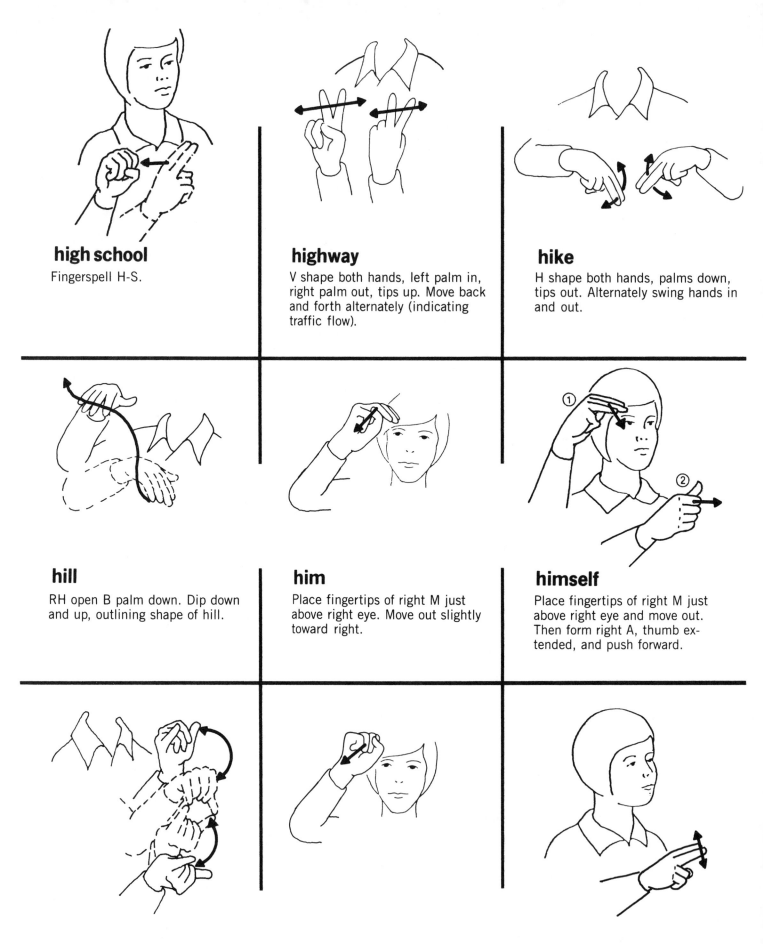

high school

Fingerspell H-S.

highway

V shape both hands, left palm in, right palm out, tips up. Move back and forth alternately (indicating traffic flow).

hike

H shape both hands, palms down, tips out. Alternately swing hands in and out.

hill

RH open B palm down. Dip down and up, outlining shape of hill.

him

Place fingertips of right M just above right eye. Move out slightly toward right.

himself

Place fingertips of right M just above right eye and move out. Then form right A, thumb extended, and push forward.

hippopotamus

Y shape both hands, left tips up, right tips down. Place right tips on left. Open wide and close again.

his

Place right S just above right eye. Move out slightly toward right.

history

H shape RH palm left, tips out. Shake up and down.

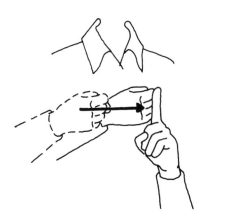

hit

Strike left index with right fist.

hitchhike

Mime hitchhiking with right fist, thumb extended.

hobby

S shape LH palm down. H shape RH palm in. Brush base of right H back and forth on back of left wrist.

hockey

LH open B palm up. Swing right X against left palm then toward body.

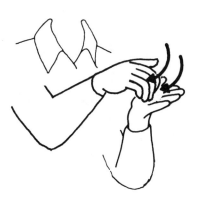

hoe

LH open B palm up, tips out. Bent RH open B palm in, tips down. Scrape left palm with right tips.

hog

H shape RH palm down, tips left. Place under chin and drop fingers.

hold

S shape both hands. Place right on top of left as if grasping rope.

hold still

Open B both hands, palms out. Push downward slightly.

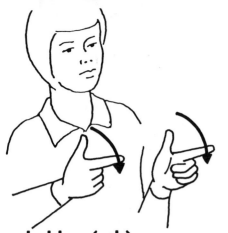

hold up (rob)

L shape both hands, palms facing, index tips out. Arc forward simultaneously.

hole

C shape LH palm and tips right, little finger side down. Circle with right index which is pointed down.

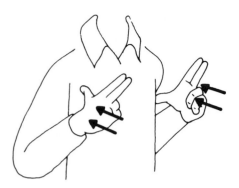

holiday

H shape both hands, palms facing, thumbs extended. Tap thumbs on upper chest several times.

hollow

C shape LH palm and tips right. Circle over LH with bent right middle finger, other fingers spread.

holly

Point left index finger to the right. Touch tip with right thumb and index finger. Then draw RH away, snapping thumb and index finger.

holster

C shape LH placed on left hip. Stick index finger of right L into left C.

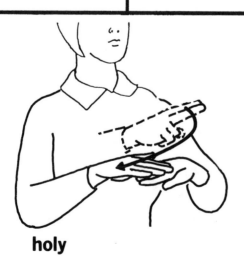

holy

Place H shape RH, palm down, over left open B. Change RH to open B shape and slide across left palm.

home

Place tips of right flat O to edge of mouth and move to upper cheek. (Sometimes made with right flat O moving to open B on cheek.)

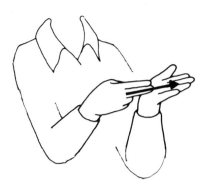

honest

LH open B palm up, tips out. H shape RH palm left, tips out. Slide RH forward on left palm.

honey

Draw index of H shape RH across chin, then flick wrist out and down.

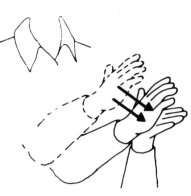

honk

Hit base of upturned left palm with base of right palm.

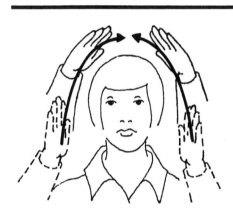

hood

Open B both hands, palms facing. Hold just above shoulders then arc up over head until fingers touch.

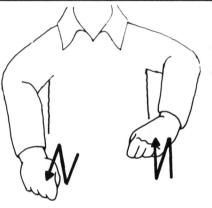

hoof

S shape both hands. Move up and down alternately (miming horse clopping along).

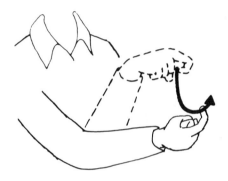

hook

X shape RH palm down. Swing downward, ending with palm up.

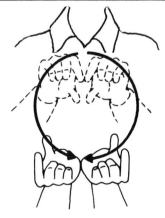

hoop

G shape both hands, palms out. Draw apart and down in circular motion, outlining hoop.

hooray!

Place fists at sides of head and simultaneously shake up and down.

hop

LH open B palm up, tips out. Place middle finger of right P on left palm then hop forward once.

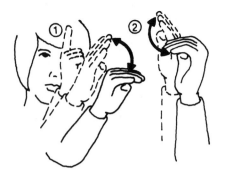

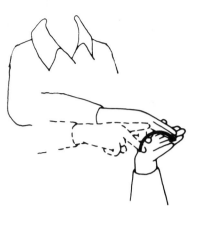

hope

Touch forehead with right index finger. Raise open B hands so they face each other, RH near right forehead, LH at the left. Simultaneously bend (and unbend) fingers of both hands toward one another.

hopscotch

LH open B palm up, tips out. Place middle finger of right P on base of left palm then hop forward, changing to H shape.

horn

C shape LH palm and tips right. S shape RH palm left. Hold RH at mouth and blow.

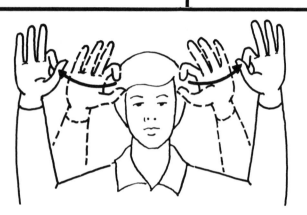

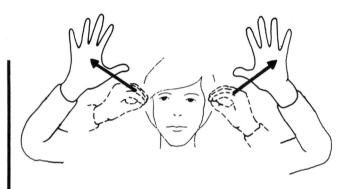

horn (animal)

Form circles with thumbs and index fingers of both hands. Place at sides of forehead and move out.

horrible

Flat O both hands, tips touching temples. Bring both hands forward suddenly, ending in 5 shapes palms out, tips up.

horror

H shape both hands, palms out, tips up. Place at left side and move down in wavy motion.

horse

H shape RH thumb extended. Place thumb on right temple. Flap H fingers downward twice.

horseback

B shape LH palm right, tips out. Straddle with right middle and index fingers and rotate in small circles, indicating a galloping motion.

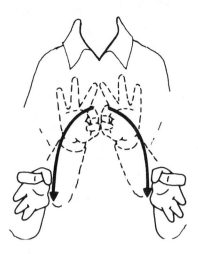

horseshoe

F shape both hands, palms out, thumbs and index fingers touching. Circle apart and down in shape of horseshoe.

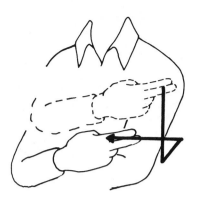

hose (water)

X shape RH palm up. Move from left to right as if watering plants or grass.

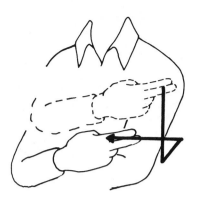

hospital

H shape RH. Make cross on upper left arm.

hot

Place tips of right claw on mouth. Twist wrist quickly so that palm faces down.

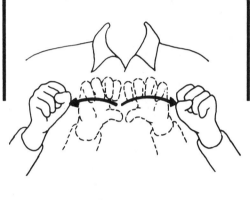

hot dog

Claw shape both hands, palms down, index fingers almost touching. Draw apart and close into S shapes.

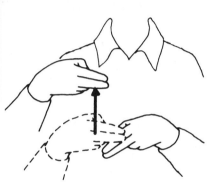

hotel

H shape both hands, left palm right, tips out; right palm in, tips left. Place right H on left H, then move up several inches.

hour

LH open B palm right, tips up. Place thumb knuckle of 1 shape RH against left palm and make a circle.

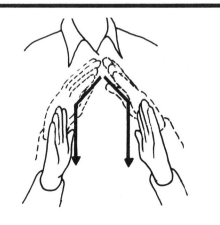

house

Place tips of both hands together to form roof. Move apart and down to form sides of house.

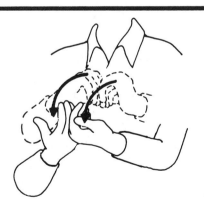

how

Hold backs of fingers together, palms down. Turn in and up.

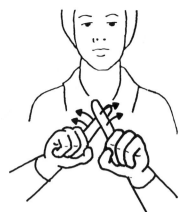

however

One shape both hands. Cross index tips and pull apart twice with short, small movements.

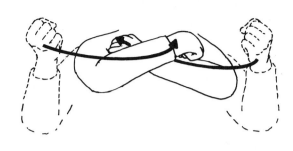

hug

S shape both hands. Cross arms on chest as if hugging something. (Sometimes H handshapes are used.)

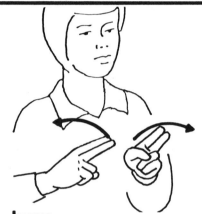

huge

H shape both hands, palms facing, tips out. Place close together then arc away from each other.

hum

Place tips of right M at lips. Move out in small, wavy motion.

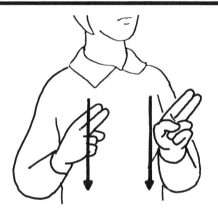

human

H shape both hands, tips out. Place wrists at sides of chest and move down.

humid

Open B shape both hands, palms up. Snap fingertips together several times while moving to the right.

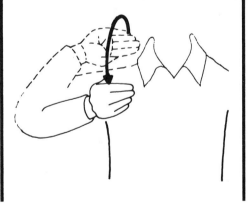

hump

B shape RH palm out, tips left, held at shoulder. Move up and down in shape of hump, ending with palm in.

hundred

Form C shape with RH. (NOTE: This sign is usually preceded by a specific number; e.g., 1 + C = one hundred, and 6 + C = six hundred.)

hungry
Draw tips of claw hand down upper chest.

hunt
L shape both hands, palms facing, index tips out. Shake up and down.

hurricane
H shape both hands, palms in, left tips up, right tips down. Circle around each other quickly.

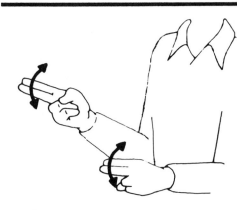

hurry
H shape both hands, palms facing, tips out. Shake up and down rapidly.

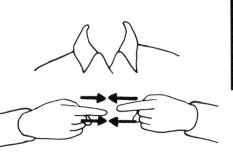

hurt
One shape both hands, palms in, tips facing. Move back and forth toward one another. (Sometimes made with H handshapes.)

husband
Place thumb of curved open B at right temple. Move down and clasp LH which is held palm up.

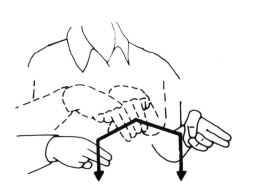

hut
H shape both hands, palms down, index fingers touching. Move apart and down, outlining shape of hut.

hydrant
Curved open B both hands, tips facing. Move up, outlining shape of hydrant.

hypnotize
Five shape both hands, palms
down. Place at eye level and move
forward, wiggling fingers.

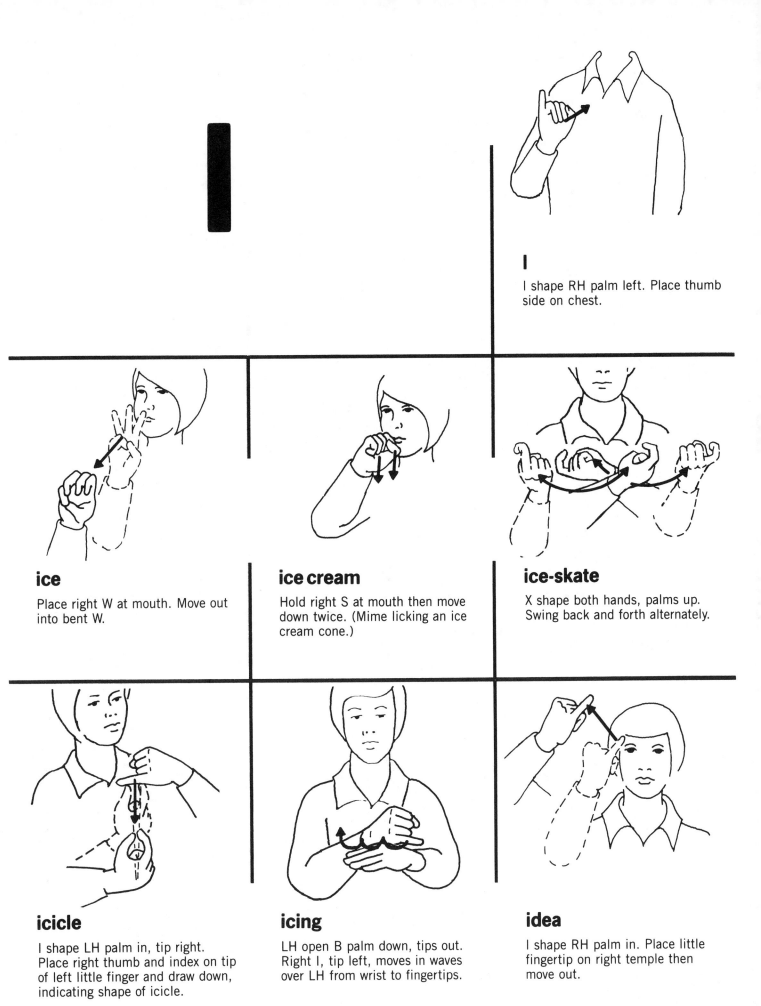

I

I shape RH palm left. Place thumb side on chest.

ice

Place right W at mouth. Move out into bent W.

ice cream

Hold right S at mouth then move down twice. (Mime licking an ice cream cone.)

ice-skate

X shape both hands, palms up. Swing back and forth alternately.

icicle

I shape LH palm in, tip right. Place right thumb and index on tip of left little finger and draw down, indicating shape of icicle.

icing

LH open B palm down, tips out. Right I, tip left, moves in waves over LH from wrist to fingertips.

idea

I shape RH palm in. Place little fingertip on right temple then move out.

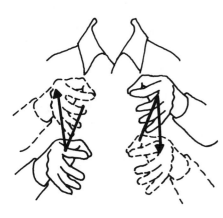

if

F shape both hands, palms facing, tips out. Move up and down alternately.

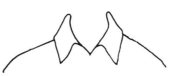

igloo

I shape both hands. Curve down, outlining shape of igloo.

ignore

Four shape RH palm left. Place tip of right index on nose then arc out and slightly to the left.

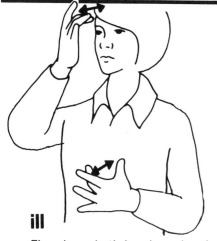

ill

Five shape both hands, palms in. Tap forehead with right middle finger and stomach with left middle finger. Repeat.

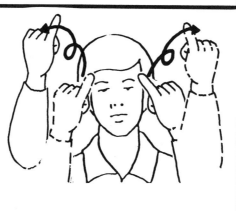

imagination

Place tips of little fingers on both sides of forehead. Alternately circle them upward and away from the head.

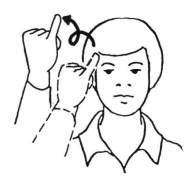

imagine

Place tip of right I on forehead. Circle it upward and away from the head.

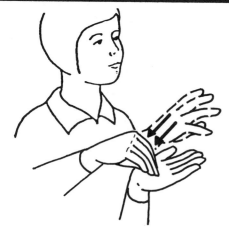

imitate

LH open B palm up, tips out. Hold RH, palm down, fingers spread, above and slightly in front of LH. Draw back into left palm, ending in flat O shape. Repeat motion.

immediate

Y shape both hands, palms in. Lower slightly.

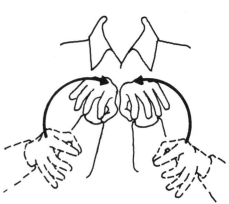

important

F shape both hands, palms facing, tips out. Draw up in semicircle until index fingers and thumbs touch.

improve

LH open B palm down. Bounce little finger side of right open B up left forearm.

in

C shape LH palm right. Place tips of right flat O into left C.

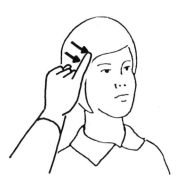

in case

Tap right side of forehead with tip of right little finger.

inch

One shape LH palm down. Slice down left index finger with right little finger.

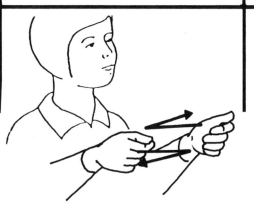

in charge

Modified A shape both hands, palms facing. Alternately move back and forth as if holding reins.

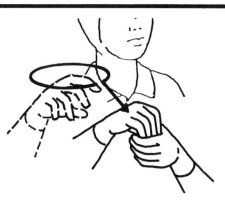

include

C shape LH palm right. Circle 5 shape RH, palm down, around and then into left C, ending with a right flat O.

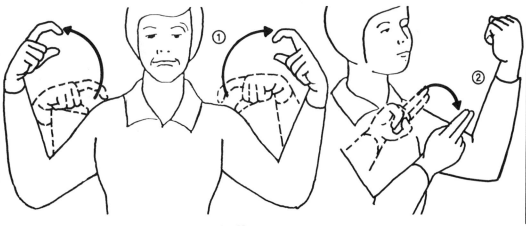

Incredible Hulk

Place curved thumb and index fingers on shoulders then move up and out. Follow with right H outlining muscle on left upper arm.

Indian (American)

Place index finger and thumb of right F on tip of nose. Move up and rest on right temple. (Sometimes made with right F moving from corner of mouth to ear.)

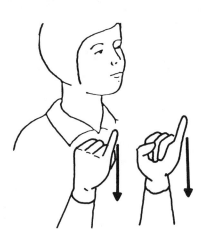

individual

I shape both hands, palms facing. Place hands in front of body then move down.

infection

Brush lips with tip of right index. Change to flat O, place on wrist, and spread into 5 shape while moving up arm.

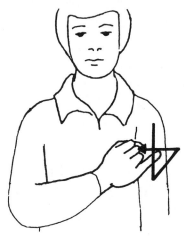

infirmary

I shape RH palm in, tips left. Outline cross on left upper arm.

influence

Place tips of right flat O on back of left hand which is held palm down. Spread fingers into 5 shape, palm down, and move in fan-like motion from left to right.

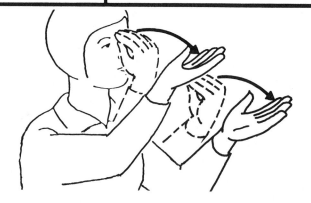

information

Flat O shape both hands, palms in. Place tips of right hand on fore-head while holding LH out and to the left. Flip both hands out simul-taneously, ending in open B shapes, palms up.

ingredient

LH open B palm in, tips up. Hold away from body. Bounce back of right little finger down left palm, indicating items on a list.

initial (noun)

H shape LH tips out, palm slanted right. Strike left index with tip of right I. Repeat motion.

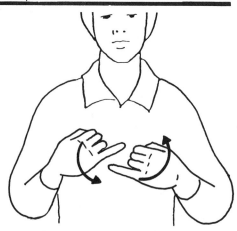

injure

I shape both hands, palms in, tips facing. Move toward each other while twisting hands in opposite directions.

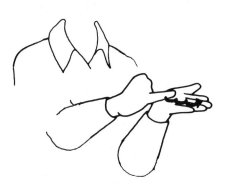

ink

LH open B palm up, tips out. Place little fingertip of right I in left palm and move forward as if writing.

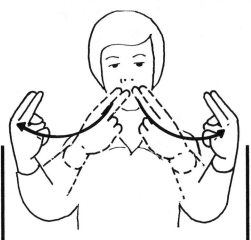

innocent

U shape both hands, palms in. Place tips on mouth then draw apart and to the sides.

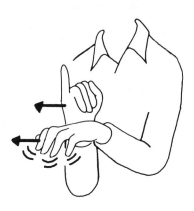

insect

Place base of left I on back of left claw hand which is held palm down. Move LH forward in crawling motion.

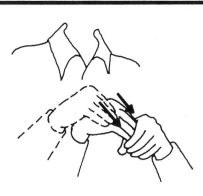

inside

C shape LH palm right. Place tips of RH in left C twice.

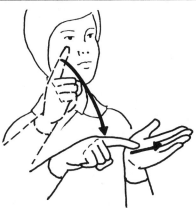

inspect

Place tip of right index under right eye. Then place on left palm and slide forward.

instant

LH open B palm right, tips up. Place thumb of right 1 shape on left palm, then flick right index forward. Follow with a quick flicking of the right thumb out from cupped fingers.

instead

F shape both hands, palms facing, tips out. Hold right above left and move under and out, reversing positions.

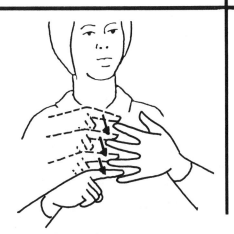

instruction

Five shape LH palm right, tips out. Consecutively touch the four fingertips of the LH with tip of right index.

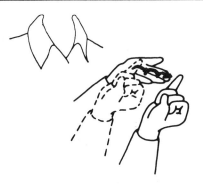

instrument

LH open B palm up, tips out. I shape RH palm up, tip left. Place tip on base of left palm and move forward in short jumps.

interest (concern)

Place open tips of middle fingers and thumbs on chest, RH above LH. Move out slightly, closing into 8 shape.

interesting

Place open tips of middle fingers and thumbs on chest, RH above LH. Arc upward and out, closing into 8 shapes.

intermediate

LH open B palm up, tips out. I shape RH little finger down. Circle right little finger over left palm then place in center of palm.

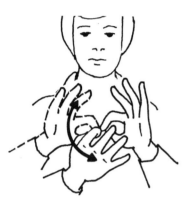

interpret

F shape both hands, fingers curved, palms facing, thumb and index tips touching. Twist RH forward. Repeat motion.

interrupt

Open B both hands, left palm right, tips out; right palm in, tips left. Strike LH between thumb and index with little finger side of right B.

interview

I shape both hands, palms facing. Place at sides of face and alternately move back and forth.

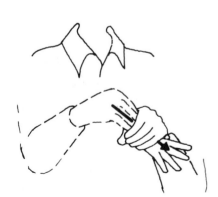

into

C shape LH palm right. Place tips of right flat O in left C and push through and forward.

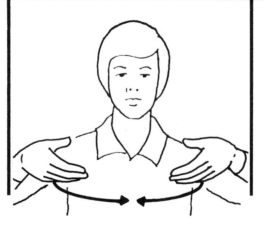

introduce

Cupped open B shape both hands, palms in. Hold out at sides of body then move in toward each other.

invent

Four shape RH palm left. Place right index tip on forehead then move up.

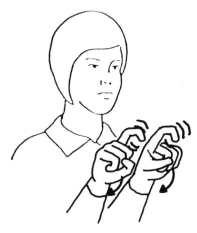

investigate

X shape both hands, palms out, right behind left. Nod hands while crooking index fingers.

invitation

RH open B palm and tips slanted left. Arc down and up toward body, ending with palm up. Then slide fingertips of right cupped hand across left palm.

invite

RH open B palm and tips slanted left. Arc down and up toward body ending with palm up.

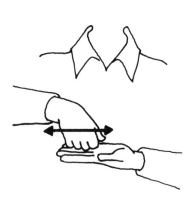

iron

Mime ironing clothes.

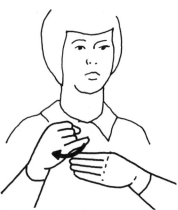

iron (noun)

B shape LH tips slanted right. Strike tip of right little finger against tip of left index and arc to right.

is

Place little finger of right I on lips and move out.

island

A shape LH palm down. Describe circle counterclockwise on back of left A with tip of right little finger.

isolate

I shape both hands, palms in, index fingers touching. Draw apart.

it

LH open B tips out. Place tip of right little finger in palm of LH.

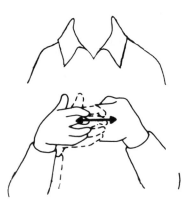

itch

Claw shape both hands, palms in. Scratch back of LH with right tips.

its

LH open B tips out. Place tip of right little finger in left palm. Then move out into S shape.

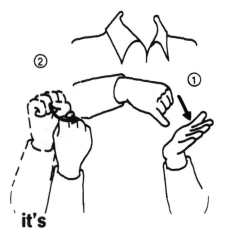

it's

LH open B tips out. Place tip of right little finger in left palm. Then move out into S shape and twist in.

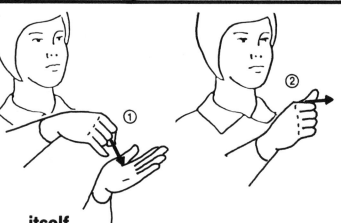

itself

LH open B tips out. Place tip of right little finger in left palm. Then form right A, palm left, and move forward.

ivy

Hold left forearm up, palm right. Move right 5 shape up left arm from elbow to wrist in a wavy motion.

J

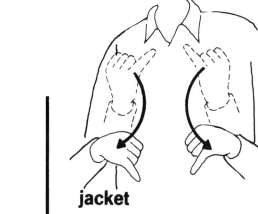

jacket

I shape both hands, palms in.
Place fingers on chest and move
down, outlining shape of lapels.

jackhammer

S shape both hands, palms down.
Rapidly bounce up and down.

jack-in-the-box

Place knuckles of right S in palm
of left bent B. Jerk up suddenly
while opening left bent B.

jack-o'-lantern

C shape both hands, palms facing.
Alternately move up and down
sides of cheeks.

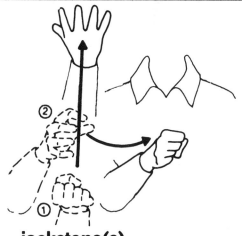

jackstone(s)

S shape RH knuckles up. Throw up
into 5 shape, come back down,
close into S shape, and twist to
left.

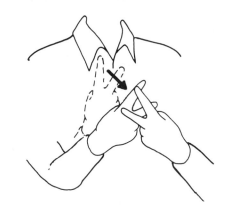

jail

V shape both hands, palms in, tips
slanted toward each other. Place
back of right V against left V.

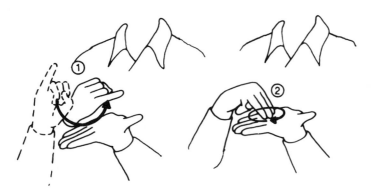

jam

LH open B palm up, tips out. Make right J over left palm, turn into M shape, and make circle in left palm with right tips.

January

LH open B palm in. Place little finger of right I (or J) on left palm, slide over fingers and down back of LH.

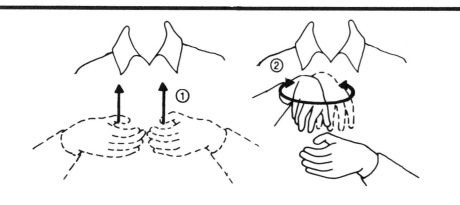

jar

C shape both hands, palms and tips facing. Raise up, outlining jar, then twist right C, palm down, above left C as if screwing on top.

jealous

Draw J shape at right side of mouth with tip of right little finger, ending with palm in.

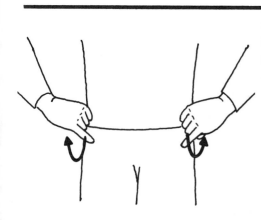

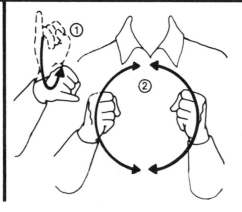

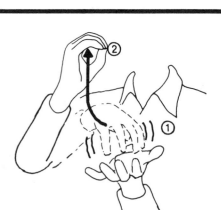

jeans

Place little fingers on hips and form J shapes.

jeep

Make a right J. Then form S shapes both hands. Move as if turning steering wheel of car.

Jell-O

LH open B palm up, tips slightly right. C shape RH palm down. Wiggle right fingers over left palm and draw up into O shape.

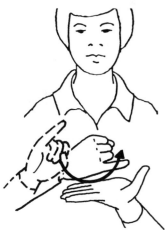

jelly

Dip right J shape into upturned palm of LH.

Jesus

Open B both hands, palms facing, tips out. Place tip of right middle finger on left palm then place tip of left middle finger on right palm.

jet

Y shape LH palm down, index finger extended. Place base of right S on left wrist and open into 5 shape several times.

jewel

Describe a J shape on ring finger of LH with right little finger.

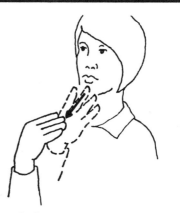

Jewish

Grab chin with fingers of RH then draw into flat O, indicating beard.

jingle

LH open B palm up. Swing right J back and forth over left palm and forearm in rhythmic motion.

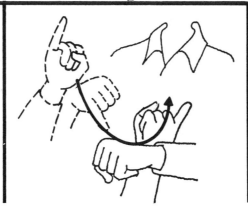

job

S shape LH, palm down. Describe J shape on back of left wrist with right little finger.

jog

S shape both hands, palms facing. Alternately swing back and forth.

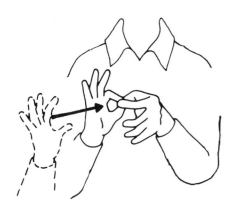

join

Open 9 shapes both hands, right in front of left. Move right hand to left and hook thumb and index fingers together.

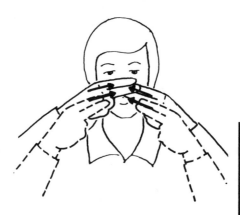

joke

H shape both hands, palms in. Move up to nose. Repeat motion.

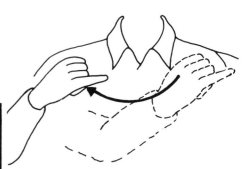

Joseph (biblical)

Place little finger of right J on left shoulder and draw across to right shoulder.

joy

I shape RH palm in, tip left. Brush tip up chest twice with short, quick motion.

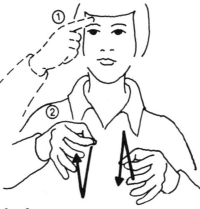

judge

Tap forehead with right index then form F shapes, palms facing, tips out, fingers spread. Move up and down alternately.

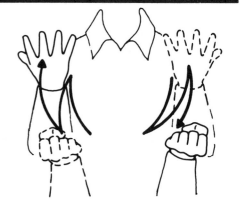

juggle

S shape both hands, knuckles up. Juggle up and down alternately, opening into 5 shapes palms in.

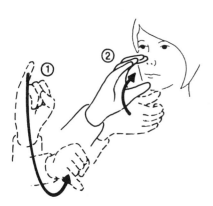

juice

Form letter J then raise cupped hand to mouth as if drinking.

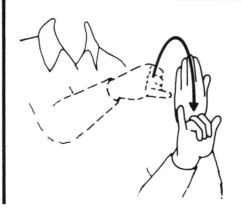

July

LH open B palm in. Outline J on left palm with right little finger, arc over fingers, and form Y shape.

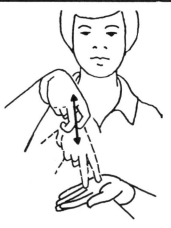

jump

LH open B palm up, tips out. Place tips of right V in left palm and pull up quickly, changing into bent V shape. Repeat motion.

jumper (clothing)

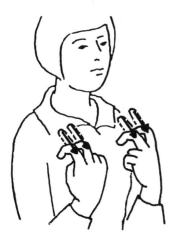

Place tips of V shape hands on upper chest. Pull out into bent V shapes.

June

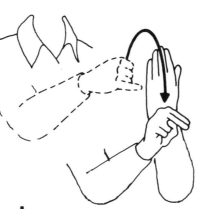

LH open B palm in. Outline J on left palm with right little finger, arc over fingers, and form N shape.

jungle

J shape RH palm left. Place right elbow on back of LH, palm down, and twist RH back and forth.

junior

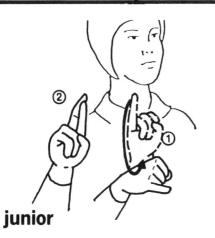

Fingerspell J-R.

junk

Describe a J in left palm with little finger of RH. Form right flat O, palm up, then toss fingers open.

just

LH open B palm right, tips up. Trace J on left palm with right little finger.

K

kangaroo

Curved open B both hands, tips out. Place right wrist on back of left wrist and hop forward twice.

karate

Open B both hands, palms down, right hand over left. Move both out in short, forceful movement.

keep

V shape both hands, tips out. Place right V on left V. (Sometimes made with K handshapes.)

keep an eye on

Place tip of right index at right eye. Then slap back of left open B with palm of right open B.

kettle

S shape LH palm right. Place right K on left S then circle forward and under so that left S rests on RH.

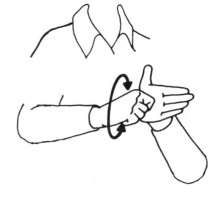

key

LH open B palm right, tips out. Twist knuckle of right index in left palm.

kick

B shape both hands. Swing index finger side of RH up against little finger side of LH.

kid (child)

K shape RH tips left. Place in front of nose and twist wrist down to left twice.

kid (goat)

Place right K on chin, then on forehead.

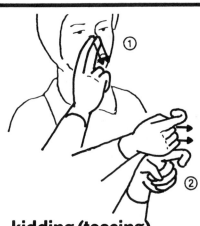

kidding (teasing)

Brush nose twice with tips of right U. Then brush base of right X off index of left X. Repeat motion.

kidnap

S shape LH palm down, arm across front of body. Place thumb of right K against left elbow. Pull back sharply toward left hand.

kill

LH open B palm out. Quickly slide right index finger across and down left palm.

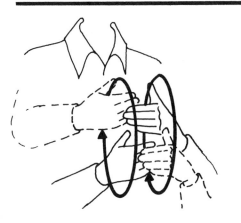

kind (virtue)

Open B both hands, palms in, left tips right, right tips left. Circle around one another moving out from the heart.

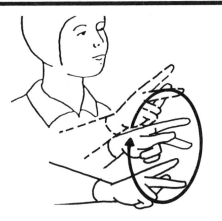

kind (of)

Place base of right K on left K. Then rotate right K around left K, ending in initial position.

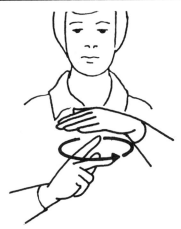

kindergarten

LH open B palm down, tips slanted right. Rotate right K counterclockwise under left palm.

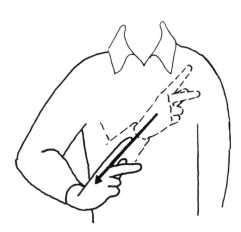

king

Place right K on upper left chest then move down to right side of waist.

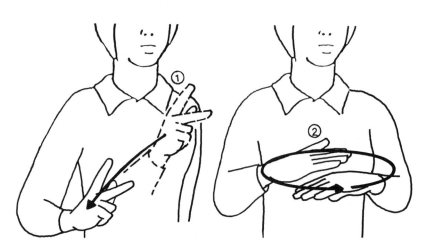

kingdom

Place right K on upper left chest then move down to right side of waist. Change to open B hand positions and rotate right hand over left hand counterclockwise.

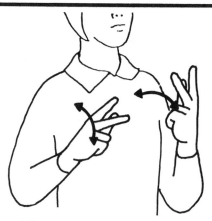

King Kong

Alternately beat thumbs of K handshapes against chest.

kiss

Place tips of right open B on mouth and move back to cheek.

kitchen

K shape RH. Shake back and forth.

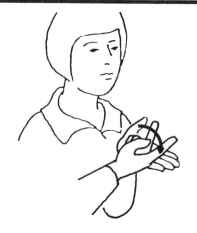

kitchen (alt.)

LH open B palm up, tips out. Place base of right K in left palm then flip over, ending with right palm up.

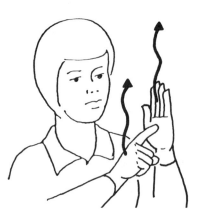

kite

Open B shape LH palm slanted right. Place tip of right index on left palm and zigzag both hands upward.

kitten

Brush side of right cheek twice with middle finger of right K.

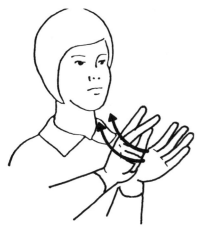

Kleenex

LH open B palm up, tips out. Brush base of right K across base of left palm toward body twice.

knee

Raise right knee and touch with tips of right hand.

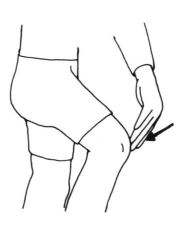

kneel

Place knuckles of bent right V in left palm.

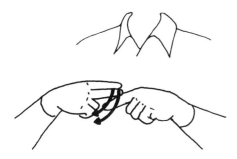

knife

Strike tips of right U against left index and move out sharply. Repeat motion.

knight

Place thumb of right K on left shoulder then move to right shoulder.

knit

Rub tips of index fingers up and down on each other, miming action of knitting needles.

knob

Mime turning doorknob.

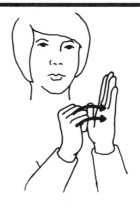

knock

LH open B palm right. Knock knuckles of right A against left palm twice.

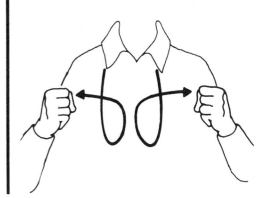

knot

S shape both hands, knuckles facing. Make motion of tying knot and pulling tight.

209

know
RH open B palm in, tips up. Pat forehead with tips.

Kool-Aid
Form right K, then mime drinking motion with cupped right hand.

L

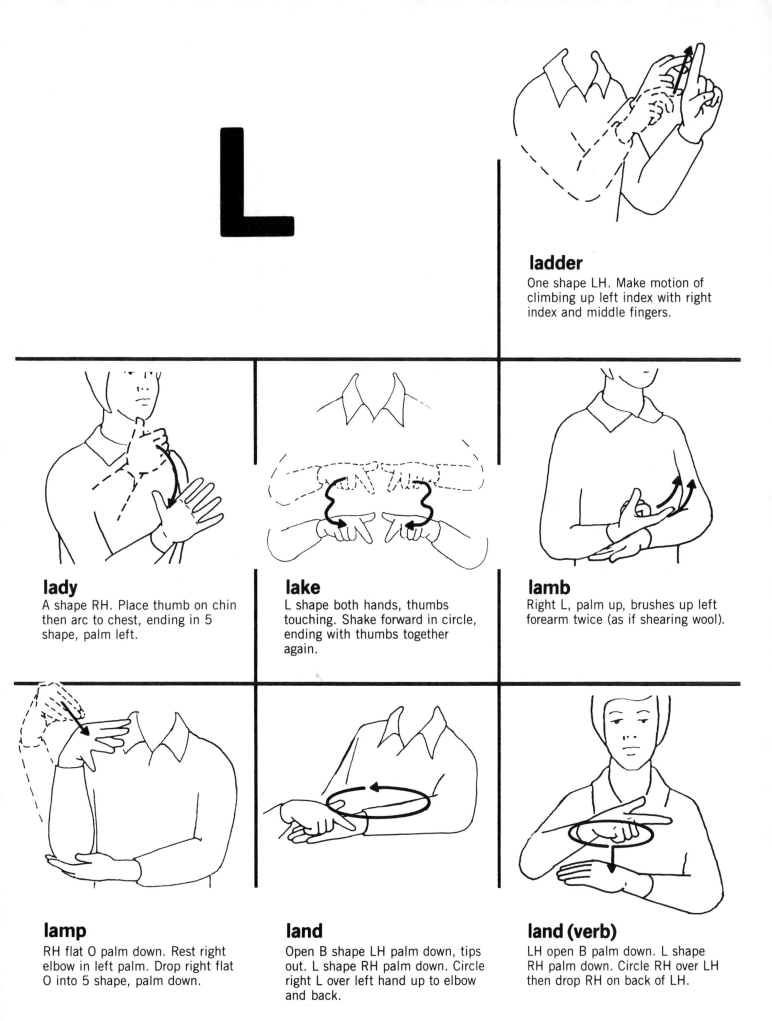

ladder
One shape LH. Make motion of climbing up left index with right index and middle fingers.

lady
A shape RH. Place thumb on chin then arc to chest, ending in 5 shape, palm left.

lake
L shape both hands, thumbs touching. Shake forward in circle, ending with thumbs together again.

lamb
Right L, palm up, brushes up left forearm twice (as if shearing wool).

lamp
RH flat O palm down. Rest right elbow in left palm. Drop right flat O into 5 shape, palm down.

land
Open B shape LH palm down, tips out. L shape RH palm down. Circle right L over left hand up to elbow and back.

land (verb)
LH open B palm down. L shape RH palm down. Circle RH over LH then drop RH on back of LH.

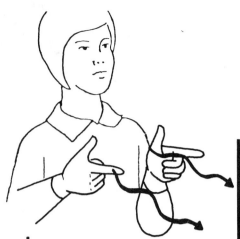

lane

L shape both hands held parallel, index tips out. Move forward with slight wavy motion.

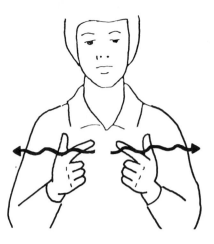

language

L shape both hands, palms facing, index tips out. Place hands close together then wiggle apart.

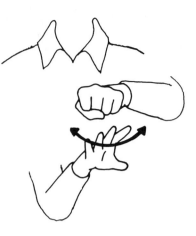

lantern

S shape LH knuckles down. Five shape RH fingers cupped, palm and tips out. Swing under left S.

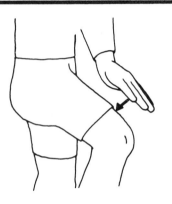

lap (person's)

Raise right knee and pat thigh with right palm several times.

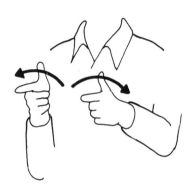

large

L shape both hands, palms facing, thumbs up. Arc hands apart.

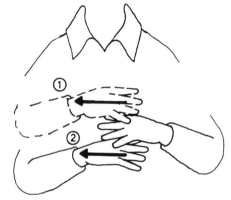

lasagna

Four shape both hands, palms down, tips opposite. Place right 4 over left, draw back to right, then place under left hand and draw back to right again (indicating layers).

last (adj. & adv.)

I shape LH tip out. Strike down tip of left little finger with right index.

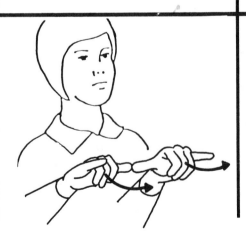

last (verb)

Y shape both hands, palms down, thumbs touching. Move both hands forward.

late

Hold right open B down by side. Wave back and forth twice.

later

L shape RH palm left, index tip up. Move up and forward in semi-circle.

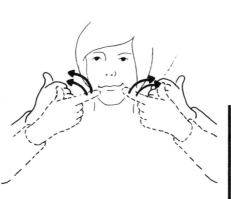

laugh

Place index fingers on sides of mouth then quickly crook index fingers two or three times.

laundry

L shape both hands, left palm up, tips slanted right; right palm down, tips slanted left. Twist hands back and forth.

law

LH open B. L shape RH. Place back of right L on fingertips, then on heel, of left palm.

lawn

B shape LH palm down, tips right. L shape RH. Outline left B with right L.

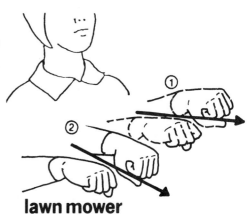

lawn mower

S shape both hands, palms down. Move both hands out to left then out to right (as if pushing mower).

lay

LH open B palm up, tips out. Lay back of right V in left palm.

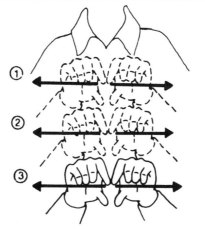

layer

G shape both hands, palms and tips out. Move apart and back three times, lowering the hands a little each time.

lazy

L shape RH palm in. Tap chest twice just below left shoulder.

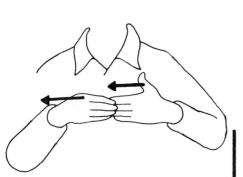

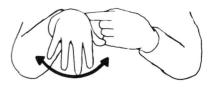

lead

LH open B palm in, tips right. Grasp with fingers and thumb of RH and pull to right.

lead (metal)

B shape LH palm and tips slanted right. L shape RH. Strike index of left B with index of right L.

leaf

One shape LH palm in, tip right. Place right wrist over left index and move hand back and forth.

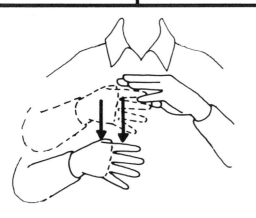
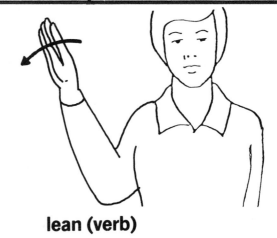

leak

Four shape both hands, left palm down, tips right; right palm in, tips left. Place under left palm and drop down twice.

lean (verb)

RH open B palm slanted right. Hold right arm up at right side then lower palm slightly.

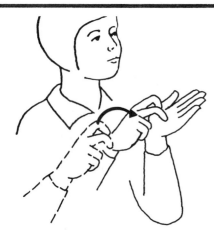
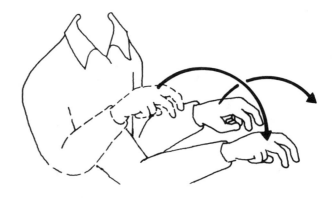

leap

LH open B palm up, tips out. Right bent V "leaps" onto left palm.

leapfrog

Bent V both hands, palms down. Leap forward alternately.

learn

LH open B palm up, fingers spread. Place fingertips of right 5 in left palm then move to forehead, changing into flat O.

learning disabled

Fingerspell L-D.

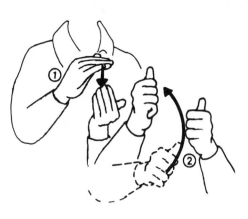

least

Bent B both hands, left palm up, right palm down. Place RH over LH and lower slightly. Now form A shape both hands, thumbs up. Brush knuckles of right A up against and past knuckles of left A.

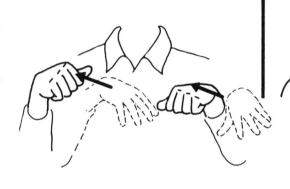

leave

Five shape both hands, palms down, tips slanted left, left hand in front of right. Draw back into A shapes.

leave (alone)

Five shape both hands, palms facing, fingers spread, left hand slightly in front of right. Arc both hands forward and down.

left (direction)

L shape RH palm out. Move from right to left.

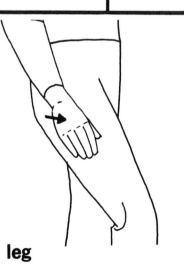

leg

Pat right thigh with right palm.

lemon

L shape RH palm left, thumb in. Tap chin with thumb.

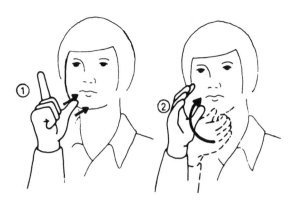

lemonade
Tap chin with thumb of right L. Change into C shape and move to mouth as if drinking.

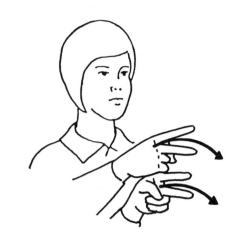

lend
V shape both hands, left palm and tips slanted right, right palm and tips slanted left. Place right V on left then arc both hands forward.

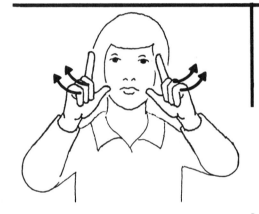

leopard
Place thumbs of L shape hands on cheeks. Brush back two or three times.

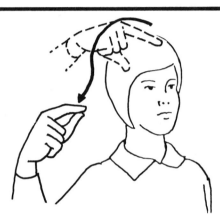

leprechaun
Place tips of right L on head. Outline shape of hat, ending with tips together.

less
Bent B both hands, left palm up, right palm down with tips left. Lower RH.

lesson
Open B both hands, RH fingers bent. Place little finger side of RH on fingertips, then heel, of left palm.

let
L shape both hands, palms facing, index tips pointed slightly down. Bring to upright position.

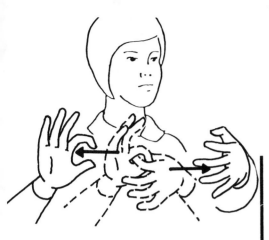

let go

Lock together thumbs and index fingers of both hands then open and move apart.

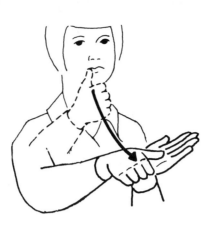

letter (mail)

Place thumb of right A on mouth and then on upturned left palm.

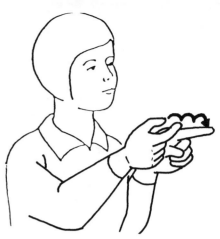

letter (alphabet)

One shape LH palm right, tip out. Place tips of right G on base of left index then move forward one or two times.

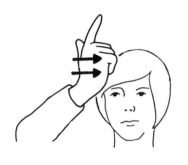

lettuce

Tap base of right L against right temple twice.

library

L shape RH. Circle in front of body.

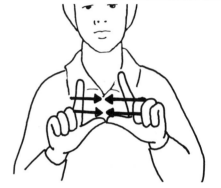

license

L shape both hands, palms out. Tap thumbs together twice.

lick

LH open B palm and tips slightly up. Place tips of right H on left palm and brush forward twice.

lid

O shape LH tips right. RH bent B tips left. Place on left O then straighten into open B shape.

lie (recline)

LH open B palm up, tips out. Draw back of right V across left palm.

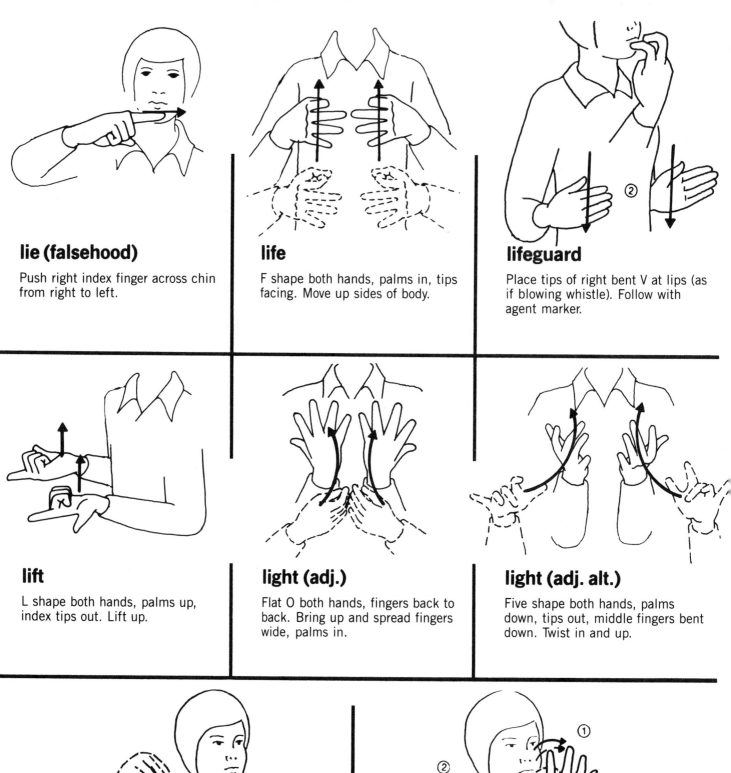

lie (falsehood)

Push right index finger across chin from right to left.

life

F shape both hands, palms in, tips facing. Move up sides of body.

lifeguard

Place tips of right bent V at lips (as if blowing whistle). Follow with agent marker.

lift

L shape both hands, palms up, index tips out. Lift up.

light (adj.)

Flat O both hands, fingers back to back. Bring up and spread fingers wide, palms in.

light (adj. alt.)

Five shape both hands, palms down, tips out, middle fingers bent down. Twist in and up.

light (noun)

Right flat O palm down. Hold up at right side then drop fingers into 5 shape palm down.

light bulb

Flick right thumb and middle finger at chin one or two times. Then mime holding and screwing in bulb with right bent 3 shape palm up.

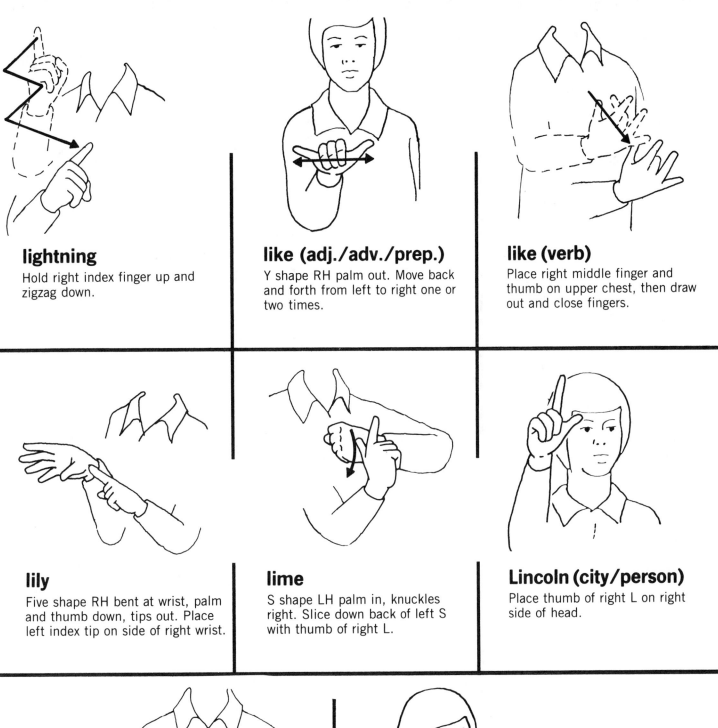

lightning
Hold right index finger up and zigzag down.

like (adj./adv./prep.)
Y shape RH palm out. Move back and forth from left to right one or two times.

like (verb)
Place right middle finger and thumb on upper chest, then draw out and close fingers.

lily
Five shape RH bent at wrist, palm and thumb down, tips out. Place left index tip on side of right wrist.

lime
S shape LH palm in, knuckles right. Slice down back of left S with thumb of right L.

Lincoln (city/person)
Place thumb of right L on right side of head.

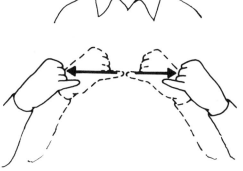

line
I shape both hands, palms in, tips touching. Draw apart in straight line.

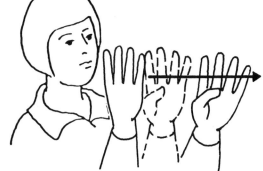

line up
Four shape both hands, left palm right, right palm left. Place right hand behind left then move LH forward.

lion

C shape RH palm and tips down, fingers slightly separated. Place on head and move back.

lip

Rub lips with right index finger.

lipread (speechread)

V shape RH palm in. Place in front of lips and move back and forth from right to left several times.

lipstick

Mime applying lipstick to lips.

liquid

C shape LH palm and tips right. Arc thumb of right L into left C.

liquor

S shape LH palm down. S shape RH palm in, index and little fingers extended. Tap back of LH with little finger side of RH.

list

LH open B palm in, held out from body. Bounce fingertips of RH down left palm, indicating items on a list.

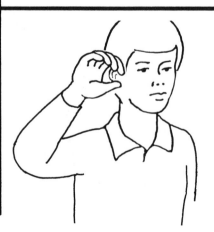

listen

Cup hand over ear.

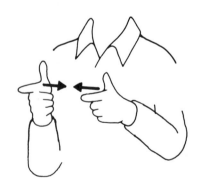

little

L shape both hands, palms facing, index tips out. Move close together.

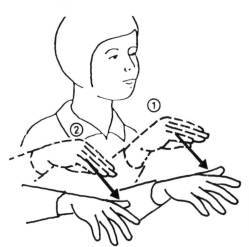

litter

Mime throwing items on ground with RH, moving from flat O to 5 shape.

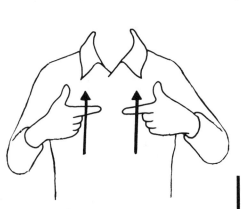

live

L shape both hands, palms in, thumbs up. Place on chest and move up.

liver

L shape LH palm in, tips right. Wiggle flesh between left thumb and index with right thumb and index.

lizard

LH open B palm right, tips up. Run right L up left palm in wiggly motion.

load

S shape LH knuckles right. L shape RH palm down, index tip left. Pass over left S toward body.

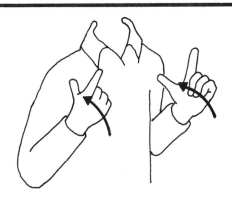

loaf (noun)

Cupped shape both hands, palms and tips down. Place thumbs and index fingers together then draw apart.

loaf (verb)

L shape both hands, palms facing, thumbs up. Draw back and place thumbs on upper chest.

lobster

V shape both hands, palms facing, tips slanted toward one another. Snap V fingers together.

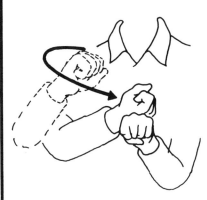

lock

S shape both hands, palms down. Turn right S over and rest on back of left S.

locker

B shape LH palm out but lowered slightly. Place thumb of right L on side of left index. Then twist to right ending with palm up.

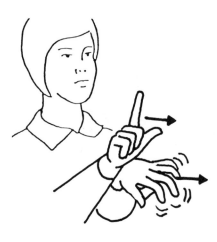

locust

Place base of right L on back of LH. Then move both hands forward while wiggling fingers of LH.

log

S shape LH palm down. Place little finger side of right L on left wrist. Then draw RH back down inside of left wrist.

lollipop

L shape RH palm left. Place index tip on mouth and brush down lips twice.

lonely

One shape RH palm left. Brush down lips. Then rotate right index, palm in, in circle counter-clockwise.

lonesome

One shape RH palm left. Brush dramatically down lips.

long

A shape LH knuckles down, arm extended. Run right index finger up left arm.

look

Point to eyes with tips of right V, then twist and point out.

look up (in a book)

LH open B palm up, tips out. Brush tip of right thumb on left palm several times.

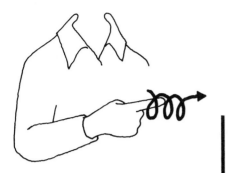

loop

One shape RH palm in, tip left. Loop forward.

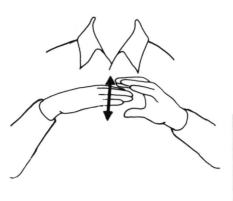

loose

C shape LH palm right. B shape RH palm down, tips left. Move up and down in left C.

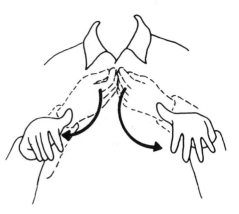

lose

Flat O shape both hands, backs of fingers touching. Drop into 5 shapes, palms down.

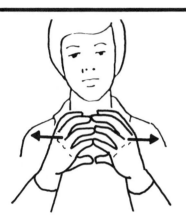

lot (quantity)

Claw shape both hands, tips touching. Pull apart.

lotion

LH open B palm up, tips out. Dip thumb of right L into left palm (as if pouring).

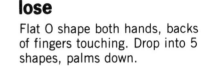
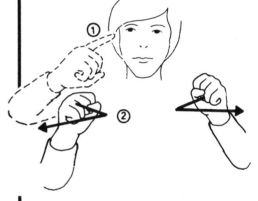

loud

Place right index at right ear, then shake S shape both hands in front of body.

lousy

Place thumb of 3 shape RH on nose. Then arc out and down.

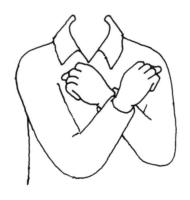

love

S shape both hands. Cross wrists and place over heart.

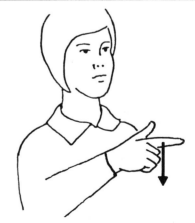

low

L shape RH palm down. Move down.

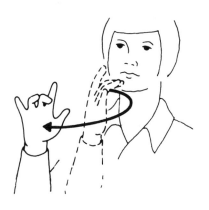

luck
Place right middle finger on chin then twist out into Y shape, index finger extended.

luggage
S shape RH knuckles down. Mime carrying suitcase.

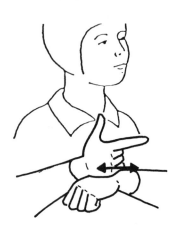

lumber
S shape LH palm down. Place base of right L on back of LH and "saw" back and forth.

lump
Outline shape of lump on back of LH with index tip of right L.

lunch
Place tips of right flat O on lips. Move out into open B, palm in, and rest elbow on back of LH which is held palm down across front of body.

lunch (alt.)
Index tip of right L, palm in, rotates in small circle in front of mouth.

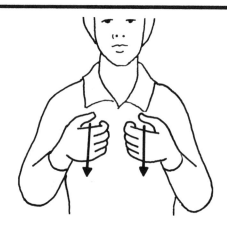

lung
Place fingertips of cupped hands on chest. Move down, outlining lungs.

M

macaroni

M shape both hands, palms down, index fingers touching. Wiggle away from each other.

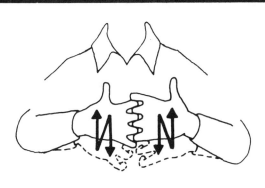

machine

Interlock fingers, palms in, and move up and down.

mad

Claw shape RH palm in. Hold in front of face and move out.

magazine

LH open B palm right, tips out. Grasp bottom of LH with right index and thumb and slide RH forward.

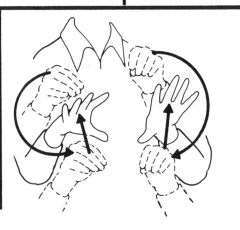

magic

Flat O shape both hands, tips out. Move away in semicircle, opening into 5 shapes palms out, tips up.

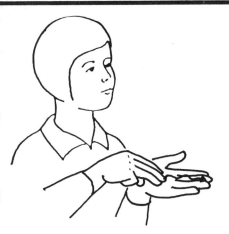

Magic Marker

LH open B palm up, tips out. Write across left palm with tips of M shape RH.

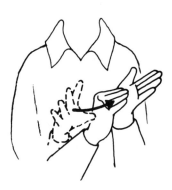

magnet

LH open B palm right, tips out. Five shape RH palm left. Close rapidly into flat O and "stick" to left palm.

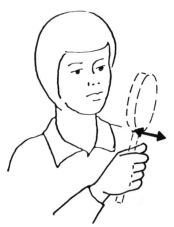

magnifying glass

Mime holding a magnifying glass in front of face and "focusing" it by moving RH in and out.

maid

Brush right cheek with tips of right M once or twice.

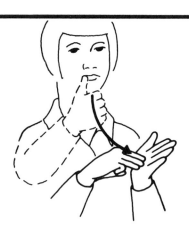

mail

Place thumb of right A on mouth. Change to M shape and place tips in upturned left palm.

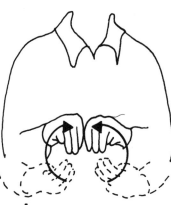

main

M shape both hands, palms up. Arc upward, ending with palms down, index fingers touching.

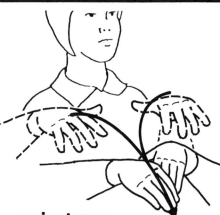

mainstream

Five shape both hands, palms down, tips out. Move toward one another while moving out from body, ending with right palm on top of LH.

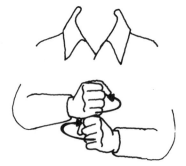

make

S shape both hands. Place little finger side of right S on thumb of left S. Twist hands in toward body.

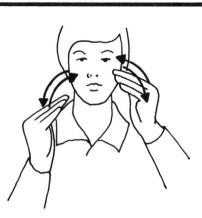

makeup (cosmetic)

Flat O both hands. Place tips on cheeks alternately.

make up (invent)

Place index tip of RH on forehead then move out in small circles.

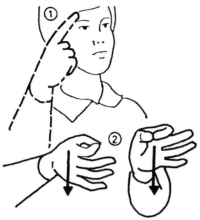

make up (one's mind)

Place tip of right index on forehead, then drop both hands into F shapes, palms facing.

male

M shape RH palm down, tips left. Place index side on forehead and slide to right.

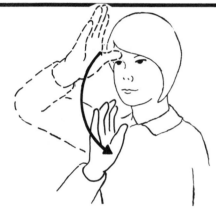

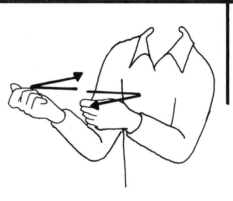

man

RH open B palm left. Touch thumb to forehead then arc down to the chest.

manage

"Loose" A shape both hands, palms up, thumbs out. Move back and forth alternately as if handling reins.

mane

Place tips of right M on hair and draw back over head.

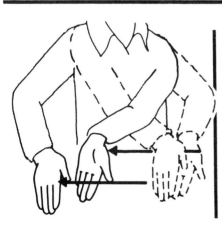

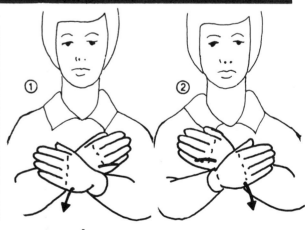

manger

Open B both hands, tips down, left palm out, right palm in. Hold at left side of body then slide to right.

manner

Move thumb of right open B into chest.

manual

Open B both hands, left palm slanted right, right palm slanted left. "Slice" left wrist with little finger side of RH. Then "slice" right wrist with LH.

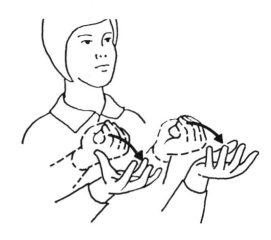

manual alphabet
Fingerspell A-B-C. (Can also be signed as a compound of *manual* plus *alphabet*.)

many
O shape both hands, tips up. Snap open quickly into 5 shapes palms up.

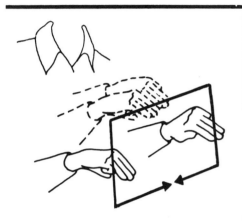

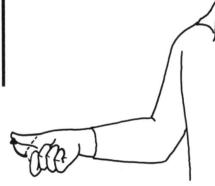

map
M shape both hands, palms down, tips out, index fingers touching. Move apart, down, and back together again.

marbles (game)
A shape RH with thumb tucked under index. Flick thumb out as if shooting a marble.

March (month)
LH open B palm in, tips up. M shape RH palm down, tips left. Place RH against left palm, slide over fingers and down.

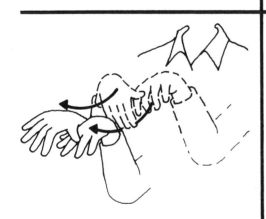

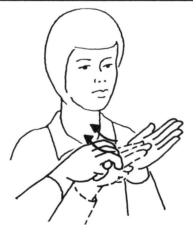

march (verb)
Five shape both hands, palms in, tips down. LH in front of right. Swing fingers back and forth while moving both hands forward.

margarine
LH open B palm up, tips out. Place tips of right M on left palm and brush inward twice.

marine
Place thumb tip of right L on right side of neck and move to center of throat (indicating "Leathernecks").

228

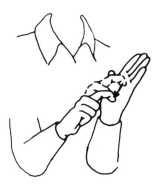

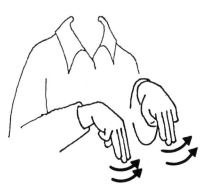

mark

LH open B palm right. X shape RH. Draw tip of right X down left palm.

market

M shape both hands. Swing fingertips forward and up twice.

marry

Clasp hands together.

marshmallow

C shape LH palm and tips right, little finger side down. Open and close right fingers in left C.

marvelous

M shape both hands, palms out. Circle outward to the sides.

Mary (biblical)

Place right M just above left shoulder. Circle over head to right shoulder.

mash

LH open B palm up, tips out. S shape RH. Strike left palm several times with little finger side of right S.

mask

M shape both hands, palms in, tips up. Place tips on bridge of nose then move to temples, ending with palms facing.

229

master

Place tips of right M on upper left chest then move down to right side of waist.

mat

B shape LH palm down. Slide tips of right M forward on back of left B.

match (noun)

LH open B palm right, tips out. Strike tips of right A upward against left palm.

match (verb)

Claw shape both hands, palms in. Interlock fingers.

mate

M shape both hands, left palm up, tips slanted right; right palm down, tips slanted left. Place right fingers on left, then reverse positions.

material

M shape RH, palm and tips up. Move slightly out and to the right in small arcing movements.

mathematics (math)

M shape both hands, palms in. Brush little finger side of right M on index finger of left M while moving hands in opposite directions. Repeat motion.

230

matter

M shape both hands, palms in, tips facing. Alternately slap tips back and forth.

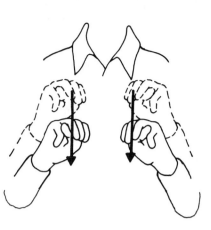

may

M shape both hands, palms down, tips slanted out. Move down.

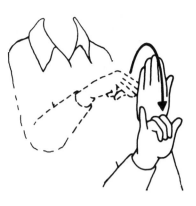

May (month)

LH open B palm in, tips up. M shape RH palm down, tips left. Place against left palm, slide over fingers and down, changing into Y shape.

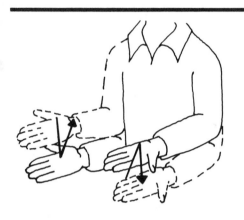

maybe

Open B both hands, palms up, tips out. Move up and down alternately.

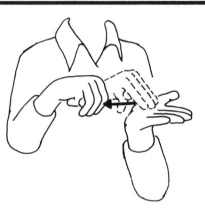

mayonnaise

LH open B palm up, tips out. Place tips of right M on heel of left palm and brush inward.

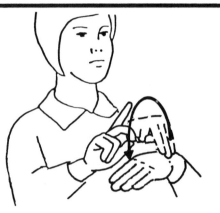

McDonald's (restaurant)

LH open B palm down, tips out. Tap back of left wrist with tips of right M. Arc forward and down on LH, ending in right D.

me

Touch chest with index finger.

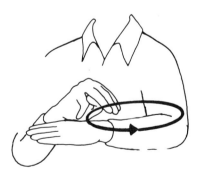

meadow

Place tips of right M on back of left wrist. Circle counterclockwise over elbow and return to original position.

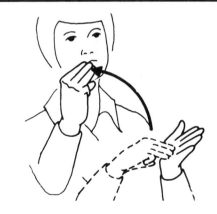

meal

LH open B palm up. Place tips of right M in left palm then move up to mouth.

mean (adj.)
A shape LH thumb up. Claw shape RH thumb extended. Brush right knuckles down left knuckles.

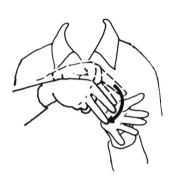

mean (verb)
LH open B palm right, tips out. V shape RH palm down. Place tips of V on left palm then reverse, ending with right palm up.

measles
Claw shape both hands. Tap tips on cheeks several times (indicating spots).

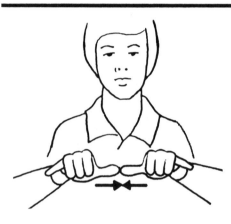

measure
Y shape both hands, palms down. Tap thumb tips together twice.

meat
LH open B palm in, tips right. Wiggle flesh between left thumb and index with right thumb and index.

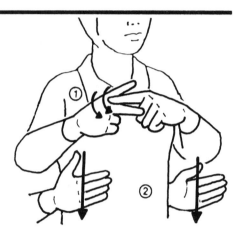

mechanic
One shape LH palm down, tip out. Place right V around left index then twist down twice. Follow with agent marker.

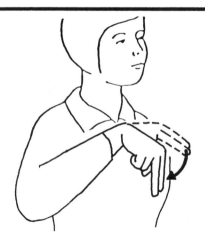

medal
U shape RH palm in, tips down. Flip tips back against upper left chest.

medicine
Circle tip of right middle finger in upturned left palm.

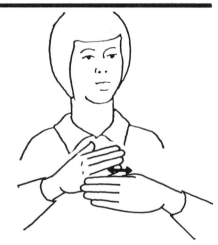

medium
B shape LH. Move little finger side of right open B back and forth slightly on middle of left index.

meet

One shape both hands, palms facing. Bring together.

meeting (noun)

Five shape both hands, palms facing, tips up. Bring tips together, forming flat O shapes.

melon

S shape LH palm down. Flick right middle finger against back of left S (as if thumping melon).

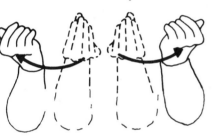

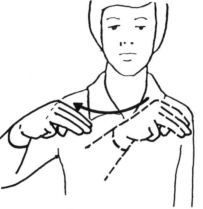

melt

Flat O shape both hands, tips up. Draw apart and slightly down, ending in A shapes.

member

Place tips of right M on left shoulder then on right shoulder.

memorize

Place tips of claw shape RH on forehead then move out into S shape keeping palm in.

memory

A shape RH palm left, thumb extended. Place thumb on forehead and twist to left.

mend

M shape both hands, left tips up, right tips down. Circle right tips around left tips.

menstruation (period)

Tap right cheek twice with flat fingers of right A.

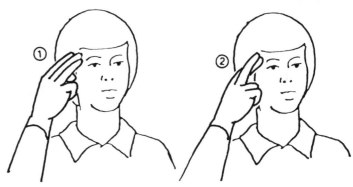

mentally retarded

Place tips of right M, then R, on right side of forehead.

menu

LH open B palm right, tips up. Bounce tips of right M down left palm.

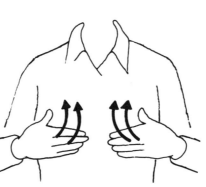

merry

Open B both hands, palms in, tips facing. Brush up chest twice.

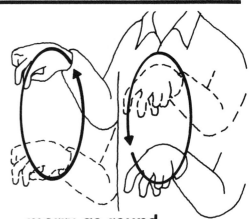

merry-go-round

Bent V shape both hands, palms down. Circle down and up alternately.

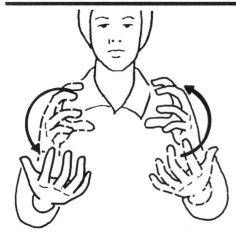

mess

Claw shape both hands, palms facing. Simultaneously twist LH inward and RH outward.

message

Place tips of right M on lips then slide across left palm.

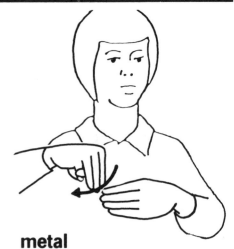

metal

B shape LH, tips slanted right. Strike tip of left index with tips of right M.

meter

Slide ring finger side of right M up and down back of left index.

Mickey Mouse

Place tips of M shape hands on head then twist forward and down, outlining shape of ears.

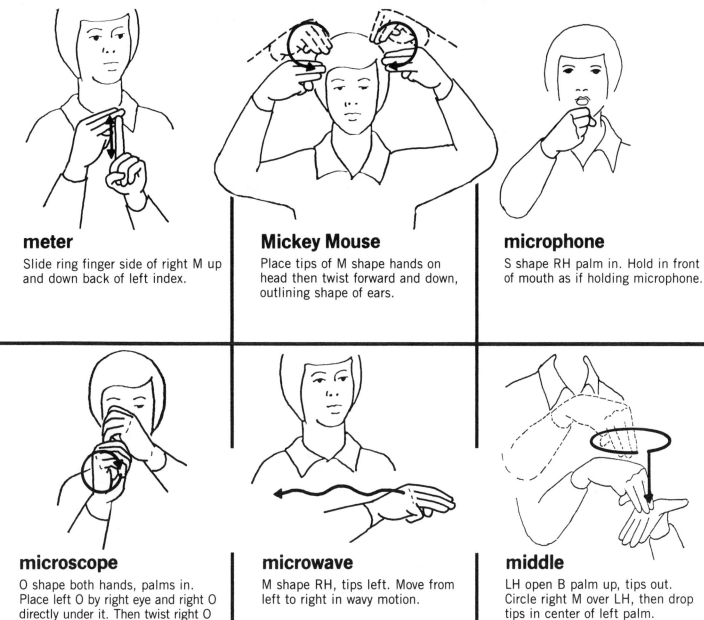

microphone

S shape RH palm in. Hold in front of mouth as if holding microphone.

microscope

O shape both hands, palms in. Place left O by right eye and right O directly under it. Then twist right O to left, as if focusing microscope.

microwave

M shape RH, tips left. Move from left to right in wavy motion.

middle

LH open B palm up, tips out. Circle right M over LH, then drop tips in center of left palm.

midget

M shape RH palm down. Lower hand and bounce slightly, indicating size of midget.

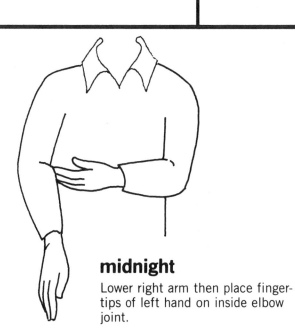

midnight

Lower right arm then place fingertips of left hand on inside elbow joint.

might

M shape both hands, palms up. Alternately move up and down.

Mighty Mouse

Place thumb and index tips of both hands on head, indicating shape of ears.

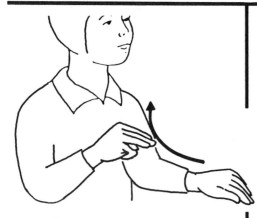

mile

LH open B palm down, arm extended. Place tips of right M on left wrist then move up arm.

milk

Claw shape both hands, palms facing. Alternately squeeze down into S shapes, as if milking cow.

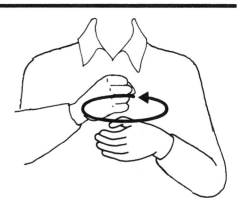

mill

C shape LH palm right, index and thumb side up. S shape RH. Circle right S over left C counterclockwise in slow, grinding motion.

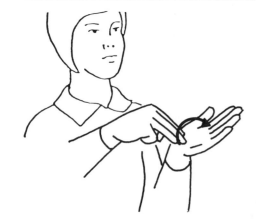

million

LH open B palm up. Place tips of right M on base of left palm then hop to fingers while moving both hands forward slightly.

mince

LH open B palm up, tips out. Chop left palm with right open B, thumb up.

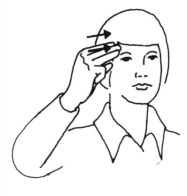

mind

Tap right temple with tips of right M.

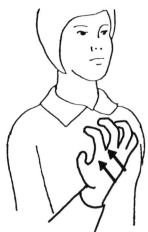

mind (care)

Tap chest twice with tips of claw shape RH.

mind (obey)

Place tips of right flat O on right side of forehead. Then move out and down, ending with 5 shape palm up.

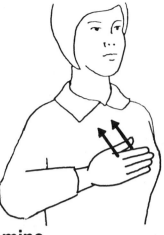

mine

Slap chest twice with palm of right open B.

minister

Place right F, palm out, at right side of head and nod forward twice. Follow with agent marker.

minus

LH open B palm out. Place side of right index horizontally across left palm.

minute

LH open B palm right, tips up. Place knuckles of right 1 shape against left palm and move forward, ending with right index tip out.

miracle

LH open B palm down, tips slanted right. Place tips of right M on back of LH then circle up.

mirror

RH open B palm in. Hold before face and twist slightly to the right. Repeat motion.

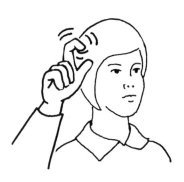

mischief

Place thumb of right L on right temple then crook and uncrook index several times.

Miss (Ms.)

M shape RH palm down, tips left. Place on right side of chin then move out.

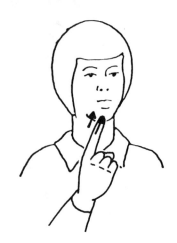

miss (feel the absence of)

Lightly tap chin with index finger of RH held palm in.

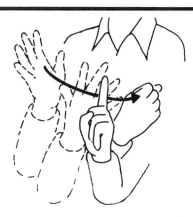

miss (verb)

One shape LH knuckles right. Make sweeping pass by left index with right claw shape ending in S.

mistake

Tap chin with knuckles of right Y twice.

misunderstand

V shape RH palm left. Place index tip on forehead. Twist inward, ending with middle fingertip on forehead.

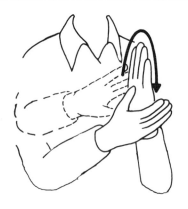

mitten

LH open B palm right, tips up. Outline with right fingers.

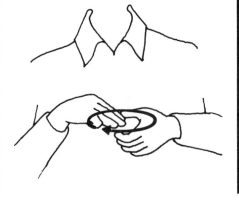

mix

C shape LH palm and tips right, little finger side down. Stir right M over left C.

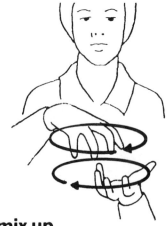

mix up

Claw shape both hands, right above left. Alternately rotate in clockwise circles.

model

LH open B palm out. Place index finger side of right M horizontally against left palm. Move both hands out.

modern

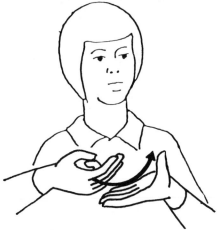

LH open B palm up. Brush back of right M across left palm in scooping motion.

moist

Flat O shape RH palm up. Tap fingertips together several times.

mold

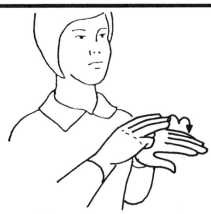

LH open B palm down. Tap across back of LH with tips of right M.

mole

Cupped open B shape both hands, index knuckles touching. Mime digging motion of mole by flapping fingers to the sides.

mommy (mama)

Five shape RH palm left, tips up. Tap chin with thumb twice.

Monday

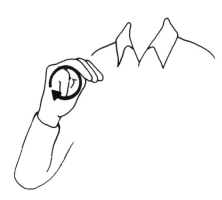

M shape RH. Move in small clockwise circle.

money

LH open B palm up, tips out. Tap left palm twice with back of right flat O.

monkey

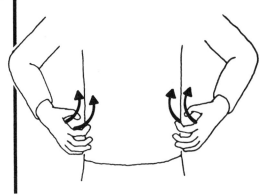

Claw shape both hands. Scratch sides of body with tips.

239

monster

Claw shape both hands, palms down. Hold at shoulder level and shake back and forth.

month

One shape both hands, left palm right; right palm in, tip left. Place right index against left and slide down.

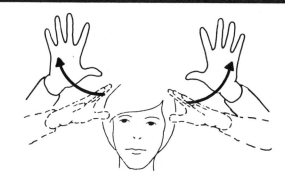

mood

Brush tips of right M up against chest.

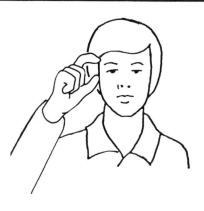

moon

Form little C with right thumb and index finger. Place at side of right eye.

moose

Five shape both hands, palms out, tips up. Place thumbs on temples and move up.

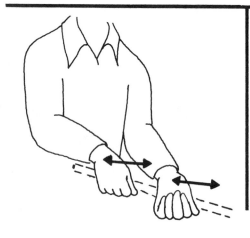

mop

A shape both hands. Mime holding and pushing a mop back and forth.

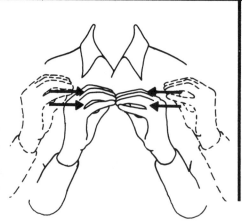

more

Flat O shape both hands, palms and tips facing. Tap tips together twice.

morning

Hold right hand out palm up. Place little finger side of left open B on inside of right elbow. Raise right arm to vertical position.

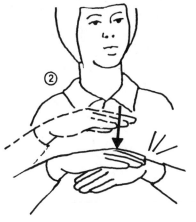

mosquito

Place thumb and index tips of right F on back of LH. Raise RH up, changing to open B, then slap back of LH.

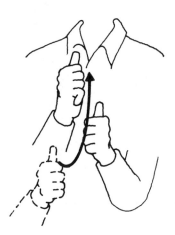

most

A shape both hands, thumbs up, left A slightly higher than right. Brush knuckles of right A up knuckles of left A.

moth

M shape both hands. Cross at wrists and flutter fingertips.

mother

Five shape RH palm left. Place thumb on chin and flutter fingers.

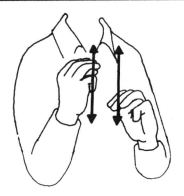

motor

M shape both hands, palms down, right tips left, left tips right. Place right M behind left then move hands up and down alternately.

motorcycle

Hold S shape hands in front of body as if grasping large handle-bars. Twist inward twice.

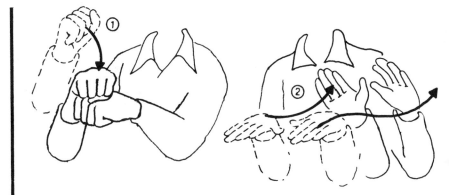

mountain

Tap back of left S with right S. Separate into open B shapes palms down, left higher than right. Move both hands up to left, outlining shape of mountains.

241

mouse

Strike tip of nose with right index finger.

mouth

Outline mouth with right index finger.

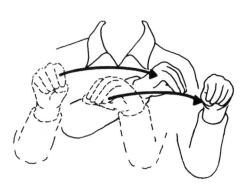

move

O shape both hands, palms down. Move from right to left or vice versa.

movie

Five shape LH palm right, tips out. Five shape RH palm left, tips up. Place palms together then gently shake right fingertips back and forth (to indicate flickering motion).

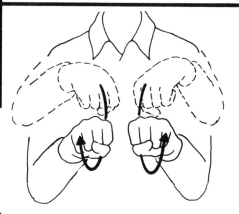

mow (verb)

S shape both hands, thumbs down. Push forward and up.

Mr.

M shape RH palm down, tips left. Place on forehead then move out to R shape.

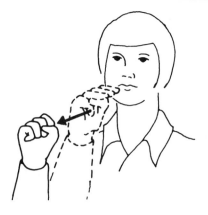

Mrs.

M shape RH palm down, tips left. Place on right side of chin then move out ending in S shape.

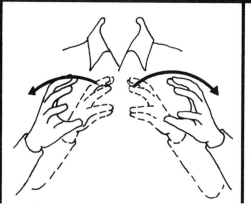

much

Claw shape both hands, palms facing. Place tips close together then arc apart.

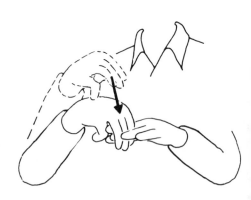

mud

LH open B palm down. Place fingers of right M between left middle and fourth fingers and push through.

muffin

LH open B palm up. Place right tips in left palm then draw up into claw shape.

mug

LH open B palm up. Place little finger side of right S in left palm then arc up to mouth.

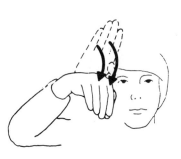

mule

B shape RH palm out, tips up. Place knuckle of right thumb on right temple and bend fingers forward twice.

multihandicapped

Fingerspell M-H.

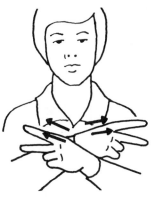

multiply

V shape both hands, palms in. Brush little finger side of right V on index finger side of left V while moving hands in opposite directions. Repeat motion.

mummy

Place right V on right eye then circle over head twice (as if peering through wrapped bandages).

mumps

Claw shape both hands. Hold at sides of neck, indicating swollen glands.

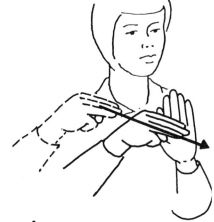

murder

LH open B palm out. Quickly slide index finger side of right M across and down left palm.

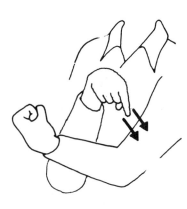

muscle

Hold LH in tight S palm up. Tap upper arm with right index.

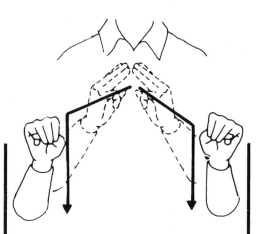

museum

M shape both hands, palms facing, tips touching. Draw apart and down, closing fingers over thumbs.

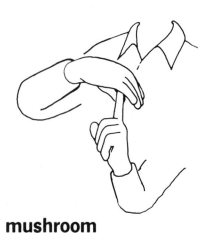

mushroom

C shape RH palm down, fingers left. Support with left index tip.

music

LH open B palm up, tips slightly right. Swing right M back and forth over left palm and forearm without touching.

must

X shape RH palm down. Jerk downward sharply.

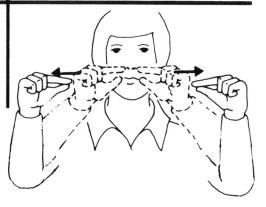

mustache

G shape both hands, knuckles and tips facing. Place under nose then draw apart, closing thumbs and index fingers.

mustard

LH open B palm up, tips out. Circle tips of right M in left palm.

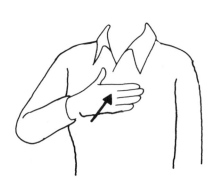

my

Place palm on chest.

myself

A shape RH, palm twisted right.
Tap chest with knuckles twice.

mystery

M shape RH palm and tips left.
Arc down across nose from right
to left.

N

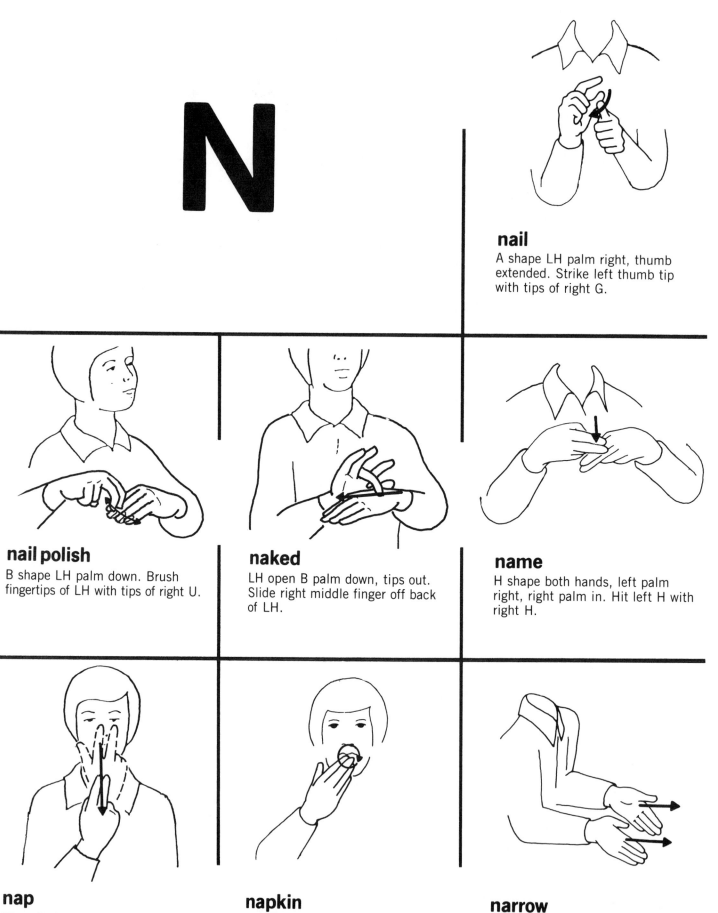

nail
A shape LH palm right, thumb extended. Strike left thumb tip with tips of right G.

nail polish
B shape LH palm down. Brush fingertips of LH with tips of right U.

naked
LH open B palm down, tips out. Slide right middle finger off back of LH.

name
H shape both hands, left palm right, right palm in. Hit left H with right H.

nap
Place 3 shape RH, palm in, in front of face then draw down into N shape.

napkin
Place tips of right fingers on mouth and make small circle clockwise.

narrow
Open B both hands, palms facing, tips slanted down. Hold close together and move forward.

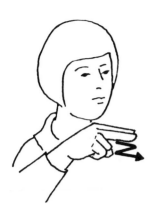

nasty

Shake right N, palm down, out from under chin.

natural

LH open B palm down, tips out. N shape RH palm down, tips left. Circle, then tap, back of LH with right N.

nature

LH open B palm in, tips right, held in front of body. Right A palm left, thumb extended. Place right A behind LH then slide under and out.

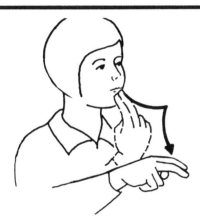

naughty

N shape RH palm in, tips up. Place tips at mouth, twist out, and jerk down.

nauseous

Circle right claw shape, palm in, clockwise at stomach.

navy

B shape both hands, tips down, index fingers touching. Place on right hip then move to left hip (indicating buttons on pants).

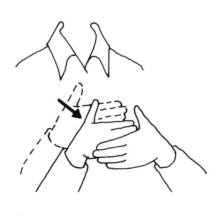

near

Open B both hands, palms in, thumbs up. Place back of right hand against palm of left.

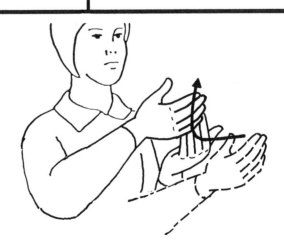

nearly

Bent LH open B palm and tips up. RH open B palm in, tips left. Slap right fingertips against back of left fingertips then slide RH up.

247

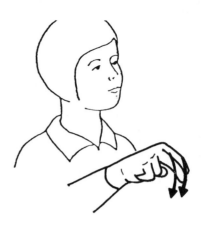

neat

LH open B palm up, tips out. Place tips of right N in left palm and slide forward.

necessary

N shape RH palm down. Nod downward twice.

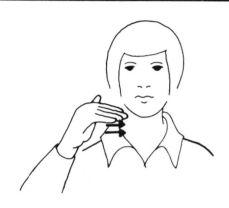

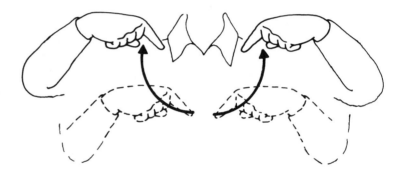

neck

Bent RH open B palm down, tips left. Tap right side of neck with tips.

necklace

One shape both hands, palms down, tips facing. Place on upper chest and slide up to shoulders, outlining shape of necklace.

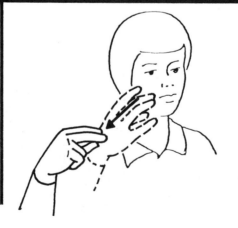

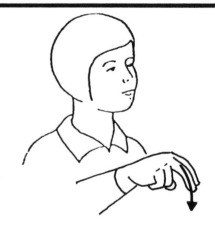

necktie

U shape RH palm in, tips up. Place at base of neck and draw down.

nectarine

Claw shape RH. Place tips on right cheek. Stroke down, ending with right N.

need

Move right N downward one time.

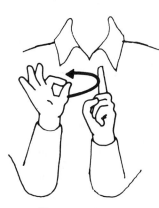

needle

One shape LH, F shape RH. Move tips of right F across tip of left index, as if threading needle.

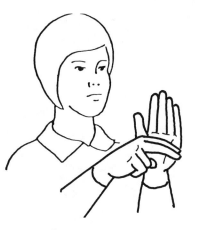

negative

LH open B palm out. N shape RH tips left. Strike left palm with the index finger side of right N.

neighbor

Open B both hands, palms in. Place right open B on back of left, then arc up and out.

neither

L shape LH palm right, index finger out. Place thumb knuckle of right N on thumb, then index, of left hand.

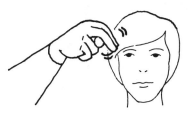

nephew

Shake right N at right temple.

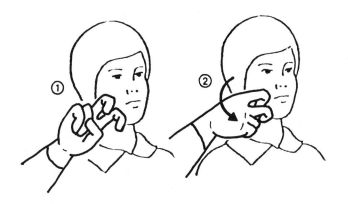

nerve

Place knuckles of right bent V, palm out, on right cheek. Twist down against cheek, ending with palm in.

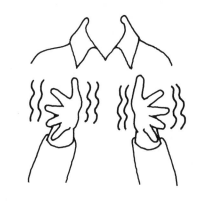

nervous

Five shape both hands, palms facing, tips out. Shake in nervous fashion.

249

nest

C shape LH palm up. Place right N in left palm.

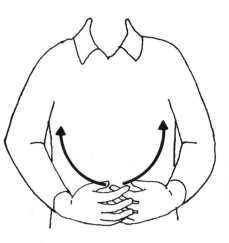

net

Open B both hands, palms up. Entwine fingers then pull apart and up.

never

B shape RH palm left, slanted up. Slash downward sharply, tips forming question mark shape.

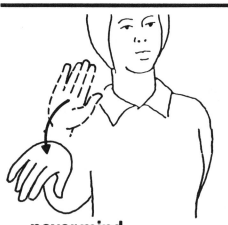

never mind

RH open B held away from body. Flap forward and down.

new

LH open B palm up, tips out. Brush back of right open B inward across left palm in a scooping motion.

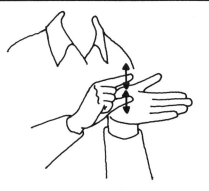

newspaper

LH open B palm up, tips out. Place thumb of right G in left palm then snap tips together two or three times.

next

Open B both hands, palms in. Place back of right fingers against left palm then arc RH over LH.

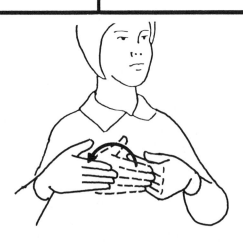

next door

LH open B palm and tips in, held away from body. Place fingers of RH against fingers of LH, then arc RH to the right.

nibble

Make nibbling motion at mouth with right thumb, index, and middle fingers.

nice

B shape LH palm and tips slanted right. Slide right N forward on left index finger.

nickel

Touch forehead with middle finger of right 5 then move hand out.

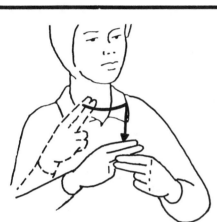

nickname

H shape both hands, left tips out, right tips left. Swing right H above left then tap middle finger of right H on index finger of left H.

niece

Shake right N at right jawline.

night

Hold left arm in front of body, palm and tips slanted down. Place heel of right open B, tips down, on left wrist.

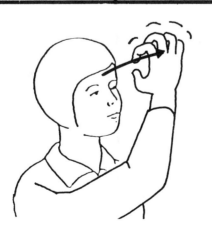

nightmare

Claw shape RH palm in, held at forehead. Crook and uncrook fingers several times while moving hand up and out.

no

Snap middle finger, index, and thumb together quickly.

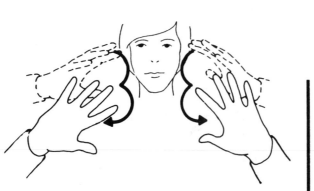

noise
Five shape both hands, index fingers held at ears. Shake hands outward.

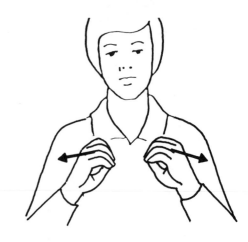

none
O shape both hands, palms and tips facing. Move forward and to the sides.

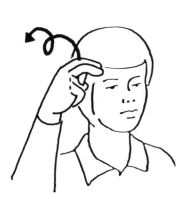

nonsense
Place tips of right N on side of forehead, then circle upward and out.

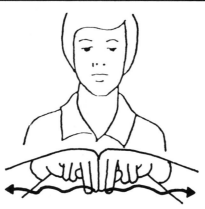

noodle
N shape both hands, palms down, index fingers touching. Wiggle away from each other.

noon
Hold right arm straight up palm left, open B shape. Rest elbow on left open B palm down, tips right.

nor
L shape LH palm right, index finger out. Place thumb knuckle of right N on left thumb. Change to O shape RH and place on left index.

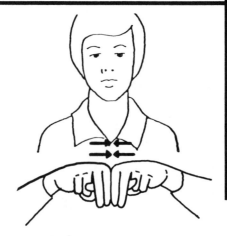

normal
N shape both hands. Tap index fingers together.

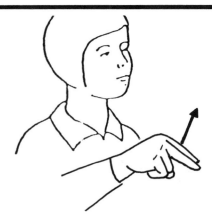

north
N shape RH tips out. Move upward.

nose

Touch right side of nose with right index finger.

nosebleed

Touch nose with right index finger. Change to 5 shape palm in and move downward while wiggling fingers.

nosy

Outline shape of large nose with right index.

not

A shape RH knuckles left, thumb extended. Place thumb under chin and move out.

note

LH open B palm up. Place fingertips of right N at eye then move across left palm.

nothing

S shape RH. Place knuckles under chin and flick out into 5 shape palm out.

notice

Place tip of right index at right eye then move down into palm of LH open B.

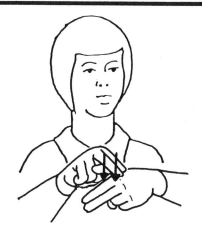

noun

H shape LH palm right, tips out. N shape RH palm left. Tap index of left H twice with base of right N.

November

LH open B palm in. Place little finger side of right N on left palm. Then slide over tips and down back of LH.

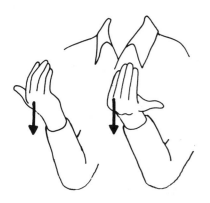

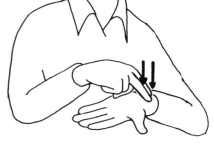

now

Bent open B both hands, palms up. Lower slightly.

number

Flat O shape both hands, left palm in, right down, tips touching. Reverse positions.

nurse

LH open B palm up. Tap left wrist twice with tips of right N.

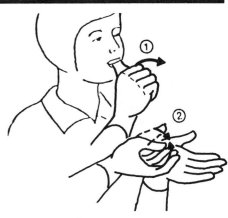

nursery

LH open B palm down, tips slanted right. Circle right N counterclockwise under left palm.

nut

Flip thumb out from under top teeth.

nutcracker

Flip thumb out from under top teeth. Then place right flat O, palm up, in left palm. Tap right fingertips together once or twice.

O

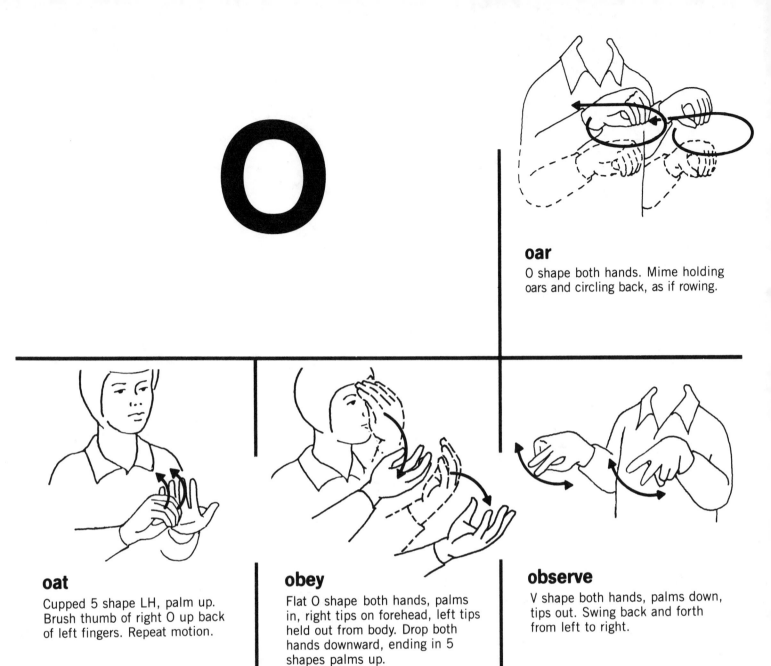

oar

O shape both hands. Mime holding oars and circling back, as if rowing.

oat

Cupped 5 shape LH, palm up. Brush thumb of right O up back of left fingers. Repeat motion.

obey

Flat O shape both hands, palms in, right tips on forehead, left tips held out from body. Drop both hands downward, ending in 5 shapes palms up.

observe

V shape both hands, palms down, tips out. Swing back and forth from left to right.

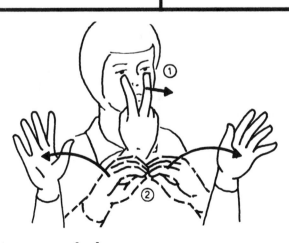

obvious

Place tips of right V at eyes and move forward. Then touch together tips of flat O shapes and spread apart, ending in 5 shapes palms out.

occupation

S shape LH palm down. Tap back of left wrist twice with base of right O.

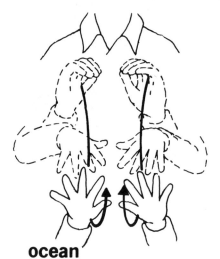

ocean

O shape both hands. Open into 5 shapes and dip forward in wavy motion.

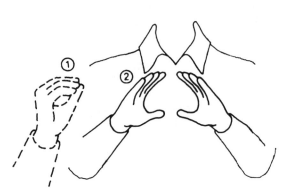

o'clock

Form right O, then C shapes both hands palms facing, as if outlining a round clock.

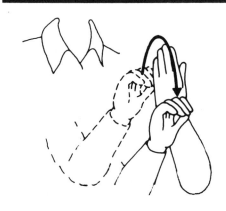

October

LH open B palm in. Place tips of right O on left palm then slide over and down back of LH.

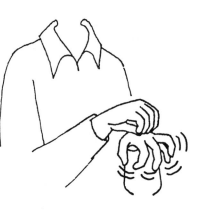

octopus

Claw shape LH palm down. Place tips of right O on back of LH then wiggle fingers.

odd

O shape RH palm and tips left. Place at right side of face and arc across eyes to lower left side of face.

of

Fingerspell O-F in quick succession as if one movement.

of course

Shake Y up and down.

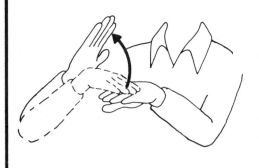

off

Open B both hands, palms down. Place right palm on back of left hand and lift off.

office

O shape both hands, tips out. Move right O left and left O right, indicating square shape.

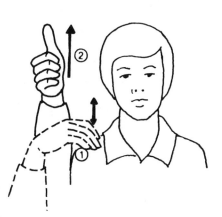

officer

Tap right shoulder with fingertips of cupped RH. Then form right A, thumb extended, and move up.

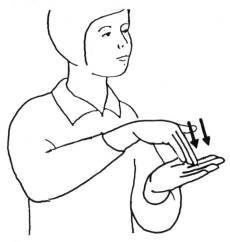

often

LH open B palm up, tips out. Strike left palm several times with tips of right bent open B.

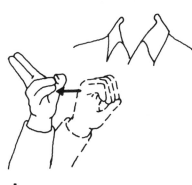

oh

Fingerspell O-H in quick succession as if one movement.

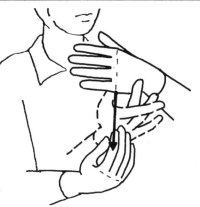

oil

LH open B palm in, tips right. Grab left palm with thumb and fingertips of RH then pull RH down, ending in flat O shape.

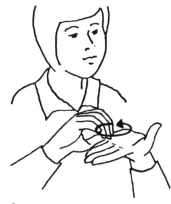

ointment

Circle thumb of right O counter-clockwise in palm of LH.

OK (okay)

Fingerspell O-K in quick succession as if one movement.

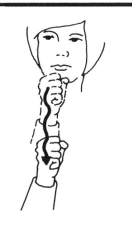

old

Place right S under chin then move down in wavy motion.

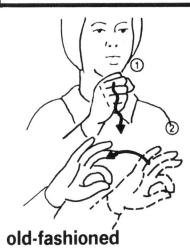

old-fashioned

Place right S under chin then move down in wavy motion. Form right F, palm down, and bounce to right.

olympic

Place hands at left and interlock thumb and index fingers. Move to right while reversing hands and interlock fingers again. Then move down while reversing hands and again interlock fingers (indicating the three interlocking circles of the olympic emblem).

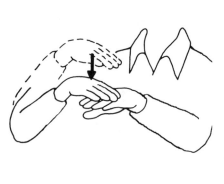

on

Open B both hands, palms down, left tips out, right tips left. Place right palm on back of left palm.

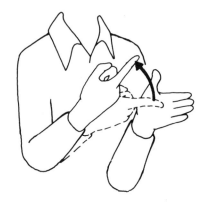

once

LH open B palm right, tips out. Place right index tip in middle of left palm and strike upward once.

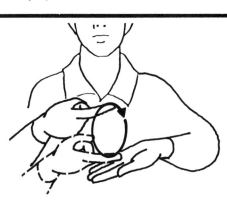

once in a while

LH open B palm up, tips out. Place tip of right index in left palm, move up in circle and back down into palm. Repeat motion.

onion

Twist X at corner of eye.

only

Hold right index finger up, palm out. Then twist, ending with palm in.

open

B shape both hands, palms down, tips out, index fingers touching. Arc apart, ending with palms up.

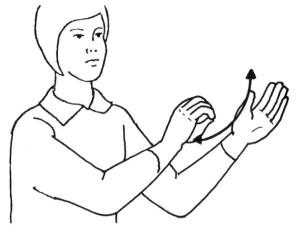

opera

LH open B palm up, arm extended. Swing right O back and forth over left palm and forearm without touching.

258

operate

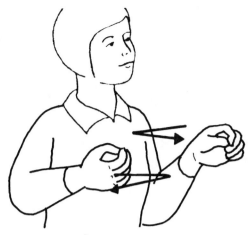

O shape both hands, palms and tips facing. Alternately move back and forth.

operation

LH open B palm out. Draw tip of right thumb down left palm.

opinion

O shape RH palm and tips left. Place at right side of forehead and nod to left twice.

opossum

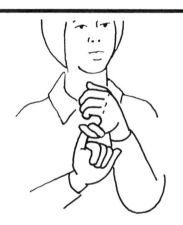

Hook little fingers together, indicating hanging by tail from tree.

opportunity

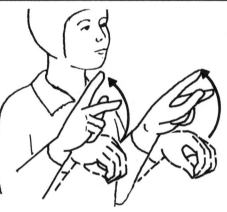

O shape both hands, palms down. Simultaneously flip upward into P shapes palms out.

opposite

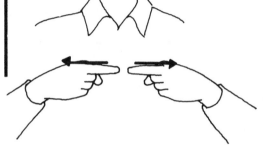

One shape both hands, palms in, tips facing. Draw apart.

or

Fingerspell O-R in quick succession as if one movement.

or (alt.)

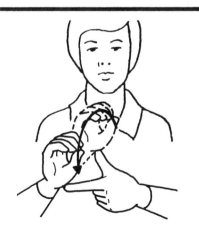

L shape LH palm right, index tip out. Place base of right O on thumb, then index tip, of left L.

oral

O shape RH palm and tips left. Circle clockwise at mouth.

259

orange

C shape RH palm and tips left. Place at mouth and "squeeze" into S shape. Repeat motion.

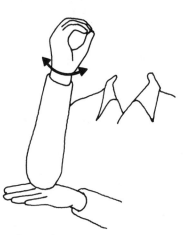

orchard

LH open B palm down held across body. O shape RH. Place right elbow on back of LH then twist right O back and forth.

orchestra

O shape both hands, palms out. Swing hands apart and back together again several times, as if conducting an orchestra.

order

Place tip of right index on lips, then turn it outward and down in forceful manner.

organization

O shape both hands, palms out, thumb and index tips touching. Draw apart and around to front, ending with palms in, little fingers touching.

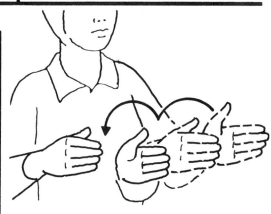

organize

Open B shape both hands, palms facing, tips out. Bounce from left to right keeping hands parallel.

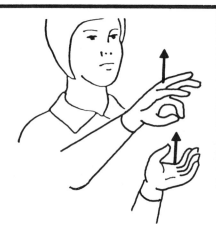

ornament

Cupped LH palm up. Extend right F, palm down, over left palm then move both hands up slightly.

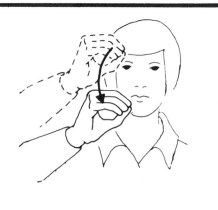

orphan

O shape RH palm and tips left. Place tips at right side of forehead then move down to chin.

orthodontist

Tap tips of right O at right side of mouth.

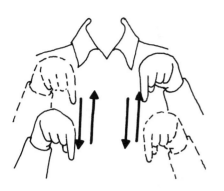

orthopedically handicapped (crippled)

One shape both hands, tips down. Move up and down alternately.

ostrich

O shape LH palm and tips right, little finger side down. G shape RH palm and tips left. Place tips of right G in left O.

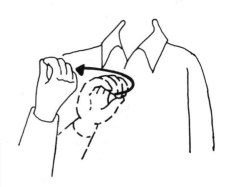

other

O shape RH tips out. Swing in semicircle to left, ending with tips up.

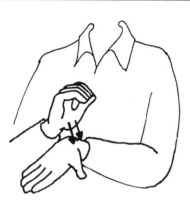

otologist

LH open B palm up, tips out. Tap left wrist with base of right O.

ought

Nod O shape RH, ending with palm down.

ounce

Fingerspell O-Z.

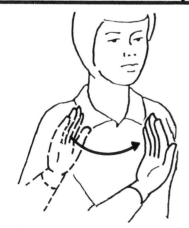

our

Place thumb of cupped RH just under right shoulder. Arc to left, ending with little finger resting just below left shoulder.

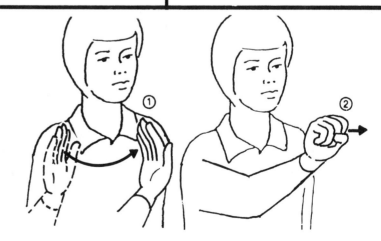

ours

Place thumb of cupped RH just under right shoulder then arc over to left shoulder. Form right S shape, palm out, and move forward slightly.

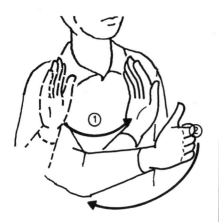

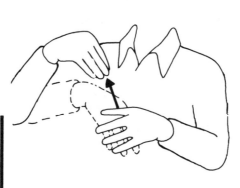

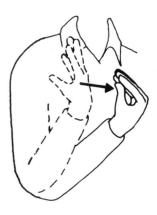

ourselves
Place thumb of cupped RH just under right shoulder. Circle to left, ending with little finger resting just below left shoulder. Extend right thumb up and sweep across front of body, moving from left to right.

out
Cupped 5 shape LH palm right. Place fingers of RH against left palm and pull out, ending in flat O shape.

outdoor
Five shape RH palm and tips in. Move out into flat O.

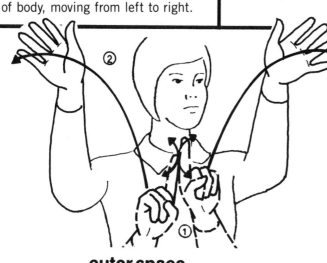

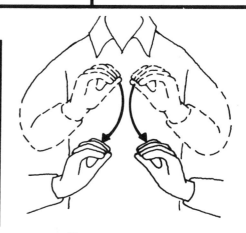

outer space
One shape both hands, palms out. Place fingers together and raise tips up and down alternately. Form 5 shapes, hands close together, then arc apart.

outfit
O shape both hands. Place thumbs on chest and brush down.

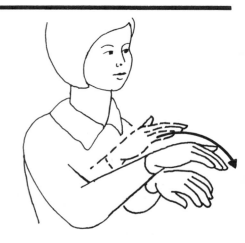

outside
Cupped 5 shape LH palm right. Place fingers of RH against left palm and pull out, ending in flat O shape. Repeat motion.

oven
LH open B palm down, tips right. O shape RH palm and tips left. Slide RH under left open B.

over
Open B both hands, palms down. Pass RH over LH without touching.

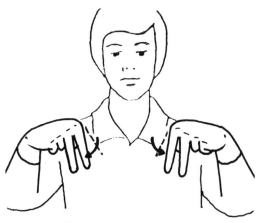

overalls

Three shape both hands, palms in, tips down. Place hands below shoulders and snap together thumb, index, and middle fingers (as if clipping straps in place).

overflow

C shape LH palm and tips right. RH open B palm down. Place right palm on top of left C and move forward while wiggling fingers.

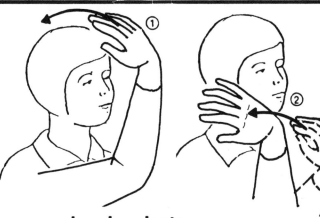

overhead projector

Pass right open B, palm down, over top of head. Form right flat O, palm in, and place at right shoulder. Open quickly into 5 shape palm in.

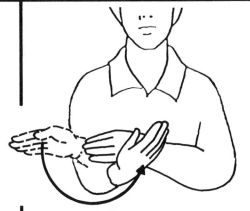

overnight

Place tips of left open B, palm in, on right wrist. Then swing right open B down and up to left, ending with palm up.

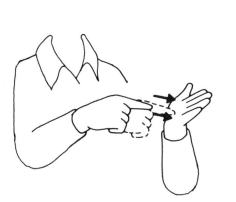

owe

LH open B palm and tips slanted left. Tap left palm several times with tip of right index.

owl

O shape both hands. Place in front of eyes and twist inward slightly. Repeat motion.

own

Slap chest dramatically with 5 shape RH.

oxygen

S shape LH palm right. Place tips of right O on top of left S then move up in wavy motion.

oyster

LH open B palm down, tips right. Place right cupped hand on back of LH then raise right fingertips up.

P

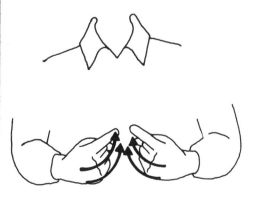

pacifier

Circle mouth with thumb and index finger of RH.

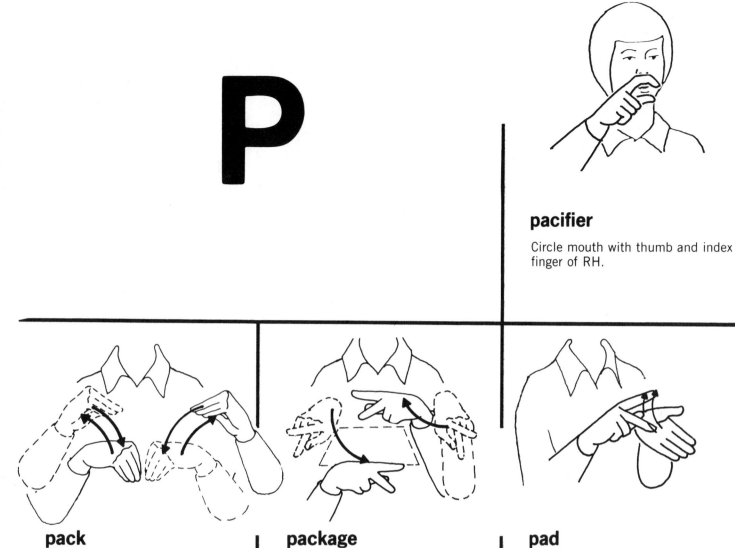

pack

Flat O both hands, palms and tips down. Move down and up alternately, as if putting things in suitcase or box.

package

P shape both hands, palms down, tips out. Swing left tips right and right tips left, outlining shape of package.

pad

LH open B palm up, tips out. Brush middle finger of right P across base of left palm toward body twice.

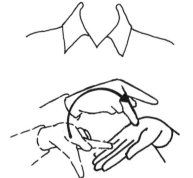

page

LH open B palm up, tips out. Place middle finger of right P on left fingertips and flip over, as if turning a page.

pail

S shape LH palm down. Place right index against left thumb, dip under, and place on left little finger.

pain

One shape both hands, palms in, tips facing. Move toward one another while arcing upward. Repeat motion.

265

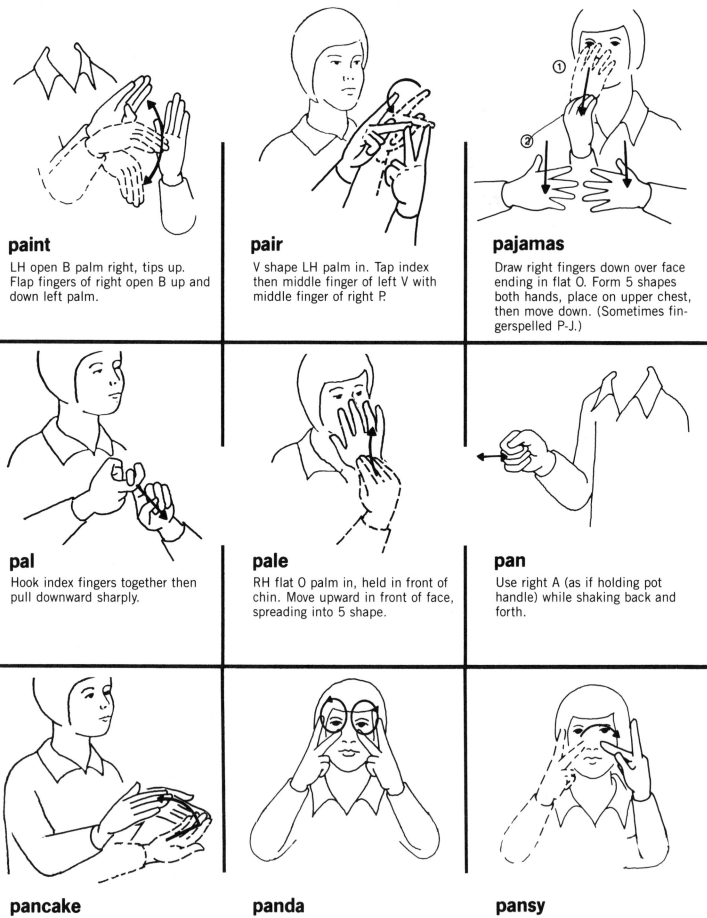

paint

LH open B palm right, tips up. Flap fingers of right open B up and down left palm.

pair

V shape LH palm in. Tap index then middle finger of left V with middle finger of right P.

pajamas

Draw right fingers down over face ending in flat O. Form 5 shapes both hands, place on upper chest, then move down. (Sometimes fingerspelled P-J.)

pal

Hook index fingers together then pull downward sharply.

pale

RH flat O palm in, held in front of chin. Move upward in front of face, spreading into 5 shape.

pan

Use right A (as if holding pot handle) while shaking back and forth.

pancake

LH open B palm up, tips out. Slide back of RH up left palm then flip RH over (as if flipping a pancake).

panda

P shape both hands, palms in, tips up. Circle eyes, left fingers to the left, right fingers to the right.

pansy

P shape RH. Place middle finger on right side of nose, then move to left side.

panther

P shape both hands, palms in, middle fingertips touching cheeks. Brush away from cheeks twice.

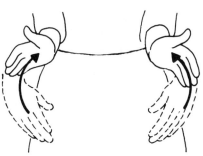

panties

Place tips of bent open B shapes on hip bones. Curve up slightly so that wrists rest on waist.

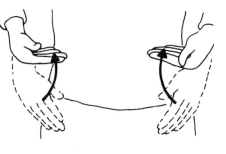

pants

Open B both hands. Place palms on hips and brush fingertips up toward waist.

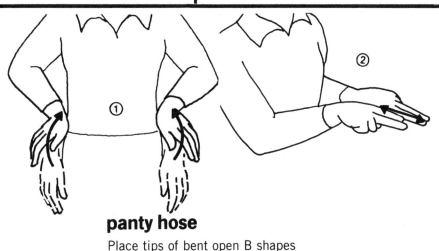

panty hose

Place tips of bent open B shapes on hip bones. Curve up slightly so that wrists rest on waist. Then form H shapes both hands, palms down. Alternately slide index fingers back and forth against each other.

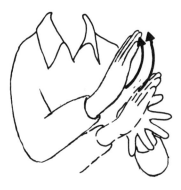

paper

Open B both hands, left palm up, tips out; right palm down, tips left. Brush base of right palm across base of left palm toward body twice.

parachute

One shape LH palm in. Claw shape RH palm down. Place right claw over left index and, with both hands, indicate back and forth and downward motion of a parachute.

parade

Four shape both hands, palms out, tips up, RH slightly back of LH. Move forward in little dips.

267

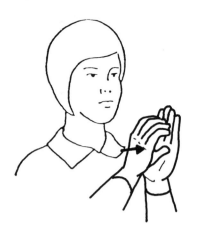

paragraph

LH open B palm right, tips up. Place fingertips of cupped RH in left palm, indicating size of a paragraph.

parakeet

Place curved right index and thumb at right side of mouth. Snap tips together twice.

pardon

LH open B palm up, tips out. Brush palm of left hand twice with fingers of right open B.

parent

P shape RH. Place middle fingertip on right side of forehead then on chin.

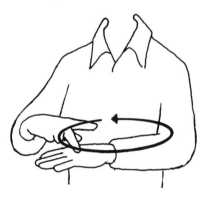

park

Open B shape LH palm down, tips out. P shape RH palm down. Circle right P over left arm up to elbow and back.

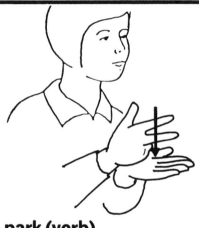

park (verb)

LH open B palm up, tips out. Three shape RH palm left, tips out. Drop base of right 3 in left palm.

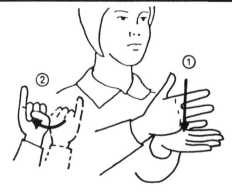

parking lot

Place base of 3 shape RH in left palm. Follow with -ing marker. Then form L shapes both hands, palms down, thumb tips almost touching. Move back toward signer while outlining square shape with thumbs.

parrot

Place curved thumb, middle, and index fingers of RH at right side of mouth. Snap tips together twice.

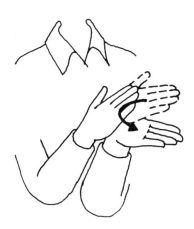

part

Open B both hands, left palm up, tips out; right palm and tips left. Slice across left palm toward body.

participate

C shape LH palm and tips right. Arc middle finger of right P into left C.

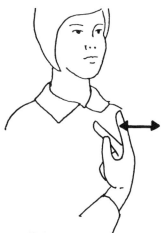

partner

P shape RH palm in, tips up. Move in and out twice.

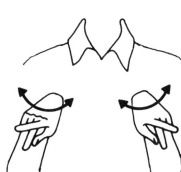

party

P shape both hands. Simultaneously swing hands to the left, then to the right, several times.

pass

Cupped RH open B palm up, tips out. Arc outward (as if passing dish at table).

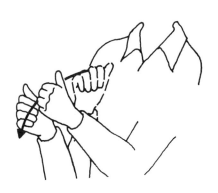

pass (go by)

A shape both hands, knuckles facing. Brush right A past left A.

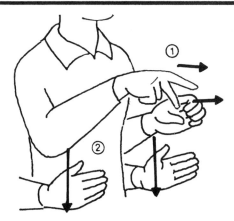

passenger

C shape LH palm and knuckles right. Place middle finger of right P in left C and move both hands forward. Follow with agent marker.

Passover

Tap left elbow twice with thumb of P shape RH.

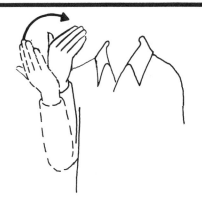

past

RH open B palm in, tips up. Place right palm above right shoulder and flip fingers back.

paste

LH open B palm up, tips out. Place middle finger of right P on left fingers, draw back over palm, turn over, and draw back to left fingertips.

pastry

LH open B palm down, tips right. P shape RH palm up. Slide RH under left hand.

pat

Pat left shoulder with right palm.

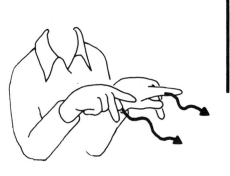

path

P shape both hands, palms down. Move forward as if following path.

patient (adj.)

Place thumb of right A against lips and draw down.

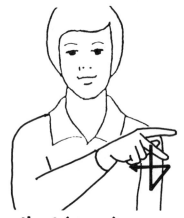

patient (noun)

Describe a cross on upper left arm with middle fingertip of right P.

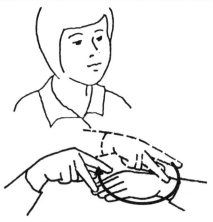

patio

B shape LH palm down. Place middle fingertip of right P on outer left wrist then arc out to tip of left middle finger.

patrol

LH open B palm down. Place base of right P on back of LH then circle both hands clockwise.

270

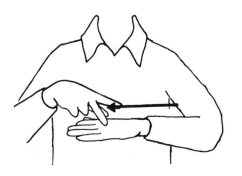

pavement

LH open B palm down. Draw middle fingertip of right P down back of LH, moving from forearm to fingertips.

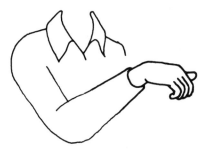

paw

RH open B fingers cupped, palm and tips down. Hold in front of body.

pay

LH open B palm up, tips out. Place middle finger of right P on left palm and flick out.

pea

One shape LH palm in, tip right. Tap from base to tip with right X.

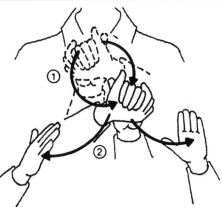

peace

Clasp together both hands, reverse positions, then clasp together again. Form open B shapes, palms down, and arc down and apart.

peach

Place tips of RH on right cheek, thumb under chin. Stroke down to right, ending in flat O.

peacock

Five shape LH. G shape RH palm and tips slanted left. Place RH against base of left palm.

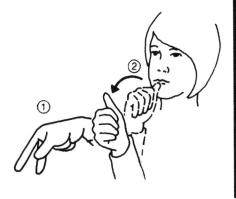

peanut

Form P with RH. Then place thumb of right A near upper teeth and flick forward.

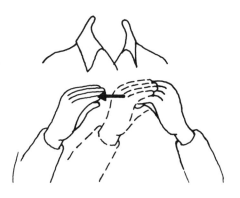

pear

LH flat O palm and tips right. Stroke left tips with right fingers, ending in flat O shape RH.

pebble

S shape LH palm down. Tap twice with back of right P.

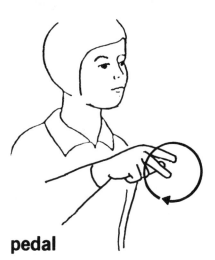

pedal

P shape RH palm down. Move down and up in circular motion.

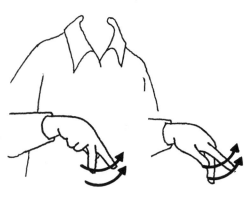

peddle

P shape both hands, palms down. Flip up, ending with palms out. Repeat.

peek

P shape RH knuckles left. Hold against right eye.

peel

LH open B palm down. F shape RH. Place RH on back of LH and move away, as if peeling a piece of fruit.

peep

Hold left B, palm right, in front of left eye. Hold right P, knuckles left, in front of right eye.

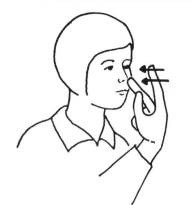

pee-pee (urination)

Tap tip of nose with middle fingertip of right P.

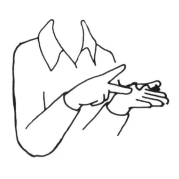

pen

LH open B palm up, tips out. "Write" in palm with middle tip of right P.

pencil

Place tips of right thumb and index finger on mouth then slide across upturned left palm.

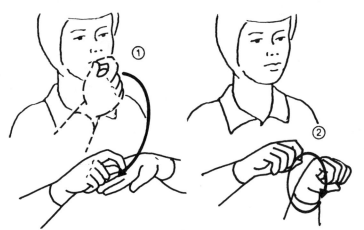

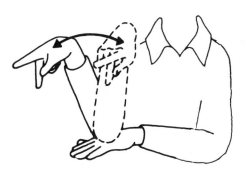

pencil sharpener

Place tips of right thumb and index finger on mouth then slide across upturned left palm. Then form S shape LH palm down. Mime turning handle of sharpener with modified A shape RH.

penguin

LH open B palm down, tips right. P shape RH. Place right elbow on back of LH and move P from right to left.

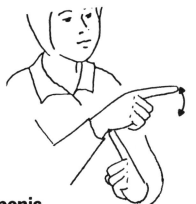

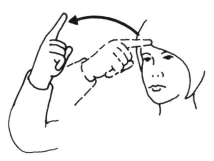

penis

One shape RH palm down. Support right wrist with left index while wiggling right index up and down slightly.

penny

Place right index on right temple then move hand out.

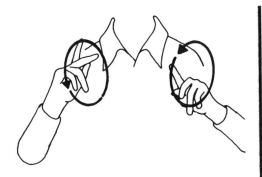

people

P shape both hands, palms out. Move up and down alternately in circular motion.

pepper

F shape RH. Mime shaking pepper shaker down to left.

peppermint

P shape RH knuckles left. Place middle finger on chin, then move out forming M shape tips left.

  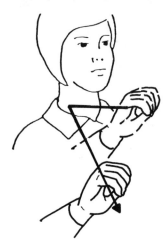

Pepsi

Describe cross on forehead with right I tip, palm in. Form C with RH, palm and tips left. Arc up to mouth, as if drinking from can.

percent

O shape RH palm out. Move to right, then down, outlining percent sign.

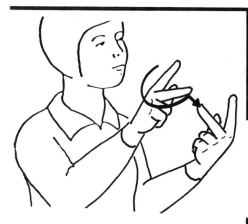 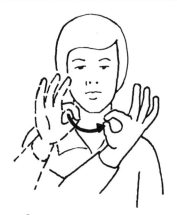 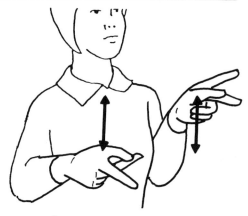

perfect

P shape both hands, left palm in, right palm out. Make semicircle with right P, then place middle fingertips together.

perfume

F shape RH. Dab thumb and index tips on both sides of neck.

perhaps

P shape both hands, palms facing. Alternately move up and down.

 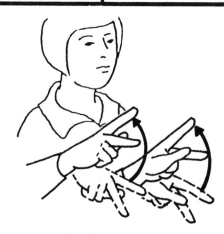

period

LH open B palm right, tips up. Place thumb knuckle of right P in left palm, then move in clockwise circle against palm.

permission

P shape both hands, palms down. Simultaneously flip up to palms out.

person

P shape both hands, middle fingertips out. Place wrists against sides
of body then move down.

personal

P shape both hands, middle fingertips out. Place back of P shapes on
chest then move down.

personality

Circle, then tap, upper left shoulder with thumb of right P.

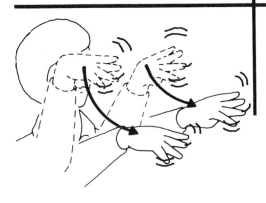

perspire (sweat)

Four shape both hands, palms
down, tips out. Place right 4 on
forehead and left 4 a little in front.
Flutter both hands forward and
down.

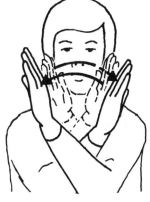

pest

Open B both hands, palms facing,
tips up. Flap in front of face, RH
behind LH.

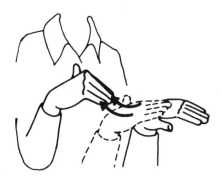

pet

Open B both hands, palms down,
tips out. Stroke back of LH with
right tips.

petal

One shape LH. Place right index
and thumb close to left index then
draw away to right.

Peter Pan

P shape RH palm in. Place middle
fingertip on upper right chest and
brush up twice.

phoney

B shape both hands, palms down, right tips left, left tips right. Place at chin, RH over LH, and alternately move back and forth.

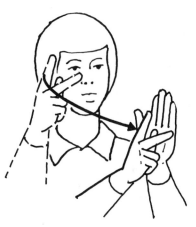

photograph

LH open B palm right, tips up, held out from body. Place thumb side of right P at right eye then move down into left palm.

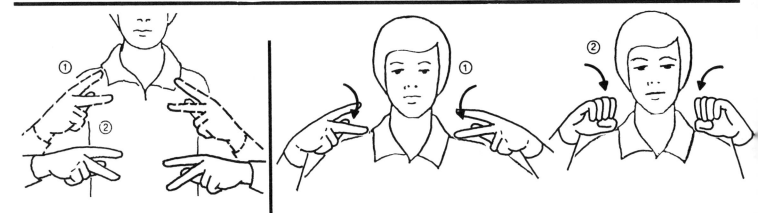

physical

P shape both hands, middle fingertips facing. Tap thumbs on upper chest then tap again at waist.

physical education

Tap middle fingertips of P shapes on shoulders. Change to E shapes and tap shoulders once again.

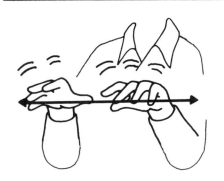

piano

Mime playing piano.

pick

G shape RH. Move up bringing index finger and thumb together.

pickle

Place middle fingertip of right P on chin then twist to left.

picnic

Place right palm on left palm. Lift both hands up until tips touch mouth.

picture

LH open B palm right, tips up. Place thumb and index finger of right C against right eye then move down to left palm.

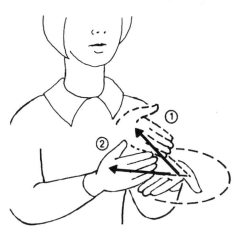

pie

Mime cutting slice of pie using left palm as pie and edge of right little finger as knife.

piece

One shape LH palm down. Strike middle fingertip of right P down against left index tip.

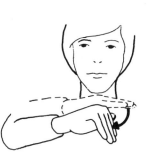

pig

Place back of RH, fingers together, under chin. Flap tips down once.

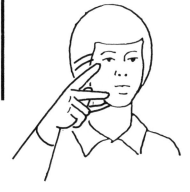

pigeon

Place thumb side of right P on side of right cheek then wiggle tips up and down.

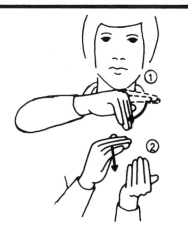

piglet

Place back of RH, fingers together, under chin and flap tips down. Now bend fingers of both hands, place RH above LH, and move down, indicating small size.

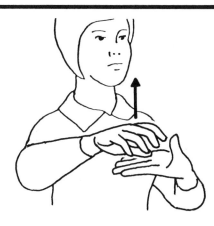

pile

LH open B palm up. Place claw shape RH, palm down, over left palm then move up.

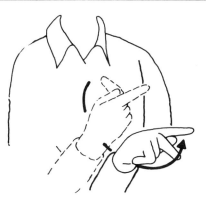

pilgrim

Place middle finger of right P on heart. Twist so that tip points out.

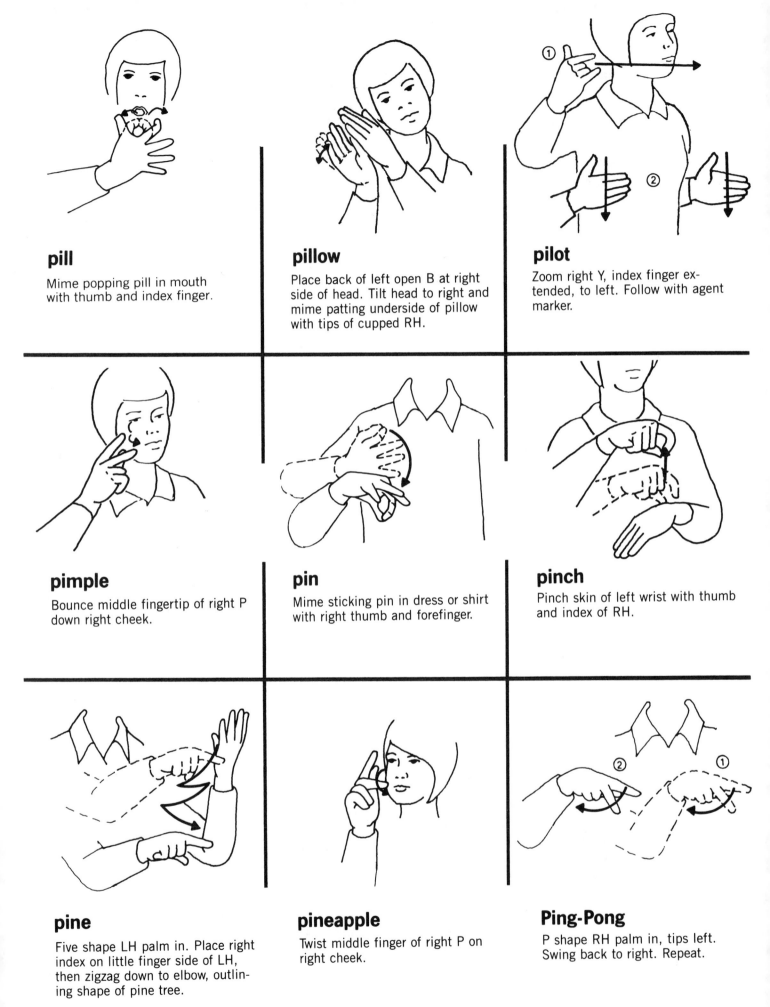

pill
Mime popping pill in mouth with thumb and index finger.

pillow
Place back of left open B at right side of head. Tilt head to right and mime patting underside of pillow with tips of cupped RH.

pilot
Zoom right Y, index finger extended, to left. Follow with agent marker.

pimple
Bounce middle fingertip of right P down right cheek.

pin
Mime sticking pin in dress or shirt with right thumb and forefinger.

pinch
Pinch skin of left wrist with thumb and index of RH.

pine
Five shape LH palm in. Place right index on little finger side of LH, then zigzag down to elbow, outlining shape of pine tree.

pineapple
Twist middle finger of right P on right cheek.

Ping-Pong
P shape RH palm in, tips left. Swing back to right. Repeat.

pink

Place middle fingertip of right P on lower lip and brush down to chin twice.

Pinocchio

Grab nose with index and thumb of G shape RH then move out.

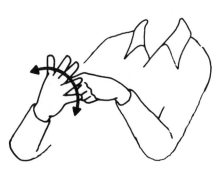

pinwheel

Five shape RH palm and tips slanted left. Place tip of left index against right palm, then twist RH down and back.

pipe

Place thumb of right Y on mouth.

pirate

Cover right eye with fingers of U shape RH palm in.

pitch

Claw shape RH palm up, held at waist. Arc upward, as if pitching a ball.

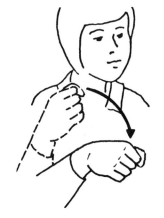

pitcher

Hold handle of pitcher with S shape RH. Mime pouring into glass.

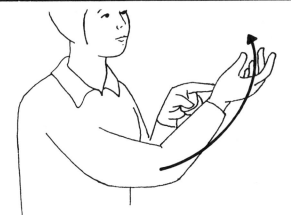

pitchfork

Place left index finger on base of RH held palm up with fingers spread and tips out. Now lift right hand forward and up.

279

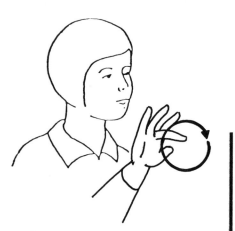

pity

Mime stroking object with extended middle finger of RH, moving in outward circular motion.

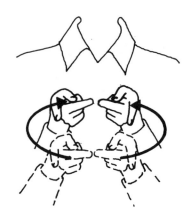

pizza

P shape RH, palm down. Draw Z shape in air with middle fingertip of right P.

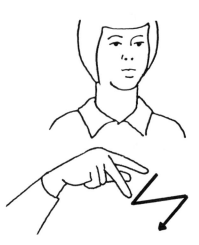

place

P shape both hands. Touch tips of middle fingers, circle back to body, and touch again.

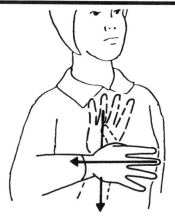

plaid

Draw back of 4 shape RH down chest. Flip to palm in, then draw across chest from left to right.

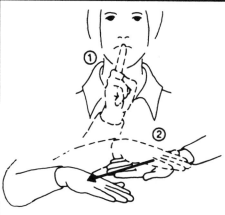

plain

LH open B palm up, tips slanted right. Place right index on lips, change to open B palm down, and brush across left palm.

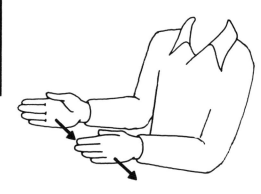

plan

Open B both hands, palms facing, tips out. Move to left or right.

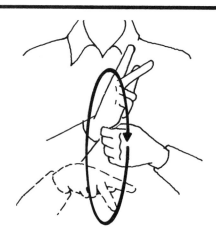

planet

Place base of right P on top of left S. Circle right P forward and under, returning to original position.

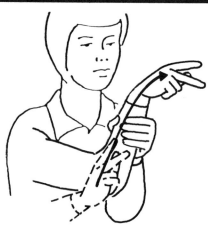

plant

Pass right P up, through, and over C shape LH palm right. (Sometimes *plant*, the verb, is signed by passing the tips of right P down through C shape LH.)

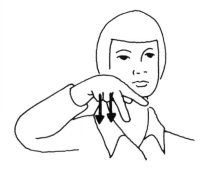

plastic

Place thumb side of right P, tips down, on right cheek. Brush down twice.

plate

Five shape both hands, palms in, middle fingers touching. Circle back toward body ending with thumbs touching.

platter

Circle left palm with middle finger-tip of right P.

play

Y shape both hands, palms in. Simultaneously twist back and forth.

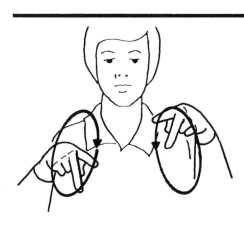

play (drama)

P shape both hands. Alternately move back in circles, brushing down chest.

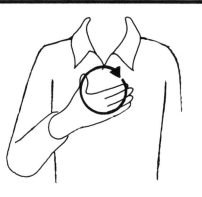

please

Rub right palm in clockwise circle against upper chest.

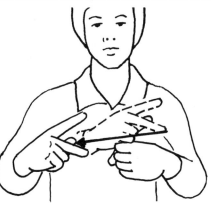

plenty

S shape LH knuckles right. Place base of right P on left S then brush right P forward, away from body.

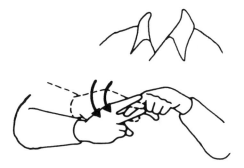

pliers

One shape LH palm down, tip out. Place right V around left index then twist right V down twice.

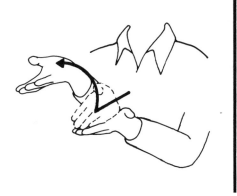

plow

LH open B palm up, tips out. Move little finger side of right open B (palm left, tips out) across left palm and turn palm up.

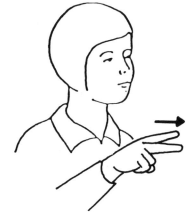

plug

V shape RH palm down, tips out. Jab forward, as if placing plug in socket.

plum

Stroke right cheek with right thumb, middle, and index fingers. Draw away, closing fingers.

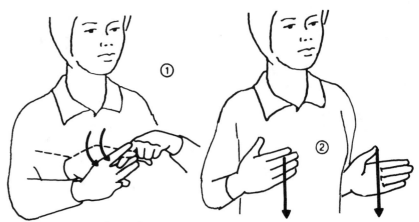

plumber

One shape LH palm down. Straddle left index with right index and middle finger of right W. Twist right W down twice. Follow with agent marker.

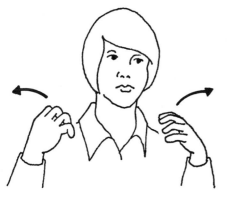

plump

Place tips of claw shape hands on shoulders then arc out from shoulders.

plus

One shape LH palm down, tip right. One shape RH palm right, tip up. Strike back of left index with right index.

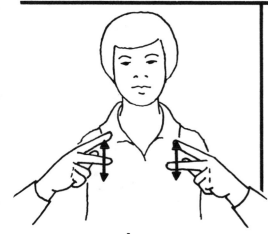

pneumonia

Rub middle fingertips of P shape hands up and down on chest.

poach

P shape LH. Flutter fingers of RH beneath left P.

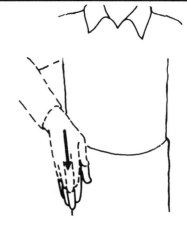

pocket

Mime placing hand in side pocket.

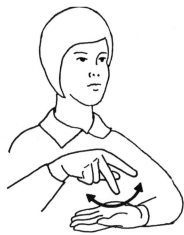

poem

LH open B palm up. Swing middle fingertip of right P, palm down, back and forth over left palm.

point

One shape LH held out from body. Touch left index tip with middle fingertip of right P.

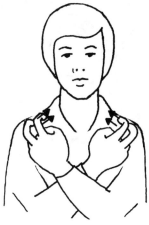

poison

Bent V shape both hands, palms in. Cross wrists on upper chest then tap chest with fingertips.

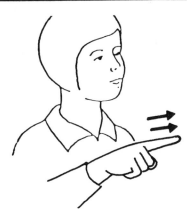

poke

Mime poking someone with right index.

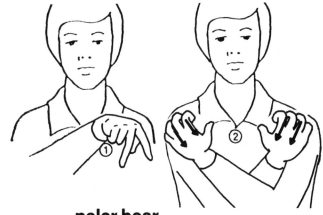

polar bear

Tap right P against left upper chest. Cross claw shape hands and place at shoulders. Scratch fingertips against upper chest twice.

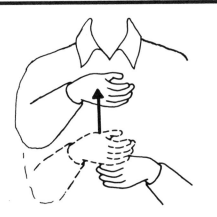

pole

C shape both hands, left tips right, right tips left. Place right C on left and then lift straight up.

police

Tap right C just below left shoulder (indicating badge).

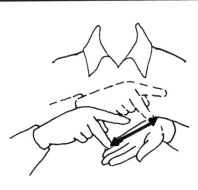

polish

LH open B palm up, tips out. Slide middle fingertip of right P back and forth on left palm.

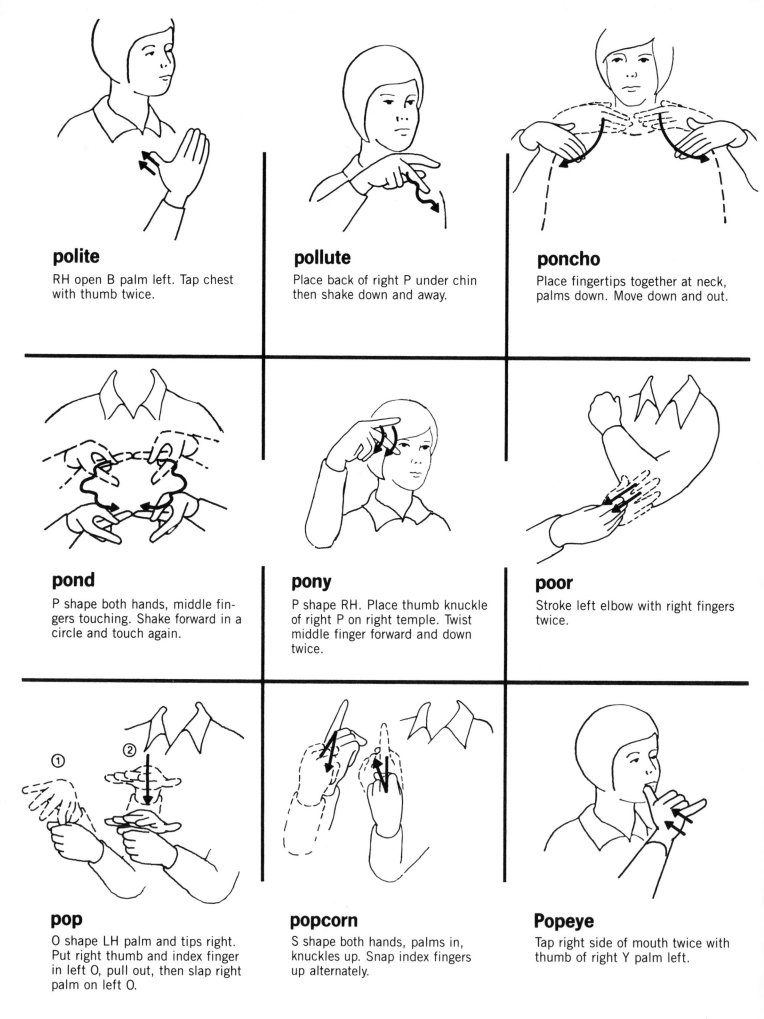

polite

RH open B palm left. Tap chest with thumb twice.

pollute

Place back of right P under chin then shake down and away.

poncho

Place fingertips together at neck, palms down. Move down and out.

pond

P shape both hands, middle fingers touching. Shake forward in a circle and touch again.

pony

P shape RH. Place thumb knuckle of right P on right temple. Twist middle finger forward and down twice.

poor

Stroke left elbow with right fingers twice.

pop

O shape LH palm and tips right. Put right thumb and index finger in left O, pull out, then slap right palm on left O.

popcorn

S shape both hands, palms in, knuckles up. Snap index fingers up alternately.

Popeye

Tap right side of mouth twice with thumb of right Y palm left.

Popsicle

V shape RH palm in. Draw down over mouth and chin. Repeat.

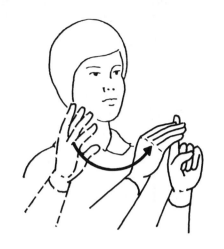

popular

One shape LH palm out. Cupped 5 shape RH palm out, held out from body. Draw fingers of RH back against left index, closing into flat O shape.

porch

LH open B palm down, arm extended. Draw shape of porch off left forearm with middle fingertip of P shape RH.

porcupine

S shape LH knuckles right. Four shape RH palm in, tips left. Place back of RH against left thumb and raise right fingers upright.

pork

P shape LH. Grasp left P with right thumb and forefinger and shake.

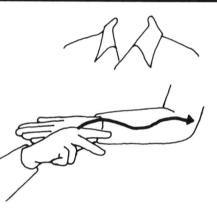

porpoise

Hold left arm before body palm down, tips right. Move right P up outside of left arm to elbow in up and down "dipping" motion.

positive

One shape LH palm down, tip right. Place tip of right index at mouth then strike against side of left index.

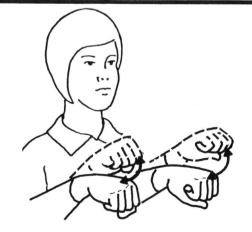

possible

S shape both hands, palms down. Shake up and down at wrists.

post (mail)

LH open B palm up. Place middle finger of right P on lips then place on left palm.

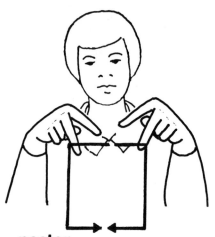

poster

P shape both hands. Move middle fingertips apart, down, then together again, outlining shape of poster.

post office

Fingerspell P-O.

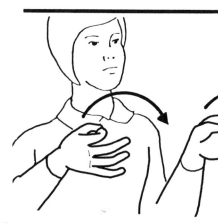

postpone

F shape both hands, tips out, LH extended out beyond RH. Arc both hands forward simultaneously.

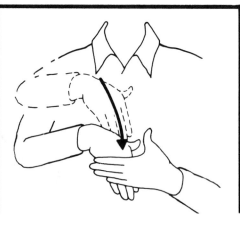

pot

P shape both hands, middle fingers touching. Arc apart and up, outlining shape of pot.

potato

S shape LH palm down. Tap back of LH with fingertips of right bent V.

potty

P shape RH palm down. Shake back and forth slightly.

pouch

Open B shape both hands, left palm in, tips right; right palm in, tips down. Slide RH down against left palm.

pound (noun)

Fingerspell L-B.

pound (verb)

LH open B palm up, tips out. Pound left palm with little finger side of right S.

pour

A shape RH. Arc to left, as if pouring into cup.

powder

C shape RH palm out. Shake to left side twice.

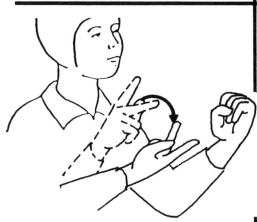

power

Hold LH in tight S palm up. Outline left bicep with middle fingertip of right P.

pox

Curve right index finger inside right thumb, then tap right cheek in several places indicating spots.

practice

One shape LH palm down, tip out. Brush knuckles of right A back and forth on left index.

pray

Place palms together, tips slanted up. Rotate toward body.

prefer

Place right open B on chest then move out into A shape thumb extended.

pregnant

Intertwine fingers of both hands. Place in front of stomach then move out.

287

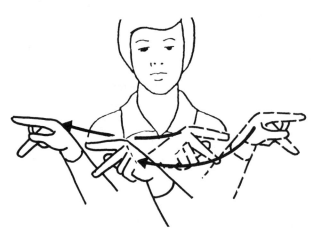

prepare

P shape both hands held parallel.
Slide from left to right.

preschool

LH open B tips right. Place back of
right P against left palm then move
right P toward body. Clap right
palm against left palm twice.

prescription

Fingerspell R-X.

present

P shape both hands. Bring up and
turn out.

president

Claw shape both hands, palms out.
Place at temples then move away,
ending in S shapes.

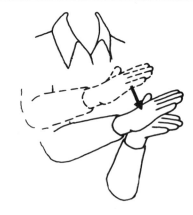

press (together)

Open B both hands, left palm up,
tips out; right palm down, tips left.
Press hands together.

pressure

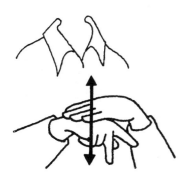

LH open B palm down. Place right P under left palm then move both hands up and down.

pretend

P shape RH palm out. Place index finger of right P on right side of forehead then circle forward.

pretty

Five shape RH palm in, tips up. Circle face from right to left ending in flat O.

pretzel

X shape both hands, left palm in, right palm down. Hook index fingers.

prevent

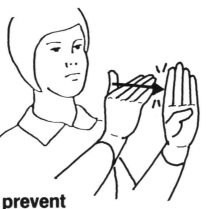

B shape LH palm right, tips up. Hit side of left index with RH open B palm down.

price

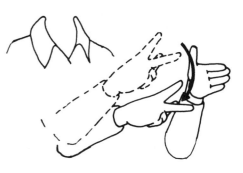

LH open B palm right, tips out. P shape RH palm and tips left. Strike middle fingertip of right P down across left palm.

priest

Place tips of right G at neck then slide to right, outlining clerical collar.

primary

LH open B palm down, tips right. Circle right P counterclockwise under left palm.

prince

Tap left shoulder, then right side of waist, with middle fingertip of right P held palm in.

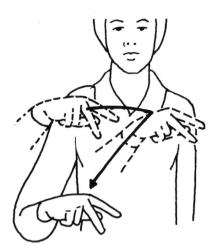

princess

Place thumb side of right P against right shoulder. Move to left shoulder then down to right side of waist.

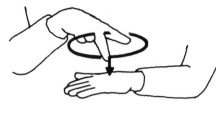

principal

LH open B palm down. Circle right P over back of left hand, then drop middle fingertip on back of LH.

print

G shape RH. Hold over left palm then draw back and snap tips together in palm.

prison

Five shape both hands, palms in, right tips up, left tips right. Slap back of right fingers against left palm.

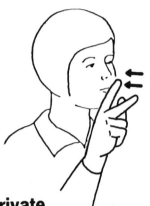

private

P shape RH palm out, tips up. Tap index finger of right P twice against lips.

prize

S shape LH knuckles right. Claw shape RH palm left. Swing RH over left S, closing into S shape; then change to A shape and circle in front of right shoulder.

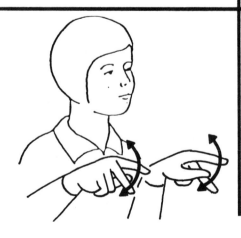

probable

P shape both hands, palms down. Shake up and down at wrists.

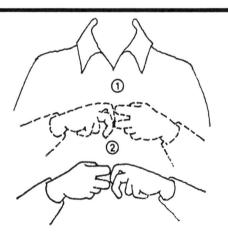

problem

Bent V shapes both hands, right palm down, left palm in. Place knuckles together then twist in opposite directions, RH rotating forward, LH rotating back.

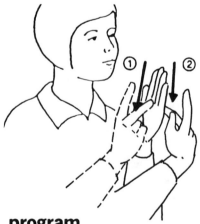

program

LH open B palm in, tips up, held away from body. Move middle fingertip of right P down left palm then down back of left hand.

290

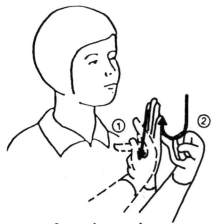

project (noun)

LH open B palm in, tips up, held away from body. Slide little finger side of right P down left palm. Then draw a J shape with right little finger on back of LH.

projector

S shape LH, 5 shape RH. Place left S against base of right thumb and "flicker" right fingers.

promise

S shape LH palm down. Place right index finger on lips, move out into open B shape, and place against LH.

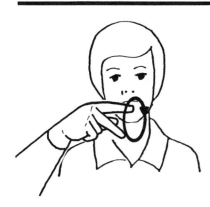

pronounce

P shape RH palm down. Hold index tip at mouth and make small circle forward.

property

Tap thumb side of right P against center of chest.

protect

S shape both hands, left slanted right, right slanted left. Place right S behind left wrist then push both hands forward.

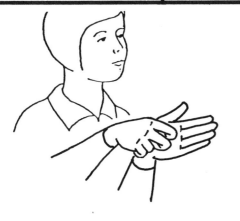

Protestant

LH open B palm right, tips out. Place knuckles of right bent V in left palm.

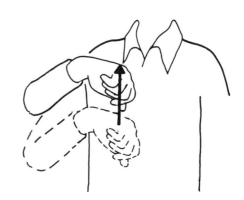

proud

A shape RH palm out, thumb down. Place on lower chest and draw up slowly.

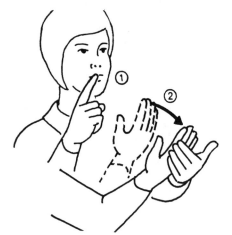

prove

Place tip of right index at lips. Then slap back of right open B into palm of left open B.

prune

Draw middle fingertip of right P, palm in, across chin from left to right.

psychiatry

LH open B palm up, tips out. Tap left wrist with middle fingertip of right P.

psychology

LH open B palm out. Strike LH between thumb and index with little finger side of right open B.

pteranodon

Hold P shape hands out to sides. Flap both wrists up and down.

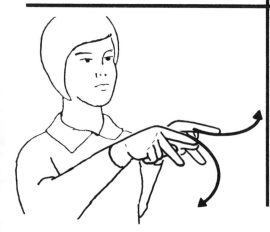

public

P shape both hands placed close together. Arc away from each other while moving out from body.

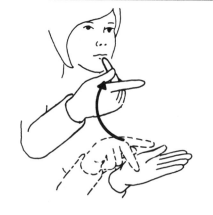

pudding

LH open B palm up, tips out. Place middle finger of right P in left palm then move up to mouth.

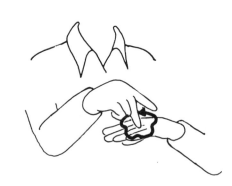

puddle

LH open B palm down. Circle right P counterclockwise over back of left B in wavy motion.

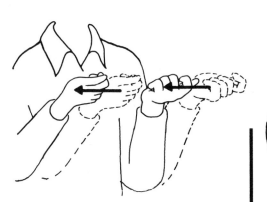

pull

A shape both hands, knuckles up, left ahead of right. Pull toward body in quick motion as if pulling a rope.

pulse

Place fingers of right hand on up-turned left wrist.

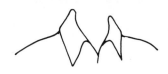

pump

Mime pumping handle of old-fashioned water pump.

pumpkin

Thump back of left S, palm down, with middle finger of right P.

punch (beverage)

P shape RH palm down. Change to C shape, palm and tips left, and move up to mouth as if drinking.

punch (verb)

One shape LH. P shape RH palm in, tips left. Swing back of left P against right index.

punish

Hold left arm in front of body, fist clenched. Strike tip of right index down against left elbow.

pupil (eye)

Place middle finger of right P at corner of right eye.

pupil (person)

LH open B palm right. Place right P on left fingers and slide down to base of palm. Repeat.

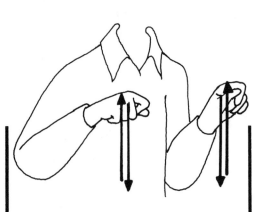

puppet

RH flat O palm out. Snap thumb and fingertips together several times, as if operating hand puppet.

puppet (alt.)

A shape both hands, palms down. Move up and down alternately, as if pulling strings.

puppy

Snap together thumb and middle finger of right P two or three times.

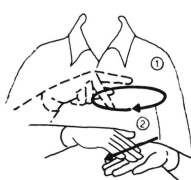

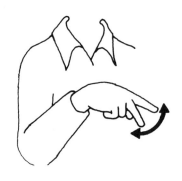

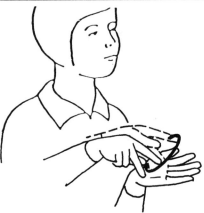

pure

LH open B palm up, tips out. Circle right P, palm down, clockwise over left palm. Then slide palm of right open B across left palm.

purple

Shake right P back and forth from wrist.

purpose

LH open B palm and tips slanted left. P shape RH. Touch left palm with middle finger of right P. Twist P forward and touch palm again.

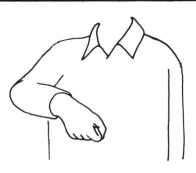

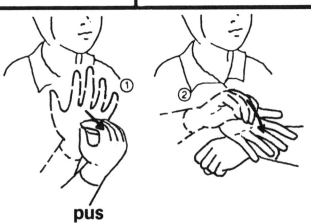

purse

A shape RH knuckles down. Hold as if carrying purse.

pus

Place 5 shape RH on chest and draw back into flat O. Then place right flat O, tips down, over left wrist and open quickly into 5 shape.

push

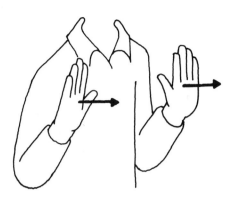

Open B both hands, palms out, tips up, left a little in front of right. Push out.

put

Flat O shape both hands, palms down. Move forward and down.

puzzle (noun)

A shape both hands, thumbs down. Make motion of fitting together.

puzzle (verb)

Place X shape RH, palm left, at right temple. Crook and uncrook right index finger several times.

pyramid

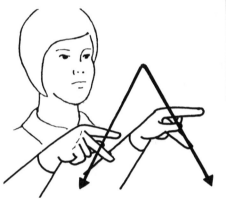

P shape both hands, thumbs and index fingers almost touching. Move apart and down, outlining shape of pyramid.

Q

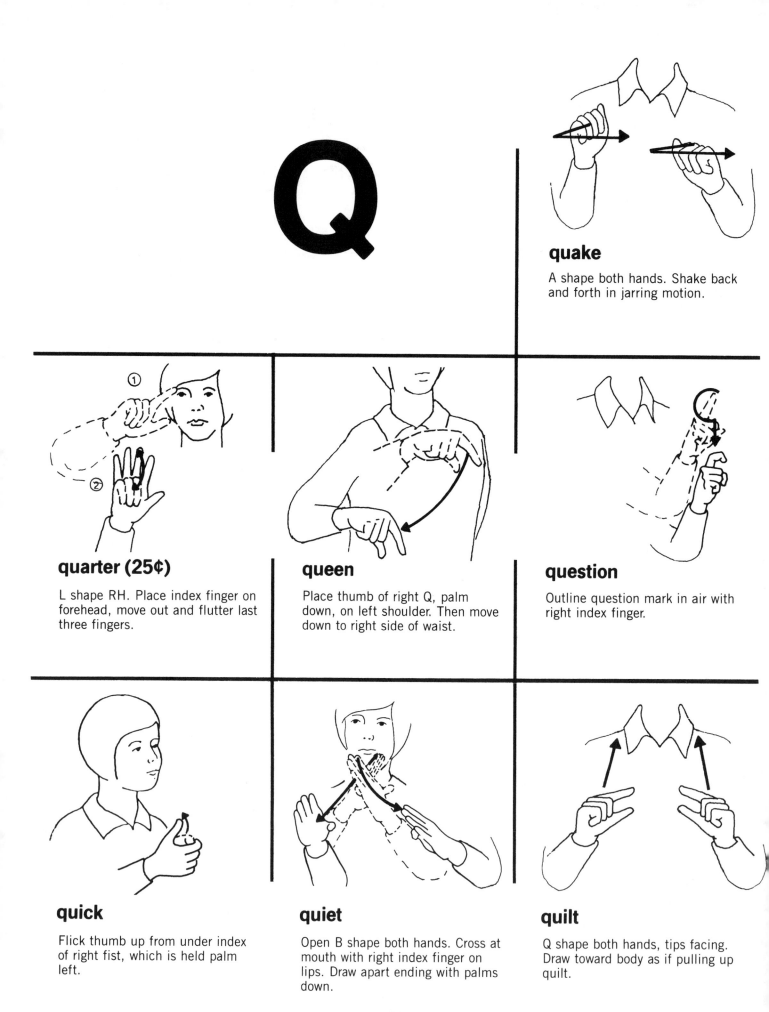

quake

A shape both hands. Shake back and forth in jarring motion.

quarter (25¢)

L shape RH. Place index finger on forehead, move out and flutter last three fingers.

queen

Place thumb of right Q, palm down, on left shoulder. Then move down to right side of waist.

question

Outline question mark in air with right index finger.

quick

Flick thumb up from under index of right fist, which is held palm left.

quiet

Open B shape both hands. Cross at mouth with right index finger on lips. Draw apart ending with palms down.

quilt

Q shape both hands, tips facing. Draw toward body as if pulling up quilt.

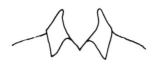

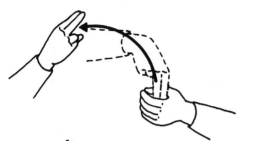

quit

O shape LH palm right. Place right middle and index fingers in left O, then pull out to right.

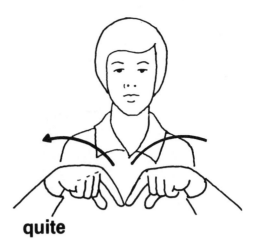

quite

Q shape both hands. Place close together then arc apart.

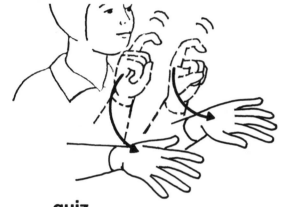

quiz

X shape both hands. Crook and uncrook fingers several times, then move out into 5 shapes, palms down.

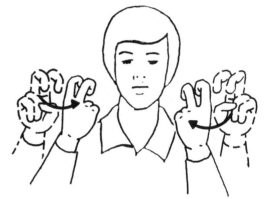

quote

Bent V shape both hands, palms out, held out from body. Twist inward, as if outlining quotation marks.

R

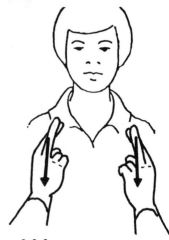

rabbi

R shape both hands, palms in. Place tips just below shoulders then draw down chest.

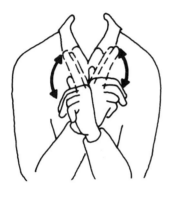

rabbit

H shape both hands. Cross at wrists then wiggle index and middle fingers up and down.

raccoon

R shape both hands, palms in. Place tips under eyes and draw back to ears.

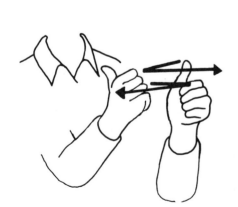

race

A shape both hands, thumbs up, knuckles facing. Alternately move forward and back.

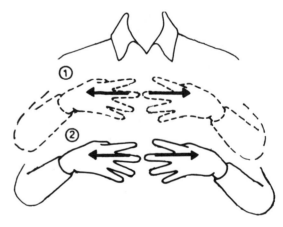

rack

Four shape both hands, palms in, tips facing. Draw apart, lower, then draw apart again.

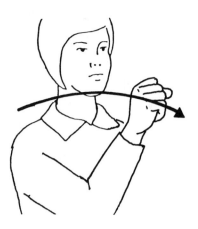

racket (sports)

Mime holding racket in front of right shoulder and batting forward.

radio

Place cupped right hand over right ear.

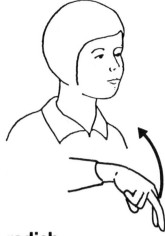

radish

R shape RH tips down. Move upward as if pulling radish from ground.

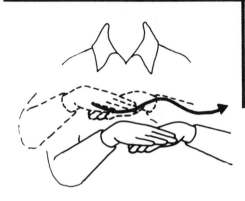

raft

B shape both hands, palms down, left tips slanted right, right tips slanted left. Place RH on back of left then move both hands forward in wavy motion.

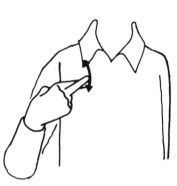

rag

R shape RH palm in. Rub tips up and down just below right shoulder.

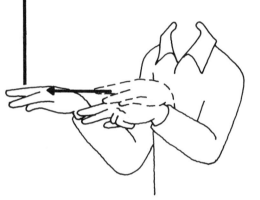

rail

V shape both hands, palms down, tips out. Slide right V forward over back of left V.

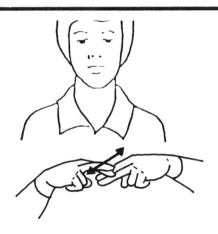

railroad

U shape LH palm down, tips out. R shape RH palm down, tips left. Rub right R back and forth on back of left U.

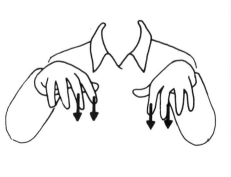

rain

Claw shape both hands, palms down. Move down sharply two or three times.

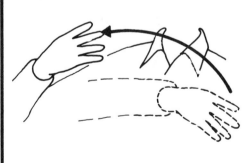

rainbow

Four shape RH palm in, tips down. Arc from left to right, outlining rainbow.

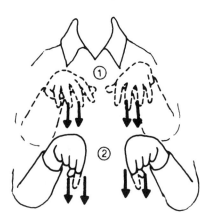

raindrop

Drop claw shape hands down sharply twice. Change to fists, palms down, and snap index fingers down alternately.

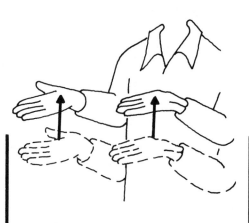

raise

Open B shape both hands, palms up, tips out. Raise up several inches.

raisin

LH open B palm in, tips down. Hop tip of right R down back of left B.

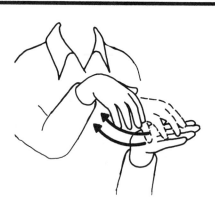

rake

Rake fingers of right claw hand across upturned left palm. Repeat motion.

ranch

Place thumb of R shape RH on left side of chin and draw across to right.

Rapunzel

R shape both hands, palms out. Place tips on ears then move down to chest, outlining long braids.

rash

Flat O shape both hands, palms in, tips up. Move up to cheeks, opening into 5 shapes.

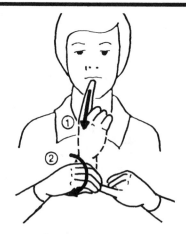

raspberry

Brush lower lip with tip of right index. Then form I shape LH, palm in, tip right. Twist fingers of claw shape RH around left little finger.

rat

Brush down tip of nose with R shape RH palm left.

rather

L shape LH palm right, index tip out. Place tips of right R on left thumb then move to tip of left index.

rattle

R shape RH. Shake back and forth.

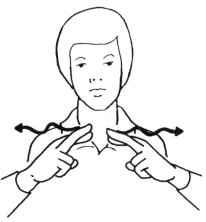

ravioli

R shape both hands, palms down, tips facing. Wiggle apart from one another.

raw

Fingerspell R-A-W.

razor

X shape RH knuckles left. Scrape down right cheek.

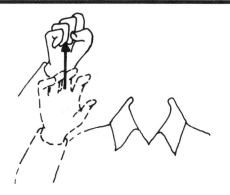

reach

Claw shape RH palm out. Raise up and close into S shape.

read

LH open B palm right, tips up. Move tips of right V down left palm in back and forth motion.

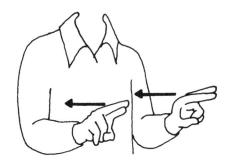

ready

R shape both hands, palms down, tips out. Move from left to right.

real

One shape RH palm left. Place finger on lips and move up and out.

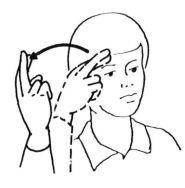

realize

Place tips of right R on right side of forehead then arc out.

reason

Circle right R, palm in, clockwise at middle of forehead.

recent

X shape RH palm in. Place at side of right cheek and wiggle index fingertip.

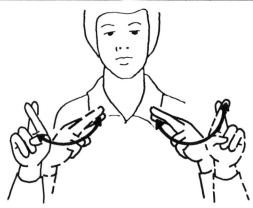

recess

R shape both hands, one palm in, one palm out. Swing back and forth two or three times.

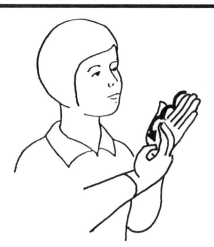

recipe

LH open B palm in, held out from body. Tap back of right R, tips left, down left palm.

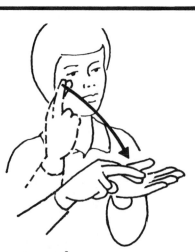

recognize

Place tips of right R at right eye then place in upturned left palm.

record

LH open B palm up, tips out. Circle tips of right R clockwise over left palm.

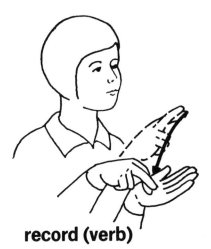

record (verb)

Hold right R above, and slightly in front of, upturned left palm. Draw tips of right R back into left palm.

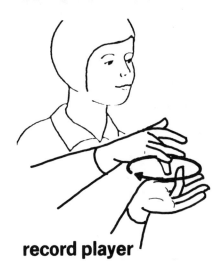

record player

Open B both hands, middle fingers extended. Rotate right middle finger clockwise around left middle finger.

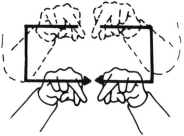

rectangle

R shape both hands, palms down, tips out. Outline shape of rectangle.

rectum

Point to rectum with right index finger then form the letter F with RH.

red

Brush lower lip with tip of right index finger. Repeat motion. (Sometimes made with R shape RH.)

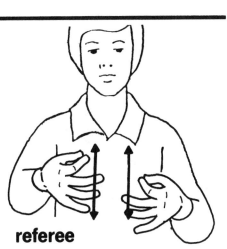

referee

F shape both hands, palms and tips facing. Alternately move up and down.

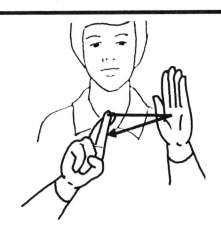

reflection

LH open B tips up, palm slanted right. Strike left palm with tips of right R, then "reflect" R back to original starting point.

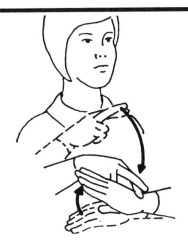

reflex

Tap back of left wrist with right R then quickly flip up LH.

303

refrigerator
R shape both hands, palms facing, tips out. Shake back and forth in "shivering" motion.

refuse (verb)
S shape RH knuckles left. Jerk back over right shoulder.

register
LH open B palm up, tips out. R shape RH palm down, tips left; place in left palm.

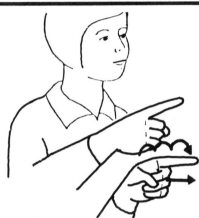

regular
One shape both hands, tips out. Tap base of left index with little finger side of RH several times while moving both hands forward.

rehearse
One shape LH palm right, tip out. Brush base of right R back and forth on left index.

reindeer
R shape both hands, thumbs extended. Place thumbs on temples and move up and out.

relative
R shape both hands, left palm up, right palm down. Place right R on left, then turn both hands over, reversing positions.

relax
R shape both hands, palms in. Cross at wrists and place both hands on upper chest.

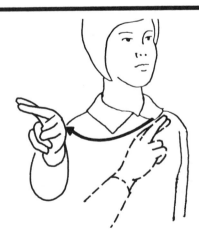

religion
Place tips of right R over heart then swing out to right.

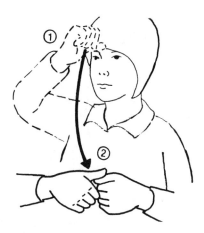

remember

Place thumb of right A on fore-head, then drop down and touch thumb of A shape LH palm right.

remind

Tap right shoulder several times with tips of bent RH.

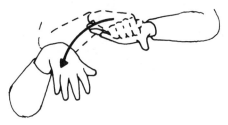

remove

LH open B palm up, tips slanted right. Place knuckles of right A in left palm, lift up, then drop into 5 shape palm down.

repair

R shape both hands, little finger sides down. Place right R on top of left R. Twist both hands in opposite directions, ending with palms in.

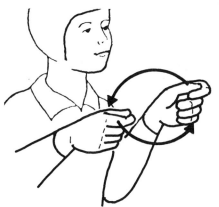

replace

Modified A shape both hands, right behind left. Simultaneously arc RH down under LH and LH up over RH.

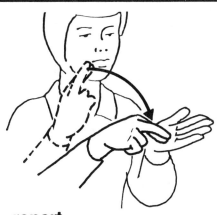

report

Place tips of right R at mouth then down into upturned left palm.

reptile

Place knuckle of right R at chin then circle forward.

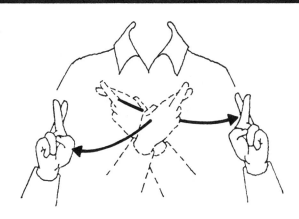

rescue

R shape both hands, palms in, crossed at wrists. Twist apart, ending with palms out.

305

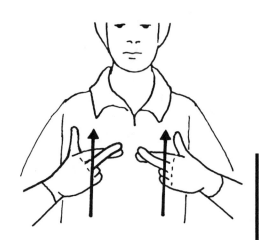

residence
R shape both hands, tips facing, thumbs extended. Move up body.

respect
R shape RH extended out from forehead. Arc in and down in front of face.

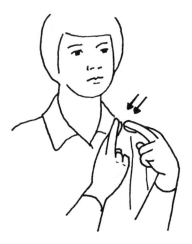

responsibility
Tap left shoulder twice with tips of R shape hands, palms in.

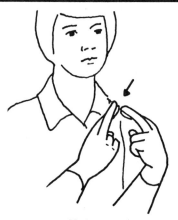

responsible
Tap left shoulder with tips of R shape hands, palms in.

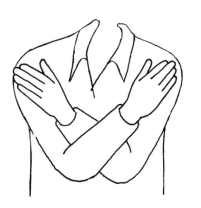

rest
Open B both hands. Fold arms and rest palms on upper chest.

restaurant
R shape RH palm left. Place on right side of mouth then move to left side.

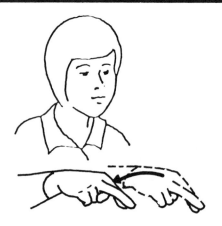

rest room
R shape RH palm down. Bounce to right.

return
R shape both hands, palms in. Move back toward body.

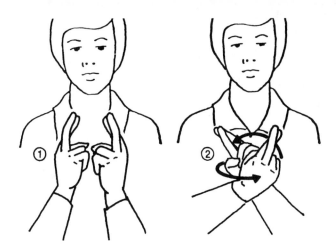

reverse

R shape both hands, palms facing. Twist at wrists, reversing positions.

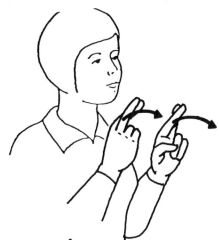

reward

R shape both hands, palms facing, tips up. Arc both hands forward, keeping R tips up.

rhinoceros

C shape RH palm left. Place on nose and move out, ending in S shape.

rhyme

LH open B palm up, tips slanted right. Swing tips of right R above left palm and forearm in rhythmic motion.

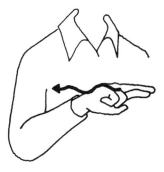

rhythm

R shape RH palm down, tips out. Move in rhythmic motion to the right.

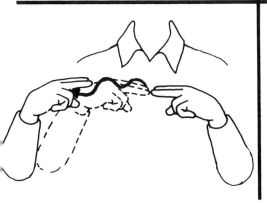

ribbon

H shape both hands, palms down, tips touching. Draw right H away from left in wavy motion.

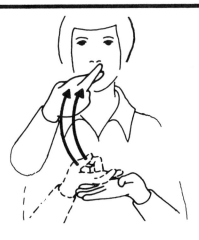

rice

LH open B palm up, tips slanted right. Place back of right R in left palm then move up to mouth. Repeat motion.

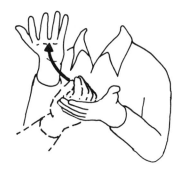

rich

Place back of right flat O in up-turned left palm. Quickly move RH up while spreading fingers into 5 shape palm up.

307

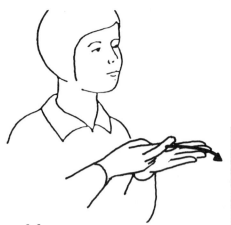

rid

Place back of right R on left palm then sweep forward sharply off palm.

riddle

Draw question mark in air with tips of right R.

ride

C shape LH palm right. Hook fingers of right H on left thumb and move both hands forward.

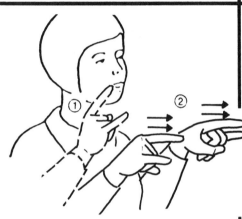

ridiculous

Extend index and little fingers of both hands, palms down. Place right index at side of mouth then move both hands forward in short jabbing motions.

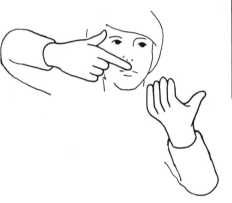

rifle

LH open B palm up, fingers curved, held out from body. Point index finger of right L at LH.

right (correct)

One shape both hands, tips out. Strike base of left index with little finger side of RH.

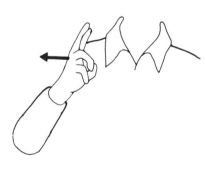

right (direction)

R shape RH. Move to right.

ring (circle)

Form circle in air with right R, tips out.

ring (jewelry)

Place right index and thumb around left fourth finger and mime putting on a ring.

ring (verb)

LH open B palm right, tips out. Strike left palm with tips of right R then move right R out in wavy motion.

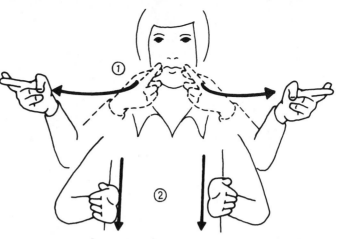

ringmaster

R shape both hands, tips on either side of mouth. Swing out to side then form agent marker.

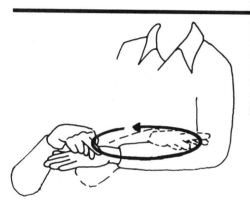

rink

LH open B palm down, tips slanted right. R shape RH palm down, tips left. Circle right R over left hand up to elbow and back.

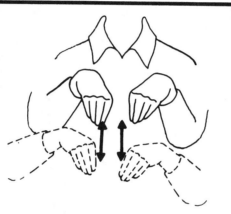

rinse

Flat O both hands, palms in, tips down. Move up and down, as if rinsing something.

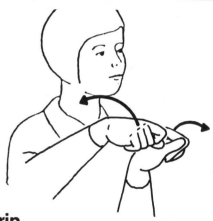

rip

Place the thumb and index tips of both hands together. Twist LH forward and RH backward, as if ripping sheet of paper.

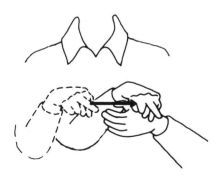

ripe

C shape LH palm and tips right, little finger side down. R shape RH palm down, tips left. Brush right R over left C toward wrist.

rise

Five shape both hands, palms down, tips out. Simultaneously move hands upward.

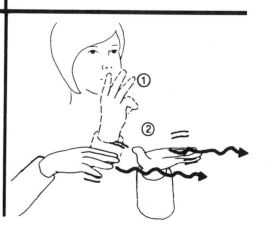

river

Place index finger of right W on mouth. Then move both hands forward, palms down, in rippling motion.

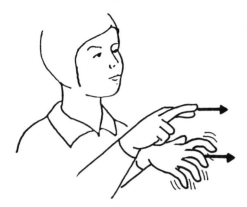

roach (cockroach)

Place base of right R on back of LH which is held palm down. Move both hands forward while wiggling fingers of LH.

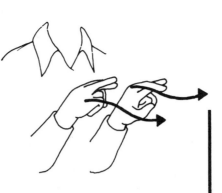

road

R shape both hands, palms down, tips out. Move forward.

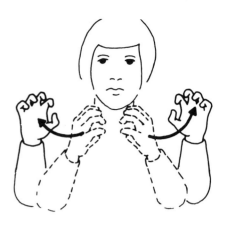

roar

Claw shape both hands, palms and tips facing. Hold at throat then swing out, ending with palms out.

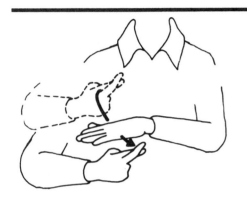

roast

LH open B palm down, tips slanting right. R shape RH palm in, tips left. Slide under left hand.

rob

Place right R, palm down, against left elbow. Jerk back to left wrist.

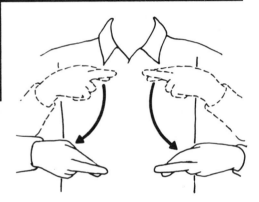

robe

R shape both hands, palms in, tips facing. Brush down chest.

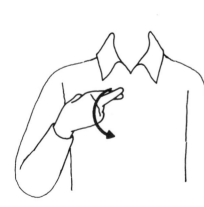

robin

R shape RH palm in, tips left. Place on chest and arc out and back in, as if outlining "red breast."

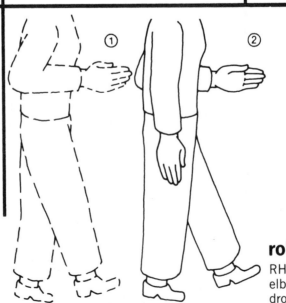

robot

RH open B palm left, tips out, elbows held at side. Walk forward, drop RH, then raise left open B in like motion.

310

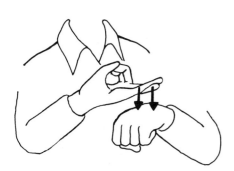

rock (noun)

S shape LH knuckles down. Tap back of left S with back of right R.

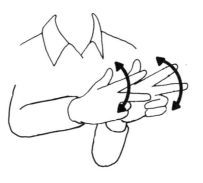

rock (verb)

Three shape both hands, palms facing, tips out. Rock back and forth.

rocket

S shape LH palm and knuckles down. Place base of right R on back of left S then raise up suddenly.

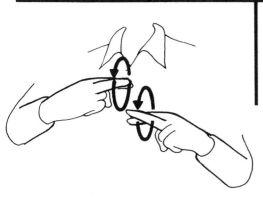

roll

R shape both hands, tips facing. Roll around each other.

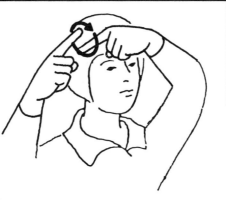

roller (hair)

One shape both hands, tips facing. Circle around one another, as if rolling hair on curler.

roller coaster

R shape RH held up to left. Move down in a wavy motion, ending in C shape.

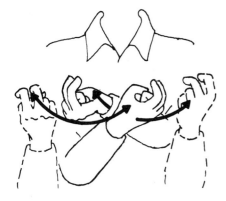

roller skate

Bent V shape both hands, palms up, right held near chest, left held out from body. Swing back and forth alternately.

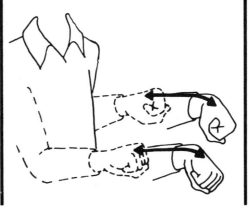

rolling pin

S shape both hands, knuckles down. Mime using a rolling pin.

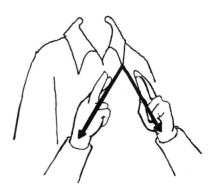

roof

R shape both hands, palms facing, tips slanted up toward each other and touching. Draw apart and down, outlining roof.

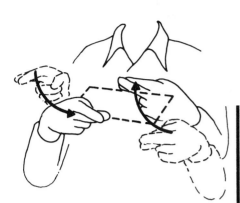

room

R shape both hands, tips out. Turn right R left and left R right to form box shape.

rooster

Three shape RH palm left. Tap forehead with thumb twice.

root

C shape LH palm and tips right. Push RH through left C until fingers show underneath.

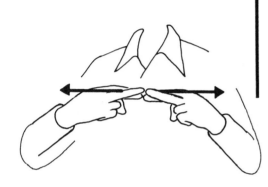

rope

R shape both hands, palms in, tips touching. Draw apart.

rose

R shape RH palm left. Place against right side of nose then move to left side.

rotten

Place tips of right R on nose then arc out and down sharply.

rough

Place fingers of right claw hand on left palm and push out.

round

C shape LH palm and tips out. R shape RH palm in, tips left. Circle left C with right R.

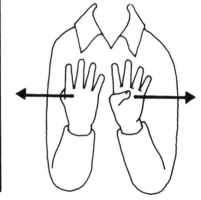

row (noun)

Four shape both hands, right palm in. Hold hands in front of body then draw apart.

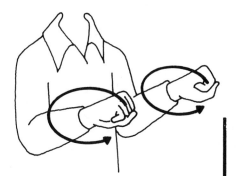

row (verb)

S shape both hands. Mime holding oars and rowing.

rub

A shape LH knuckles down. RH open B palm down, tips left. Place RH on back of left A and rub back and forth.

rubber

X shape RH palm out. Rub down side of right cheek twice.

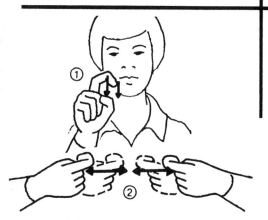

rubber band

Rub right X down side of cheek twice. Then move X shape hands, palms in, apart and back, as if stretching rubber band.

rude

One shape both hands, palms down, tips out. Move right index forward several times, striking against base of left index at each pass.

Rudolph (the red-nosed reindeer)

Tap right side of nose with tips of right R.

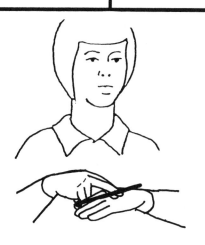

rug

LH open B palm down, tips out. R shape RH palm down, tips left. Place RH on left wrist and slide to fingertips.

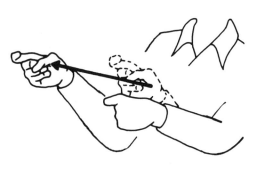

ruin

X shape both hands, right on top of left. Sharply brush right X forward.

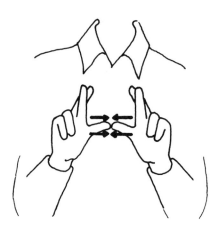

rule

LH open B palm right. R shape RH palm left. Tap fingers, then base, of left hand with tips of right R.

ruler

R shape both hands, thumbs extended. Tap thumbs together.

Rumpelstiltskin

R shape both hands, left tips out, right tips left. Tap left R twice with right R.

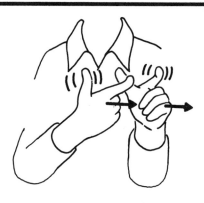

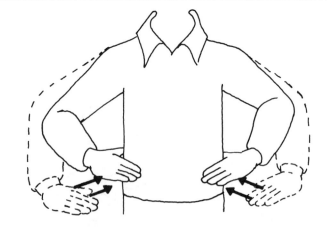

run

L shape both hands, index tips out, LH a little ahead of right. Hook right index finger around left thumb. Wiggle L shape fingers while moving both hands forward.

runway

LH open B palm up, tips out. Y shape RH palm down, index finger extended. Slide palm of RH across palm of LH.

rush

R shape both hands, palms facing, tips out. Shake hands up and down rapidly.

Russia

Open B both hands, palms down, left tips right, right tips left. Tap against sides of waist several times.

rye

Five shape LH palm up, fingers curved. Brush tips of right R up back of left fingers twice.

S

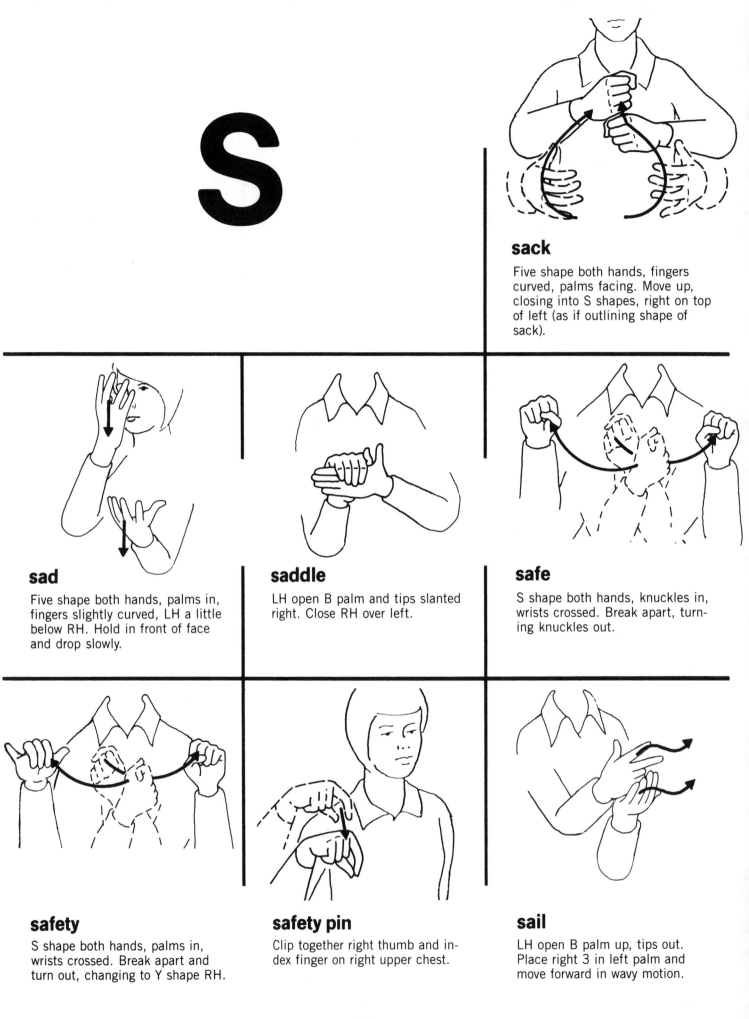

sack

Five shape both hands, fingers curved, palms facing. Move up, closing into S shapes, right on top of left (as if outlining shape of sack).

sad

Five shape both hands, palms in, fingers slightly curved, LH a little below RH. Hold in front of face and drop slowly.

saddle

LH open B palm and tips slanted right. Close RH over left.

safe

S shape both hands, knuckles in, wrists crossed. Break apart, turning knuckles out.

safety

S shape both hands, palms in, wrists crossed. Break apart and turn out, changing to Y shape RH.

safety pin

Clip together right thumb and index finger on right upper chest.

sail

LH open B palm up, tips out. Place right 3 in left palm and move forward in wavy motion.

saint

LH open B palm up, tips out. Circle right S, palm down, over LH then brush across left palm.

salad

Three shape both hands, palms up, fingers curved. Mime tossing salad with small upward movements.

salad dressing

Mime pouring dressing on salad with A shape RH thumb down.

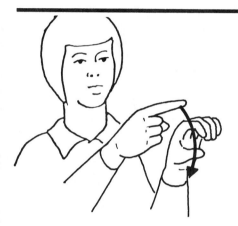

salami

C shape LH palm slanted down. Strike right index down against thumb and index finger of left C (as if slicing a roll of salami).

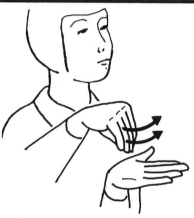

sale

LH open B palm up, tips out. Place tips of right flat O over left palm and flip up twice without touching.

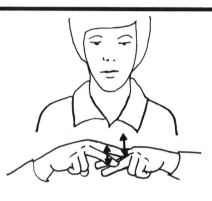

salt

Tap right V on back of left V two or three times. (Sometimes the fingers of the right V move alternately against fingers of left V.)

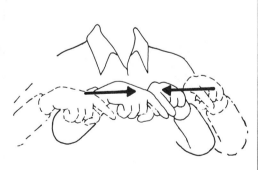

same

One shape both hands, palms down, tips out. Bring index fingers together.

sample

LH open B palm out. Place right S against left palm and move both hands forward.

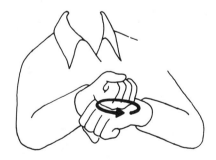

sand

S shape both hands, left S down, right S up. Place right S on back of left S and move in small circle counterclockwise.

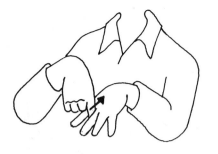

sandal

Five shape LH palm down. Slide right index finger, pointed down, between left index and middle fingers.

sandwich

Open B both hands, palms up. Slide right hand between thumb and fingers of LH (as if inserting filling into sandwich).

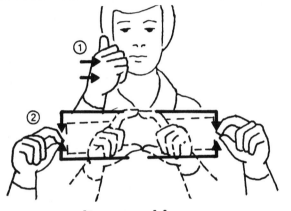

sanitary napkin

Tap knuckles of right A on right cheek twice. Then place tips of index fingers and thumbs together. Draw apart and close, outlining napkin.

sanitation

LH open B palm up, tips out. Rub knuckles of right S twice across left palm.

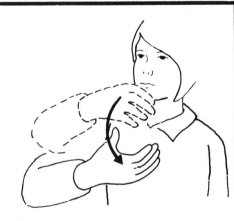

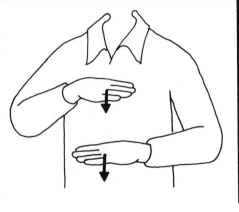

Santa Claus

C shape RH palm in. Place index on chin and arc down to

satisfy

Open B both hands, palms down. Place on chest, RH above LH, then move down slightly.

Saturday

Circle right S clockwise.

sauce

LH open B palm up. Circle right A, thumb down, over left palm, as if pouring.

saucer

Tap base of left X twice with palm of RH.

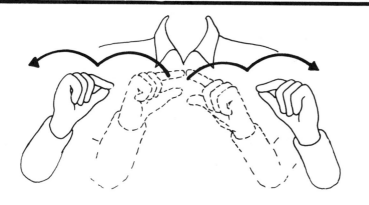

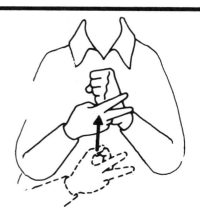

sausage

G shape both hands, palms and tips out, index fingers touching. Draw apart while opening and closing fingers, outlining links.

save

Tap little finger side of left S with tips of right V.

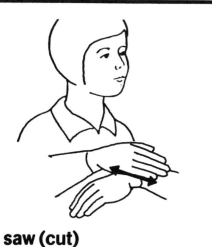

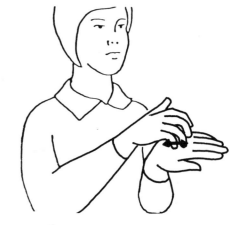

saw (cut)

Move little finger side of right open B back and forth on wrist of left open B, palm down.

say

One shape RH palm in, tip left. Hold at mouth and make small circle forward.

scab

Move fingers of claw shape RH back and forth on back of LH.

scale

LH open B palm in, tips right. Slide thumb side of right S across back of LH from right to left.

scare

S shape both hands, knuckles facing. Move toward one another sharply while opening into 5 shapes.

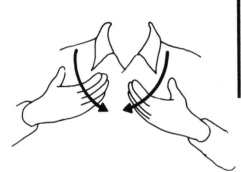

scarf

C shape both hands, palms and tips in. Place tips on shoulders then draw down and together, outlining scarf.

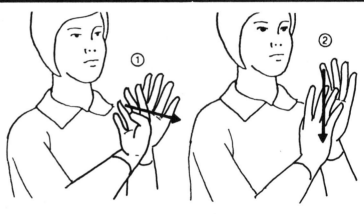

schedule

Five shape LH palm right. Move back of 4 shape RH across left palm. Then flip RH over and brush tips down left palm.

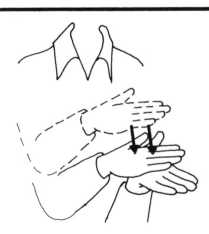

school

Open B both hands, left palm up, tips out; right palm down, tips left. Clap hands twice.

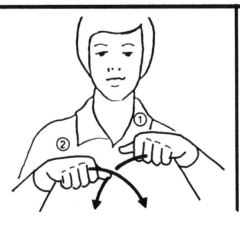

science

A shape both hands. Alternately arc thumbs down, as if pouring from vials.

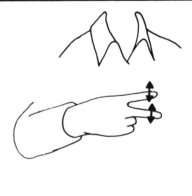

scissors

V shape RH palm in, tips left. Open and close fingers like scissor blades.

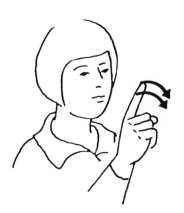

scold

Shake right index finger up and down vigorously.

scoop

Move fingertips of right C in scooping motion across upturned left palm.

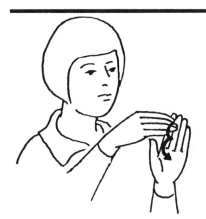

score

LH open B palm right. Bounce tips of RH down left palm.

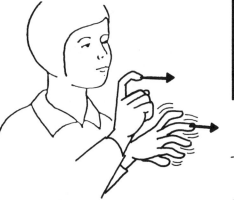

scorpion

Place base of right X on back of LH. Move both hands forward while wiggling fingers of LH.

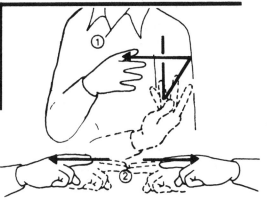

Scotch tape

Make a cross on upper left arm with fingers of 4 shape RH. Then form H shape both hands, palms down, tips touching. Draw apart in straight line.

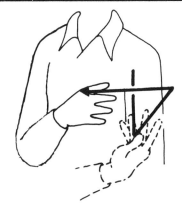

Scotland

Place back of 4 shape RH on upper left arm and move down. Then flip to palm in and move across arm, forming cross shape.

scout (noun)

Place together index, middle, and fourth fingers of RH. Hold up near right shoulder, palm out.

scout (verb)

B shape LH palm down, tips right. Place on forehead. V shape RH palm down, tips out. Wave from left to right beneath left B.

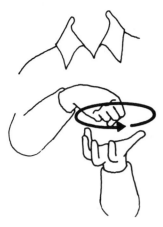

scramble

Claw shape LH palm up. S shape RH knuckles down. Circle RH over left palm.

scrapbook

Mime pasting down pictures on left palm with RH. Then place palms together, thumbs up, and open.

scrape

LH open B palm up, tips out. Slide little finger side of right open B off left palm. Repeat motion.

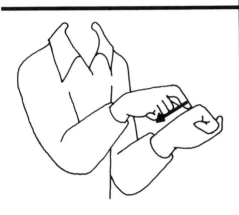

scratch

Scratch back of left S with right index finger.

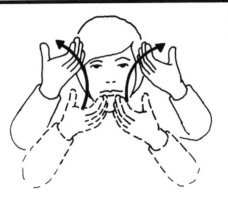

scream

C shape both hands, palms in. Hold under chin then move up and out.

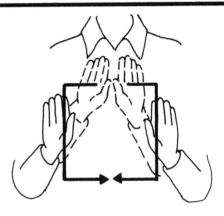

screen

Hold hands in front of body, palms out, tips up. Draw apart, down, and back again, outlining shape of screen.

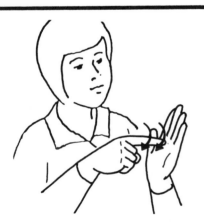

screw

LH open B palm right. Twist tip of right index forward in left palm. Repeat motion.

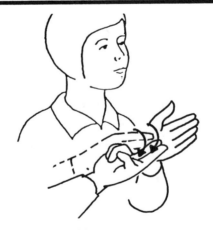

screwdriver

LH open B palm right. Twist tips of right H forward in left palm. Repeat motion.

scribble

LH open B palm up, tips out. Move right thumb and index tip forward on left palm in scribbling motion.

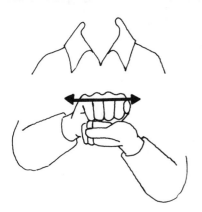

scrub

A shape both hands, left knuckles up, right knuckles down. Rub right knuckles back and forth across left knuckles in scrubbing motion.

sea

S shape both hands, palms down. Open into 5 shapes and dip forward in wavy motion.

seal

S shape LH palm down. Place right open B on top of left S and flap fingers down twice.

search (look for)

C shape RH palm and tips left. Circle clockwise in front of face two or three times.

season

LH open B palm right, tips up. Rotate thumb side of right S clockwise against left palm.

seat

S shape LH knuckles right, thumb side up. RH bent V palm and tips down; place on top of left S.

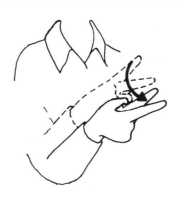

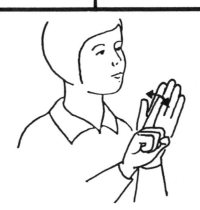

second

Two shape RH palm out. Twist so that palm faces in.

second (unit of time)

LH open B palm right, tips up. Place right thumb knuckle against left palm and move back and forth in small movements.

323

secret

Tap thumb of right A against lips.

secretary

LH open B palm up, tips out. K shape RH. Place middle finger on right cheek, then move down to left palm and slide forward.

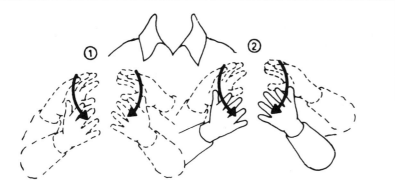

section

Cupped shape both hands, palms and tips facing. Twist down then move to left and repeat.

see

V shape RH palm in. Place tips at eyes then move forward.

seed

Rub fingers of RH together while moving from right to left, as if dropping seeds into soil.

seek

C shape RH palm and tips left. Circle clockwise in front of right eye.

seem

RH bent B palm and tips left. Twist inward twice.

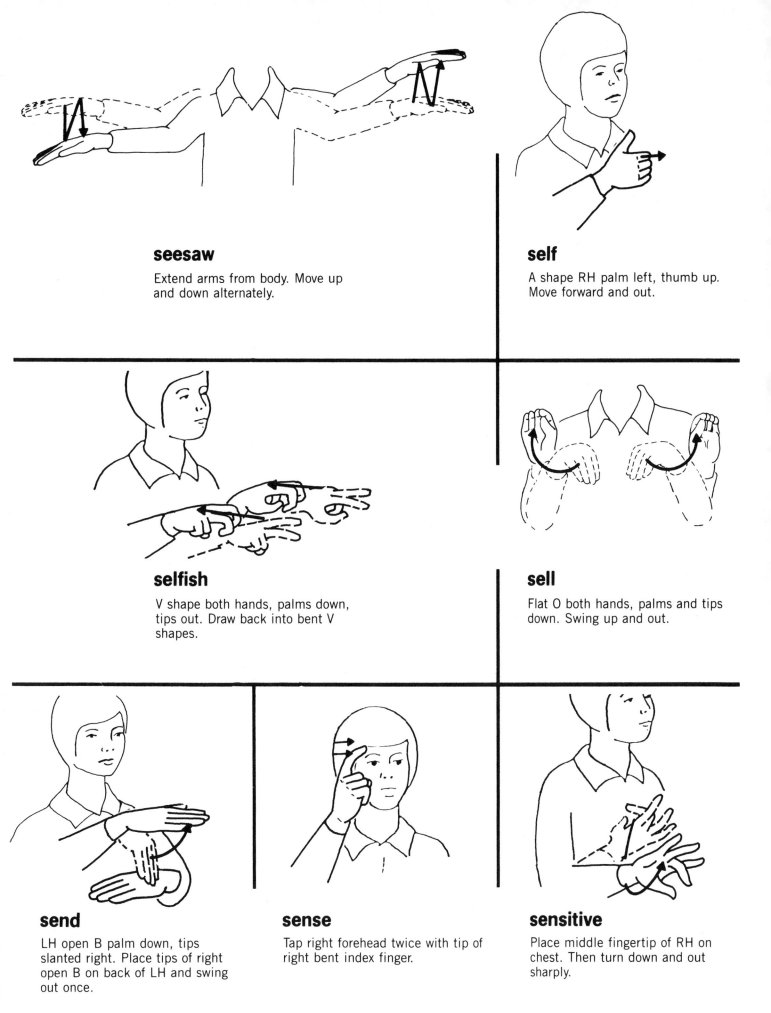

seesaw

Extend arms from body. Move up
and down alternately.

self

A shape RH palm left, thumb up.
Move forward and out.

selfish

V shape both hands, palms down,
tips out. Draw back into bent V
shapes.

sell

Flat O both hands, palms and tips
down. Swing up and out.

send

LH open B palm down, tips
slanted right. Place tips of right
open B on back of LH and swing
out once.

sense

Tap right forehead twice with tip of
right bent index finger.

sensitive

Place middle fingertip of RH on
chest. Then turn down and out
sharply.

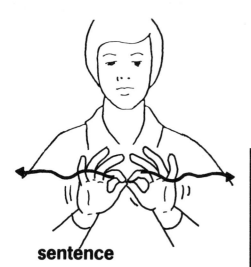

sentence

F shape both hands, thumb and index fingertips touching. Move apart while shaking hands slightly.

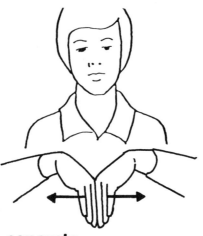

separate

Bent open B both hands, backs of fingers touching. Move apart.

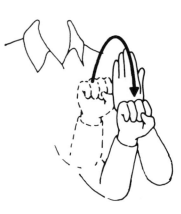

September

RH open B palm in. Place right S against left palm and slide over fingers and down.

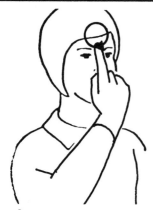

serious

One shape RH palm in. Form small circle at center of forehead with tip of right index.

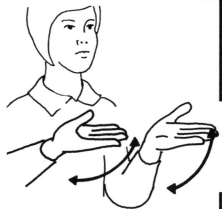

serve

Open B both hands, palms up, tips out. Swing to left and back.

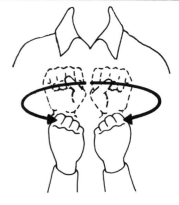

set (noun)

S shape both hands, palms out, thumbs touching. Circle out and around, ending with little fingers touching.

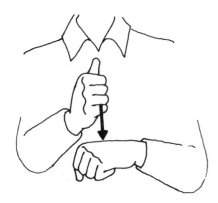

set (verb)

S shape LH knuckles down. A shape RH knuckles left, thumb extended. Place right A on left S.

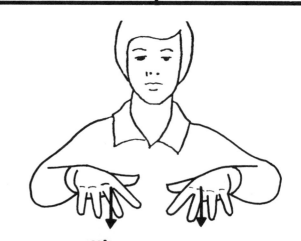

settle

Five shape both hands, palms down. Lower slowly.

several

Loose A shape RH palm up. Pass thumb along the fingers while opening them up.

sew

Nine shape both hands, palms facing, tips out. Make motion of stitching with needle and thread.

sex

Touch right temple, then right cheek, with right X.

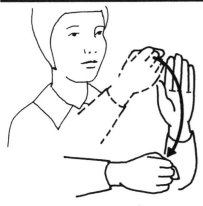

shade

LH open B palm out. S shape RH palm in. Pass right S down in front of left palm.

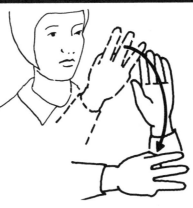

shadow

LH open B palm out. W shape RH palm in. Pass right W down in front of left palm.

shake

Five shape both hands, palms down. Shake.

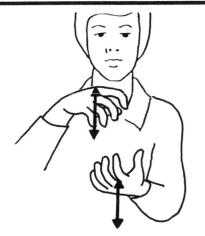

shake (alt.)

Claw shape both hands, right palm above left palm. Shake both hands up and down.

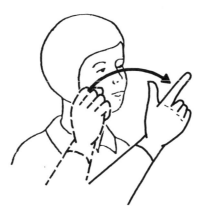

shall

S shape RH palm left. Place near right cheek and move out to L shape.

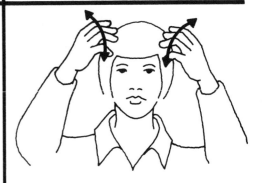

shampoo

Claw shape both hands. Place tips on head and rub back and forth, as if shampooing hair.

shape

A shape both hands. Curve downward, outlining shape of body.

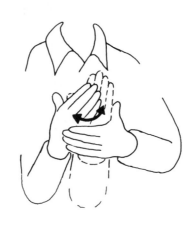

share

LH open B. Brush little finger side of right open B back and forth between left thumb and index finger.

shark

Open B both hands, left palm down, tips out; right palm left, tips up. Place RH between left middle and fourth fingers and move forward in swimming motion.

sharp

LH open B palm and tips down. Place right middle finger on back of LH and jerk up and out.

shave

Y shape RH palm left. Draw thumb down right cheek, as if shaving.

she

E shape RH knuckles left. Place on right cheek then move forward.

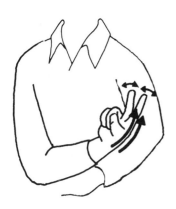

sheep

Clip together tips of right V, palm up, on left forearm (as if clipping wool). Repeat motion.

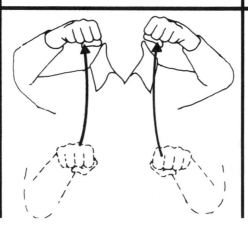

sheet

S shape both hands, knuckles down. Draw up from waist to shoulders, as if pulling up sheet.

shelf

Open B both hands held high, palms down, tips out. Hold together then move apart in straight line.

shell

S shape LH palm down. X shape RH palm up. Tap back of left S with back of right X.

shine

LH open B palm and tips down. Place right middle finger on back of LH then wiggle up in shimmering motion.

ship

LH open B palm up, tips out. Place right 3 in left palm and move forward twice.

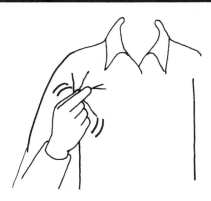

shirt

Grasp clothing on right upper chest with thumb and index finger of RH and tug slightly.

shiver

A shape both hands, thumbs up. Hold close to body and "shiver".

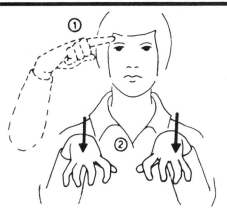

shock

Place right index finger on right temple. Then form claw shape both hands, palms down.

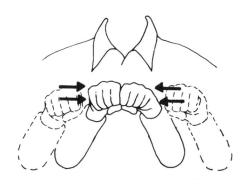

shoe

S shape both hands, palms down. Strike together several times.

shoot

L shape RH palm left, thumb up. Change to X shape, as if pulling trigger.

shop (noun)

S shape both hands, palms facing. Turn right S left and left S right to form box shape.

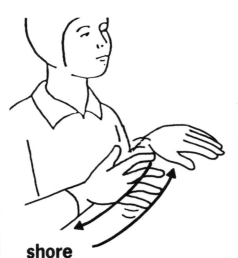

shop (verb)

LH open B palm up, tips out. Place back of right flat O on left palm and move out twice.

shore

LH open B palm down, tips out. RH open B palm down, tips left. Move RH up against, then back from, inside of LH while wiggling fingers.

short

H shape both hands, left palm right, tips out; right palm in, tips left. Rub right H back and forth on top of left H.

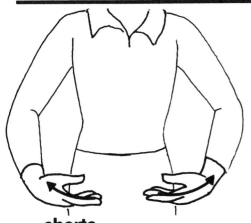
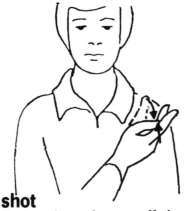
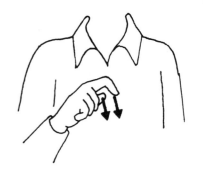

shorts

Open B both hands. Place fingertips on inside of thighs and move out, outlining bottom of shorts.

shot (hypodermic needle)

Place back of right V, thumb extended, on left upper arm. Push thumb against fingers, as if injecting needle.

should

X shape RH knuckles down. Move down. Repeat.

shoulder

Pat shoulder twice with RH open B.

shout

Claw shape RH palm and tips in. Hold in front of mouth, then raise up and out.

shovel

LH open B palm up, tips out. Dig back of right open B into left palm and turn over toward body.

show (noun)

S shape both hands, palms out. Alternately move back in circles, brushing down chest.

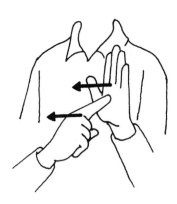

show (verb)

LH open B palm out, tips up. Place right index tip in middle of left palm and move both hands forward.

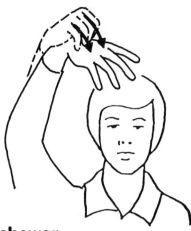

shower

S shape RH palm down. Hold above head and open into 5 shape. Repeat motion.

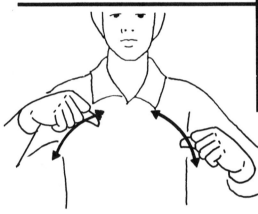

show off

A shape both hands, thumbs extended. Alternately punch upper chest with thumbs.

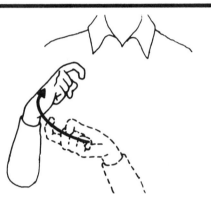

shrimp

X shape RH palm up. Circle up and turn palm down.

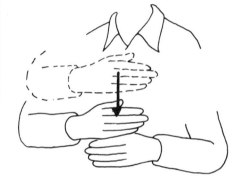

shut

B shape both hands, palms in, left tips right, right tips left. Bring little finger side of RH down on index side of LH.

shy

Place knuckles of right A on right cheek and twist forward while spreading fingers slightly.

sick

Five shape RH palm in. Tap forehead with middle finger.

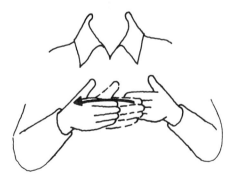

side

Open B both hands, palms in, left tips right, right tips left. Place RH on back of LH and slide to right.

sigh

Place thumb side of right S against chest. Open fingers into cupped 5 shape then close again into S shape.

sight

Place right S between the eyes and left S on little finger of right S. Draw apart into C shapes.

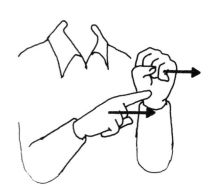

sign (noun)

S shape LH palm out. Place right index on base of left thumb then move both hands forward.

sign (language)

One shape both hands, palms out. Alternately circle index fingers in toward body.

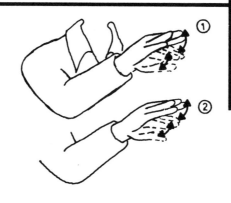

signal

RH flat O palm and tips out. Move forward, opening into 5 shape. Lower hand and repeat motion.

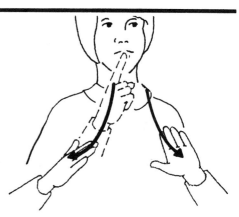

silent

Place right index on lips. Then form open B shapes palms facing, tips slanted up. Draw apart, ending with palms down.

silly

Y shape RH. Shake in front of nose.

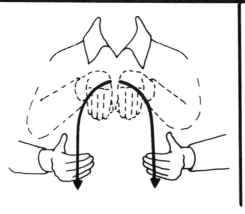

silo

Bent B both hands, palms and tips down, index fingers touching. Draw apart and down, outlining shape of silo.

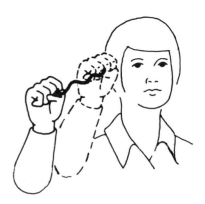

silver

Hold right S against right temple then shake out and down.

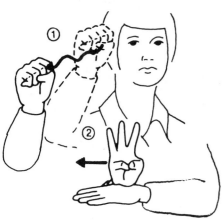

silverware

LH open B palm down, tips right. Hold right S against right temple then shake out and down. Change to W shape and slide across back of LH.

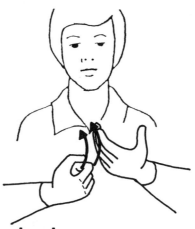

simple

Cupped LH palm up. Brush little finger side of right S up back of left fingers. Repeat motion.

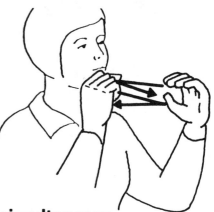

simultaneous communication

C shape LH palm right. S shape RH palm left. Alternately move back and forth at mouth.

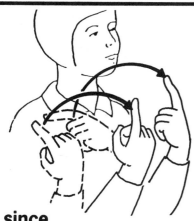

since

Touch right shoulder with tips of index fingers then arc both hands forward and out.

sing

LH open B palm up. Swing fingers of right open B above left forearm and palm in rhythmic motion.

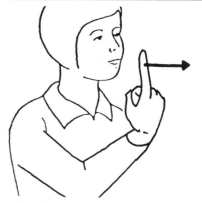

single

One shape RH palm in. Move forward with short, sharp movement.

sink

C shape LH palm and tips right, little finger side down. S shape RH. Place right arm in left C and slowly wiggle down (sink out of sight).

sip

Arc tips of right G up to mouth.

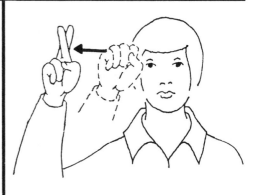

sir

Place right S, palm out, at right temple. Move forward, changing into R shape.

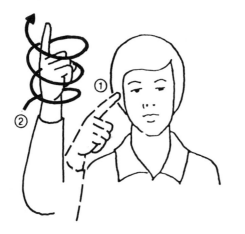

siren

Point to ear with right index then move finger upward in spiraling motion.

sister

One shape LH palm down, tip out. Place right thumb on right cheek. Change to 1 shape RH and place index fingers together.

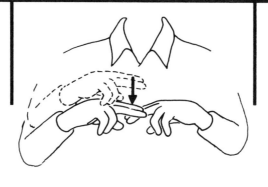

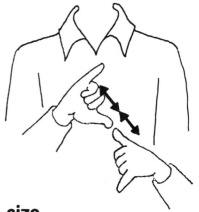

sister (alt.)

L shape both hands, thumbs up. Touch right cheek with right thumb then drop right L on index finger of left L.

sit

H shape both hands, palms down, left tips slanted right, right tips slanted left. Rest right H on left.

size

Y shape both hands, left palm in, right palm out. Place right Y above left Y and tap thumb tips together several times.

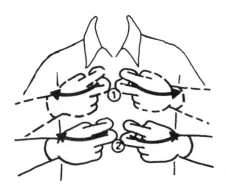

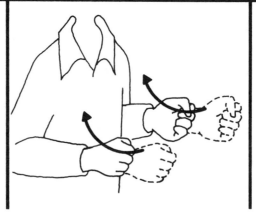

skeleton

Bent V both hands. Scratch outward across chest. Lower hands and repeat motion.

ski

S shape both hands, knuckles facing. Mime grasping and using ski poles.

skin

Pull at right cheek with thumb and index of right A.

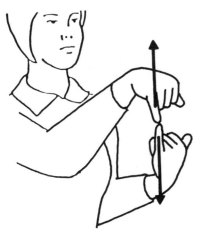

skinny

I shape both hands, right above left. Place little fingertips together then draw apart.

skip

LH open B palm and tips slanted right. Place middle finger of right K on base of left palm, then twist forward quickly so that index tip rests on fingers.

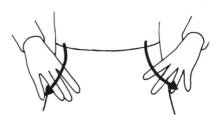

skirt

Five shape both hands, thumbs on waist. Brush down.

skunk

P shape RH palm down, index tip left. Place thumb on forehead and draw back over crown of head.

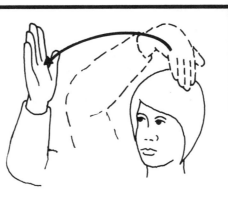

sky

Place RH open B, palm down, to left over head. Arc from left to right, ending with fingertips pointing to sky.

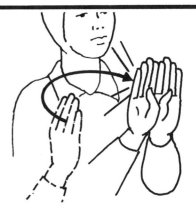

slam

B shape both hands, left palm out. Swing right B back against thumb of left B in forceful manner.

slap

One shape LH. Slap once with right open B.

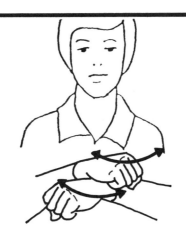

slave

S shape both hands, palms down. Cross at wrists then swing both hands back and forth.

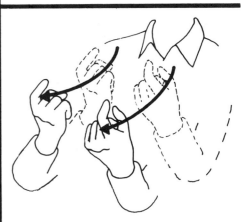

sled

X shape both hands, palms up. Move slightly down and out (indicating runners).

sleep

Draw open fingers of RH down over face, ending in flat O.

sleeve

Grasp upper left arm with right hand and slide down to left wrist.

sleigh

X shape both hands, palms in, tips up. Arc outward ending with palms up and draw back to body.

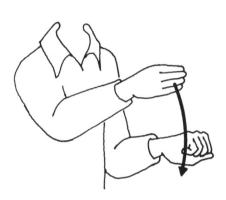

slice

S shape LH palm down. B shape RH palm left, tips out. Move RH down past left in slicing motion.

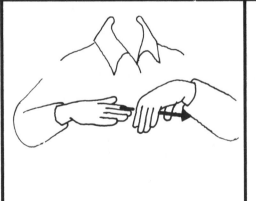

slide

B shape RH palm down held at shoulder. Bring down in sweeping movement.

slip (clothing)

One shape LH. C shape RH. Drop right C down around left index.

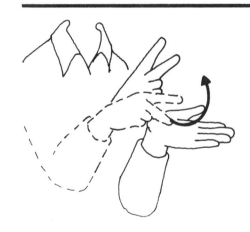

slip (verb)

LH open B palm up, tips out. Place middle finger of right P in left palm and slip forward and up.

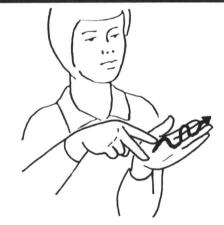

slipper

C shape LH palm down. RH open B palm down, tips left. Slide RH under left palm.

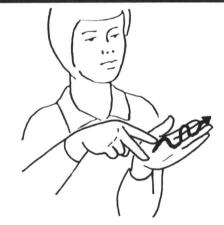

slippery

LH open B palm up. Move tips of right V in wavy motion across left palm.

sliver/splinter

One shape LH. Jab down side of left index with tip of bent right index.

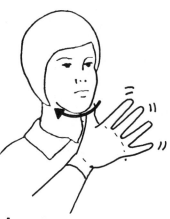

sloppy

Place thumb of 5 shape RH under chin and move to right while fluttering fingers.

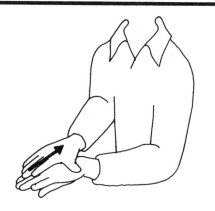

slow

Draw palm of RH slowly up back of LH.

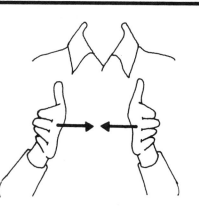

small

Open B both hands, palms facing, tips out. Draw close together.

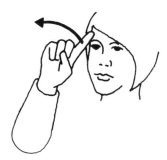

smart

Place right index on right temple then move out quickly.

smell

RH open B palm up, tips left. Hold under nose and brush upward.

smile

L shape both hands. Place index fingers at sides of mouth and move up to cheeks.

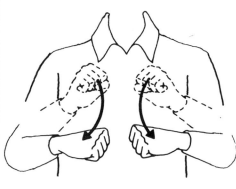

smock

Place thumbs of S shape hands on upper chest then swing down and out.

337

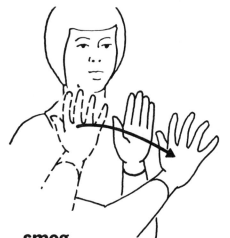

smog

LH open B palm out. Five shape RH palm in. Wiggle tips of RH past left palm, moving from right to left.

smoke

Cupped 5 shape both hands, left palm up, tips slanted right. Place tips of RH in left palm then move up in spiraling motion.

smoke (cigarette)

Tap lips with tips of V shape RH palm in.

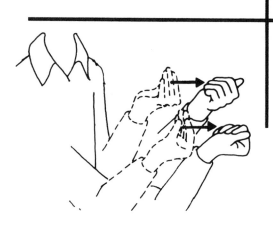

smooth

Flat O both hands, palms and tips up. Move forward while changing into A shapes.

snack

LH open B palm up, tips out. Place thumb and index tips of right F in left palm, then raise to mouth.

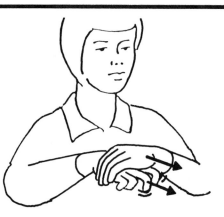

snail

Place cupped LH over V shape RH palm down. Move both hands forward, wiggling fingers of right V.

snake

Place back of bent V under chin then circle forward.

snap

Snap right thumb and middle finger.

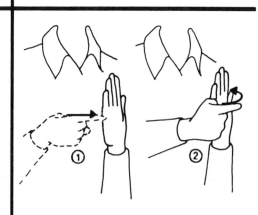

sneak

LH open B palm right. Slide right index finger past left little finger then around back of LH.

338

sneeze

Hold right index under nose and bob head.

sniff

Place right X against nose and sniff.

snob

Extend index and little finger of RH. Brush up tip of nose with tip of right index.

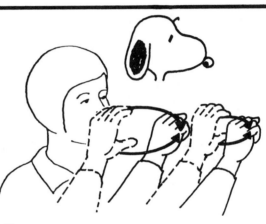

Snoopy

C shape RH palm left. Place at nose and move out into S shape. Then open and close hands once again, outlining shape of Snoopy's nose.

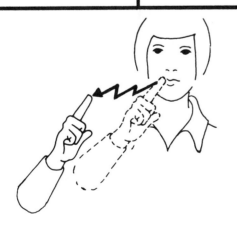

snore

Place right index against mouth, then move out in a zigzag motion.

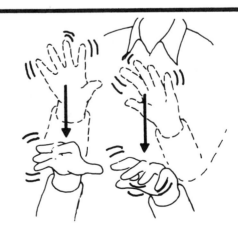

snow

Five shape both hands, palms down. Wiggle fingers while moving down slowly.

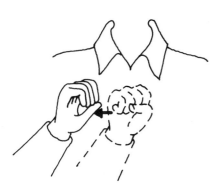

so
Fingerspell S-O in quick succession as if one movement.

soak
Place index finger of right W on chin. Then place back of RH in left palm and tap fingertips together several times.

soap
Open B both hands, left palm up, tips out; right palm in, tips down. Draw right fingers backward across left palm ending in A shape.

soccer
S shape LH palm down. Hit base of left wrist with index side of right B.

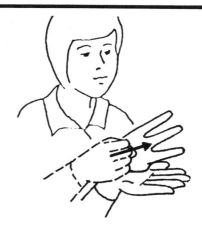

social work
LH open B palm up, tips out. Put little finger side of right S in left palm then change to W shape.

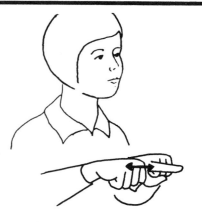

sock
S shape RH palm down. Brush back and forth along side of left index held tip out, palm down.

socket
LH open B palm right, tips up. V shape RH palm down. Jab tips of right V in middle of left palm.

soda
C shape LH palm and tips right, little finger side down. Place RH in left C, tips down, then pull up and out fluttering fingers.

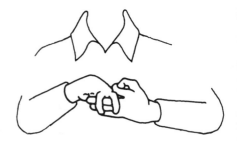

sofa
F shape LH palm in. Hang right V over left middle finger.

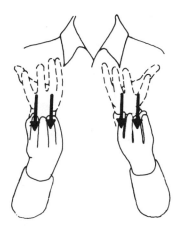

soft

Claw shape both hands, palms up. Lower into flat O shapes palms up. Repeat.

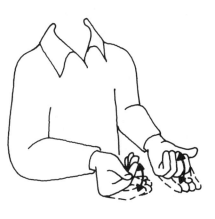

soil

Loose flat O both hands, palms up. Rub finger and thumb tips together several times.

soldier

S shape both hands, palms in. Place right S on left upper chest and left S just underneath as if holding a rifle.

solid

LH open B palm down. Hit little finger side of right bent V against back of LH.

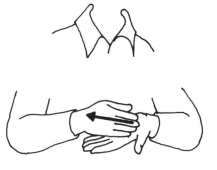

some

LH open B palm up. Draw little finger side of right open B across left palm.

somersault

Place tips of right V in left palm, lift up into a bent V, circle around, and land tips back in center of left palm.

sometimes

LH open B palm right, tips out. Place right index tip in center of left palm and slowly strike upward. Repeat motion.

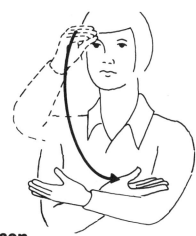

son

Place thumb side of right flat O on forehead. Arc down into crook of left elbow, opening into open B shape.

song

LH open B palm up, tips out. Swing right S above left palm and forearm in rhythmic motion.

soon

LH open B palm right, tips up. Place side of right S in left palm and make a one-quarter turn forward.

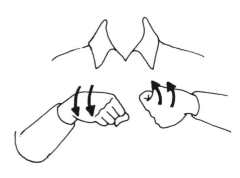

sore

S shape both hands, palms down. Twist in opposite directions while moving toward each other. Repeat motion.

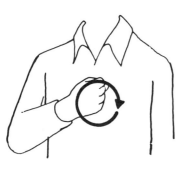

sorry

Circle right S on chest.

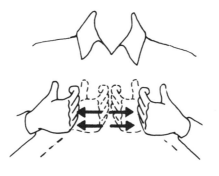

sort

Bent B both hands, palms and tips in, fingers back to back. Draw apart.

sound

Tap right ear with right S.

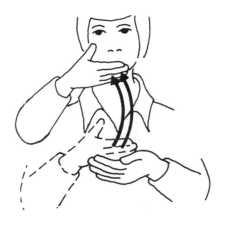

soup

Place back of RH in left palm, then move up to mouth as if drinking soup. Repeat motion.

sour

Place right index finger on chin, palm left. Twist so that palm faces in.

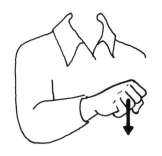

south
S shape RH. Lower in front of body.

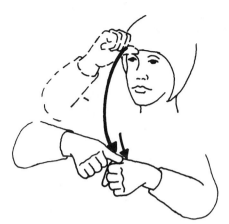

souvenir
S shape LH palm right. A shape RH. Place right thumb on forehead then on left S and tap left thumb once or twice.

space
S shape both hands, knuckles down, fingers touching. Circle back to body and touch again.

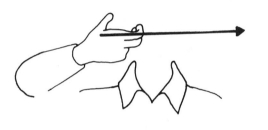

spaceship
H shape RH palm in, tips left, thumb extended. Bend finger and move swiftly to the left.

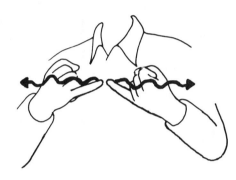

spaghetti
I shape both hands, palms in, tips touching. Wiggle away from each other.

spank
Strike palm of right open B against palm of left open B.

spark
One shape LH, S shape RH. Hold together, then flick right index finger up twice.

sparrow
S shape RH. Change to G shape, then place on chin and snap index and thumb together twice.

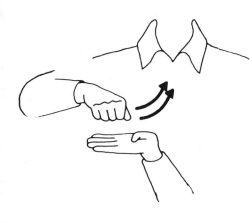

spatula

LH open B palm up, tips slanted right. A shape RH palm down. Dip RH over left palm twice.

speak

Four shape RH palm left. Move in and out from mouth.

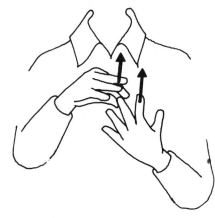

special

Five shape LH palm in. Grasp middle finger with right thumb and index and pull up.

speech

S shape RH. Change to bent V, palm in, and circle at mouth.

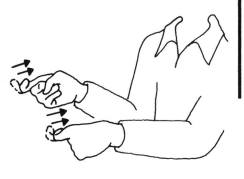

speed

X shape both hands, palms facing, little finger sides down, RH a little ahead of LH. Crook index fingers quickly twice.

spell

Five shape RH palm down, tips out. Wiggle fingers while moving hand to right. (Also used for *fingerspell*.)

spend

LH open B palm up, tips out. Place back of right flat O in left palm and lift out changing to A shape.

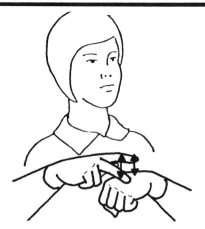

spice

S shape LH palm down. Tap back of left S with fingers of right V. (Sometimes the fingers of the V move alternately against back of left S.)

spider

Five shape both hands, palms down. Cross RH over LH, interlock little fingers, and wiggle all fingers while moving forward.

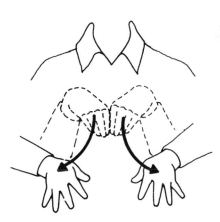

spill

Flat O both hands, palms and tips down, index fingers touching. Spread down into 5 shapes.

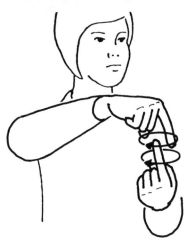

spin

Place right index finger, palm down, over left index finger. Rotate fingers quickly.

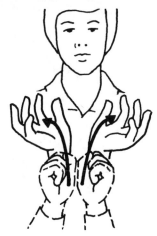

spinach

S shape both hands, palms facing, thumbs touching. Spread apart into claw shape hands, palms up.

spit

S shape RH knuckles left. Place on mouth then arc out ending in 1 shape tip out.

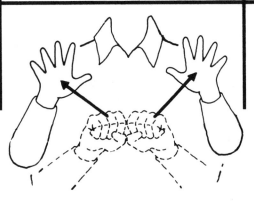

splash

S shape both hands, knuckles down, index fingers touching. Open up into 5 shapes while moving hands apart and up.

split

Hold LH up, palm in. Now split the middle and fourth fingers apart with little finger side of right open B, palm left, tips out.

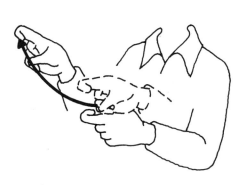

spoil

X shape both hands, little finger sides down. Place right X on top of left, then slide right X forward, arcing upward.

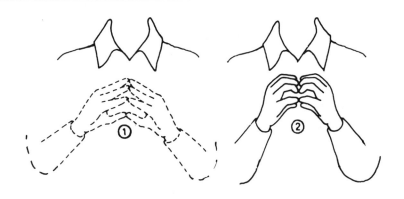

sponge

Place tips of open hands together and close as if squeezing sponge.

spooky

S shape both hands, palms out, held to left. Move down in wavy motion.

spool

S shape LH little finger side down. Circle right index over left S.

spoon

LH open B palm up. Place back of right H on left palm then raise to mouth, as if eating from spoon. Repeat motion.

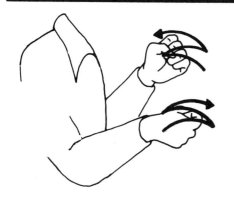

sport

S shape both hands, palms facing. Move back and forth alternately.

spot

F shape RH index finger curved inside thumb. Place on chest.

sprain

Bent V shape both hands, left palm in, right palm down. Twist left V down and right V up.

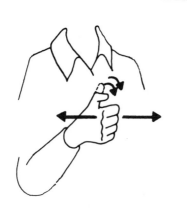

spray

A shape RH palm left, thumb extended. Move from left to right while pushing thumb down.

spread

Flat O shape both hands, palms down, thumb and index tips touching. Spread out into 5 shapes.

346

spring (season)

Push right flat O up through left C, opening into 5 shape. Repeat motion.

sprinkle

S shape RH. Open into 5 shape palm down, tips out. Repeat.

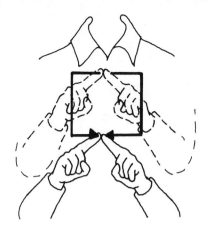

square

One shape both hands, palms out, index tips touching. Move apart, down, and back together, outlining shape of square. (Sometimes made with S handshapes.)

squash (noun)

C shape both hands, palms and tips out, index fingers touching. Swing right C away and up to the right.

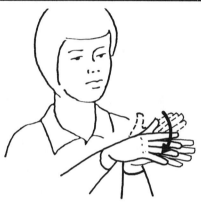

squash (verb)

LH open B palm up, tips out. Press right open B, tips left, in left palm and twist forward.

squeak

Grasp throat with right C and wiggle slightly.

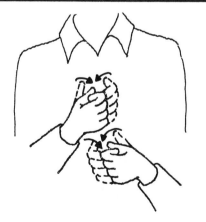

squeeze

S shape both hands, palms in, right held above left. Make squeezing motion with both hands.

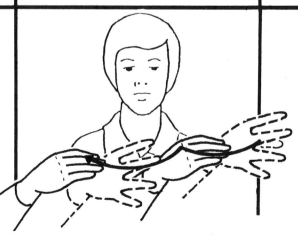

squid

Imitate movement of squid by opening and closing fingers of RH, palm left, moving from left to right.

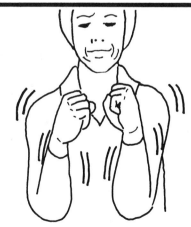

squirm

S shape both hands. Place arms against chest and move body in squirming motion.

squirrel

Bent V shape both hands, palms facing, wrists touching. Tap tips of V shapes together at mouth.

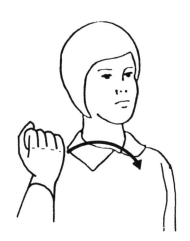

stab

Mime holding knife with S shape RH and plunging it into left upper chest.

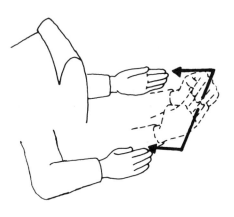

stable (noun)

Bent B both hands, palms in, tips opposite. Place right B inside left B. Now draw apart, straighten tips, and move back toward body.

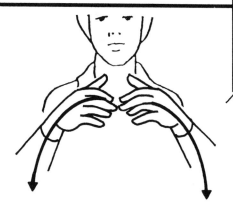

stack

Five shape both hands, palms down. Place close together then arc apart and down, outlining stack.

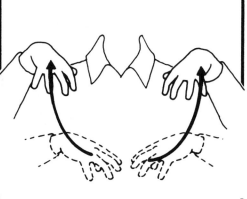

stadium

Five shape both hands, palms down, tips facing, fingers slightly curved. Move apart and up in semicircular motion.

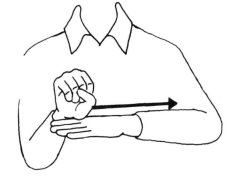

stage

LH open B palm down. Slide base of right S up left forearm, beginning at fingertips.

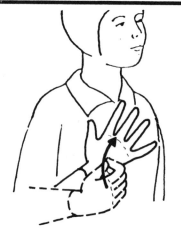

stain

RH flat O palm in. Place tips on chest then spread into 5 shape.

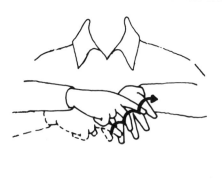

stair

Five shape LH palm down, tips out. "Walk" over back of left fingers with right middle and index fingers.

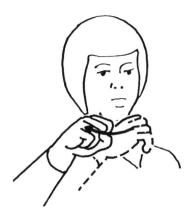

stale

S shape RH palm left. Place on left side of chin then slide over to the right side.

348

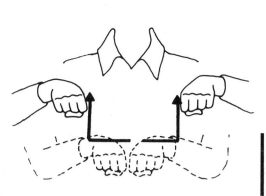

stall (noun)

S shape both hands, palms down, knuckles out. Place together, then move apart and up, outlining shape of stall.

stamp

LH open B palm up, tips out. Place tips of right H on lips then move down and place in left palm.

stand

LH open B palm up. Stand tips of right V on left palm.

staple

Open B both hands, left palm up, tips out; right palm down, tips left and slightly bent. Strike base of left palm with base of right.

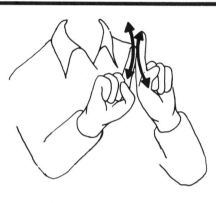

star

One shape both hands, palms out. Alternately strike index fingers upward against each other.

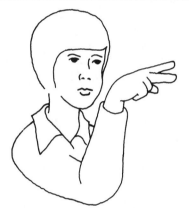

stare

V shape RH palm down, tips out. Hold in front of face.

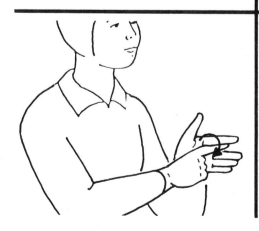

start

Five shape LH palm and tips slanted right. Place right index between left index and middle fingers and make half turn.

startle

S shape both hands. Hold at eyes then open into C shape suddenly.

starve

S shape RH palm in. Place on upper chest and slide down slowly.

349

state

LH open B palm right. Place thumb and index finger side of right S on left fingertips then arc down to heel.

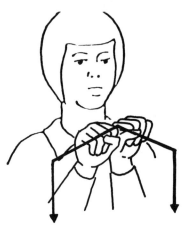

station

Place S shape hands together then draw apart and down, outlining shape of building.

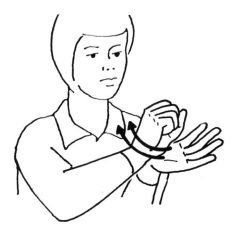

stationery

LH open B palm up, tips out. Brush base of right S across base of left palm toward body. Repeat motion.

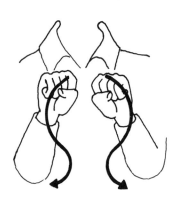

statue

S shape both hands. Move down, outlining shape of statue.

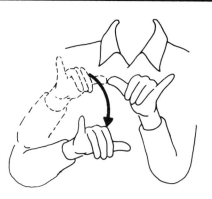

stay

Y shape both hands, palms down, thumbs touching. Arc RH forward.

steak

S shape LH palm down. Grasp with right thumb and index finger and shake slightly.

steal

Place right V palm down against left elbow. Pull back sharply toward wrist, ending in bent V.

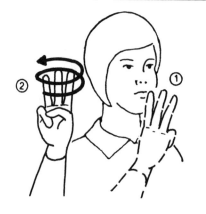

steam

Place index finger of W shape RH on chin then spiral upward.

steel

B shape LH tips slanted right. S shape RH. Strike tip of left index with base of right S, ending with RH palm out.

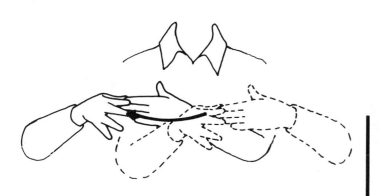

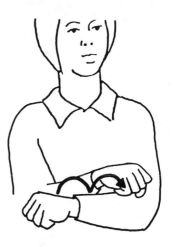

steer (verb)

LH open B palm in, tips right. Grasp tips with thumb and index finger of right F and pull to right.

stegosaurus

S shape both hands, palms down. Bounce right S up left forearm, starting at left wrist.

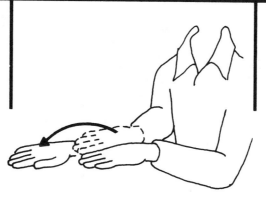

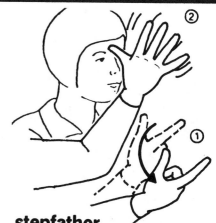

stem

One shape LH. Place right thumb and index at base of left index and slide up.

step

Open B both hands, palms down, tips out. Move right B forward.

stepfather

L shape RH palm left, index tip out. Flip over to palm up. Then place thumb of 5 shape RH on forehead and wiggle fingers.

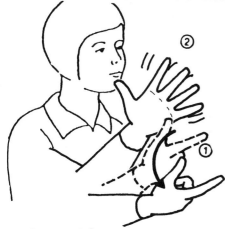

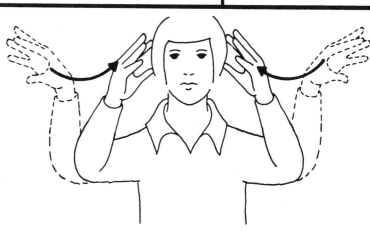

stepmother

L shape RH palm left, index tip out. Flip over to palm up. Then place thumb of 5 shape RH on chin and wiggle fingers.

stereo

Cupped 5 shape both hands, left palm left, right palm right. Twist in and place on ears.

stethoscope

Three shape RH palm in. Place tips on chest and take a deep breath.

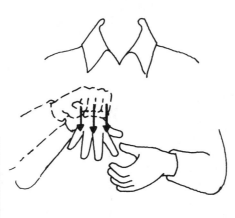

stew

C shape LH palm and tips right, little finger side down. Hold right S over left C and open into 5 shape several times.

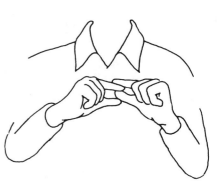

stick

G shape both hands, tips facing. Fit together.

stick (in)

Five shape LH palm down. Stick fingertips of right V down between left index and middle fingers.

stick (out)

Five shape LH palm down. Stick fingertips of right V up between left index and middle fingers.

sticky

Five shape both hands, palms out. Tap together thumb and middle fingertips several times.

still

Y shape RH palm down. Arc down then up, ending with palm out.

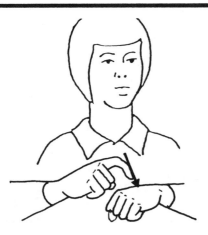

sting

S shape LH palm down. Tap back of LH with bent right index finger.

stink

Hold nose with thumb and index finger of RH.

stir

C shape LH palm and tips right, little finger side down. Stir right A over left C.

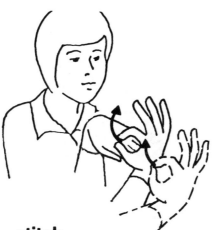

stitch

Mime stitching back of left hand with tips of F shape RH.

stocking

Place index fingers together palms down. Rub back and forth (as if knitting).

stomach

Pat stomach with palm of right open B.

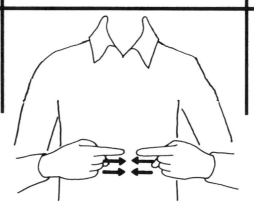

stomachache

One shape both hands, palms in, tips facing. Move back and forth toward one another in front of stomach.

stone

S shape both hands, left palm down, right palm up. Tap back of left S twice with back of right S.

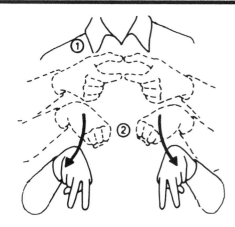

stool

Outline round seat of stool with thumbs and forefingers. Now drop into S shapes, then V shapes pointed down.

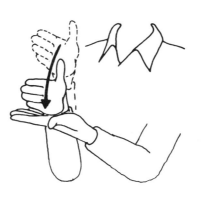

stop

LH open B palm up, tips out. Strike little finger side of right open B down on left palm.

store (noun)

Flat O shape both hands, tips down. Swing out twice.

353

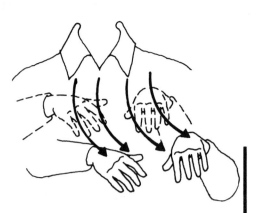

storm

Cupped 5 shape both hands, palms down. Sweep to the left. Repeat motion.

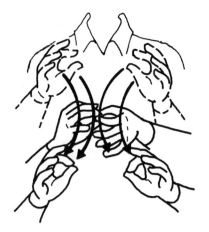

story

Open 9 shape both hands. Move down, link thumbs and index fingers, then pull apart, ending in 9 shapes. Repeat motion.

stove

S shape RH palm in. Place at mouth then twist wrist quickly so that palm faces down.

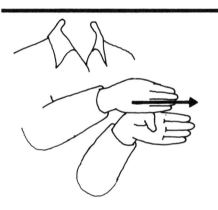

straight

B shape both hands, left palm right, right palm left, tips out. Move little finger side of right B straight out across index finger of left B.

strange

C shape RH. Place at right side of face and arc across eyes to lower left side of face.

straw

Cupped 5 shape LH palm up. Brush thumb side of right S up back of left fingers. Repeat motion.

straw (drinking)

G shape both hands, tips facing. Place right G on left G then raise right G to mouth.

strawberry

Nine shape RH. Place index and thumb on mouth and flick out.

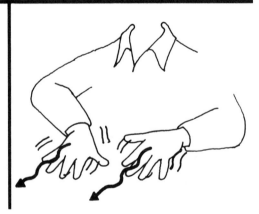

stream

Five shape both hands, palms down, tips out. Move forward in rippling motion.

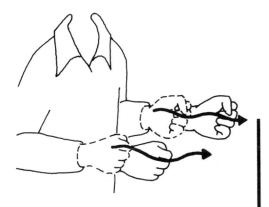

street

S shape both hands, palms facing, little finger sides down. Move forward.

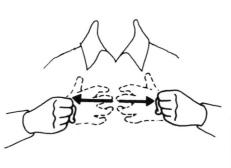

stretch

Claw shape both hands, palms in, tips close together. Pull apart into S shapes.

strike (hit)

LH open B palm right, tips up. Strike left palm with knuckles of right S.

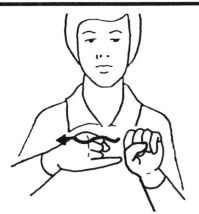

string

S shape LH palm out. Place tip of right I on left S then shake away to the right.

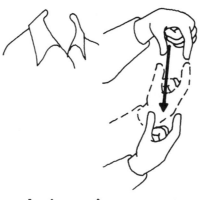

strip (noun)

G shape both hands, left tips down, right tips up. Place right G under left G, then drop down.

stripe

Four shape RH palm in, tips left. Draw across chest from left to right.

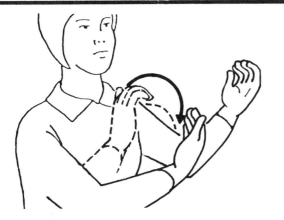

strong

Hold left forearm up. Outline shape of left bicep with the cupped RH.

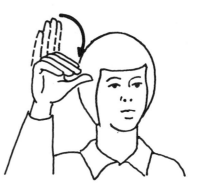

stubborn

Place thumb of right open B on right temple then flap fingers forward and down.

355

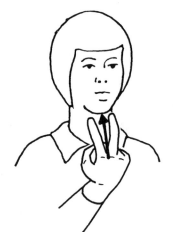

stuck

V shape RH palm in. Touch front of neck with tips of right V.

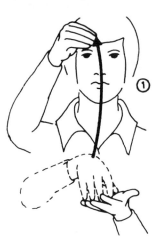
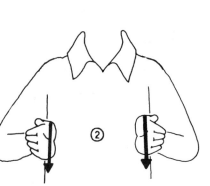

student

LH open B palm up, tips slanted right. Place right tips in left palm then lift up to forehead closing into flat O. Follow with agent marker.

study

LH open B palm up, tips out. Wiggle fingertips of RH, palm down, above left palm.

stuff (noun)

S shape RH palm up. Move out and to the right in small bouncing movements.

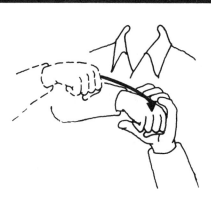

stuff (verb)

Stuff right S down into left C.

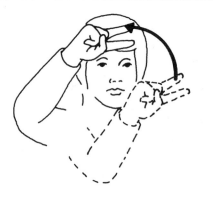

stupid

Slap back of V shape RH against middle of forehead.

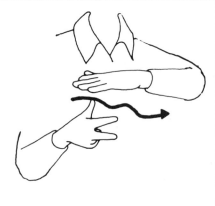

submarine

LH open B palm down. Three shape RH tips left. Move RH under LH in wavy motion.

substitute

S shape both hands, right behind left. Simultaneously arc right S under left and left S over right.

356

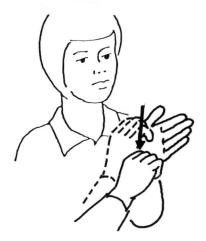

subtract

LH open B palm right, tips out.
Scratch fingertips of right C downward on left palm, ending in A shape RH.

subway

LH open B palm down, tips right.
One shape RH palm down, tip out.
Slide forward under left B.

success

One shape both hands, palms in.
Twist out, raise hands slightly, and twist out again.

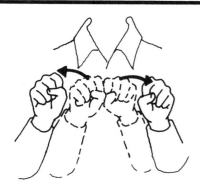

such

S shape both hands, knuckles out, index fingers touching. Draw up and apart.

suck

Hold RH palm down, then draw up to mouth, ending in flat O.

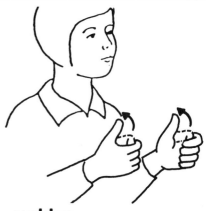

sudden

Flick thumbs out from under index fingers of both hands.

sugar

H shape RH palm in. Stroke tips down chin twice.

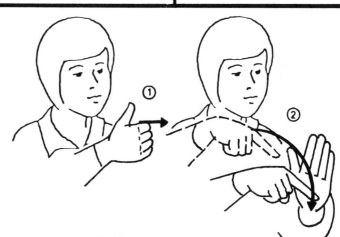

suicide

A shape RH palm left, thumb up.
Move forward. Then strike index finger down across left palm.

357

suit (clothes)

Y shape both hands, palms in, thumbs up. Place on chest and brush down to waist.

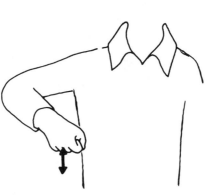

suitcase

Hold right arm down by side with fist clinched, as if carrying a heavy suitcase.

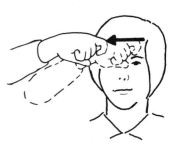

summer

X shape RH palm down, knuckles left. Draw across forehead from left to right

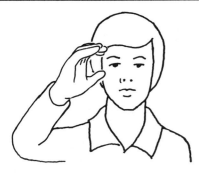

sun

Place right C against side of right eye.

sundae

C shape LH palm and tips right, little finger side down. A shape RH palm down, thumb extended. Circle over left C while spiraling upward.

Sunday

Open B both hands, palms out. Circle away from each other.

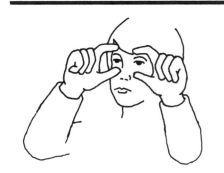

sunglasses

Circle eyes with index fingers and thumbs.

sunrise

LH open B palm down, tips right. C shape RH palm and tips left. Place right C against outer side of left wrist then move up slowly.

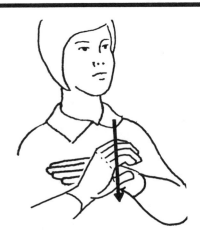

sunset

LH open B palm down, tips right. C shape RH palm and tips left. Place right C just above outer side of left wrist then lower slowly.

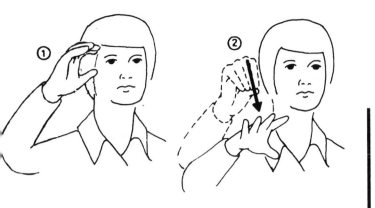

sunshine

Place right C at side of right eye.
Change into flat O palm down.
Then open into 5 shape palm
down.

super

LH open B palm down, tips right.
Place right S on back of LH then
arc RH upward in semicircle.

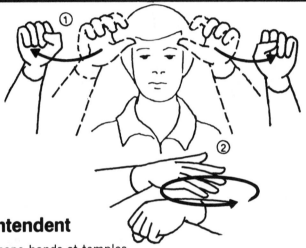

superintendent

Place C shape hands at temples
and move out into S shapes. Then
circle right open B, palm down,
over hand and forearm of left S,
palm down.

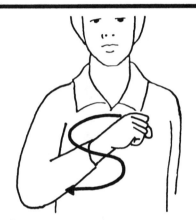

Superman

Draw large S on chest with S shape
RH, moving from upper left to
lower right.

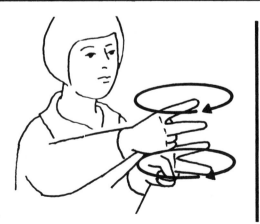

supervise

V shape both hands, tips out, right
on top of left. Move both hands in
horizontal clockwise circle.

supper

S shape RH palm in, little finger
side down. Rotate in small circle in
front of mouth.

suppose

Tap right temple gently with right little finger.

sure

One shape RH palm left. Place index finger on mouth then move forward.

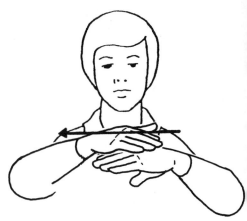

surface

Open B both hands, palms down. Rub right palm across back of LH.

surprise

Place index fingers and thumbs at edges of eyes. Snap open into L shapes.

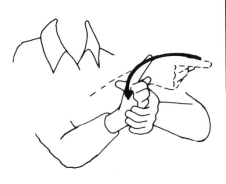

swallow

C shape LH palm and tips right, little finger side down. G shape RH. Hold RH over left C then draw back and down into left C.

swan

LH open B palm down, tips right. RH flat O palm down, tips slanted down and left. Place right elbow on back of left hand.

swat

Mime using fly swatter.

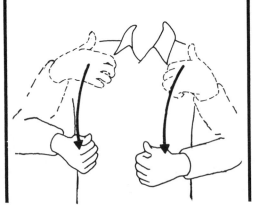

sweater

Claw shape both hands, palms in, tips in. Place on chest and move to waist, ending in A shapes.

sweep

Open B both hands, left palm up. Sweep little finger side of RH on left palm twice toward body.

sweet

RH open B palm in, tips up. Place tips on chin and brush down.

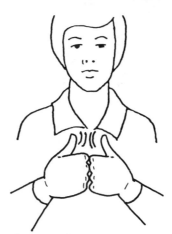

sweetheart

Place knuckles of hands together than wiggle thumbs toward one another.

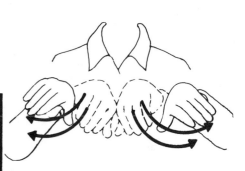

swim

Hands together palms down. Move forward and out (miming breast-stroke).

swing

Hook right V over left H, palms down. Swing both hands back and forth.

switch (verb)

One shape both hands, left palm up, tip out; right palm down, tip left. Place right index on left, then reverse positions.

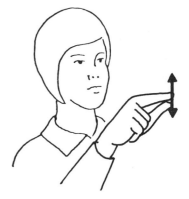

switch (noun)

Mime moving switch up and down with tips of right thumb and index finger.

swollen

Place claw hands over eyes, then move out, indicating swelling.

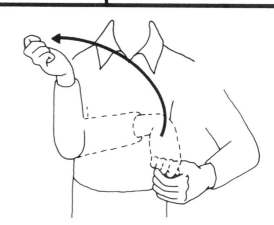

sword

Hold left C at waist, palm and tips right, little finger side down. Mime pulling sword out with right A and jab forward.

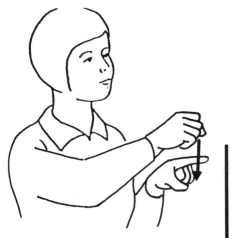

syllable

One shape LH palm down, tip out. Brush right S, palm left, down side of left index.

synagogue

LH open B palm down. Tap back of LH twice with base of right S, palm out.

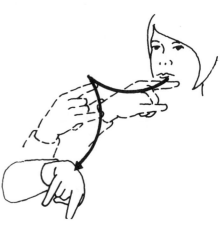

syrup

Extend right little and index fingers. Wipe chin with index and flip wrist out.

T

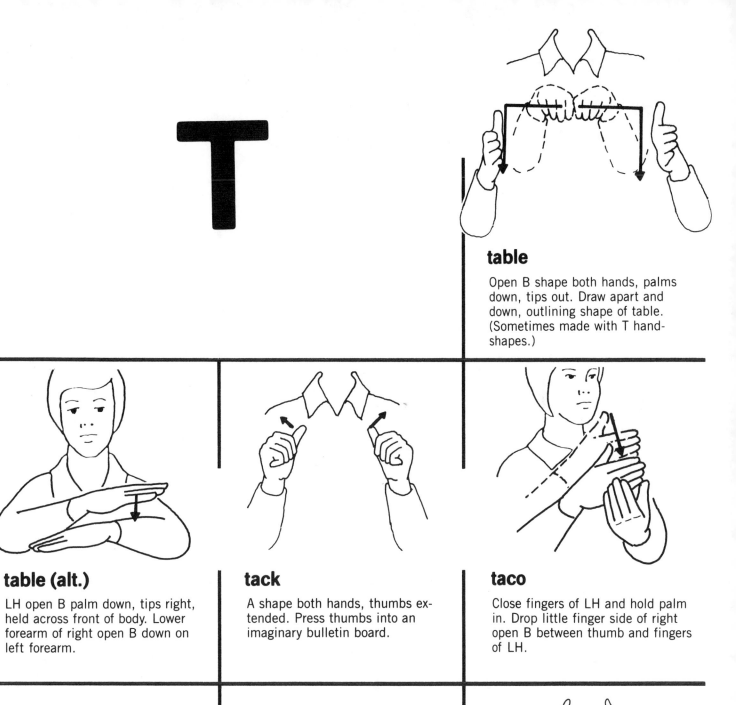

table

Open B shape both hands, palms down, tips out. Draw apart and down, outlining shape of table. (Sometimes made with T hand-shapes.)

table (alt.)

LH open B palm down, tips right, held across front of body. Lower forearm of right open B down on left forearm.

tack

A shape both hands, thumbs extended. Press thumbs into an imaginary bulletin board.

taco

Close fingers of LH and hold palm in. Drop little finger side of right open B between thumb and fingers of LH.

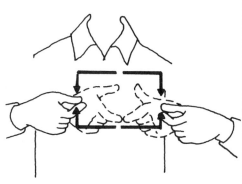

tag (card)

G shape both hands, palms in. Place tips on upper left chest, then draw apart, closing tips.

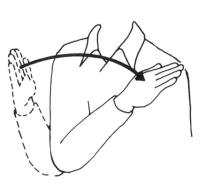

tag (game)

"Tag" left shoulder with right hand once.

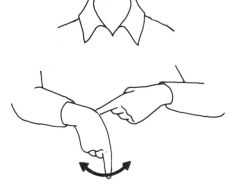

tail

One shape RH tip down. Place left index under right wrist then wag right hand from left to right.

 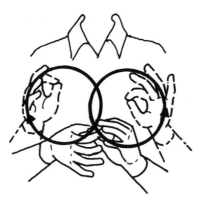 

take

Five shape RH palm down, fingers slightly curved. Draw up quickly, ending in fist.

tale

Open 9 shape both hands. Interlock thumbs and index fingers and pull apart in fluid, circular motion. Repeat.

talk

Place index tips on mouth, alternately moving back and forth.

 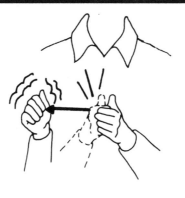 

tall

LH open B palm out, tips up. Run right index finger up left palm.

tambourine

LH open B palm right, tips out. Hit left palm with right A then shake RH away to the right.

tame

LH open B palm down, tips out. Stroke back of left hand with knuckles of right T twice toward body.

tampon

Tap right cheek with knuckles of right A twice. Form F shapes, tips touching, and draw apart, outlining shape of tampon.

tan

Place index finger of right T on right cheek and slide down.

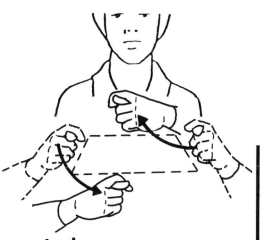

tank

T shape both hands, thumb tips out. Swing right T to left and left T to right, outlining square shape.

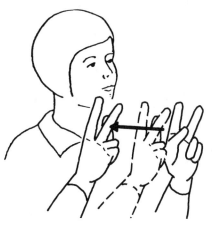

tank (vehicle)

K shape both hands, left palm right, right palm left. Place little finger side of right K on thumb of left K then draw right K back toward body.

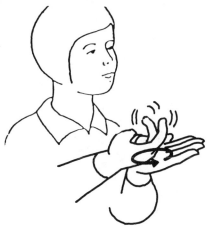

tantrum

LH open B palm up, tips out. Place back of right bent V in left palm, then move in counterclockwise circle while wiggling middle and index fingers.

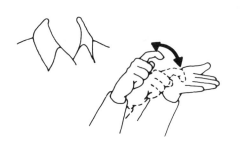

tap

LH open B palm up, tips out. Tap left palm with tip of right X.

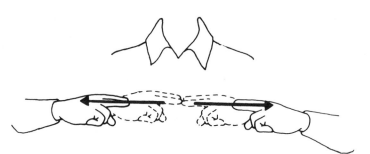

tape

H shape both hands, palms down, tips touching. Draw apart in straight line.

tape recorder

One shape both hands, tips down. Move in horizontal circles, RH moving clockwise, LH moving counterclockwise.

tarantula

Five shape RH palm in, fingers bent. Slowly "climb up" upper left arm with fingers of RH (miming a crawling tarantula).

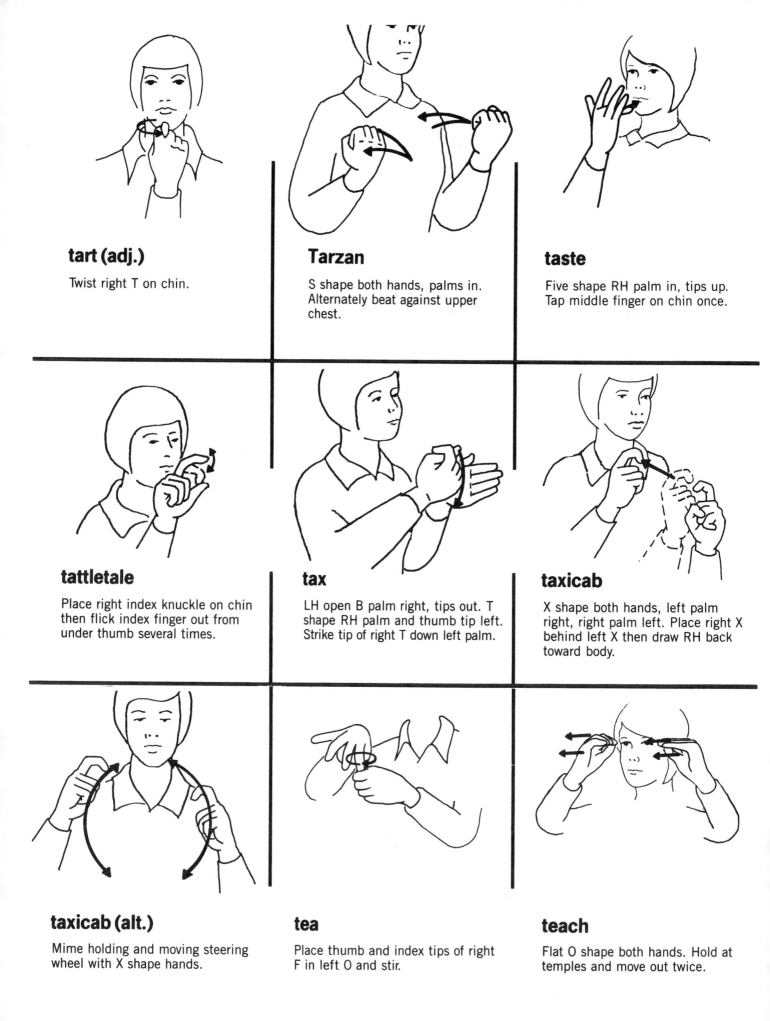

tart (adj.)

Twist right T on chin.

Tarzan

S shape both hands, palms in. Alternately beat against upper chest.

taste

Five shape RH palm in, tips up. Tap middle finger on chin once.

tattletale

Place right index knuckle on chin then flick index finger out from under thumb several times.

tax

LH open B palm right, tips out. T shape RH palm and thumb tip left. Strike tip of right T down left palm.

taxicab

X shape both hands, left palm right, right palm left. Place right X behind left X then draw RH back toward body.

taxicab (alt.)

Mime holding and moving steering wheel with X shape hands.

tea

Place thumb and index tips of right F in left O and stir.

teach

Flat O shape both hands. Hold at temples and move out twice.

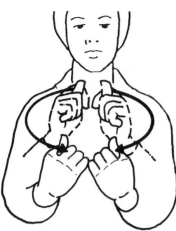

team

T shape both hands, palms out, held close together. Draw apart and around to front.

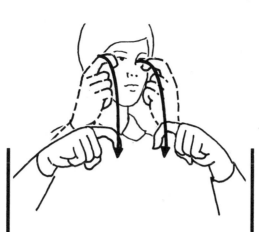

tear (noun)

Place tips of bent index fingers below eyes then move out and down.

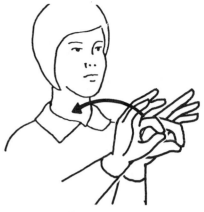

tear (verb)

F shape both hands, palms down, thumb and index tips touching. Arc right F back as if tearing paper.

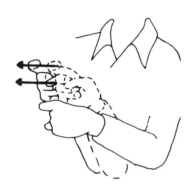

tease

X shape both hands, left palm right, right palm left, little finger sides down. Slide right X forward on left X twice.

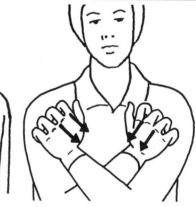

teddy bear

Tap upper left shoulder with T shape RH. Then cross wrists of claw hands and scratch upper chest twice.

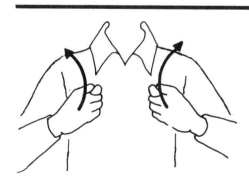

teenager

T shape both hands, palms in. Place knuckles on chest and brush upwards.

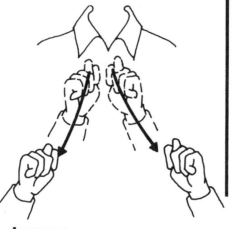

teepee

T shape both hands, palms facing, knuckles touching. Draw down and apart, outlining shape of teepee.

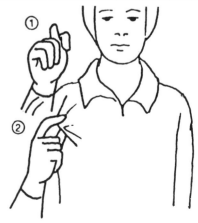

tee shirt

Form T with RH. Then grasp clothing on right upper chest with thumb and index finger of RH and tug slightly.

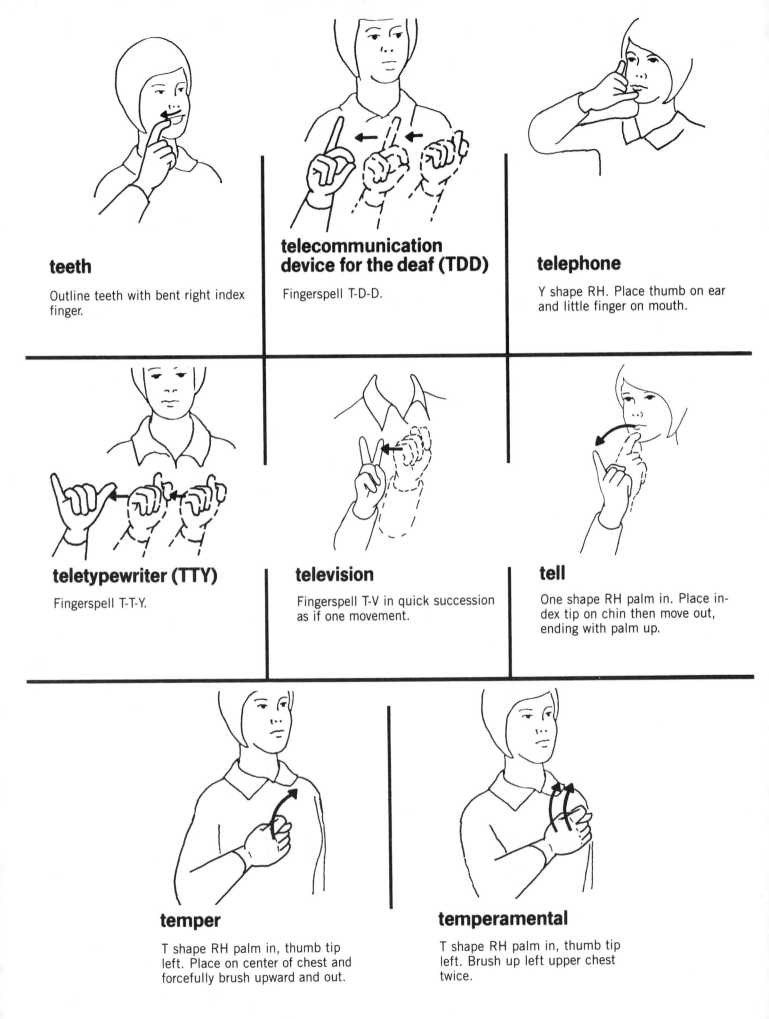

teeth

Outline teeth with bent right index finger.

telecommunication device for the deaf (TDD)

Fingerspell T-D-D.

telephone

Y shape RH. Place thumb on ear and little finger on mouth.

teletypewriter (TTY)

Fingerspell T-T-Y.

television

Fingerspell T-V in quick succession as if one movement.

tell

One shape RH palm in. Place index tip on chin then move out, ending with palm up.

temper

T shape RH palm in, thumb tip left. Place on center of chest and forcefully brush upward and out.

temperamental

T shape RH palm in, thumb tip left. Brush up left upper chest twice.

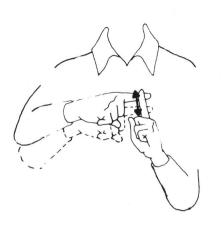

temperature

One shape both hands, left palm out, right palm down. Rub right index up and down back of left index.

temple

S shape LH palm down. Tap back of LH twice with base of right T.

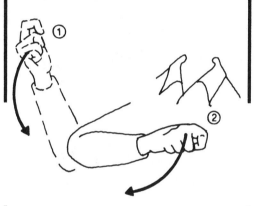

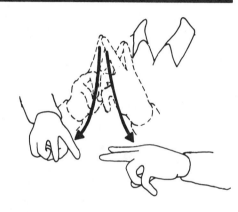

tempt

Hold left arm up, palm in, fingers closed. Tap elbow with right X.

tennis

Mime swinging tennis racket.

tent

V shape both hands, palms facing, tips touching. Draw apart, ending with palms down.

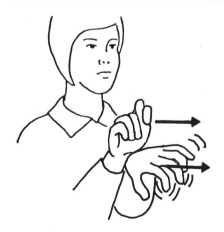

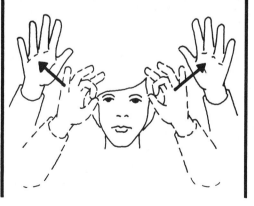

termite

Place base of right T on back of LH held palm down. Move both hands forward while wiggling LH fingers.

terrible

Eight shape both hands. Place on temples. Snap forward into 5 shapes, palms out.

terrific

Open B both hands, palms out, tips up. Bounce slightly forward several times.

369

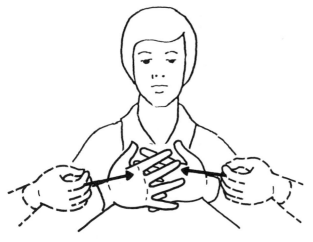

terrify

Flat O shape both hands, tips facing, held near chest. Move toward one another sharply while opening into 5 shapes, fingers overlapping.

test

X shape both hands, palms out. Crook and uncrook index fingers several times while moving hands downward.

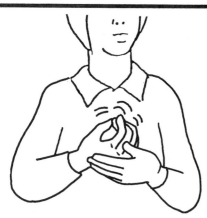

texture

Place back of RH in palm of LH, then rub RH fingers together several times.

than

Bent open B shape both hands, palms down. Slap down left fingertips with right fingertips.

thank (you)

RH open B palm in, tips up. Place tips on chin or lips. Move out as if throwing a kiss.

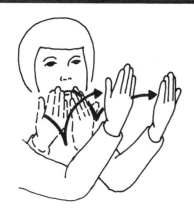

Thanksgiving

Open B both hands, palms in. Place tips on mouth, then arc out and down and up again.

that

Place knuckles of right Y on upturned left palm.

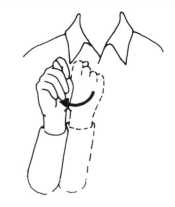

the

T shape RH palm in. Twist out.

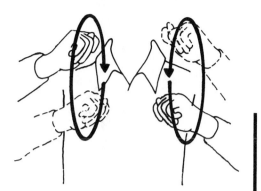

theater
T shape both hands. Alternately circle inward, brushing against chest.

their
RH open B palm up, tips out. Slide from left to right, twisting to R shape RH palm out.

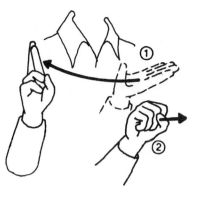

theirs
RH open B palm up, tips out. Slide from left to right, twisting to R shape RH palm out. Then form right S shape and move forward slightly.

them
RH open B palm up, tips out. Slide from left to right, twisting to M shape RH.

themselves
RH open B palm up, tips out. Slide from left to right, twisting to M shape RH. Then form right A, thumb up, and push forward twice.

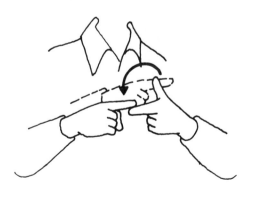

then
L shape LH thumb up, index tip out. Place right index behind left thumb then move to tip of left index.

therapy
T shape RH little finger side down. Place on left palm and move both hands up.

371

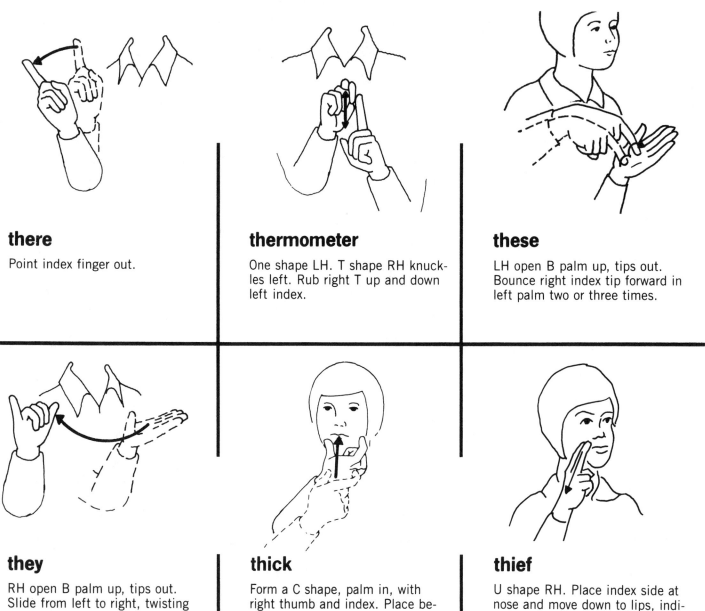

there
Point index finger out.

thermometer
One shape LH. T shape RH knuckles left. Rub right T up and down left index.

these
LH open B palm up, tips out. Bounce right index tip forward in left palm two or three times.

they
RH open B palm up, tips out. Slide from left to right, twisting into Y shape palm out.

thick
Form a C shape, palm in, with right thumb and index. Place below chin and move up a little above mouth then out.

thief
U shape RH. Place index side at nose and move down to lips, indicating mustache.

thigh
Tap upper right thigh with palm of T shape RH.

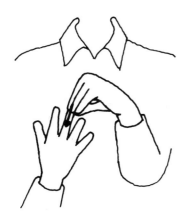

thimble

Mime pushing thimble on middle finger.

thin

Five shape RH palm in, tips left. Draw index finger and thumb down sides of mouth.

thing

RH open B palm up, tips out. Move out and to the right in small bouncing movements.

think

Place tip of index finger on forehead.

third

Three shape RH palm out. Twist to palm in, tips left.

thirsty

Point right index finger to throat and draw down.

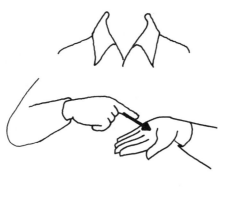

this

LH open B palm up, tips out. Tap LH with right index finger.

thorn

One shape LH. Place tips of right thumb and index on left index, then pull back to right, as if pulling thorn out.

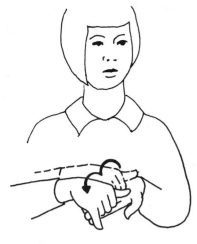

those

LH open B palm up, tips out. Tap knuckles of right Y on base of left palm, then on fingers.

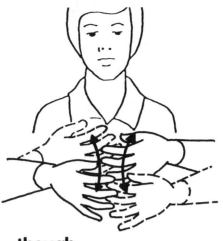

though

Open B shape both hands, palms in, fingers slightly spread. Alternately slap tips several times, moving hands forward and back.

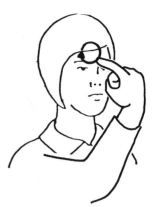

thoughtful

One shape RH palm in. Circle right index clockwise at center of forehead.

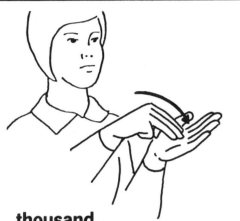

thousand

Place tips of right M in upturned left palm.

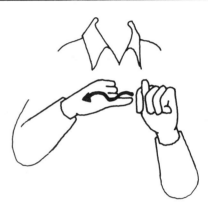

thread

T shape LH. Place tip of right little finger (other fingers closed) on base of left T, then draw away to right in wavy motion.

threaten

Tap left forearm sharply with right palm.

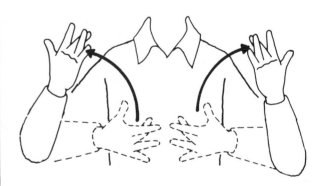

thrill

Five shape both hands, palms in, tips facing. Place tips of middle fingers on chest, then brush up and away from each other.

374

throat

G shape RH palm in. Place tips on throat and move down.

throne

Mime clasping arms of throne with claw shape hands, arms extended.

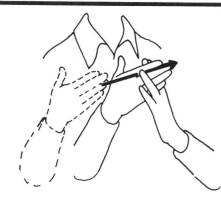

through

Five shape LH, open B shape RH. Pass right tips outward through left middle and fourth fingers.

throw

Hold right S over shoulder. Move forward into open handshape (as if throwing ball).

thumb

Extend thumb of A shape RH palm left.

thunder

S shape both hands. Draw left S back while moving right S forward. Repeat.

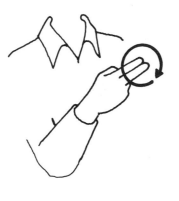

Thursday

Circle right H clockwise.

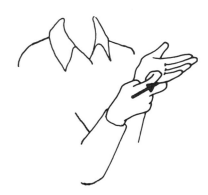

ticket

LH open B palm up, tips out. RH bent V palm in, knuckles left. Slide RH onto side of left palm.

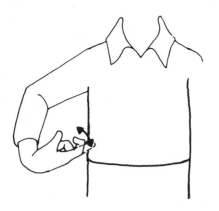

tickle

Make tickling motion at right side of waist with right index finger.

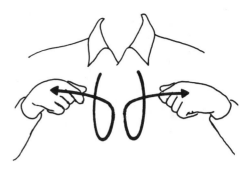

tie

Mime tying a knot and pulling it tight.

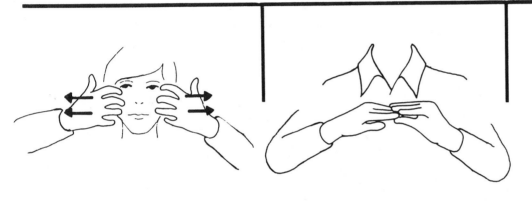

tiger

Claw shape both hands, palms in. Place tips on cheeks then move out. Repeat motion.

tight

RH open B palm down, tips left. Grasp with left fingers and hold tightly.

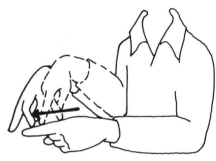

tightrope

One shape LH palm right, tip out. "Walk" along left index with right middle and index fingers.

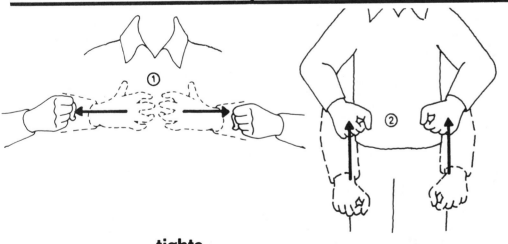

tights

Claw shape both hands, palms in, tips facing. Draw apart, closing into S shapes, then mime pulling on tights.

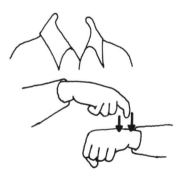

time

Tap back of left wrist with right index finger which is slightly bent.

time out

Open B shape both hands, left palm right, right tip left. Tap tips of LH twice with palm of RH.

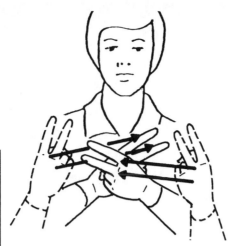

times (multiply)

V shape both hands, palms in. Brush back of RH against thumb of left V while moving hands in opposite directions. Repeat motion.

Tinkerbell

F shape RH palm down. Shake hand as if ringing bell.

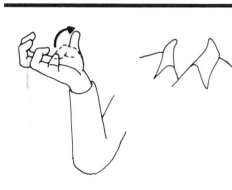

tiny

Claw shape RH palm up. Flick little finger with thumb.

tip (noun)

Tap tip of left index finger with right index finger.

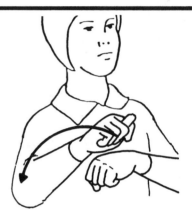

tip (verb)

S shape LH palm down. Place base of right T on back of LH then tip forward.

tiptoe

One shape both hands, palms in, tips down. Move forward alternately as if tiptoeing.

tire (noun)

T shape RH palm left. Rotate forward in circular motion.

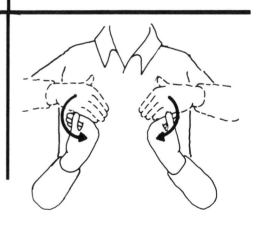

tired

Bent open B shape both hands, palms in. Place tips on chest then let hands drop, ending with little finger sides against chest.

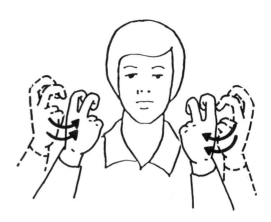

tissue
LH open B palm up, tips out. T shape RH palm down, knuckles left. Brush base of right T across base of left palm twice.

title
Bent V shape both hands, palms out, held out from body. Twist inward twice.

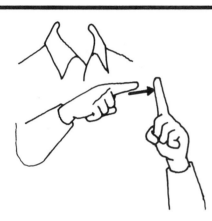

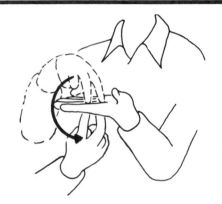

to
One shape both hands. Direct right index toward left and touch. (Note: As part of an infinitive, *to* is often fingerspelled.)

toad
LH open B held across front of body. V shape RH palm down, tips under thumb. Place on back of LH and move up forearm while flicking tips of V out several times.

toast
Place tips of right V in left palm. Circle under and touch back of LH.

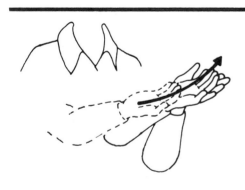

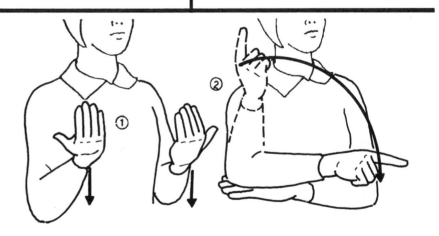

toboggan
Open B both hands, palms up, tips out. Slide RH forward on left palm.

today
Drop cupped hands in front of body with palms up. Then rest elbow of right D on back of LH which is held across front of body. Arc thumb and index of right D down to inside of left elbow.

378

toe

LH open B palm down, tips out. Place right T on left thumb then circle around to little finger.

together

T shape both hands, thumbs out. Bring together.

toilet

Shake right T from left to right several times.

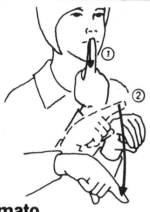

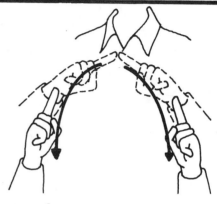

tomato

LH flat O palm and tips down. Brush right index down lips then down side of left flat O.

tomb

Place tips of index fingers together, palms facing. Draw apart and down, outlining shape of tomb.

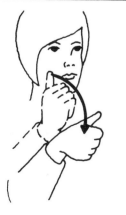

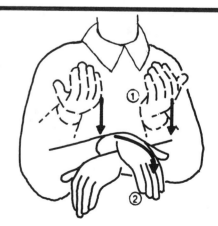

tomorrow

A shape RH. Place thumb side on right cheek and arc forward.

tongue

Point to tip of tongue with right index finger.

tonight

Drop cupped hands, palms up, in front of body. Then, with hands cupped palms down, drop RH down over left wrist.

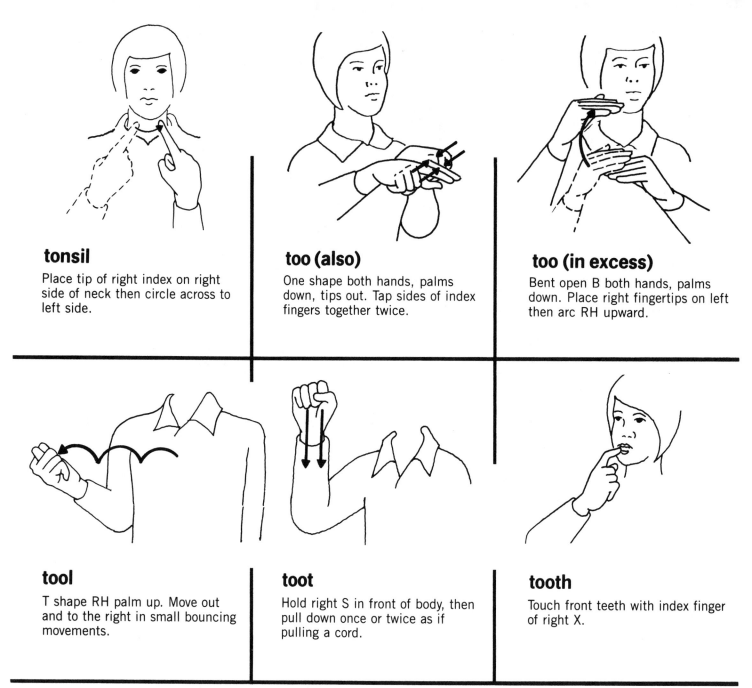

tonsil

Place tip of right index on right side of neck then circle across to left side.

too (also)

One shape both hands, palms down, tips out. Tap sides of index fingers together twice.

too (in excess)

Bent open B both hands, palms down. Place right fingertips on left then arc RH upward.

tool

T shape RH palm up. Move out and to the right in small bouncing movements.

toot

Hold right S in front of body, then pull down once or twice as if pulling a cord.

tooth

Touch front teeth with index finger of right X.

toothache

One shape both hands, palms in, tips facing. Move back and forth at lower side of right cheek.

toothbrush

Rub edge of right index finger back and forth over teeth.

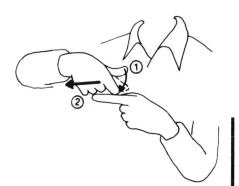

toothpaste

Mime spreading paste on tooth-brush.

top

B shape both hands, left palm right, tips up; right palm down, tips left. Rest right palm on left tips.

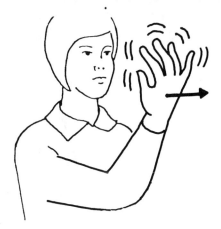

torch

Five shape RH palm in. Move forward while wiggling fingers.

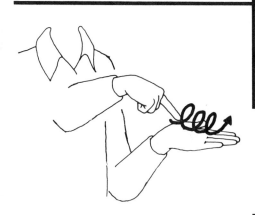

tornado

LH open B palm up, tips out. Hold tip of right index over base of left palm then move out over fingers in whirling motion.

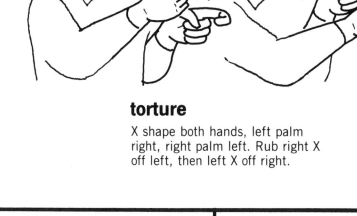

torture

X shape both hands, left palm right, right palm left. Rub right X off left, then left X off right.

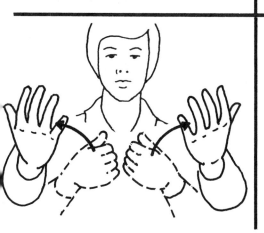

toss

A shape both hands, palms in, thumbs up. Toss apart into 5 shapes palms in.

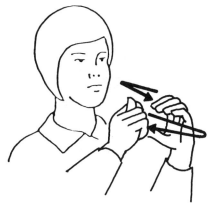

total communication

C shape LH palm right. T shape RH palm left. Alternately move back and forth in front of mouth.

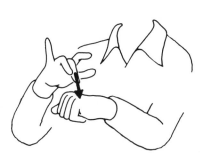

touch

A shape LH palm down. Touch back of LH with tip of right middle finger.

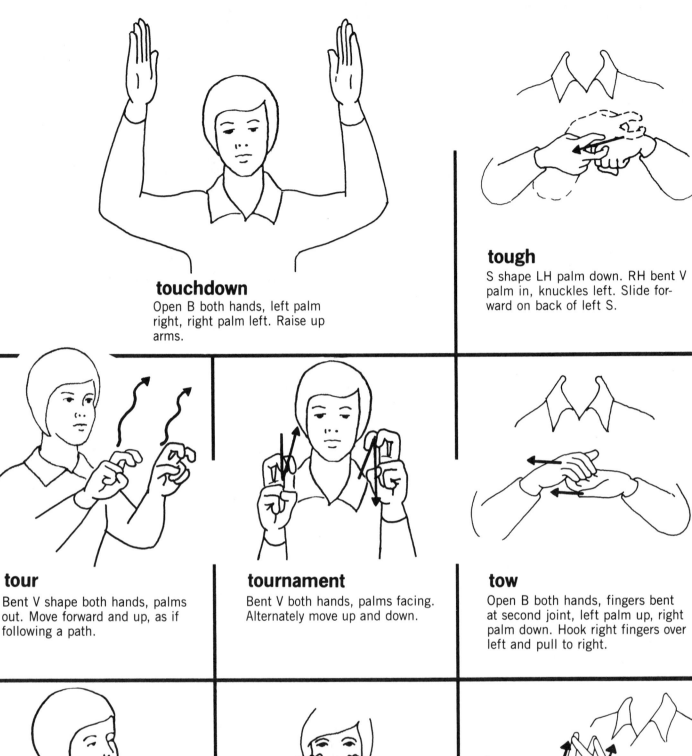

touchdown
Open B both hands, left palm right, right palm left. Raise up arms.

tough
S shape LH palm down. RH bent V palm in, knuckles left. Slide forward on back of left S.

tour
Bent V shape both hands, palms out. Move forward and up, as if following a path.

tournament
Bent V both hands, palms facing. Alternately move up and down.

tow
Open B both hands, fingers bent at second joint, left palm up, right palm down. Hook right fingers over left and pull to right.

toward
One shape LH palm out. Move right index toward center of left index but do not touch.

towel
Open B both hands, palms facing, tips up. Circle palms on cheeks.

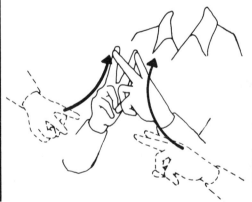

tower
V shape both hands, palms down, tips facing. Move up, ending with palms facing and tips touching.

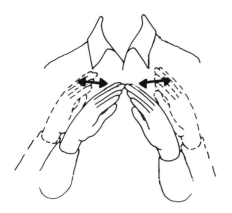

town

Open B both hands, palms facing, tips up. Tap tips together (indicating roofs of many buildings).

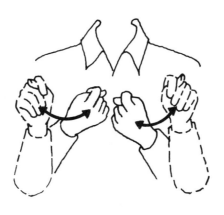

toy

T shape both hands. Swing in and out two or three times.

trace

LH open B palm right. Slide right T down left palm as if tracing something.

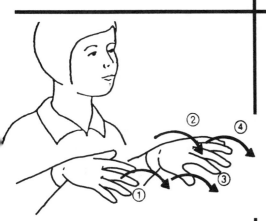

track

Five shape both hands, palms down. Alternately move out from body step by step.

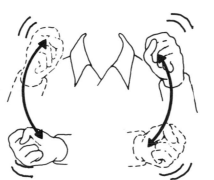

tractor

S shape both hands. Mime holding large steering wheel and turn in bouncy motions.

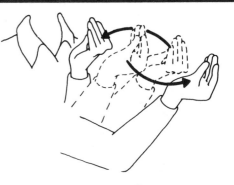

trade

Flat O both hands, palms up, left ahead of right. Reverse positions.

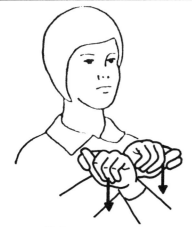

tradition

T shape both hands. Cross at wrists and move down.

traffic

Five shape both hands. Place hands together and move back and forth alternately in rapid succession.

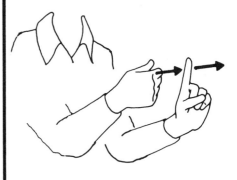

trail

One shape LH palm right. A shape RH palm left. Place RH behind left index then move both hands forward.

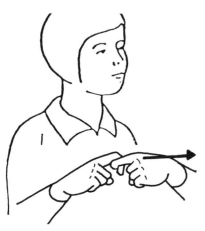

trailer
X shape both hands. Link index fingers and move to right or left.

train (noun)
H shape both hands, palms down, left tips out, right tips left. Rub right H back and forth on left H.

train (verb)
One shape LH palm down, tip out. Brush base of right T back and forth on left index.

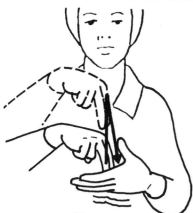

trampoline
LH open B palm up. Bounce tips of right V ("person") down and up in left palm while left palm ("trampoline") moves down and up.

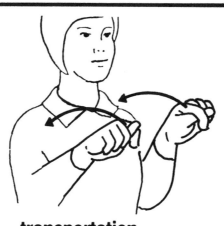

transportation
T shape both hands, palms down. Simultaneously arc from left to right.

trap
One shape LH palm out. Push index and middle fingers of right V around left index.

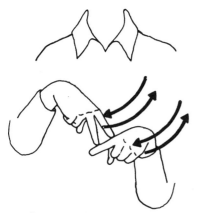

trapeze
One shape LH palm down, tip out. Place tips of right V on left index then swing both hands back and forth.

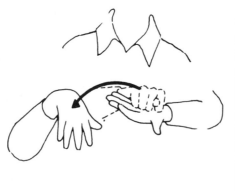

trash
LH open B palm up. Place palm of right T in left palm, lift out, then drop into 5 shape palm down.

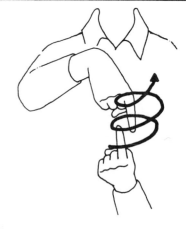

travel
One shape both hands, palms in, right tip down. Circle around one another while spiraling upward.

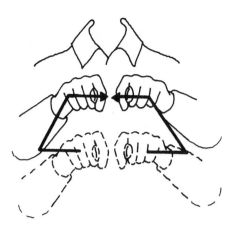

tray

T shape both hands, palms down, thumb tips out. Draw apart, back to body, then together, outlining shape of tray.

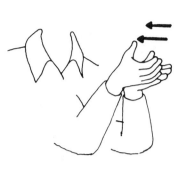

treasure

LH open B palm up, tips slanted right. Curved RH open B palm in. Scrape RH back over left palm twice.

treat (noun)

T shape both hands. Turn forward and up.

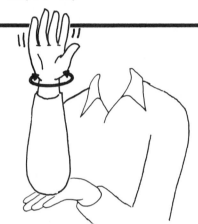

tree

Five shape RH palm left. Place right elbow on back of LH and shake RH rapidly.

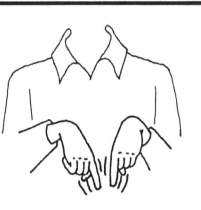

tremble

One shape both hands, palms and tips down. Hold close together and shake slightly.

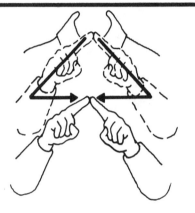

triangle

One shape both hands, palms out, tips touching. Outline shape of triangle. (Sometimes made with T handshapes.)

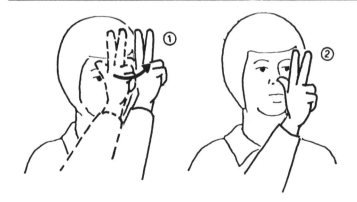

triceratops

Move thumb of 3 shape RH from right to left side of forehead. Then place on nose.

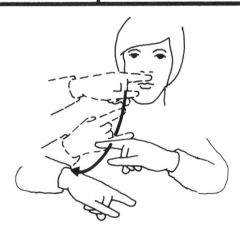

trick

Extend little and index fingers of both hands, palms down. Place right index under nose then pass under LH.

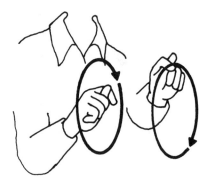

tricycle

T shape both hands. Circle alternately as if pedaling.

trim

H shape LH palm down, tips out. V shape RH palm down, tips left. Make snipping motion with right V on back of left H.

trip (noun)

RH bent V. Move forward in circular motion.

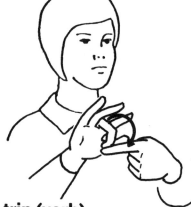

trip (verb)

One shape LH palm down. "Trip" middle fingertip over left index.

triple

LH open B palm up. Place middle fingertip of right 3 in left palm then brush inward and up.

troop

T shape both hands, RH slightly back of LH. Move forward in little dips.

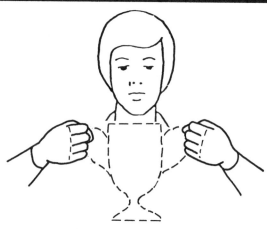

trophy

Hold S shape hands in front of body as if grasping handles of a trophy.

trouble

B shape both hands, palms slanted out. Alternately circle inward toward front of face.

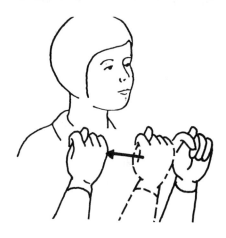

truck

T shape both hands, left palm right, right palm left. Place little finger side of right T on left thumb then draw RH back toward body.

truck (alt.)

Mime holding and moving steering wheel with T shape hands, palms facing.

true

Place right index on mouth then move straight out. Repeat.

trunk (elephant)

C shape RH palm left. Place at nose and curve down, outlining shape of elephant's trunk.

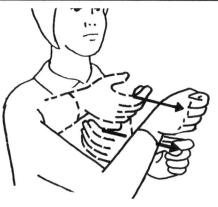

trust

Cupped shape both hands, right above left. Drop down and out, closing into S shapes (as if grabbing rope).

truth

LH open B palm up, tips out. Slide little finger side of right T across left palm.

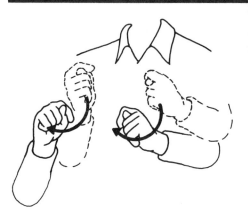

try

T shape both hands, palms facing. Move forward while arcing downward.

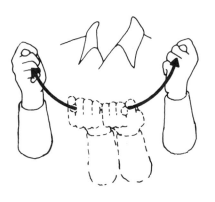

tub

T shape both hands, palms up, little fingers touching. Move apart and up, outlining shape of tub.

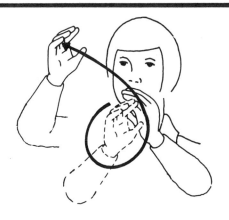

tuba

C shape both hands, left palm right, right palm left, left C held at mouth. Place right C against left; then circle out, under, and up again, outlining shape of tuba.

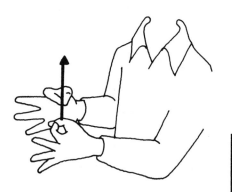

tube

F shape both hands, palms facing, tips out. Place right F on left then move up.

Tuesday

Move right T in small circle.

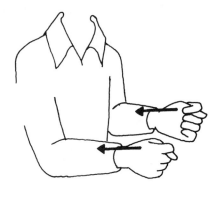

tug

T shape both hands, palms facing. Pull back to body.

tulip

Place right T at right side of nose then arc to left side.

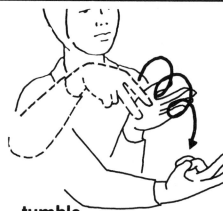

tumble

LH open B palm up. Place tips of right V in left palm then roll forward and down.

tuna

LH open B palm in, tips right. T shape RH palm left, knuckles out. Place left tips on right wrist, then move both hands forward, fluttering right T.

tunnel

Hold LH palm down, fingers slightly curved. Pass right T under and out.

turkey

Place back of right Q on tip of nose then shake down in front of chest.

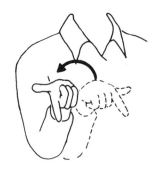

turn

L shape RH palm down. Turn so that palm faces up.

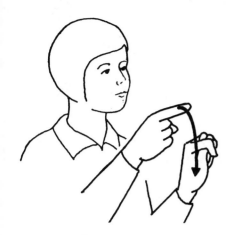

turnip

T shape LH palm out. Slice right index down against side of left T.

turtle

Place right A under curved LH. Extend thumb and wiggle.

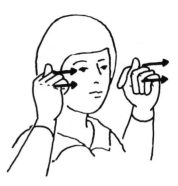

tutor

T shape both hands. Hold at temples and move out twice.

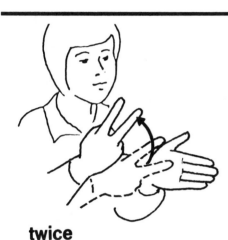

twice

Place middle fingertip of right V in upturned left palm. Brush RH toward body once.

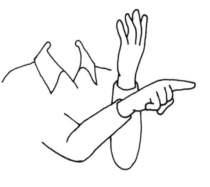

twig

Four shape LH palm in. One shape RH palm down, tip left. Place RH against left wrist.

twin

T shape RH palm left. Place at left side of chin then move to right.

twinkle

Snap right index finger and thumb at edge of right eye. Repeat.

twist

A shape both hands, palms down, thumbs facing. Twist in opposite directions.

type (kind)

Circle right T on upper left chest.

typewrite

Mime typing on typewriter.

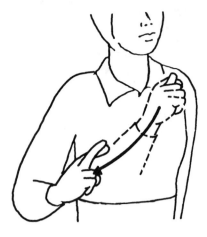

tyrannosaurus rex

Place right T on left shoulder then move down to right side of waist, changing to R shape.

U

ugly

X shape RH palm down. Draw across nose from left to right.

umbrella

Rest right S on left S and move RH up as if opening umbrella.

umpire

Open B shape LH palm down. Place base of U shape RH, palm down, on back of LH.

unbutton

Mime unbuttoning shirt or blouse with index fingers and thumbs.

uncle

U shape RH. Wiggle at right temple.

unconscious

Place right index on right side of forehead. Then drop hands down into cupped 5 shapes, palms down.

under

LH open B palm down. Pass right A, thumb extended, under left palm.

underline

LH open B palm right, tips out. Draw straight line under left palm with right index finger.

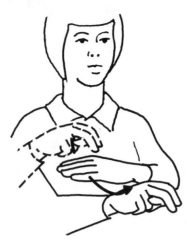

underneath

LH open B palm down. Pass N shape RH under left palm.

understand

S shape RH palm in. Place on or near right temple then snap index finger up.

underwear

C shape LH palm in, tips on chest. RH open B palm in, tips down. Slide RH into left C.

undress

Place tips of claw shape hands on chest then pull apart. Lower hands slightly and repeat motion.

unicorn

Place C shape RH on middle of forehead. Move out into S shape, indicating shape of horn.

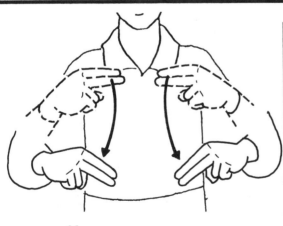

uniform

U shape both hands, palms in, tips facing. Place on upper chest then brush down.

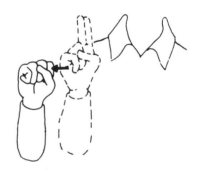

United States

Fingerspell U-S in quick succession as if one movement.

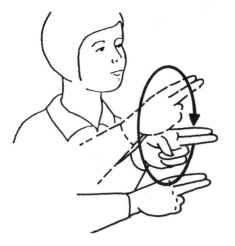

universe

U shape both hands, tips out, right on top of left. Circle right U forward and under left U, returning to original position.

unless

U shape LH palm in. Pull up tips of left U with thumb and index finger of RH.

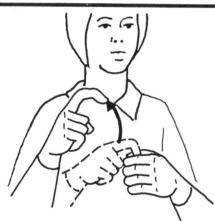

unlock

Pull tip of right X out from thumb and index finger of O shape LH.

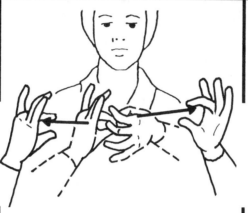

untie

Lock together middle fingers and thumbs of both hands then snap open and apart.

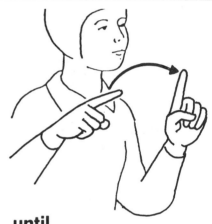

until

One shape both hands. Arc tip of right index over to tip of left index.

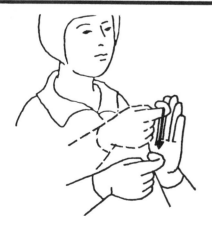

unzip

LH open B palm right, tips up. Slide knuckles of right X down left fingers and palm.

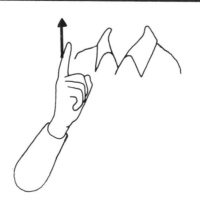

up

Point index finger up.

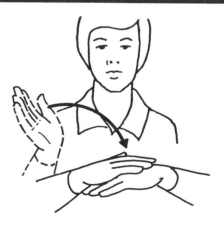

upon

Open B both hands, left palm down, right palm up. Arc RH down on top of LH.

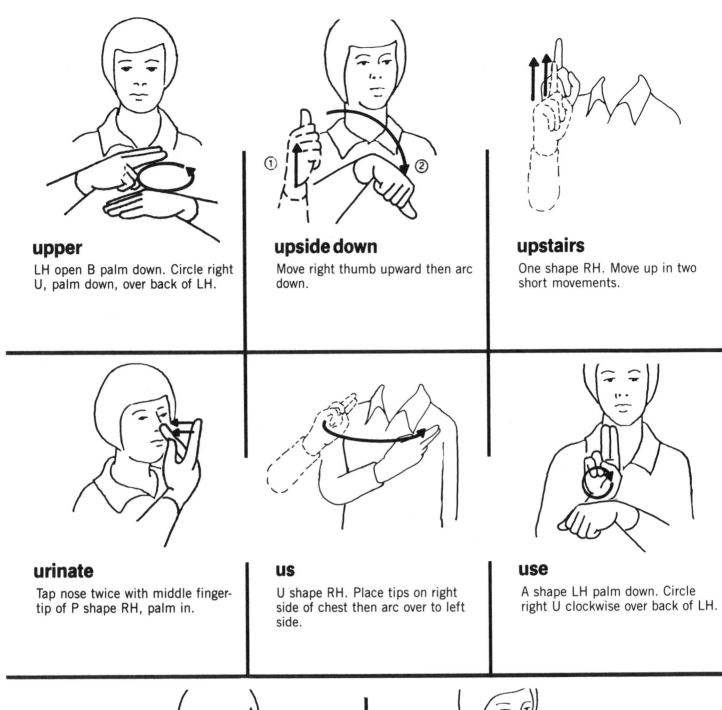

upper
LH open B palm down. Circle right U, palm down, over back of LH.

upside down
Move right thumb upward then arc down.

upstairs
One shape RH. Move up in two short movements.

urinate
Tap nose twice with middle finger-tip of P shape RH, palm in.

us
U shape RH. Place tips on right side of chest then arc over to left side.

use
A shape LH palm down. Circle right U clockwise over back of LH.

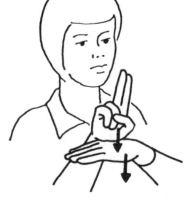

used to (accustomed to)
LH open B palm down. Place base of right U on back of LH then move both hands down.

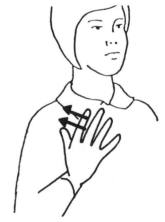

used to (did in the past)
Tap right shoulder with thumb tip of 5 shape RH, palm left.

usual

LH open B palm down. Drop base
of right U on back of left palm.

V

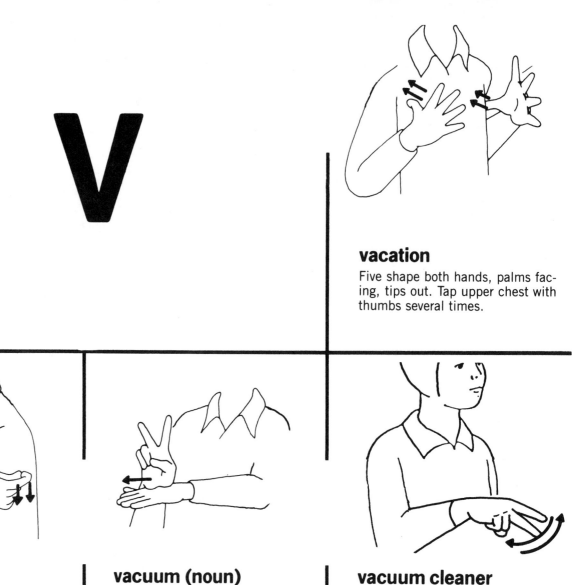

vacation
Five shape both hands, palms facing, tips out. Tap upper chest with thumbs several times.

vaccination
Scratch left upper arm with right thumb and index finger.

vacuum (noun)
LH open B palm down, tips out. Place base of right V on back of left B then slide forward.

vacuum cleaner
V shape RH palm down, tips out. Move back and forth, as if vacuuming.

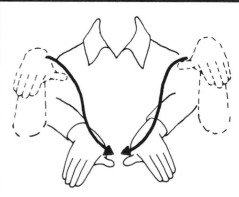

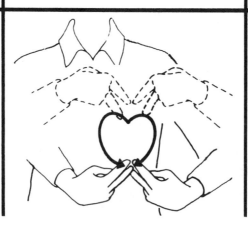

vagina (vulva)
Place index tips and thumb tips together with index tips pointing down.

valentine
Outline heart shape on left chest with tips of V shape hands.

valley
Open B both hands, palms down, tips out. Swoop down and level off, outlining shape of valley.

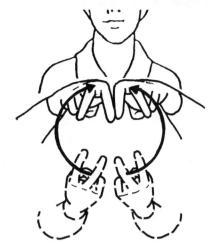

valuable

V shape both hands, palms up. Circle up and together, ending with palms down, index fingers touching.

vampire

Place tips of right bent V against side of neck.

van

V shape both hands, left palm right, right palm left. Place right V behind left V then draw RH back toward body.

vane

V shape RH palm left, tips out. Place left index on right wrist then move RH back and forth.

vanilla

LH open B palm down. Circle base of right V counterclockwise on back of LH.

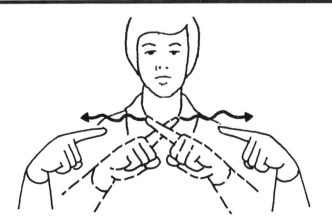

variety

One shape both hands. Cross index tips then pull apart with wiggling motion.

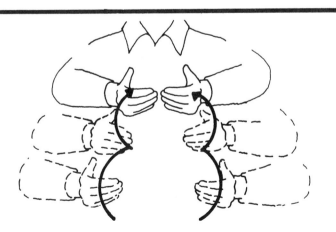

vase

Curved open B shape both hands, palms and tips facing. Move up, outlining shape of vase.

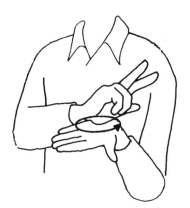

Vaseline

LH open B palm up. Circle base of right V counterclockwise in left palm.

veal

V shape LH. Grasp side with right thumb and index finger and shake.

vegetable

V shape RH. Touch right side of cheek with index finger then twist inward, ending with middle finger on cheek.

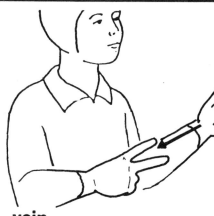

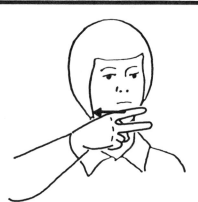

vein

Run tips of right V, palm down, up left forearm held palm up.

velvet

Place back of RH against upper right chest, then rub fingers together as if feeling velvet.

verb

V shape RH palm in, tips left. Slide across chin, moving from left to right.

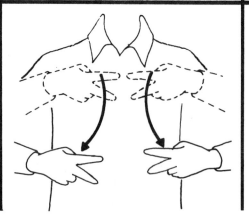

very

V shape both hands, palms facing. Place tips together and draw apart.

vest

V shape both hands, palms in, tips facing. Place on chest then move down and apart.

veterinarian

Fingerspell V-E-T.

vibration

Five shape both hands, palms down. Wiggle slightly.

videotape

LH open B palm right, tips up. Circle right V, then T, against palm of LH.

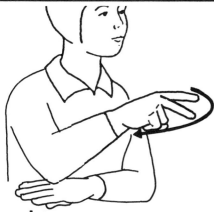

view

Place elbow of right V on back of LH, then move right V in scanning motion from left to right or right to left.

village

LH open B palm right, tips up. V shape RH, palm out. Tap hands together twice.

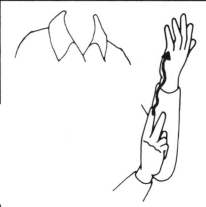

vine

LH open B palm in. Run right V up left arm from elbow to fingers in wavy motion.

vinegar

V shape RH palm left. Tap chin with index finger.

violet

Place index finger of right V on right side of nose, then middle finger on left side of nose.

violin

Mime holding and playing a violin.

virgin

Move V shape RH over head and down right side of face (as if outlining shawl).

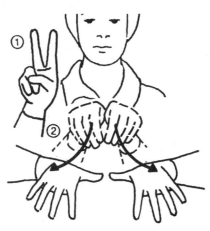

virus

V shape RH. Then place thumb and index tips of flat O shapes together and spread apart.

visit

V shape both hands, palms in, tips up. Rotate away from body alternately.

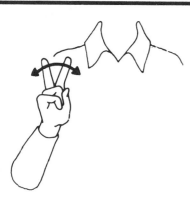

vitamin

Shake right V from left to right.

vocabulary

One shape LH palm right, tip out. Tap side of left index with tips of V shape RH.

voice

V shape RH palm in. Place tips on throat then arc upward and out.

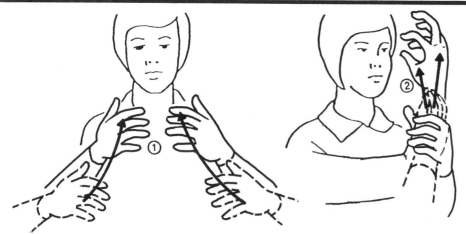

volcano

Move cupped hands upward and toward each other. Then place tips of right flat O in C shape LH. Move RH up, ending in claw shape, palm in. Repeat motion.

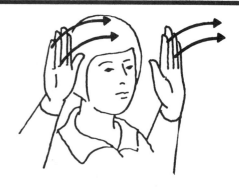

volleyball

Open B both hands, palms out. Place at sides of head and push up and forward, as if hitting ball. Repeat motion.

volunteer

Tug cloth on right upper chest with thumb and index finger of RH, other fingers extended.

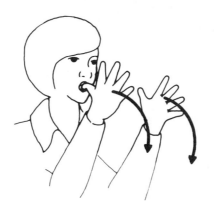

vomit (throw up)

Five shape both hands, palms facing, right thumb on mouth. Move both hands forward and down in sudden motion.

vote

Flat O shape LH, little finger side down. Place thumb and index finger of right F into left O.

vowel

One shape LH palm right, tip out. Place base of right V on tip of left index.

vulture

V shape RH palm down, tips left. Place under nose then draw fingers back to right ending in bent V shape.

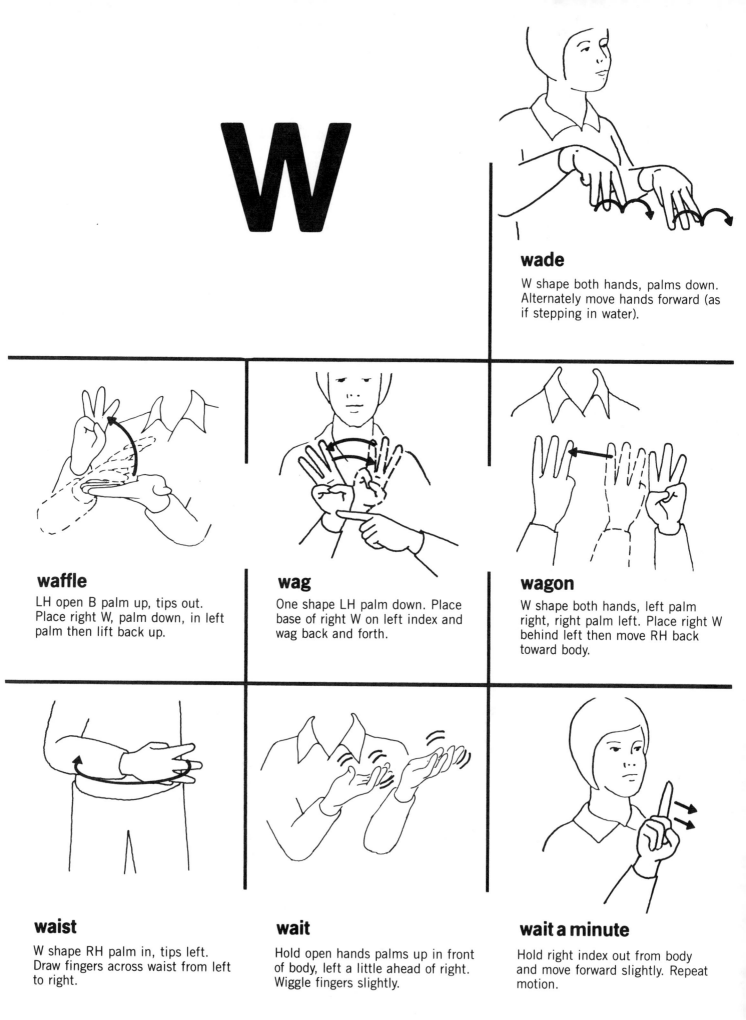

W

wade

W shape both hands, palms down. Alternately move hands forward (as if stepping in water).

waffle

LH open B palm up, tips out. Place right W, palm down, in left palm then lift back up.

wag

One shape LH palm down. Place base of right W on left index and wag back and forth.

wagon

W shape both hands, left palm right, right palm left. Place right W behind left then move RH back toward body.

waist

W shape RH palm in, tips left. Draw fingers across waist from left to right.

wait

Hold open hands palms up in front of body, left a little ahead of right. Wiggle fingers slightly.

wait a minute

Hold right index out from body and move forward slightly. Repeat motion.

402

waiter
Snap right flat O on forehead. Change to open B palm up, tips slanted back, as if balancing tray.

waitress
Brush thumb of right A down right cheek. Change to open B shape palm up, tips slanted back, as if balancing tray.

 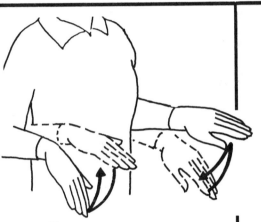 

wake up
Hold index fingers and thumbs over eyes. Snap open into L shapes.

walk
Open B both hands, palms down, tips out. Flap forward several times alternately.

walkie-talkie
C shape RH. Place at mouth then move to right ear, as if holding earpiece.

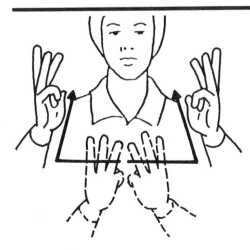 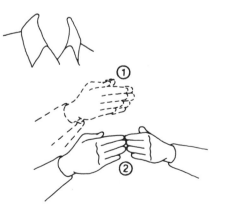 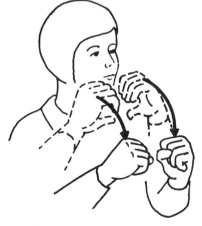

wall
W shape both hands, palms in, held close together. Move hands apart then back, outlining shape of wall.

wallet
Open B both hands, palms together, tips out. Open so that palms face in and tips touch.

walrus
C shape both hands, palms facing. Place at sides of mouth then arc down into S shapes.

403

Walt Disney
W shape RH palm left. Place at right temple then circle forward, changing into D shape.

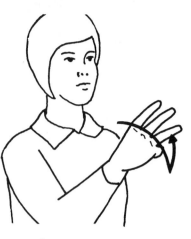

wand
W shape RH palm left, held out from body. Mime tapping object with a wand.

wander
One shape RH palm down, tip out. Move forward while weaving finger back and forth from left to right.

want
Five shape both hands, palms up, fingers slightly curved. Draw back to body.

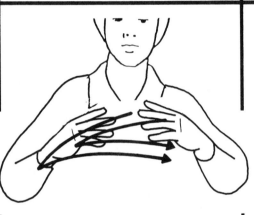

war
Bent 4 shape both hands, palms in, tips facing. Move both hands to one side then to the other.

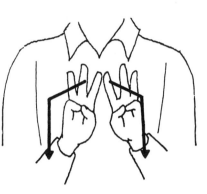

warehouse
W shape both hands, index tips touching. Move apart and down, outlining shape of building.

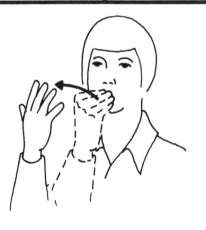

warm
Place tips of right O at mouth then open up fingers into 5 shape.

warn
S shape LH palm down. Tap back of LH twice with tips of RH open B.

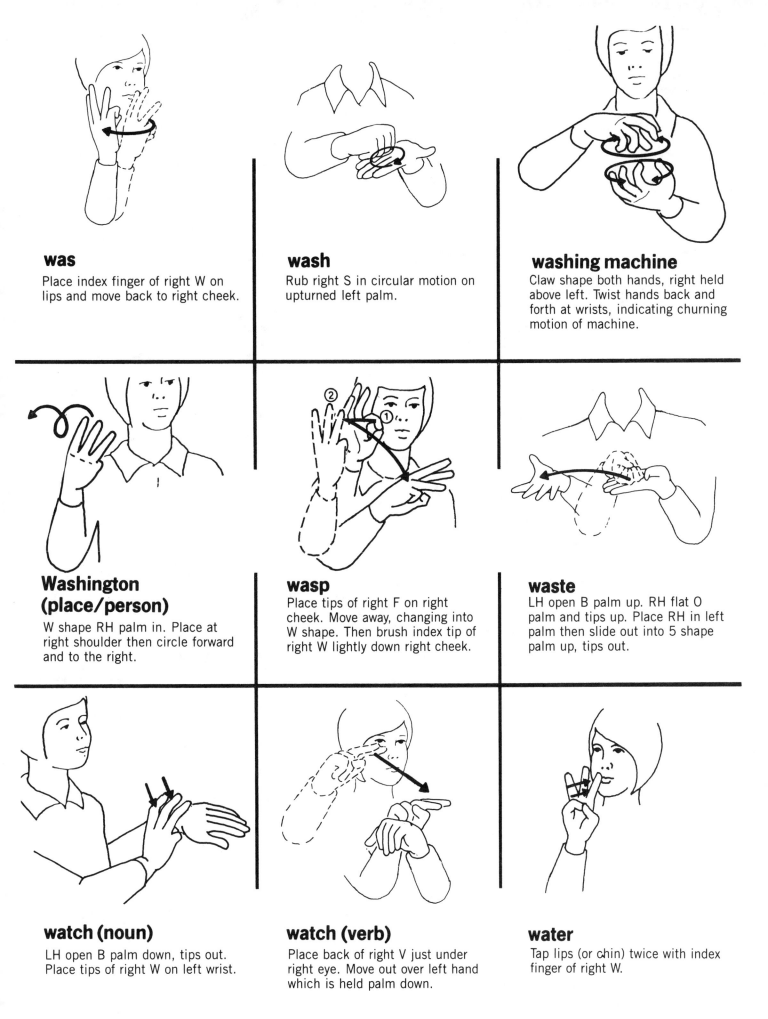

was

Place index finger of right W on lips and move back to right cheek.

wash

Rub right S in circular motion on upturned left palm.

washing machine

Claw shape both hands, right held above left. Twist hands back and forth at wrists, indicating churning motion of machine.

Washington (place/person)

W shape RH palm in. Place at right shoulder then circle forward and to the right.

wasp

Place tips of right F on right cheek. Move away, changing into W shape. Then brush index tip of right W lightly down right cheek.

waste

LH open B palm up. RH flat O palm and tips up. Place RH in left palm then slide out into 5 shape palm up, tips out.

watch (noun)

LH open B palm down, tips out. Place tips of right W on left wrist.

watch (verb)

Place back of right V just under right eye. Move out over left hand which is held palm down.

water

Tap lips (or chin) twice with index finger of right W.

405

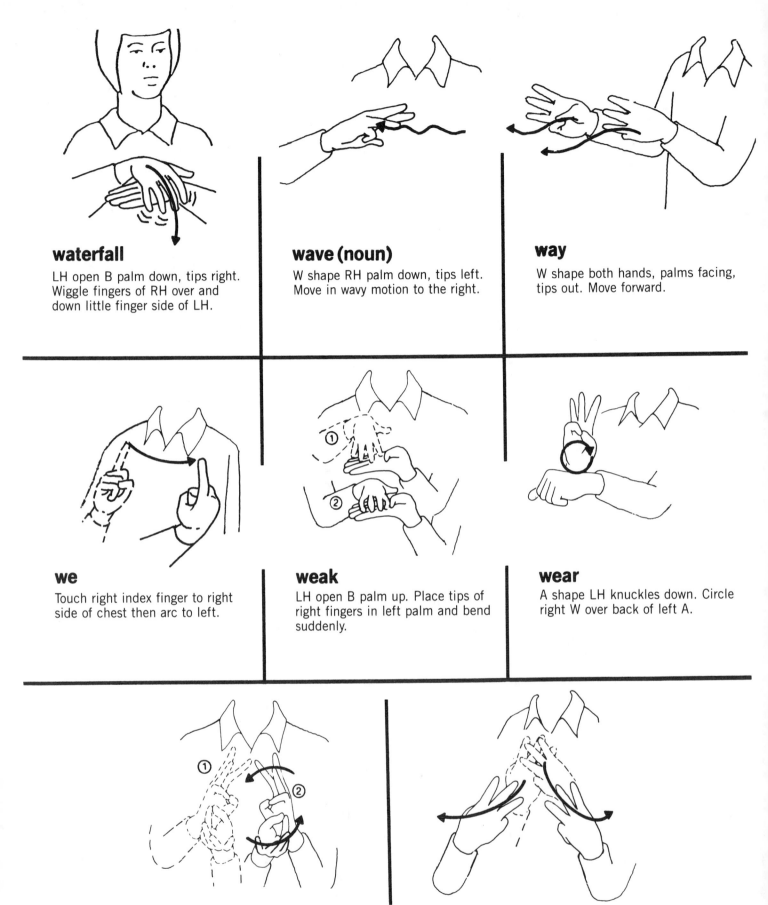

waterfall
LH open B palm down, tips right. Wiggle fingers of RH over and down little finger side of LH.

wave (noun)
W shape RH palm down, tips left. Move in wavy motion to the right.

way
W shape both hands, palms facing, tips out. Move forward.

we
Touch right index finger to right side of chest then arc to left.

weak
LH open B palm up. Place tips of right fingers in left palm and bend suddenly.

wear
A shape LH knuckles down. Circle right W over back of left A.

weather
W shape both hands, left palm up, tips out; right palm down, tips left. Place right wrist on left then reverse.

web
W shape both hands, palms in, tips slanted up. Place right W against left W. Draw down and apart.

406

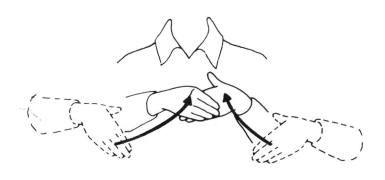

wedding

Open B both hands, palms in, tips slanted down. Arc toward one another, ending with RH clasping LH.

Wednesday

Move right W in small clockwise circle.

weed

C shape LH, little finger side down. Pass right W up through left C.

week

LH open B palm up, tips out. One shape RH palm down, tip left. Slide RH across left palm from base to tip.

weekend

Slide palm of 1 shape RH, tip left, across left palm then drop down into open B.

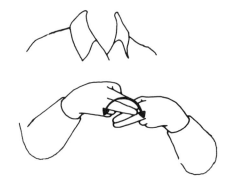

weigh

H shape both hands, palms slanted in, left tips slanted right, right tips slanted left. Place right H on left and move back and forth as if balancing.

weight

Fingerspell W-T.

weird

W shape RH palm left. Move from right to left in front of eyes while crooking and uncrooking fingers.

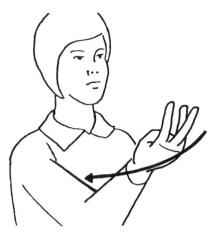

welcome

W shape RH tips slanted left, held out to right of body. Arc in toward body, ending with palm up.

well (adj. & adv.)

LH open B palm up. W shape RH palm in. Place tips on mouth, then move out and down to left palm.

well (noun)

W shape both hands, palms facing, tips out. Drop both hands down.

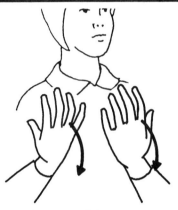

well (interj.)

Five shape both hands, palms in, tips slanted up. Hold at sides of chest then arc out, ending with palm up.

were

Place right R on lips and move back to right cheek.

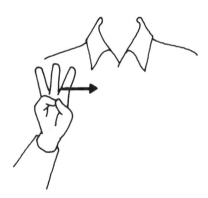

west

W shape RH. Move to left.

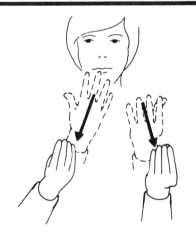

wet

Five shape both hands, palms in, fingers slightly curved. Place right index tip on mouth then drop both hands into flat O shapes.

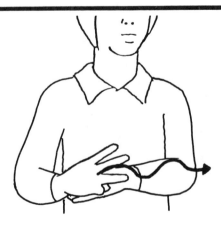

whale

Hold left arm before body, palm down, tips right. Move right W up outside of left arm to elbow in wavy motion.

whale (alt.)

LH open B palm in, tips right. W shape RH tips out. Place left tips on right wrist then flutter tips of right W back and forth from left to right while moving forward.

what

LH open B tips out, fingers slightly spread. Brush right index tip down across left fingers.

wheat

Five shape LH palm up, fingers cupped. Brush fourth finger of right W up against back of left fingers several times.

wheel

W shape RH palm left, tips out. Rotate outward in circular motion.

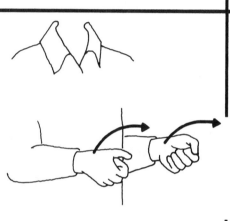

wheelbarrow

A shape both hands, thumbs out. Hold some distance apart and push forward, as if pushing a wheelbarrow.

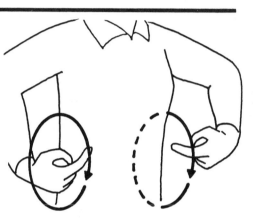

wheelchair

One shape both hands, tips facing. Circle outward at hips.

when

One shape LH palm in, held out from body. Circle LH with right index finger and then touch tips.

where

One shape RH. Wave from left to right.

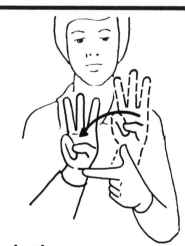

whether

L shape LH index tip out. Place base of right W on thumb, then index tip, of left L.

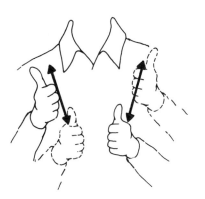

which

A shape both hands, palms facing, thumbs up. Move up and down alternately.

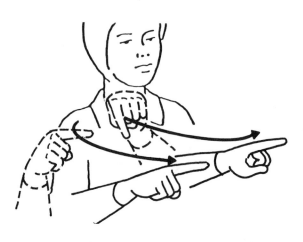

while

One shape both hands, palms down, slightly separated. Place tips near right shoulder then swing down and forward.

whip

C shape LH palm down. Make whipping motion at side of left C with right A.

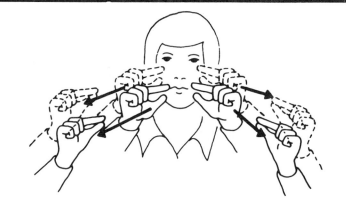

whisker

G shape both hands, palms and tips facing. Place on cheeks then draw away. Repeat.

whisper

B shape RH palm left. Place on left side of nose.

whistle

Place tips of right bent V on lips and mime whistling.

white

Five shape RH palm in, tips left. Place tips on chest and bring out into flat O shape.

who
Circle right index finger around mouth clockwise.

whole
LH open B palm up, tips out. Circle LH with right W, ending with back of right W resting in left palm.

whom
Circle right index finger around mouth then form right M.

whose
Circle right index finger around mouth then form right S.

why
RH open B palm in, tips up. Place tips on forehead and move out into Y shape.

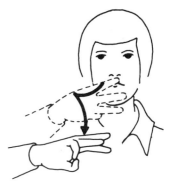

wicked
W shape RH palm in, tips left. Place on mouth then twist out and down.

wide
W shape both hands, palms facing, tips out. Place close together then arc apart to sides.

wife
Cupped shape LH palm up. Move thumb of right A down right cheek then clasp hands together.

wig
Place tips of right W on top of head and move down.

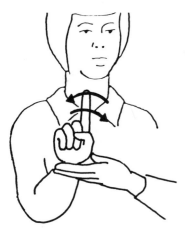

wiggle

LH open B palm up. One shape RH. Place base of right 1 in left palm and shake back and forth.

wigwam

W shape both hands, tips touching. Draw down and apart, outlining shape of wigwam.

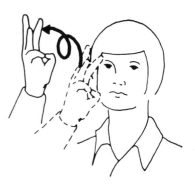

wild

Place tips of right W on right temple then loop forward and up.

will

Place palm of right open B near right cheek and move out.

win

S shape LH knuckles right. Make sweeping pass with right C over left S closing C into S shape.

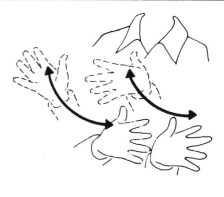

wind

Five shape both hands, palms facing, tips out. Swing back and forth.

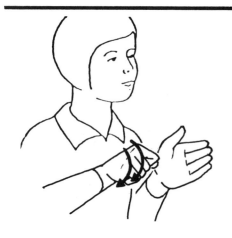

wind (up)

LH open B palm right, tips out. Place right thumb and index finger together. Twist them forward several times in front of left palm.

windmill

One shape LH palm in. W shape RH palm in. Rotate right W in front of left index finger.

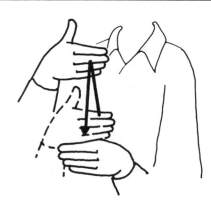

window

Open B both hands, palms in, tips opposite. Place right little finger on left index. Move up then down.

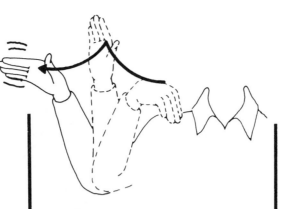

wine
W shape RH palm left. Circle at right cheek.

wing
Bent open B shape RH palm down, tips on right shoulder. Swing to palm out and flutter fingers slightly.

wink
Snap right thumb and index finger in front of right eye. Open slightly and snap again.

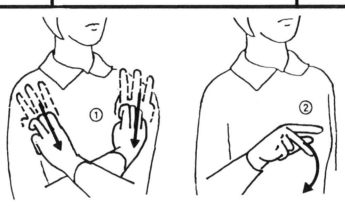

Winnie the Pooh
Cross W shape hands and place on upper chest. Scratch chest with tips of W shapes. Then place thumb side of right P on chest. Arc out and back against stomach, outlining potbelly.

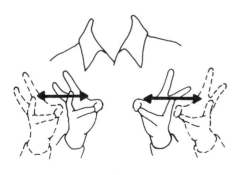

winter
W shape both hands, palms facing, tips out. Press upper arms against body, then shake hands back and forth in shivering motion.

wipe
LH open B palm up. Rotate right open B in left palm, as if wiping something.

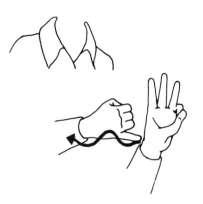

wire

W shape LH. I shape RH palm in, tip left. Place tip of right little finger on inside of left wrist, then draw back to the right in wavy line.

wise

Nod right X up and down at forehead several times.

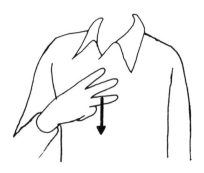

wish

W shape RH palm in. Place on chest and move down slightly.

wishbone

One shape both hands, palms facing. Press tips together.

witch

X shape both hands, left palm up. Place back of right X on nose, move out and down, and tap index tips.

with

A shape both hands, knuckles facing, thumbs up. Bring together.

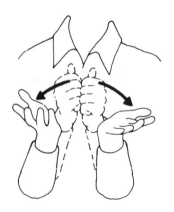

without

A shape both hands, thumbs up. Place together then draw apart, ending with fingers spread, both palms up.

wolf

Place tips of RH around nose then draw away into flat O shape.

woman

Brush thumb of A shape RH down chin then place on chest, opening into open B shape.

wonder
Circle right index tip at right side of forehead.

wonderful
Five shape both hands, palms out. Push up and out.

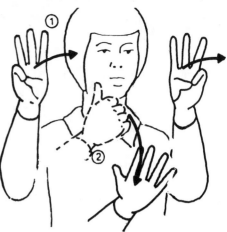

Wonder Woman
Hold up W shape hands and push forward. Brush thumb of right A down chin then place on chest, opening into open B shape.

won't
A shape RH knuckles left. Jerk back over right shoulder.

wood
A shape RH palm down. Slide little finger side of right W back and forth on left wrist as if sawing wood.

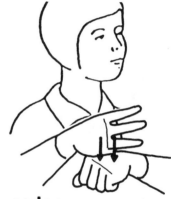

wooden
A shape RH palm down. Tap little finger side of right W on back of left A.

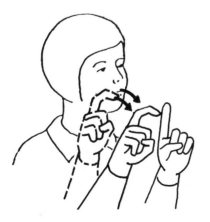

woodpecker
Place right X at right side of mouth then move out and tap side of left index finger with tip of right X.

woods
W shape RH palm left. LH open B palm down, held across front of body. Place right elbow on back of LH then twist right wrist back and forth.

Woody Woodpecker

Slide little finger side of right W back and forth on left wrist. Place right X at side of mouth, then move out and tap side of left index with tip of right X.

wool

W shape RH palm up. Brush up left forearm twice.

word

One shape LH palm right, tip out. Place tips of right G against tip of left index finger.

work

S shape both hands, palms down. Hit back of left S with right S. Repeat motion.

workshop

W shape both hands, palms out, index tips touching. Draw apart and around to front, changing to S shapes palms in, little fingers touching.

world

W shape both hands, tips out. Place right W on top of left. Circle right W forward and under left W, returning to original position.

worm

LH open B palm slanted out. Move right X across left palm while crooking and uncrooking right index finger (to indicate wiggling worm).

worn-out

A shape both hands, thumb tips touching and knuckles touching. Drop down and apart, ending in 5 shapes.

worry

W shape both hands, palms slanted out. Alternately circle inward in front of face.

worse

V shape both hands, palms in. Cross in front of body.

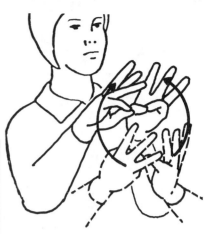

worth

W shape both hands, palms up, fourth fingers touching. Circle up and together, ending with palms down, index fingers touching.

would

Place palm of right open B near right cheek then move out. Repeat.

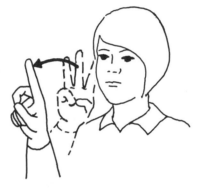

would (alt.)

Place palm of right W near right cheek then move out, ending in D shape.

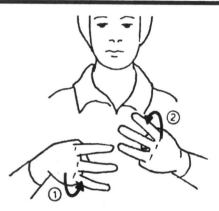

wound

W shape both hands, tips facing. Twist wrists in opposite directions while moving fingers toward one another.

wow

Fingerspell W-O-W in rapid succession.

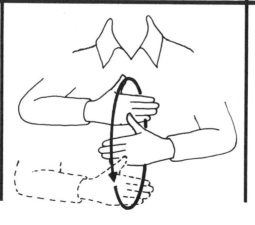

wrap

Open B both hands, palms in, left tips right, right tips left. Circle left hand with right.

wreath

C shape both hands, palms out, thumbs touching. Circle down so that little fingers touch. (Sometimes made with W handshapes.)

wreck

One shape LH. W shape RH palm in, tips left. Strike left index with back of right W.

wrench (noun)

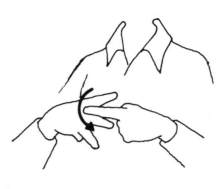

One shape LH tip out. Straddle left index with index and middle finger of right W. Twist right W downward.

wrestle

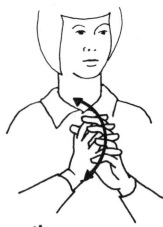

Entwine fingers of both hands. Twist wrists up and down.

wring

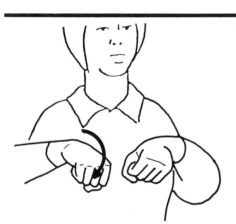

S shape both hands, palms down. Move RH in twisting motion, as if wringing out cloth.

wrinkle

LH open B palm up. W shape RH palm down. Move right W over left palm in wavy motion.

wrist

S shape LH palm down. Place right thumb and index finger around left wrist.

write

Mime writing in upturned left palm with thumb and index finger of RH (other fingers closed).

wrong

Strike chin with knuckles of Y shape RH.

X

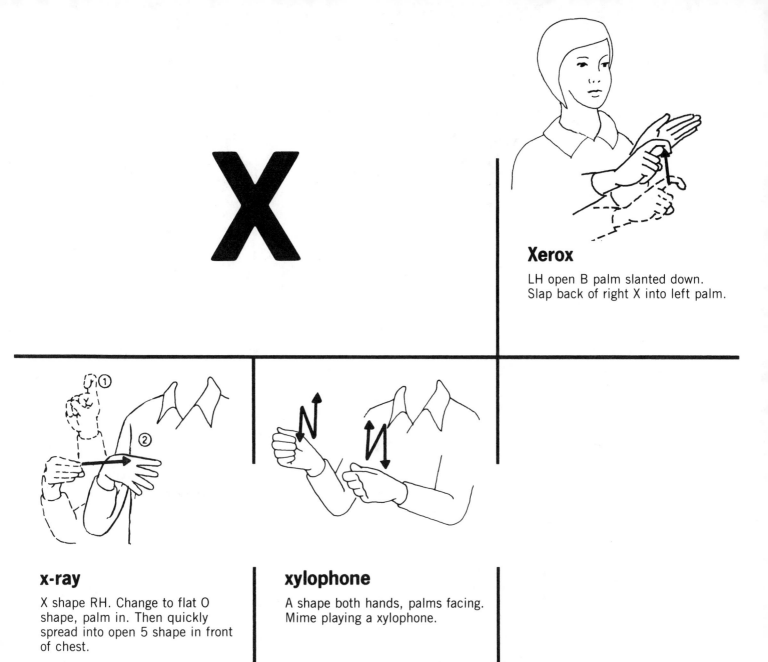

Xerox

LH open B palm slanted down.
Slap back of right X into left palm.

x-ray

X shape RH. Change to flat O
shape, palm in. Then quickly
spread into open 5 shape in front
of chest.

xylophone

A shape both hands, palms facing.
Mime playing a xylophone.

Y

yard (measurement)

Slide knuckles of right Y up left arm.

yard (place)

LH open B palm down. Y shape RH palm down. Circle right Y over left hand and forearm.

yarn

Y shape LH palm out. Place tip of right little finger on left thumb then draw back to the right in wavy line.

yawn

Hold right S at mouth then open up into bent 3 shape.

year

S shape both hands. Place right S on top of left. Circle right S forward and under left S, ending in original position.

420

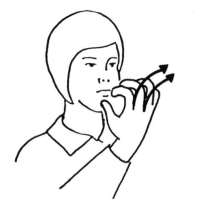

yell

Claw shape RH palm in. Place at mouth then move up and out sharply once or twice.

yellow

Y shape RH. Shake in and out.

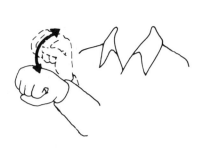

yes

S shape RH. Shake up and down at wrist.

yesterday

Place thumb of right A on right cheek. Arc back and touch back of cheek near ear. (Sometimes made with Y handshape.)

yet

Hold Y shape RH palm in, tips down, near waist. Flap backward twice.

yield

Y shape both hands, palms down. Arc up and back sharply, ending with palms out.

yogurt

C shape LH, little finger side down. Mime spooning yogurt into mouth with Y shape RH.

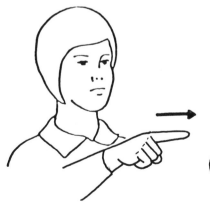

you

Point index finger at person being addressed.

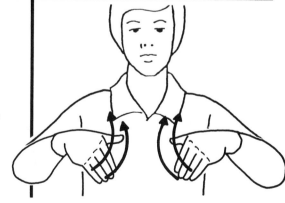

young

Bent open B shape both hands, thumbs up. Place tips of fingers on upper chest and brush up twice.

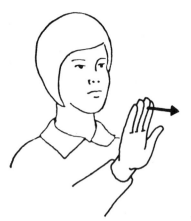

your

Push palm forward toward person being addressed.

you're welcome

W shape RH palm in. Place tips at mouth and arc forward and down, ending with palm up.

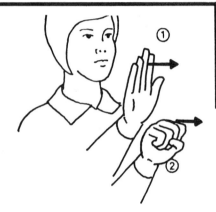

yours

Push right palm forward. Then form right S and move forward slightly.

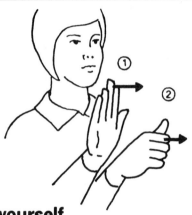

yourself

Push right palm forward. Then form right A, thumb up, and move forward slightly.

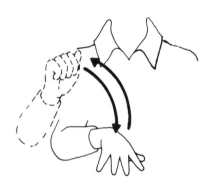

yo-yo

A shape RH. Drop down into 5 shape, palm and tips slanted down. Repeat.

yucky

Flick middle fingertips of both hands out from under thumbs.

Z

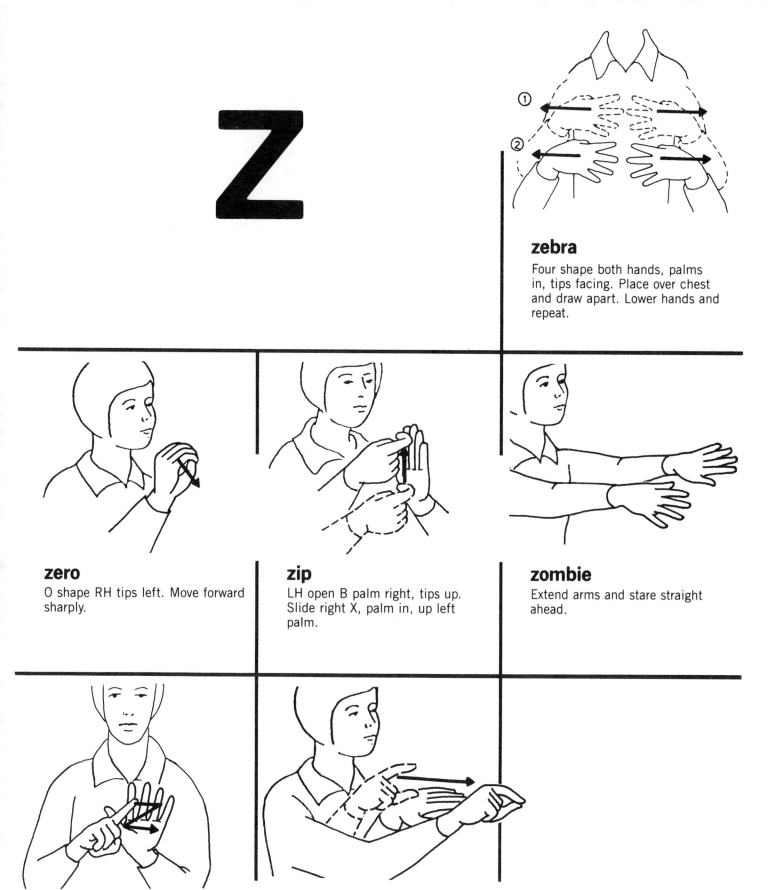

zebra

Four shape both hands, palms in, tips facing. Place over chest and draw apart. Lower hands and repeat.

zero

O shape RH tips left. Move forward sharply.

zip

LH open B palm right, tips up. Slide right X, palm in, up left palm.

zombie

Extend arms and stare straight ahead.

zoo

Five shape LH. Trace Z on left palm with right index finger.

zoom

LH open B palm down. G shape RH tips left. Place thumb of right G on back of LH then quickly slide forward, ending with thumb and index tips touching.

Appendix A
Why and How We Developed the *Signed English* Series

The basic idea of representing a spoken language manually is not new. It has been tried in a number of countries over the last hundred years. A very readable account of many of these efforts can be found in Savage, Evans, and Savage (1981). The principal conclusions that we have drawn from these past efforts are as follows: They were not subjected to rigorous, objective evaluation, nor were they modified in part or in whole as a consequence of such evaluation. And, of course, they lacked today's considerable and growing body of information on natural sign languages, the demography of deafness, and the educational practices used with deaf children and adults.

Unrealistic Expectations

We do feel, however, that some common threads exist between the past and present which are unfortunate. For example, unrealistic expectations abound among many who are involved in the education of the deaf. A good manual system will *not* serve every hearing-impaired child's needs. It will *not* raise the average English-language level of deaf children to the average found with hearing children, and neither will good oral programs. The evidence supporting these assertions is so overwhelming that it is sheer dishonesty to claim otherwise. Notwithstanding these facts, there has been and there continues to be the practice of using a select group of successful children as proof of the value of a particular communication approach. What happens again and again is that parents and teachers soon learn that, for a variety of reasons, the vast majority of children do not perform at the advertised level. They become frustrated and disillusioned and turn to some new approach, which in turn is also billed *as the method* which enables deaf children to perform as well as the general population.

In contrast, the Signed English Project from its inception has attempted to measure the performance of unselected children taught in school settings where no special enrichment or experimental treatments have been employed. We have learned that, on the average, young children exposed to Signed English do better in English than those exposed to other techniques. These results have been reported in the *American Annals of the Deaf.* We have also acquired information which, when coupled with findings obtained by other investigators, has enabled us to suggest new ways to use Signed English. Further, these findings have reinforced the basic intuition which caused us to begin this effort in the first place: the belief that simplicity is the key element to a workable system.

The SEE Systems

In the U.S., the best known and probably most influential manual English system in the early '70s was Seeing Essential English. It has since been greatly surpassed in popularity by a spin-off called Signing Exact English. A second derivative, Linguistics of Visual English, quickly fell into disuse. These SEE systems use signs to represent a combination of sound, spelling, and meaning of English words and word parts. They have designed a large number of affixes for use in unlimited combination and employ relatively large sign vocabularies.

In addition to the SEE systems, a sizeable number of local sign books were prepared during this period. As far as we know, the amount of vocabulary included in these works is relatively limited and greatly overlapping. None contain significant differences in system logic. Indeed, most do not present any system logic at all. Early, when there was a dearth of books on signs, there may have been a place for such works. Now that several books are available nationally, there isn't much point in using a local sign book, little of which is unique.

We developed the *Signed English* series because we believe that the SEE systems have very serious shortcomings. We felt and still feel that gestures or signs best represent meaning or concepts only. The orthography of a word is surely well represented by the manual alphabet, and other techniques seem better suited to represent sound. By attempting to represent sound and spelling as well as meaning, the SEE systems include rules which lead to the creation of a number of synthetic signs that not only differ in character from those found in American Sign Language but often take longer to execute or form.

Complex Sign Systems

More importantly there is now abundant evidence to indicate that much of this sign system complexity is nonfunctional; most of the affix signs and resulting sign combinations are simply not used. Even worse, we suspect that system complexity may be counterproductive.

How is system complexity nonfunctional? Very simply, parents and teachers do not use complex sentences with very young children. Moreover, they use a relatively small number of affixes. When communicating with older children, teachers tend to use only those elements that contain information necessary for understanding the message. Sometimes they substitute ASL constructions for English phrases. This comes about because their speech is probably more rapid, their sentences more complex, and their concern about being an English language model less important to them than a quick exchange of ideas. Complex systems are simply too cumbersome for most people to use in secondary and postsecondary educational settings. We hope that our suggestions on how to use Signed English meet most of these problems.

How are complex sign systems counterproductive or self-defeating? They are clearly much more difficult for parents and teachers to learn. Indeed, they are so formidable looking that they may even tend to discourage some would-be learners. In the unlikely event that they are used in their entirety, they may be difficult for children to process (read) effectively. Finally, complex systems are seductive in that their very design suggests that the teacher and parent will be able to provide a manual model rich enough for the average child to develop a complex language. We doubt that this is true. We believe that adults are more likely to keep their spoken language relatively simple in order to reduce the manual or signing burden which accompanies their speech. We suspect that deaf children will develop a rich language primarily through intensive and continuous exposure to a processable (readable) sign system, coupled with good learning experiences and the development of reading and writing skills.

Rationale for Signed English

Although Signed English is simpler than the SEE systems, even a simple system is difficult to learn and to use. Gestures or signs are used to represent specific English words in a set of more than 3,100 vocabulary items used most frequently by and with children. The signs do not represent sounds, syllables, or phonemes, nor do they represent English spelling; they represent just the specific English word, with all its various meanings.

Of course, 3,100 words are not all the words in the English language, and 14 markers do not reflect all the structural features of English. Observations of students' language behavior suggests, however, that this system is large and flexible enough to meet most of their needs. It can be supplemented with the use of a very simple existing technique: the manual alphabet. Quite simply, the manual alphabet can be used to spell any words that cannot be handled by the Signed English system. This strategy has been devised because the frequency with which words outside of the selected 3,100 are used is quite low, and we felt that the payoff for learning such signs is not great enough.

How did we develop and/or select the signs for the *Signed English* series? First, we began with the cardinal rule in this work, that one sign (gesture) is designated to represent one English word. Second, where possible, a sign from American Sign Language is used for this purpose. Please note again that a sign represents the meaning and not the sound or spelling of a word. Consequently, sign words do not necessarily have the same constituent parts as do English words. For example, the sign words that represent the English words *today* and *yesterday* do not have a common gesture element that represents *day.* Some sign words do have elements in common, but this either reflects convenience or derives from the usual growth of a natural language, in this case American Sign Language. Remember that common gesture elements from sign word to sign word are a convenience and not a rule in Signed English.

Choosing the Signs

We chose natural signs from ASL because they are more likely to be attractive and suitable for the manual medium. We also want to make it easier for the child to communicate with users of ASL and Pidgin Sign English variants. Older students who learn to use Signed English as we have suggested should be able to communicate with those who use a form of Pidgin Sign English that is close to English. However, they probably will have difficulty communicating with those who sign in ASL but who don't use a pidgin.

Because American Sign Language is not English, there is not a perfect relationship between the word in the spoken language and the gesture in the signed language. Moreover, there are some structures present in one language which are not directly present in the other or which are expressed in entirely different ways. The articles *the, an,* and *a* are examples of words that do not exist in ASL. We have either invented signs for such words or used those invented by other system makers. Additionally, there are a great many cases where one ASL sign is now used for more than one English word, such as *glad* and *happy*. We arbitrarily decided that the ASL sign would represent only one of these words—*happy*—and invented a second sign, a variant of the original sign, to represent *glad*. This, of course, applies to other like cases. Space does not allow us to describe how ASL treats, for example, plurality and verb endings.

We have followed standard English dictionary practice in treating separate dictionary entries as different words. With only a few exceptions, one sign word represents one separate dictionary entry. Consequently, we have assigned two signs for each of such English words as *mean* and *rock*, because the dictionary lists two different entries for each of these words.

When only one of two similar dictionary entries is used frequently by school children, we offer only one sign word. The infrequently used word is fingerspelled. For example, we have a sign word for *bear*, meaning the animal. With other meanings, the word is fingerspelled.

Probably the greatest departure from American Sign Language usage consists of using signs in English word order and in using sign markers to represent or to parallel English structural meanings. This is not to suggest that American sign order is totally different from English word order or that ASL does not have structural markers. There are some similarities in order and structure. The comparative marker, as one example, is taken directly from ASL and retains roughly the same meaning.

All of the exceptions to the rules described in this appendix are discussed in the introductory section, About Signed English.

APPENDIX B
Name Signs

Although names for people, establishments, and geographical locations can always be fingerspelled, it is often convenient and much more personal to devise "name signs," especially for family members and friends. As in American Sign Language (ASL), there are three general approaches to creating name signs. These are (1) to use English initials (initialization), (2) to focus on an important or colorful characteristic of the person or place, or (3) to use the literal meaning of existing signs in a somewhat unusual way.

Because of its personal nature, a name sign is best chosen or created by family members. Do not leave the choice to a teacher. If you are in doubt about the aesthetics of a particular name sign, discuss the matter with a deaf adult.

I. Initialization

For people: The first letter of the person's first (or sometimes last) name is placed on the body in a clearly seen location above the waist. Common locations are on the center of the chest, on the chest above the heart, along the left arm, on the elbow, and on the wrist.

Manual letters may also be placed so that they indicate the sex of the person, i.e., at the forehead for males and at the chin for females. For example, W for Walter might be placed at the forehead level, while T for Tamara would be placed at the chin level. Oftentimes the first letter of the person's first name is placed in the fingerspelling position and shaken gently from side to side.

Within the family: Initials may be preceded by the signs for grandmother, grandfather, aunt, uncle, or cousin. Parents should have name signs in addition to mother and father for use in social situations outside the home.

Within a large social group: A recent trend is to use the initials of the first and last names. For example, Mike Smith would be referred to as M-S. The full monograms of prominent people are used for name signs, too. The initials are formed in the normal fingerspelling position. For example, one would fingerspell J-F-K for John F. Kennedy and H-H-H for Hubert H. Humphrey.

For stores, cities, states, and countries: Many are signed by using their English abbreviations. Again, these letters are placed in the fingerspelling position. Examples are S-F for San Francisco, M-D for Maryland, and U-S for United States. Similar abbreviations are used for smaller stores and cities, but these are often understood only regionally. Examples are S-S for Silver Spring, Maryland, or W-L for Woodward and Lothrop, a department store.

B for Bob on
chest above heart

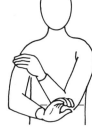

C for Carol
on elbow

Shake E
for Elizabeth

W for Walter
at forehead

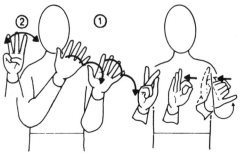

Grandmother and W
for Grandmother Wheeler

J-F-K for
John F. Kennedy

II. Important Characteristics

The location of the initial(s) or name sign is often coupled with an outstanding feature of the person, place, or thing.

For people: The initial letter of the name may be placed at eye level for a person who wears eyeglasses, or at the middle of the chest for a man who always wears a tie. Historical figures and fantasy characters are dealt with similarly, e.g., L at the top of the head for Abraham Lincoln's tall hat and two Ms outlining big ears on the head for Mickey Mouse. The initial of a child who is highly thought of may be incorporated into a sign with a favorable or positive meaning. For example, the initial R following the location and movement of the sign for king or queen might be the sign for Roger or Ruth. Although letters can also be incorporated into negative concept signs, such as "to lie," we emphatically recommend that you not adopt this practice. Furthermore, any letters placed on the nose would be considered derogatory in nature.

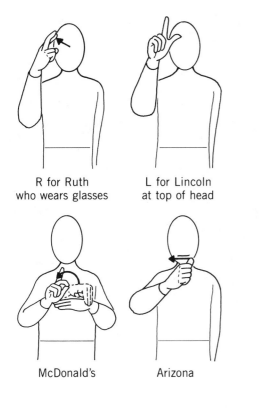

R for Ruth
who wears glasses

L for Lincoln
at top of head

McDonald's

Arizona

For places: Here, too, a letter can be incorporated into an existing sign or mime which characterizes an organization, state, or country. In many areas, for example, the letters M-D arched above the left wrist mimics McDonald's "golden arches." An A grafted upon the sign for dry is the sign for Arizona because the state is dry. Name signs for countries can represent some characteristic of their people, too. For example, an S circling at the forehead suggests the blondes of Sweden.

III. Existing Signs Used in Unusual Ways

For people: Occasionally name signs are signed literally, by using existing signs from the various sign systems. For example, the name Pat Brown may be signed as a combination of the verb pat and the color brown. The name Rose can utilize the sign for the flower, rose. Be careful about this practice, because many such signs are not especially attractive.

Pat Brown

For places: Signs for stores can follow this practice, too. For example, Giant Food can be signed as a combination of the signs for giant and food. Burger King is signed as a combination of hamburger and king. Most prominent stores, cities, states, and countries have established name signs, only a few of which have been included in this dictionary.

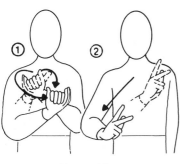

Burger King

429

Appendix C
A Model for the Visual Representation of Speech

Because Signed English is intended to be an aid to language development and a supplement to speech, we wish to present to the user consistent and accurate relationships between printed word, signed word, and appearance of the lips while that word is spoken. To do this we show the most distinctive shape of the first visible lip movement for most words.

Because some different sounds appear the same on the lips, we decided that nine different lip shapes could be used to represent reasonably the speech sounds. By consulting the model you can tell which sound has been drawn for any word in a given text. However, there are certain exceptions. For example, when an emotion such as surprise or excitement is involved, the lips usually represent the emotion rather than the sound.

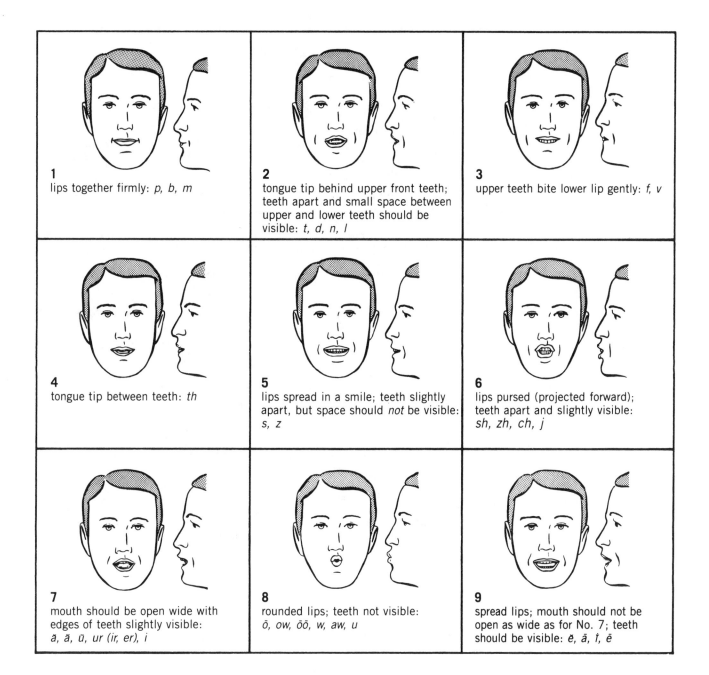

1 lips together firmly: *p, b, m*

2 tongue tip behind upper front teeth; teeth apart and small space between upper and lower teeth should be visible: *t, d, n, l*

3 upper teeth bite lower lip gently: *f, v*

4 tongue tip between teeth: *th*

5 lips spread in a smile; teeth slightly apart, but space should *not* be visible: *s, z*

6 lips pursed (projected forward); teeth apart and slightly visible: *sh, zh, ch, j*

7 mouth should be open wide with edges of teeth slightly visible: *ă, ä, ŭ, ur (ir, er), i*

8 rounded lips; teeth not visible: *ō, ow, ōō, w, aw, u*

9 spread lips; mouth should not be open as wide as for No. 7; teeth should be visible: *ĕ, ā, ĭ, ē*

Bibliography

Anthony D. A. *Signing essential English.* Unpublished master's thesis, Eastern Michigan University, 1966.

Anthony D. A., and associates (Eds.). *Seeing essential English* (2 vols.). Anaheim, Calif.: Educational Services Division, Anaheim Union High School District, 1971.

Babb, R. *A study of the academic achievement and language acquisition levels of deaf children of hearing parents in an educational environment using Signing Exact English as the primary mode of communication.* Unpublished doctoral dissertation, University of Illinois, 1979.

Beier, E. G., Starkweather, J. A., and Miller, D. E. Analysis of word frequencies in spoken language of children. *Language and Speech,* 1967, *10,* 217–227.

Bellugi, U., and Fischer, S. A comparison of sign language and spoken language: Rate and grammatical mechanisms. *Cognition,* 1972, *1,* 173–200.

Bornstein, H. *Reading the manual alphabet.* Washington, D.C.: Gallaudet University Press, 1965.

Bornstein, H. A description of some current sign systems designed to represent English. *American Annals of the Deaf,* 1973, *118,* 454–463.

Bornstein, H. Signed English: A manual approach to English language development. *Journal of Speech and Hearing Disorders,* 1974, *39,* 330–343.

Bornstein, H. Sign language in the education of the deaf. In I. Schlesinger and L. Namir (Eds.), *Sign language of the deaf: Psychological, linguistic, and social perspectives.* New York: Academic Press, 1978, 333–359.

Bornstein, H. Systems of sign. In L. Bradford & W. Hardy (Eds.), *Hearing and hearing impairment.* New York: Academic Press, 1979, 333–361.

Bornstein, H. Towards a theory of use for Signed English: From birth through adulthood. *American Annals of the Deaf,* 1982, *127,* 26–31.

Bornstein, H., and Kannapell, B. M. *New signs for instructional purposes* (Report 6-1924). Washington, D.C.: Office of Education, 1969.

Bornstein, H., and Hamilton, L. B. Recent national dictionaries of signs. *Sign Language Studies,* 1973, *1,* 42–63.

Bornstein, H., Saulnier, K., and Hamilton, L. B. Signed English: A first evaluation. *American Annals of the Deaf,* 1980, *125,* 467–481.

Bornstein, H., and Saulnier, K. Signed English: A brief follow-up to the first evaluation. *American Annals of the Deaf,* 1981, *126,* 69–72.

Brasel, K., and Quigley, S. The influence of certain language and communication environments in early childhood on the development of language in deaf individuals. *Journal of Speech and Hearing Research,* 1977, *20,* 95–107.

Burch, D., Zier, C., and Thomas, B. *An introduction to instructional signs for pre-school primary science.* Washington, D.C.: Kendall Demonstration Elementary School, Gallaudet University, 1978.

Carroll, J. B., Davies, P., and Richman, B. *The American Heritage word frequency book.* Boston: Houghton Mifflin, 1971.

Custer, D., Mitchell, M., and Taggart, M. *Index to American Sign Language.* St. Paul, Minn.: St. Paul Technical Vocational Institute, n.d.

Gentile, A., and DiFrancesca, S. *Academic achievement test performance of hearing impaired students in the United States: Spring 1969* (Series D, No. 1). Washington, D.C.: Gallaudet University Office of Demographic Studies, 1969.

Gorman, P., and Paget, G. *The Paget Gorman sign system.* London: Association for Experiment in Deaf Education, 1971.

Greenberg, B., and Withers, S. *Better English usage.* Indianapolis: Bobbs-Merrill, 1964.

Gustason, G., Pfetzing, D., and Zawolkow, E. *Signing exact English* (Rev. ed. and Supplements 1 and 2). Rosmoor, Calif.: Modern Signs Press, 1972.

Howes, D. H. A word count of spoken English. *Journal of Verbal Learning and Verbal Behavior,* 1966, *5,* 572–606.

Kannapell, B. M., Hamilton, L. B., and Bornstein, H. *Signs for instructional purposes.* Washington, D.C.: Gallaudet University Press, 1969.

Karchmer, M., and Wolk, S. *Louisiana state survey of hearing impaired and deaf-blind children* (Series C, No. 5). Washington, D.C.: Gallaudet University Office of Demographic Studies, 1980.

Kluwin, T. The grammaticality of manual representation of English in classroom settings. *American Annals of the Deaf,* 1981, *126,* 417–421.

Madsen, W. J. *Intermediate conversational sign language.* Washington, D.C.: Gallaudet University Press, 1982.

Marmor, G., and Pettito, L. Simultaneous communication in the classroom: How grammatical is it? *Sign Language Studies,* 1979, *23,* 99–136.

Moog, J. S., and Geers, A. E. *Grammatical analysis of elicited language: Simple sentence level.* St. Louis, Mo.: Central Institute for the Deaf, 1979.

Moses, W. A., et al. *Communication evaluation and remediation task force report to the school of communication.* Washington, D.C.: Gallaudet University, 1981.

Murphy, H. A. The spontaneous speaking vocabulary of children in primary grades. *Boston University Journal of Education,* No. 140, December 1957.

O'Rourke, T. J. (Ed.). *Psycholinguistics and total communication.* Silver Spring, Md.: American Annals of the Deaf, 1972.

Rawlings, B. *Characteristics of hearing impaired students by hearing status, U.S. 1970–71* (Series D, No. 10). Washington, D.C.: Gallaudet University Office of Demographic Studies, 1973.

Reich, P., and Bick, M. An empirical investigation of some claims made in support of visible English. *American Annals of the Deaf,* 1976, *121,* 573–577.

Savage, R. D., Evans, L., and Savage, J. F. *Psychology and communication in deaf children.* Sydney, Australia: Grune and Stratton, 1981.

Stokoe, W. C., Jr., Casterline, D. C., and Croneberg, C. G. *A dictionary of American Sign Language on linguistic principles.* Washington, D.C.: Gallaudet University Press, 1965.

Trybus, R., and Jensema, C. *Communication patterns and educational achievement of hearing impaired students* (Series T, No. 2). Washington, D.C.: Gallaudet University Office of Demographic Studies, 1978.

Wampler, D. W. *Linguistics of visual English: Morpheme list one, an introduction to the spatial symbol system, questions and answers.* Santa Rosa, Calif.: Linguistics of Visual English, n.d.

Bibliography (continued)

Washburn, A. O. *A SEE Thesaurus.* Dubuque, Iowa: Kendall/Hunt Publishing, 1973.

Watson, D. O. *Talk with your hands* (2 vols.). Menasha, Wis.: George Banta Co., 1973.

Wepman, J. M., and Hass, W. *A spoken word count (children—ages 5, 6, and 7).* Chicago: Language Research Associates, 1969.

Index

dawn	111	dinner (alt.)	117	dough	123
day	112	dinosaur	117	doughnut	123
daydream	112+125	dip	118	dove	123
dead	112	diplodocus	118	down	123
deaf	112	diploma	118	downstairs	123
deaf (alt.)	112	direct	118	downtown	123+383
deal (noun)	112	direction	118	dozen	123
dear	112	dirt	118	Dracula	123
death	112	disabled	118	drag	124
December	112	disagree	118	dragon	124
decide	112	disappear	118	drain	124
decorate	113	disappoint	119	drapes	124
deep	113	discover	119	draw	124
deer	113	discuss	119	drawbridge	124
defeat	113	disease	119	drawer	124
degree	113	disguise	119	dream	125
delicious	113	disgust	119	dress	125
deliver	113	dish	119	dresser	125
demonstrate	113	Disney	119	drill	125
den	114	Disneyland	119+211	drink	125
dental hygienist	114	Disney World	119+416	drip	125
dentist	114	disobey	119	drive	125
deodorant	114	disposal	120	driveway	125
department	114	dissolve	120	drop	126
depend	114	distance	120	drown	126
depress	114	disturb	120	drug	126
describe	114	dive	120	drugstore	126
desert	115	divide	120	drum	126
design	115	divorce	120	drunk	126
desk	115	dizzy	120	dry	126
desk (alt.)	115	do	121	duck	126
dessert	115	dock	121	duckling	127
dessert (alt.)	115	doctor	121	dull	127
destroy	115	doctor (alt.)	121	dumb	127
detective	115	does	21	dump	127
devil	116	doesn't	121	during	127
diamond	116	dog	121	dust	127
diaper	116	doll	121	dustpan	127
diarrhea	116	dollar	121	dwarf	128
dice	116	dolphin	122	dye	128
dictionary	116	donkey	122		
did	21	don't	122		
didn't	116	door	122	**E**	
die	116	doorbell	122		
diet	116	doorknob	122+209	each	129
different	117	doorstep	122+351	eagle	129
difficult	117	dope	122	ear	129
dig	117	dormitory	122	earache	129
dime	117	dot	122	early	129
dimple	117	double	122	ear mold	129
dine	117	doubt	123	earn	129
dinner	117	doubt (alt.)	123	earring	130
				earth	130

441

Compounds

About 150 compounds in this dictionary combine two sign words exactly like the combined English words.

somewhere

everything

haystack

A number of English words, usually compounds, are represented by American Sign Language compounds that differ in order and kind from those found in the comparable English words.

today

breakfast

gentleman

Approximately 100 other English compounds in this dictionary are represented either by simple traditional or simple new signs, that is, signs which cannot be broken down into two other sign words.

sometimes

downstairs

toothbrush

Contractions

The Basic Rule

A simple and widely-used technique is followed in forming most contractions. As shown below, you first execute the sign word, then the right hand forms the appropriate manual letter and quickly twists it *inward*. The table below gives all the contraction parallels.

English Spelling:	'd	'll	'm	n't	're	've	's
Manual Letter:	D	L	M	N	R	V	S

haven't

I'm

wouldn't   couldn't   shouldn't